msdn

msdn training

2559B: Introduction to Visual Basic® .NET Programming with Microsoft® .NET

Demo code
2559

Greg Woods

Installed
C:\Program Files\msdntrain\2559

Robert Rrivera
BSA
BA

Microsoft®

Course Number: 2559B
Part Number: X10-28227
Released: 07/2002

END-USER LICENSE AGREEMENT FOR MICROSOFT OFFICIAL CURRICULUM COURSEWARE -STUDENT EDITION

PLEASE READ THIS END-USER LICENSE AGREEMENT ("EULA") CAREFULLY. BY USING THE MATERIALS AND/OR USING OR INSTALLING THE SOFTWARE THAT ACCOMPANIES THIS EULA (COLLECTIVELY, THE "LICENSED CONTENT"), YOU AGREE TO THE TERMS OF THIS EULA. IF YOU DO NOT AGREE, DO NOT USE THE LICENSED CONTENT.

1. GENERAL. This EULA is a legal agreement between you (either an individual or a single entity) and Microsoft Corporation ("Microsoft"). This EULA governs the Licensed Content, which includes computer software (including online and electronic documentation), training materials, and any other associated media and printed materials. This EULA applies to updates, supplements, add-on components, and Internet-based services components of the Licensed Content that Microsoft may provide or make available to you unless Microsoft provides other terms with the update, supplement, add-on component, or Internet-based services component. Microsoft reserves the right to discontinue any Internet-based services provided to you or made available to you through the use of the Licensed Content. This EULA also governs any product support services relating to the Licensed Content except as may be included in another agreement between you and Microsoft. An amendment or addendum to this EULA may accompany the Licensed Content.

2. **GENERAL GRANT OF LICENSE.** Microsoft grants you the following rights, conditioned on your compliance with all the terms and conditions of this EULA. Microsoft grants you a limited, non-exclusive, royalty-free license to install and use the Licensed Content solely in conjunction with your participation as a student in an Authorized Training Session (as defined below). You may install and use one copy of the software on a single computer, device, workstation, terminal, or other digital electronic or analog device ("Device"). You may make a second copy of the software and install it on a portable Device for the exclusive use of the person who is the primary user of the first copy of the software. A license for the software may not be shared for use by multiple end users. An "Authorized Training Session" means a training session conducted at a Microsoft Certified Technical Education Center, an IT Academy, via a Microsoft Certified Partner, or such other entity as Microsoft may designate from time to time in writing, by a Microsoft Certified Trainer (for more information on these entities, please visit www.microsoft.com). WITHOUT LIMITING THE FOREGOING, COPYING OR REPRODUCTION OF THE LICENSED CONTENT TO ANY SERVER OR LOCATION FOR FURTHER REPRODUCTION OR REDISTRIBUTION IS EXPRESSLY PROHIBITED.

3. DESCRIPTION OF OTHER RIGHTS AND LICENSE LIMITATIONS

3.1 *Use of Documentation and Printed Training Materials.*

3.1.1 The documents and related graphics included in the Licensed Content may include technical inaccuracies or typographical errors. Changes are periodically made to the content. Microsoft may make improvements and/or changes in any of the components of the Licensed Content at any time without notice. The names of companies, products, people, characters and/or data mentioned in the Licensed Content may be fictitious and are in no way intended to represent any real individual, company, product or event, unless otherwise noted.

3.1.2 Microsoft grants you the right to reproduce portions of documents (such as student workbooks, white papers, press releases, datasheets and FAQs) (the "Documents") provided with the Licensed Content. You may not print any book (either electronic or print version) in its entirety. If you choose to reproduce Documents, you agree that: (a) use of such printed Documents will be solely in conjunction with your personal training use; (b) the Documents will not republished or posted on any network computer or broadcast in any media; (c) any reproduction will include either the Document's original copyright notice or a copyright notice to Microsoft's benefit substantially in the format provided below; and (d) to comply with all terms and conditions of this EULA. In addition, no modifications may made to any Document.

Form of Notice:

© 2002. Reprinted with permission by Microsoft Corporation. All rights reserved.

Microsoft and Windows are either registered trademarks or trademarks of Microsoft Corporation in the US and/or other countries. Other product and company names mentioned herein may be the trademarks of their respective owners.

3.2 *Use of Media Elements.* The Licensed Content may include certain photographs, clip art, animations, sounds, music, and video clips (together "Media Elements"). You may not modify these Media Elements.

3.3 *Use of Sample Code.* In the event that the Licensed Content includes sample code in source or object format ("Sample Code"), Microsoft grants you a limited, non-exclusive, royalty-free license to use, copy and modify the Sample Code; if you elect to exercise the foregoing rights, you agree to comply with all other terms and conditions of this EULA, including without limitation Sections 3.4, 3.5, and 6.

3.4 *Permitted Modifications.* In the event that you exercise any rights provided under this EULA to create modifications of the Licensed Content, you agree that any such modifications: (a) will not be used for providing training where a fee is charged in public or private classes; (b) indemnify, hold harmless, and defend Microsoft from and against any claims or lawsuits, including attorneys' fees, which arise from or result from your use of any modified version of the Licensed Content; and (c) not to transfer or assign any rights to any modified version of the Licensed Content to any third party without the express written permission of Microsoft.

3.5 *Reproduction/Redistribution Licensed Content.* Except as expressly provided in this EULA, you may not reproduce or distribute the Licensed Content or any portion thereof (including any permitted modifications) to any third parties without the express written permission of Microsoft.

4. **RESERVATION OF RIGHTS AND OWNERSHIP.** Microsoft reserves all rights not expressly granted to you in this EULA. The Licensed Content is protected by copyright and other intellectual property laws and treaties. Microsoft or its suppliers own the title, copyright, and other intellectual property rights in the Licensed Content. You may not remove or obscure any copyright, trademark or patent notices that appear on the Licensed Content, or any components thereof, as delivered to you. **The Licensed Content is licensed, not sold.**

5. **LIMITATIONS ON REVERSE ENGINEERING, DECOMPILATION, AND DISASSEMBLY.** You may not reverse engineer, decompile, or disassemble the Software or Media Elements, except and only to the extent that such activity is expressly permitted by applicable law notwithstanding this limitation.

6. **LIMITATIONS ON SALE, RENTAL, ETC. AND CERTAIN ASSIGNMENTS.** You may not provide commercial hosting services with, sell, rent, lease, lend, sublicense, or assign copies of the Licensed Content, or any portion thereof (including any permitted modifications thereof) on a stand-alone basis or as part of any collection, product or service.

7. **CONSENT TO USE OF DATA.** You agree that Microsoft and its affiliates may collect and use technical information gathered as part of the product support services provided to you, if any, related to the Licensed Content. Microsoft may use this information solely to improve our products or to provide customized services or technologies to you and will not disclose this information in a form that personally identifies you.

8. **LINKS TO THIRD PARTY SITES.** You may link to third party sites through the use of the Licensed Content. The third party sites are not under the control of Microsoft, and Microsoft is not responsible for the contents of any third party sites, any links contained in third party sites, or any changes or updates to third party sites. Microsoft is not responsible for webcasting or any other form of transmission received from any third party sites. Microsoft is providing these links to third party sites to you only as a convenience, and the inclusion of any link does not imply an endorsement by Microsoft of the third party site.

9. **ADDITIONAL LICENSED CONTENT/SERVICES.** This EULA applies to updates, supplements, add-on components, or Internet-based services components, of the Licensed Content that Microsoft may provide to you or make available to you after the date you obtain your initial copy of the Licensed Content, unless we provide other terms along with the update, supplement, add-on component, or Internet-based services component. Microsoft reserves the right to discontinue any Internet-based services provided to you or made available to you through the use of the Licensed Content.

10. **U.S. GOVERNMENT LICENSE RIGHTS**. All software provided to the U.S. Government pursuant to solicitations issued on or after December 1, 1995 is provided with the commercial license rights and restrictions described elsewhere herein. All software provided to the U.S. Government pursuant to solicitations issued prior to December 1, 1995 is provided with "Restricted Rights" as provided for in FAR, 48 CFR 52.227-14 (JUNE 1987) or DFAR, 48 CFR 252.227-7013 (OCT 1988), as applicable.

11. **EXPORT RESTRICTIONS**. You acknowledge that the Licensed Content is subject to U.S. export jurisdiction. You agree to comply with all applicable international and national laws that apply to the Licensed Content, including the U.S. Export Administration Regulations, as well as end-user, end-use, and destination restrictions issued by U.S. and other governments. For additional information see <http://www.microsoft.com/exporting/>.

12. **TRANSFER.** The initial user of the Licensed Content may make a one-time permanent transfer of this EULA and Licensed Content to another end user, provided the initial user retains no copies of the Licensed Content. The transfer may not be an indirect transfer, such as a consignment. Prior to the transfer, the end user receiving the Licensed Content must agree to all the EULA terms.

13. **"NOT FOR RESALE" LICENSED CONTENT.** Licensed Content identified as "Not For Resale" or "NFR," may not be sold or otherwise transferred for value, or used for any purpose other than demonstration, test or evaluation.

14. **TERMINATION.** Without prejudice to any other rights, Microsoft may terminate this EULA if you fail to comply with the terms and conditions of this EULA. In such event, you must destroy all copies of the Licensed Content and all of its component parts.

15. **DISCLAIMER OF WARRANTIES. TO THE MAXIMUM EXTENT PERMITTED BY APPLICABLE LAW, MICROSOFT AND ITS SUPPLIERS PROVIDE THE LICENSED CONTENT AND SUPPORT SERVICES (IF ANY) *AS IS AND WITH ALL FAULTS,* AND MICROSOFT AND ITS SUPPLIERS HEREBY DISCLAIM ALL OTHER WARRANTIES AND CONDITIONS, WHETHER EXPRESS, IMPLIED OR STATUTORY, INCLUDING, BUT NOT LIMITED TO, ANY (IF ANY) IMPLIED WARRANTIES, DUTIES OR CONDITIONS OF MERCHANTABILITY, OF FITNESS FOR A PARTICULAR PURPOSE, OF RELIABILITY OR AVAILABILITY, OF ACCURACY OR COMPLETENESS OF RESPONSES, OF RESULTS, OF WORKMANLIKE EFFORT, OF LACK OF VIRUSES, AND OF LACK OF NEGLIGENCE, ALL WITH REGARD TO THE LICENSED CONTENT, AND THE PROVISION OF OR FAILURE TO PROVIDE SUPPORT OR OTHER SERVICES, INFORMATION, SOFTWARE, AND RELATED CONTENT THROUGH THE LICENSED CONTENT, OR OTHERWISE ARISING OUT OF THE USE OF THE LICENSED CONTENT. ALSO, THERE IS NO WARRANTY OR CONDITION OF TITLE, QUIET ENJOYMENT, QUIET POSSESSION, CORRESPONDENCE TO DESCRIPTION OR NON-INFRINGEMENT WITH REGARD TO THE LICENSED CONTENT. THE ENTIRE RISK AS TO THE QUALITY, OR ARISING OUT OF THE USE OR PERFORMANCE OF THE LICENSED CONTENT, AND ANY SUPPORT SERVICES, REMAINS WITH YOU.**

16. **EXCLUSION OF INCIDENTAL, CONSEQUENTIAL AND CERTAIN OTHER DAMAGES. TO THE MAXIMUM EXTENT PERMITTED BY APPLICABLE LAW, IN NO EVENT SHALL MICROSOFT OR ITS SUPPLIERS BE LIABLE FOR ANY SPECIAL, INCIDENTAL, PUNITIVE, INDIRECT, OR CONSEQUENTIAL DAMAGES WHATSOEVER (INCLUDING, BUT NOT**

LIMITED TO, DAMAGES FOR LOSS OF PROFITS OR CONFIDENTIAL OR OTHER INFORMATION, FOR BUSINESS INTERRUPTION, FOR PERSONAL INJURY, FOR LOSS OF PRIVACY, FOR FAILURE TO MEET ANY DUTY INCLUDING OF GOOD FAITH OR OF REASONABLE CARE, FOR NEGLIGENCE, AND FOR ANY OTHER PECUNIARY OR OTHER LOSS WHATSOEVER) ARISING OUT OF OR IN ANY WAY RELATED TO THE USE OF OR INABILITY TO USE THE LICENSED CONTENT, THE PROVISION OF OR FAILURE TO PROVIDE SUPPORT OR OTHER SERVICES, INFORMATION, SOFTWARE, AND RELATED CONTENT THROUGH THE LICENSED CONTENT, OR OTHERWISE ARISING OUT OF THE USE OF THE LICENSED CONTENT, OR OTHERWISE UNDER OR IN CONNECTION WITH ANY PROVISION OF THIS EULA, EVEN IN THE EVENT OF THE FAULT, TORT (INCLUDING NEGLIGENCE), MISREPRESENTATION, STRICT LIABILITY, BREACH OF CONTRACT OR BREACH OF WARRANTY OF MICROSOFT OR ANY SUPPLIER, AND EVEN IF MICROSOFT OR ANY SUPPLIER HAS BEEN ADVISED OF THE POSSIBILITY OF SUCH DAMAGES. BECAUSE SOME STATES/JURISDICTIONS DO NOT ALLOW THE EXCLUSION OR LIMITATION OF LIABILITY FOR CONSEQUENTIAL OR INCIDENTAL DAMAGES, THE ABOVE LIMITATION MAY NOT APPLY TO YOU.

17. **LIMITATION OF LIABILITY AND REMEDIES. NOTWITHSTANDING ANY DAMAGES THAT YOU MIGHT INCUR FOR ANY REASON WHATSOEVER (INCLUDING, WITHOUT LIMITATION, ALL DAMAGES REFERENCED HEREIN AND ALL DIRECT OR GENERAL DAMAGES IN CONTRACT OR ANYTHING ELSE), THE ENTIRE LIABILITY OF MICROSOFT AND ANY OF ITS SUPPLIERS UNDER ANY PROVISION OF THIS EULA AND YOUR EXCLUSIVE REMEDY HEREUNDER SHALL BE LIMITED TO THE GREATER OF THE ACTUAL DAMAGES YOU INCUR IN REASONABLE RELIANCE ON THE LICENSED CONTENT UP TO THE AMOUNT ACTUALLY PAID BY YOU FOR THE LICENSED CONTENT OR US$5.00. THE FOREGOING LIMITATIONS, EXCLUSIONS AND DISCLAIMERS SHALL APPLY TO THE MAXIMUM EXTENT PERMITTED BY APPLICABLE LAW, EVEN IF ANY REMEDY FAILS ITS ESSENTIAL PURPOSE.**

18. **APPLICABLE LAW.** If you acquired this Licensed Content in the United States, this EULA is governed by the laws of the State of Washington. If you acquired this Licensed Content in Canada, unless expressly prohibited by local law, this EULA is governed by the laws in force in the Province of Ontario, Canada; and, in respect of any dispute which may arise hereunder, you consent to the jurisdiction of the federal and provincial courts sitting in Toronto, Ontario. If you acquired this Licensed Content in the European Union, Iceland, Norway, or Switzerland, then local law applies. If you acquired this Licensed Content in any other country, then local law may apply.

19. **ENTIRE AGREEMENT; SEVERABILITY.** This EULA (including any addendum or amendment to this EULA which is included with the Licensed Content) are the entire agreement between you and Microsoft relating to the Licensed Content and the support services (if any) and they supersede all prior or contemporaneous oral or written communications, proposals and representations with respect to the Licensed Content or any other subject matter covered by this EULA. To the extent the terms of any Microsoft policies or programs for support services conflict with the terms of this EULA, the terms of this EULA shall control. If any provision of this EULA is held to be void, invalid, unenforceable or illegal, the other provisions shall continue in full force and effect.

Should you have any questions concerning this EULA, or if you desire to contact Microsoft for any reason, please use the address information enclosed in this Licensed Content to contact the Microsoft subsidiary serving your country or visit Microsoft on the World Wide Web at http://www.microsoft.com.

Si vous avez acquis votre Contenu Sous Licence Microsoft au CANADA :

DÉNI DE GARANTIES. Dans la mesure maximale permise par les lois applicables, le Contenu Sous Licence et les services de soutien technique (le cas échéant) sont fournis *TELS QUELS ET AVEC TOUS LES DÉFAUTS* par Microsoft et ses fournisseurs, lesquels par les présentes dénient toutes autres garanties et conditions expresses, implicites ou en vertu de la loi, notamment, mais sans limitation, (le cas échéant) les garanties, devoirs ou conditions implicites de qualité marchande, d'adaptation à une fin usage particulière, de fiabilité ou de disponibilité, d'exactitude ou d'exhaustivité des réponses, des résultats, des efforts déployés selon les règles de l'art, d'absence de virus et d'absence de négligence, le tout à l'égard du Contenu Sous Licence et de la prestation des services de soutien technique ou de l'omission de la 'une telle prestation des services de soutien technique ou à l'égard de la fourniture ou de l'omission de la fourniture de tous autres services, renseignements, Contenus Sous Licence, et contenu qui s'y rapporte grâce au Contenu Sous Licence ou provenant autrement de l'utilisation du Contenu Sous Licence. PAR AILLEURS, IL N'Y A AUCUNE GARANTIE OU CONDITION QUANT AU TITRE DE PROPRIÉTÉ, À LA JOUISSANCE OU LA POSSESSION PAISIBLE, À LA CONCORDANCE À UNE DESCRIPTION NI QUANT À UNE ABSENCE DE CONTREFAÇON CONCERNANT LE CONTENU SOUS LICENCE.

EXCLUSION DES DOMMAGES ACCESSOIRES, INDIRECTS ET DE CERTAINS AUTRES DOMMAGES. DANS LA MESURE MAXIMALE PERMISE PAR LES LOIS APPLICABLES, EN AUCUN CAS MICROSOFT OU SES FOURNISSEURS NE SERONT RESPONSABLES DES DOMMAGES SPÉCIAUX, CONSÉCUTIFS, ACCESSOIRES OU INDIRECTS DE QUELQUE NATURE QUE CE SOIT (NOTAMMENT, LES DOMMAGES À L'ÉGARD DU MANQUE À GAGNER OU DE LA DIVULGATION DE RENSEIGNEMENTS CONFIDENTIELS OU AUTRES, DE LA PERTE D'EXPLOITATION, DE BLESSURES CORPORELLES, DE LA VIOLATION DE LA VIE PRIVÉE, DE L'OMISSION DE REMPLIR TOUT DEVOIR, Y COMPRIS D'AGIR DE BONNE FOI OU D'EXERCER UN SOIN RAISONNABLE, DE LA NÉGLIGENCE ET DE TOUTE AUTRE PERTE PÉCUNIAIRE OU AUTRE PERTE

DE QUELQUE NATURE QUE CE SOIT) SE RAPPORTANT DE QUELQUE MANIÈRE QUE CE SOIT À L'UTILISATION DU CONTENU SOUS LICENCE OU À L'INCAPACITÉ DE S'EN SERVIR, À LA PRESTATION OU À L'OMISSION DE LA 'UNE TELLE PRESTATION DE SERVICES DE SOUTIEN TECHNIQUE OU À LA FOURNITURE OU À L'OMISSION DE LA FOURNITURE DE TOUS AUTRES SERVICES, RENSEIGNEMENTS, CONTENUS SOUS LICENCE, ET CONTENU QUI S'Y RAPPORTE GRÂCE AU CONTENU SOUS LICENCE OU PROVENANT AUTREMENT DE L'UTILISATION DU CONTENU SOUS LICENCE OU AUTREMENT AUX TERMES DE TOUTE DISPOSITION DE LA U PRÉSENTE CONVENTION EULA OU RELATIVEMENT À UNE TELLE DISPOSITION, MÊME EN CAS DE FAUTE, DE DÉLIT CIVIL (Y COMPRIS LA NÉGLIGENCE), DE RESPONSABILITÉ STRICTE, DE VIOLATION DE CONTRAT OU DE VIOLATION DE GARANTIE DE MICROSOFT OU DE TOUT FOURNISSEUR ET MÊME SI MICROSOFT OU TOUT FOURNISSEUR A ÉTÉ AVISÉ DE LA POSSIBILITÉ DE TELS DOMMAGES.

LIMITATION DE RESPONSABILITÉ ET RECOURS. MALGRÉ LES DOMMAGES QUE VOUS PUISSIEZ SUBIR POUR QUELQUE MOTIF QUE CE SOIT (NOTAMMENT, MAIS SANS LIMITATION, TOUS LES DOMMAGES SUSMENTIONNÉS ET TOUS LES DOMMAGES DIRECTS OU GÉNÉRAUX OU AUTRES), LA SEULE RESPONSABILITÉ 'OBLIGATION INTÉGRALE DE MICROSOFT ET DE L'UN OU L'AUTRE DE SES FOURNISSEURS AUX TERMES DE TOUTE DISPOSITION DEU LA PRÉSENTE CONVENTION EULA ET VOTRE RECOURS EXCLUSIF À L'ÉGARD DE TOUT CE QUI PRÉCÈDE SE LIMITE AU PLUS ÉLEVÉ ENTRE LES MONTANTS SUIVANTS : LE MONTANT QUE VOUS AVEZ RÉELLEMENT PAYÉ POUR LE CONTENU SOUS LICENCE OU 5,00 $US. LES LIMITES, EXCLUSIONS ET DÉNIS QUI PRÉCÈDENT (Y COMPRIS LES CLAUSES CI-DESSUS), S'APPLIQUENT DANS LA MESURE MAXIMALE PERMISE PAR LES LOIS APPLICABLES, MÊME SI TOUT RECOURS N'ATTEINT PAS SON BUT ESSENTIEL.

À moins que cela ne soit prohibé par le droit local applicable, la présente Convention est régie par les lois de la province d'Ontario, Canada. Vous consentez Chacune des parties à la présente reconnaît irrévocablement à la compétence des tribunaux fédéraux et provinciaux siégeant à Toronto, dans de la province d'Ontario et consent à instituer tout litige qui pourrait découler de la présente auprès des tribunaux situés dans le district judiciaire de York, province d'Ontario.

Au cas où vous auriez des questions concernant cette licence ou que vous désiriez vous mettre en rapport avec Microsoft pour quelque raison que ce soit, veuillez utiliser l'information contenue dans le Contenu Sous Licence pour contacter la filiale de succursale Microsoft desservant votre pays, dont l'adresse est fournie dans ce produit, ou visitez écrivez à : Microsoft sur le World Wide Web à http://www.microsoft.com

Contents

Module 5: Decision Structures and Loops

Module 6: Validating User Input

Module 7: Object-Oriented Programming in Visual Basic .NET

Module 8: Handling Errors and Exceptions

Module 9: Enhancing the User Interface

Module 10: Web Forms and XML Web Services

Module 11: Using ADO.NET

Module 12: Deploying Applications

About This Course

This section provides you with a brief description of the course, audience, suggested prerequisites, and course objectives.

Description

The goal of this course is to enable developers with programming experience in a non-graphical environment, in addition to developers with limited programming experience in a graphical environment, to design and develop a simple graphical user interface (GUI)–based application by using Microsoft® Visual Basic® .NET and the Microsoft Visual Studio® .NET development environment.

Audience

This course is intended for developers who:

- Understand the basics of structured programming, including concepts such as flow control, variables and parameters, and function calls.
- Have some experience (at least three months) in developing applications in either a graphical or non-graphical environment.
- Have little or no experience with object-oriented programming concepts.

Student prerequisites

This course requires that students meet the following prerequisites:

- Have an understanding of and experience with structured programming.

  Microsoft MSDN® Training Course 2667, *Introduction to Programming,* might help students gain basic skills in programming techniques. However, additional experience writing code is necessary for students to fully benefit from attending Course 2559B, *Introduction to Visual Basic .NET Programming with Microsoft .NET.*
- Be familiar and comfortable with using a mouse and keyboard to perform common tasks—such as navigating the file system, opening files, and saving files—in a GUI-based application environment such as Microsoft Word or Microsoft Internet Explorer.

Course objectives

After completing this course, students will be able to:

- Create a simple Visual Basic .NET application based on the Microsoft Windows® Application template.
- Use forms and controls to create a user interface.
- Create and use variables and arrays.
- Create and use **Sub** and **Function** procedures, including predefined functions.
- Implement decision structures and loops by using conditional expressions.
- Validate user input for fields, controls, and forms.
- Apply object-oriented programming techniques to create classes, add methods, and add properties.
- Handle syntax, run-time, and logic errors by using the debugger and structured exception handling.
- Enhance the user interface by adding menus, status bars, and toolbars.
- Create a simple Visual Basic .NET–based Web Forms application that uses an XML Web service.
- Access and manipulate data in a Microsoft Access or Microsoft SQL Server™ database by using Microsoft ADO.NET.
- Build, package, and deploy an application.

Student Materials Compact Disc Contents

The Student Materials compact disc contains the following files and folders:

- *Autorun.exe.* When the compact disc is inserted into the CD-ROM drive, or when you double-click the **Autorun.exe** file, this file opens the compact disc and allows you to browse the Student Materials compact disc.
- *Autorun.inf.* When the compact disc is inserted into the compact disc drive, this file opens Autorun.exe.
- *Default.htm.* This file opens the Student Materials Web page. It provides you with resources pertaining to this course, including additional reading, review and lab answers, lab files, multimedia presentations, and course-related Web sites.
- *Readme.txt.* This file explains how to install the software for viewing the Student Materials compact disc and its contents and how to open the Student Materials Web page.
- *2559B_ms.doc.* This file is the Manual Classroom Setup Guide. It contains a description of classroom requirements, classroom setup instructions, and the classroom configuration.
- *Addread.* This folder contains additional reading pertaining to this course.
- *Democode.* This folder contains demonstration code.
- *Flash.* This folder contains the installer for the Macromedia Flash 5.0 browser plug-in.
- *Fonts.* This folder contains fonts that are required to view the PowerPoint presentation and Web-based materials.
- *Labfiles.* This folder contains files that are used in the hands-on labs. These files may be used to prepare the student computers for the hands-on labs.
- *Media.* This folder contains files that are used in multimedia presentations for this course.
- *Mplayer.* This folder contains the setup file to install Microsoft Windows Media™ Player.
- *Practices.* This folder contains files that are used in the hands-on practices.
- *Webfiles.* This folder contains the files that are required to view the course Web page. To open the Web page, open Windows Explorer, and in the root directory of the compact disc, double-click **Default.htm** or **Autorun.exe**.
- *Wordview.* This folder contains the Word Viewer that is used to view any Word document (.doc) files that are included on the compact disc.

Document Conventions

The following conventions are used in course materials to distinguish elements of the text.

Convention	Use
Bold	Represents commands, command options, and syntax that must be typed exactly as shown. It also indicates commands on menus and buttons, dialog box titles and options, and icon and menu names.
Italic	In syntax statements or descriptive text, indicates argument names or placeholders for variable information. Italic is also used for introducing new terms, for book titles, and for emphasis in the text.
Title Capitals	Indicate domain names, user names, computer names, directory names, and folder and file names, except when specifically referring to case-sensitive names. Unless otherwise indicated, you can use lowercase letters when you type a directory name or file name in a dialog box or at a command prompt.
ALL CAPITALS	Indicate the names of keys, key sequences, and key combinations—for example, ALT+SPACEBAR.
`monospace`	Represents code samples or examples of screen text.
[ ]	In syntax statements, enclose optional items. For example, [*filename*] in command syntax indicates that you can choose to type a file name with the command. Type only the information within the brackets, not the brackets themselves.
{ }	In syntax statements, enclose required items. Type only the information within the braces, not the braces themselves.
|	In syntax statements, separates an either/or choice.
▶	Indicates a procedure with sequential steps.
...	In syntax statements, specifies that the preceding item may be repeated.
. . .	Represents an omitted portion of a code sample.

msdn® training

Introduction

Contents

Microsoft®

Introduction

- Name
- Company affiliation
- Title/function
- Job responsibility
- Programming, networking, database experience
- Product experience
- Expectations for the course

Your instructor will ask you to introduce yourself and provide a brief overview of your background, addressing the bulleted items on the slide as appropriate.

Course Materials

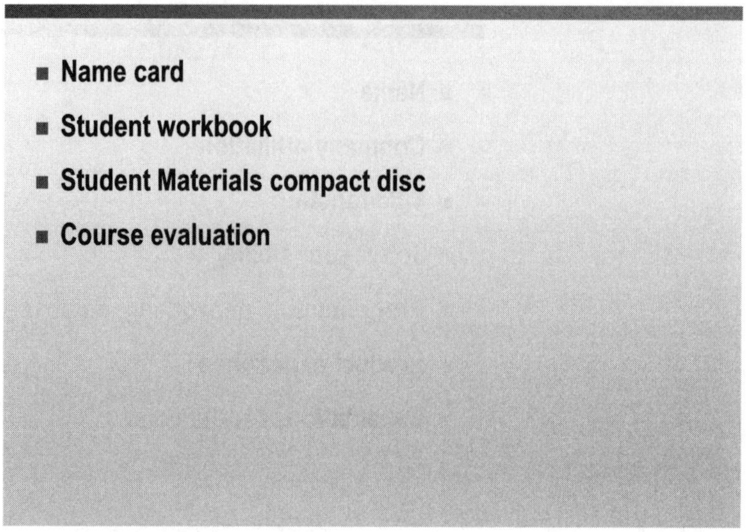

The following materials are included with your kit:

- *Name card.* Write your name on both sides of the name card.
- *Student workbook.* The student workbook contains the material covered in class, in addition to the hands-on lab exercises.
- *Student Materials compact disc.* The Student Materials compact disc contains the Web page that provides you with links to resources pertaining to this course, including additional readings, review and lab answers, lab files, multimedia presentations, and course-related Web sites.

  Note To open the Web page, insert the Student Materials compact disc into the CD-ROM drive, and then in the root directory of the compact disc, double-click **Autorun.exe** or **Default.htm**.

- *Course evaluation.* To provide feedback on the course, training facility, and instructor, you will have the opportunity to complete an online evaluation near the end of the course.

  To provide additional comments or inquire about the Microsoft® Certified Professional program, send e-mail to mcphelp@microsoft.com.

Prerequisites

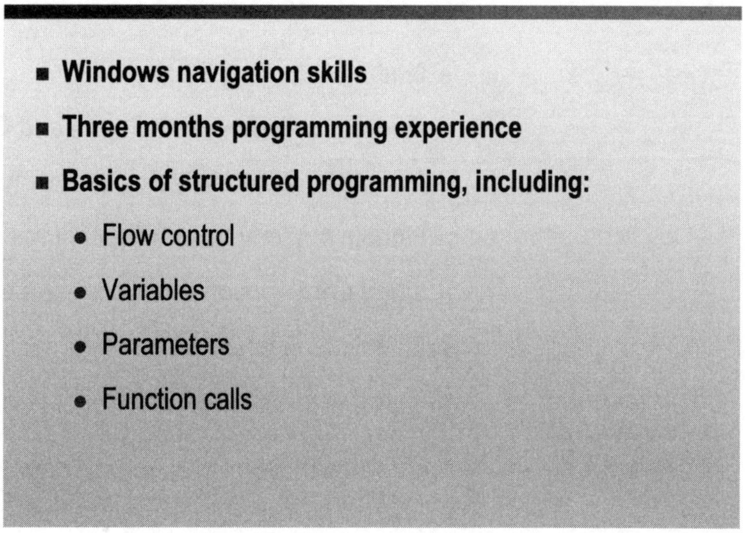

This course requires that students meet the following prerequisites:

- Microsoft Windows® navigation skills.
- Experience (at least 3 months) developing applications in either a graphical or non-graphical environment.

  –And–
- Completion of Microsoft MSDN® Training Course 2667, *Introduction to Programming*.

  –Or–
- Understanding of the basics of structured programming, including concepts such as flow control, variables and parameters, and function calls.

Course Outline

- **Module 1: Getting Started**
- **Module 2: Working with Forms and Controls**
- **Module 3: Using Variables and Arrays**
- **Module 4: Working with Procedures**
- **Module 5: Decision Structures and Loops**
- **Module 6: Validating User Input**

Module 1, "Getting Started," introduces Visual Basic .NET and explains how it fits into the Microsoft .NET platform. It explains how to use the programming tools in Microsoft Visual Studio® .NET and provides enough practice so that students can create their first application in Visual Basic .NET.

Module 2, "Working with Forms and Controls," explains fundamental programming concepts, including event-driven programming, classes, objects, properties, methods, and events. This module also explains how to use forms and controls to create a user interface, which includes the following: how to create a form, set properties, call methods, and write code for events; how to add controls to a form; how to manage multiple forms, how to use message boxes; how to use naming conventions, and how to format and document code.

Module 3, "Using Variables and Arrays," explains how to name, declare, assign values to, and use variables and constants. It explains how to declare variables with different levels of scope, how to create your own data structures, and how to convert variable values from one data type to another. It also describes how to store data in an array.

Module 4, "Working with Procedures," describes how to create and use **Sub** and **Function** procedures, including predefined functions, and how to structure code for increased reusability.

Module 5, "Decision Structures and Loops," explains how to implement decision structures and loop structures to control program output and execution.

Module 6, "Validating User Input," explains how to validate user input at both the field level and the form level in applications. It describes how to handle invalid input by providing error messages and guiding users through the process of finding and fixing errors. It describes how to use control properties and methods to restrict and validate data entry.

Course Outline *(continued)*

- Module 7: Object-Oriented Programming in Visual Basic .NET
- Module 8: Handling Errors and Exceptions
- Module 9: Enhancing the User Interface
- Module 10: Web Forms and XML Web Services
- Module 11: Using ADO.NET
- Module 12: Deploying Applications

Module 7, "Object-Oriented Programming in Visual Basic .NET," explains how to create and use classes. The module explains the concepts of abstraction, encapsulation, instantiation, initialization, constructors, and destructors. This module also describes inheritance, polymorphism, and namespaces.

Module 8, "Handling Errors and Exceptions," explains types of errors that can occur in a program, and explains how to use the debugging tools provided with Visual Basic .NET to help diagnose and correct the errors. These tools include the Visual Studio .NET debugger, debugging windows, and structured exception handling.

Module 9, "Enhancing the User Interface," explains how to create menus, status bars, and toolbars to enhance the usability of an application.

Module 10, "Web Forms and XML Web Services," explains how to use Web Forms to create a Web application, and how to invoke a simple XML Web service from a Web application.

Module 11, "Using ADO.NET," explains how to use Microsoft ADO.NET with a Windows Forms application to create, read, update, and delete records in Microsoft Access and Microsoft SQL Server™ databases.

Module 12, "Deploying Applications," explains various deployment options available in Visual Basic .NET, and how to deploy applications based on Windows.

Microsoft Official Curriculum

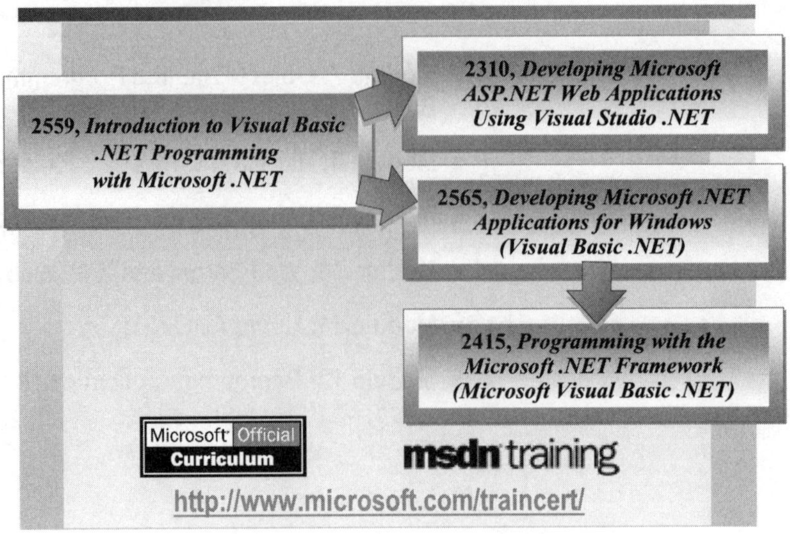

Introduction

Microsoft Training and Certification develops Microsoft Official Curriculum (MOC), including MSDN Training, for computer professionals who design, develop, support, implement, or manage solutions using Microsoft products and technologies. These courses provide comprehensive skills-based training in instructor-led and online formats.

Additional recommended courses

Each course relates in some way to another course. A related course may be a prerequisite, a follow-up course in a recommended series, or a course that offers additional training.

To learn more about developing Windows-based applications by using Visual Basic. NET, it is recommended that you take the following courses in this order:

Course	Title and description
2565	*Developing Microsoft .NET Applications for Windows (Visual Basic .NET)* This three-day, instructor-led course is a part of the Visual Basic .NET curriculum and will cover the major topics for Windows client application programming on the Microsoft .NET Framework. These topics include: Windows Forms, GDI+, simple data access, interoperating with unmanaged code, threading and asynchronous programming issues, simple remoting, Web access, XML Web services consumption, debugging, security, and deployment issues for desktop applications.
2415	*Programming with the Microsoft .NET Framework (Microsoft Visual Basic .NET)* This five-day, instructor-led course will help application developers understand the .NET Framework. In addition to offering an introduction to key concepts and terminology, the course provides a series of labs, which explain .NET Framework features that are used to code, debug, tune, and deploy applications. Topics include working with assemblies, versioning, the common type system, memory management, file and network I/O, serialization, remoting, and XML Web services.

After taking Course 2559B, *Introduction to Visual Basic .NET Programming with Microsoft .NET*, you can also take the following course if you are interested in learning more about developing Web applications:

Course	Title and description
2310	*Developing Microsoft ASP.NET Web Applications Using Visual Studio .NET* This five-day, instructor-led course will teach Visual Basic programmers and beginning Web developers the fundamentals of Web application implementation with ASP.NET and Visual Basic .NET. This course focuses on using the Visual Studio .NET environment and the .NET platform to create an ASP.NET Web application that delivers dynamic content to the Web.

Other related courses may become available in the future, so for up-to-date information about recommended courses, visit the Training and Certification Web site.

Microsoft Training and Certification information

For more information, visit the Microsoft Training and Certification Web site at http://www.microsoft.com/traincert/.

6:00 til 10:30

* MCAD Microsoft Certified Applications Developer

MCSD Microsoft Certified Solutions Developer

Microsoft Certified Professional Program

Introduction

Microsoft Training and Certification offers a variety of certification credentials for developers and IT professionals. The Microsoft Certified Professional program is the leading certification program for validating your experience and skills, keeping you competitive in today's changing business environment.

MCP certifications

The Microsoft Certified Professional program includes the following certifications.

- MCSA on Microsoft Windows 2000

  The Microsoft Certified Systems Administrator (MCSA) certification is designed for professionals who implement, manage, and troubleshoot existing network and system environments based on Microsoft Windows 2000 platforms, including the Windows .NET Server family. Implementation responsibilities include installing and configuring parts of the systems. Management responsibilities include administering and supporting the systems.

- MCSE on Microsoft Windows 2000

  The Microsoft Certified Systems Engineer (MCSE) credential is the premier certification for professionals who analyze the business requirements and design and implement the infrastructure for business solutions based on the Microsoft Windows 2000 platform and Microsoft server software, including the Windows .NET Server family. Implementation responsibilities include installing, configuring, and troubleshooting network systems.

- MCAD

  The Microsoft Certified Application Developer (MCAD) for Microsoft .NET credential is appropriate for professionals who use Microsoft technologies to develop and maintain department-level applications, components, Web or desktop clients, or back-end data services, and for those who work in teams that develop enterprise applications. The credential covers job tasks that include developing, deploying, and maintaining the solution.

- MCSD

  The Microsoft Certified Solution Developer (MCSD) credential is the premier certification for professionals who design and develop leading-edge business solutions with Microsoft development tools, technologies, platforms, and the Microsoft Windows DNA architecture. The types of applications MCSDs can develop include desktop applications and multi-user, Web-based, N-tier, and transaction-based applications. The credential covers job tasks ranging from analyzing business requirements to maintaining solutions.

- MCDBA on Microsoft SQL Server 2000

  The Microsoft Certified Database Administrator (MCDBA) credential is the premier certification for professionals who implement and administer Microsoft SQL Server databases. The certification is appropriate for individuals who derive physical database designs, develop logical data models, create physical databases, create data services by using Transact-SQL, manage and maintain databases, configure and manage security, monitor and optimize databases, and install and configure SQL Server.

- MCP

  The Microsoft Certified Professional (MCP) credential is for individuals who have the skills to successfully implement a Microsoft product or technology as part of a business solution in an organization. Hands-on experience with the product is necessary to successfully achieve certification.

- MCT

  Microsoft Certified Trainers (MCTs) demonstrate the instructional and technical skills that qualify them to deliver Microsoft Official Curriculum through Microsoft Certified Technical Education Centers (Microsoft CTECs).

Certification requirements

The certification requirements differ for each certification category and are specific to the products and job functions addressed by the certification. To become a Microsoft Certified Professional, you must pass rigorous certification exams that provide a valid and reliable measure of technical proficiency and expertise.

For More Information See the Microsoft Training and Certification Web site at http://www.microsoft.com/traincert/.

You can also send e-mail to mcphelp@microsoft.com if you have specific certification questions.

Acquiring the skills tested by an MCP exam

Microsoft Official Curriculum (MOC) and MSDN Training Curriculum can help you develop the skills that you need to do your job. They also complement the experience that you gain while working with Microsoft products and technologies. However, no one-to-one correlation exists between MOC and MSDN Training courses and MCP exams. Microsoft does not expect or intend for the courses to be the sole preparation method for passing MCP exams. Practical product knowledge and experience is also necessary to pass the MCP exams.

To help prepare for the MCP exams, use the preparation guides that are available for each exam. Each Exam Preparation Guide contains exam-specific information, such as a list of the topics on which you will be tested. These guides are available on the Microsoft Training and Certification Web site at http://www.microsoft.com/traincert/.

Facilities

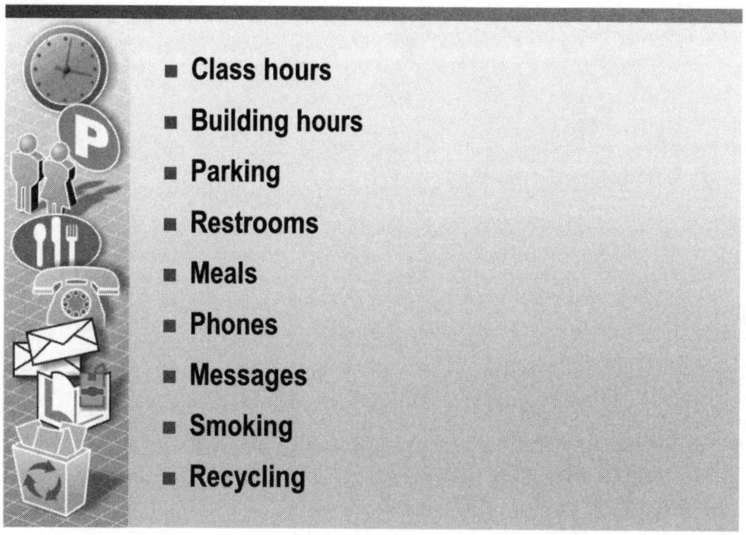
Class hours
Building hours
Parking
Restrooms
Meals
Phones
Messages
Smoking
Recycling

msdn® training

Module 1: Getting Started

Contents

Microsoft®

Overview

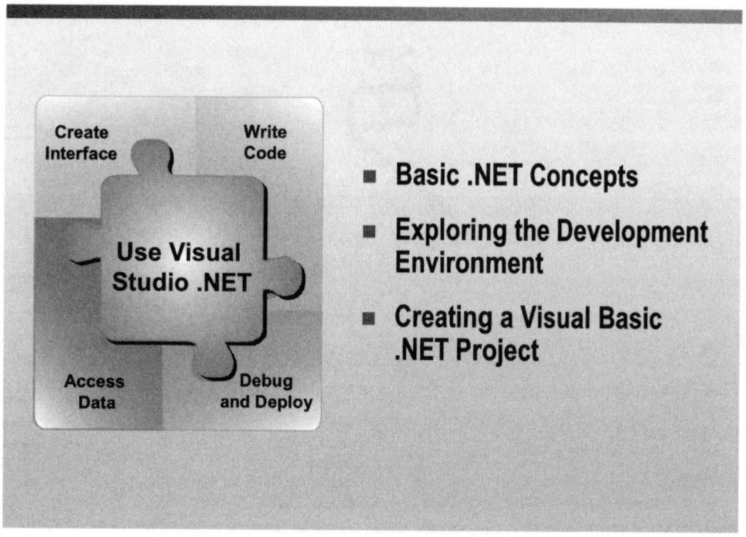

Introduction

This module introduces Microsoft® Visual Basic® .NET and explains how it fits into the Microsoft .NET platform. It explains how to use the programming tools in Microsoft Visual Studio® .NET and provides enough practice so that you can create your first application in Visual Basic .NET.

Objectives

After completing this module, you will be able to:

- Start a Visual Basic .NET project that is based on the Microsoft Windows® Application template.
- Use the standard toolbar, programming tools, and programming windows in the development environment to work with applications.
- Create a simple application in Visual Basic .NET.

Multimedia: Tour of Visual Studio .NET

Introduction

This multimedia demonstration takes you on a tour through Visual Studio .NET. It shows how to create a simple Visual Basic .NET–based application by using Visual Studio .NET. It demonstrates many of the commonly used features of the development environment.

Lesson: Basic .NET Concepts

Introduction

Visual Basic .NET is the newest version of the Visual Basic development system. Before you start creating applications in Visual Basic .NET, you will find it useful to understand some basic .NET concepts.

Lesson agenda

This lesson includes the following topics and activities:

- What Is the .NET Platform?
- How the .NET Framework Works
- What Is Visual Studio .NET?
- How to Use the Start Page
- What Is an Application Template?
- How to Use Solution Explorer
- Practice: Working with a Visual Basic .NET Project

Lesson objectives

This lesson provides an overview of the .NET platform and how it benefits developers. It explains how to use the programming tools in the Visual Studio .NET development environment to create applications in Visual Basic .NET.

After completing this lesson, you will be able to:

- Describe the key elements of the .NET platform.
- Explain the benefits that the Microsoft .NET Framework offers to developers.
- Describe the role of Visual Studio .NET and Visual Basic .NET in the .NET platform.
- Use the Visual Studio Start Page to access developer news and to set user preferences.
- Start a Visual Basic .NET project that is based on the Windows Application template.
- Use Solution Explorer to examine solution files and code.

What Is the .NET Platform?

Marketing Ploy

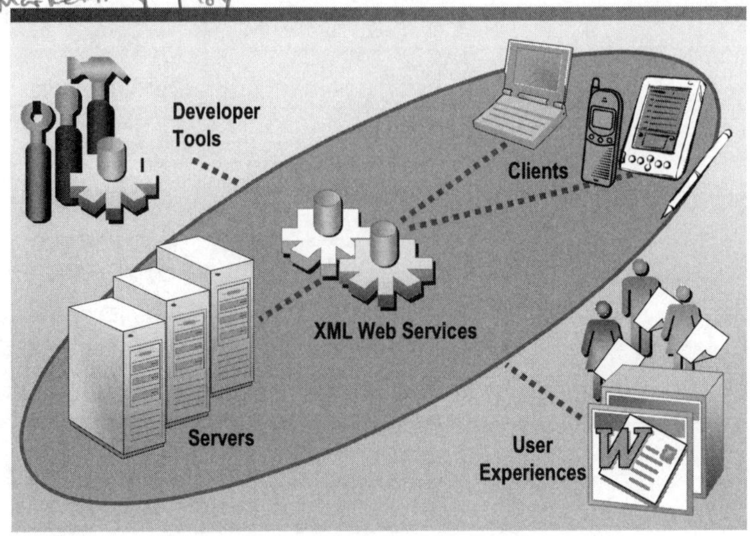

Introduction

The .NET platform provides the foundation for the next generation of software that connects disparate systems, information, devices, and users in a more unified and personalized way. It includes XML Web services as the means to enable different technologies to interoperate. It provides software developers the tools and technology to quickly and efficiently deliver business solutions that span multiple applications and multiple client devices across many organizations. It enables users to control how, when, and what information is delivered to them.

Case study

The following is an example of how the .NET platform can help companies integrate solutions and share data to improve the user experience.

An airline partner approached a car rental company, one of the world's largest car rental companies, with the opportunity to link the company's reservations system with the airline partner's Web site. The challenge for the car rental company was to determine how to easily transfer reservation requests and related data between this large airline, which uses UNIX systems, and the company, which primarily uses Windows technologies.

The car rental company chose to build its solution with .NET technologies and XML Web services. The solution enabled the company to quickly build a translation system between the UNIX system at the airline and the company's VMS system. The solution was developed by two people in only two months—two to three times faster than the company had anticipated.

Using traditional methods of creating a unique solution for this particular airline was certainly an option. But by building the system with XML Web services, the car rental company is capable of extending its service to multiple airlines and partners. If other partners or corporate customers want to connect directly with the company's reservations systems, all the company needs to do is give them the XML schema.

Family of .NET products

The .NET platform includes a comprehensive family of products created to comply with XML and Internet standards. These products provide the following components for working with XML-based solutions:

- Tools to develop solutions
- Servers to manage, build, and deploy solutions
- Services to integrate, connect, and reuse solutions
- Hardware and software clients to provide unprecedented user experiences

Key elements

The following table provides definitions and examples for each of the key elements in the .NET platform.

Element	Definition	Examples
Developer tools	The programming interfaces and tools for designing, creating, running, and deploying solutions for the .NET platform.	.NET Framework Visual Studio .NET
Servers	The infrastructure for building, deploying, and operating solutions for the .NET platform.	Microsoft Windows 2000 Server Microsoft .NET Enterprise Servers
XML Web services	A core set of predefined services that perform common and routine tasks, and the means for developers to develop their own services.	Microsoft .NET My Services
Clients	Devices running on operating systems that integrate and interact with all of the other .NET elements.	Microsoft Windows CE for handheld devices Microsoft Windows XP for computers
User experiences	Traditional client software integrated with XML Web services to present everything users need in a way that makes sense to them.	Future versions of Microsoft bCentral™ Microsoft MSN®

How the .NET Framework Works

inside framework

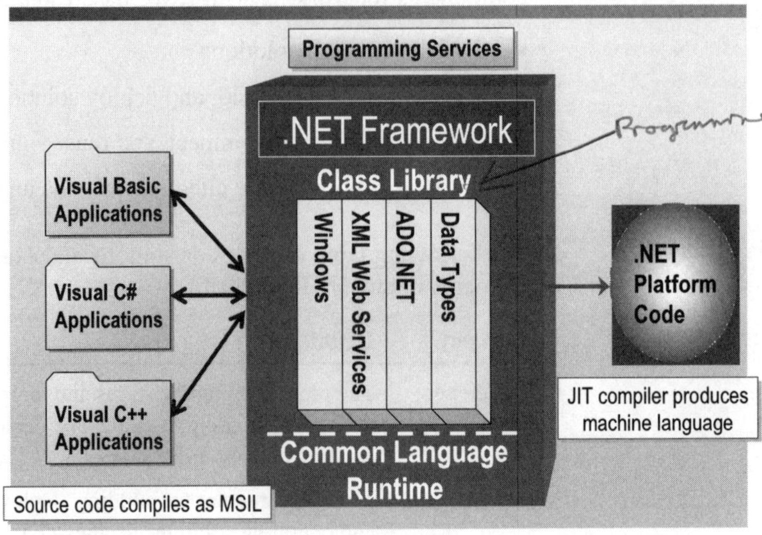

CLR Common Language Runtime

Introduction

The .NET Framework is a set of programming services designed to simplify application development in the highly distributed environment of the Internet. The .NET Framework has two main components: the common language runtime and the class library.

How applications interact with the .NET Framework

When you create a new Windows-based application in Visual Basic .NET, you are provided with starter code that includes the **System.Windows.Forms** namespace and the **Form** class. With this class, you can easily create windows, buttons, menus, toolbars, and other screen elements. When you compile the application, it is translated into the runtime's common language, Microsoft intermediate language (MSIL). After the application is compiled, the runtime manages the execution of the application.

The runtime includes a feature called just-in-time (JIT) compilation that translates the MSIL code into the machine language of the system on which the application will run. When a client device on the .NET platform launches the Visual Basic .NET application, it starts running in the machine language of the client system and can fully integrate and interact with other .NET-based applications and services regardless of the language in which it was developed.

ms training & cert:

http://www.microsoft.com/Learning/training/default.asp

Managed code - code that runs within the framework

unmanaged code - code that does not run within framework (native code)

Terms and definitions

To understand how the .NET Framework works, you need to be familiar with the following terminology:

- Class

  A *class* is a named programming entity that comprises a common set of methods, properties, and attributes. For example, **Form** is one of the classes in the **System.Windows.Forms** namespace that is used to create Windows Forms.

- Namespace

  A *namespace* identifies a collection of related classes and/or other namespaces in the .NET Framework. Examples of namespaces include the following:

  - **System**
  - **System.Windows.Forms**

- Class library

  The *class library* is a comprehensive object-oriented collection of reusable classes that are organized by their functionality into hierarchical namespaces. You can use the class library to develop applications ranging from traditional client applications to applications based on the latest innovations provided by Microsoft ASP.NET and XML Web services.

- Common language runtime

  The *common language runtime* is the foundation of the .NET Framework. In the .NET environment, programmers develop applications in the .NET-compatible language of their choice, the code is compiled into MSIL, and the runtime manages and runs the compiled code.

Note In addition to Microsoft languages such as Visual Basic, Microsoft Visual C#™, Microsoft Visual C++®, and Microsoft JScript®, alternative languages including Perl, Smalltalk, and Eiffel are being modified for compatibility with the .NET platform.

What Is Visual Studio .NET?

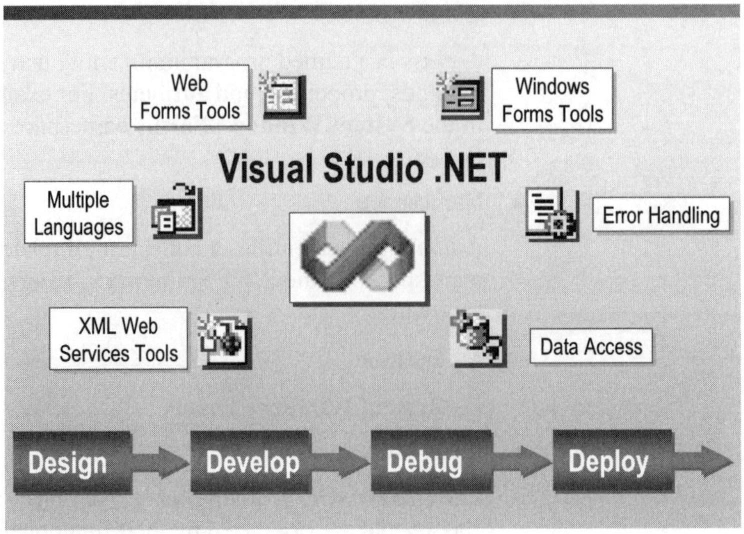

Introduction

Visual Studio .NET is an integrated development environment that helps you to quickly design, develop, debug, and deploy .NET Framework solutions. You can access a common set of tools, designers, and editors from any Visual Studio .NET programming language. You can create Windows Forms and Web Forms applications that integrate data and business logic.

Definitions

Visual Studio .NET includes the programming features described in the following table.

Feature	Description
Windows Forms Designer	A graphical design surface enables you to quickly create the user interface for an application. You can drag or draw controls onto this surface.
Tools for Windows Forms	A Windows Forms Designer, a Windows Application template, essential project references, and starter code are provided to help you create standard Windows Forms applications.
Tools for Web Forms	A Web Forms Designer, an ASP.NET Web Application template, essential project references, and starter code are provided to help you build Web Forms applications in which the primary user interface is a browser.
Tools for XML Web services	An ASP.NET Web Services template is provided. This template constructs a Web application project structure on a development Web server and a Visual Studio .NET solution file on your local computer.
Multiple language support	All of the .NET platform programming languages, including Visual Basic .NET and Visual C#, are integrated into the development environment.
Data access	Components for creating applications that share data, visual database tools for accessing data, and a robust set of Microsoft ADO.NET classes make it easy to work with all types of data.
Error handling	Debugging tools with cross-language support help you to find and fix errors in your code, and you can use structured exception classes to build error handling into your application.
Wizards	Wizards help you to quickly complete common and perhaps complex tasks. Each page of a wizard helps you set options, configure settings, and customize projects.

How to Use the Start Page

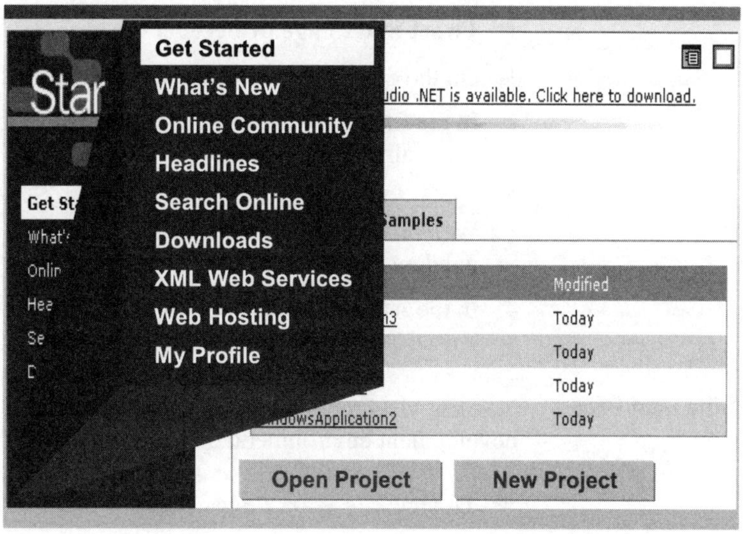

Introduction

You use the Visual Studio .NET Start Page to open projects, to create your own profile, and to set your preferences. You can also read recent Microsoft developer news, participate in .NET online communities, search the Microsoft MSDN® Library, and download software upgrades.

Opening projects

You can choose whether you want to start a new project or open an existing project from the Start Page.

▶ **To open a new project**

- Click **Get Started** in the list on the left side of the page (if it is not selected already), and then click **New Project**.

▶ **To open an existing project**

- Click **Get Started** in the list on the left side of the page, and then click **Open Project**.

Showup on help

Setting Visual Studio .NET preferences

You can choose a pre-existing profile, such as Visual Basic Developer, or you can modify each profile item manually.

► **To set Start Page preferences**

1. On the Start Page, click **My Profile** in the list on the left side of the page.
2. In the first drop-down list under Profile, click **Visual Basic Developer** (if it is not already selected).
3. Under **Show Help**, choose whether you want Help content to appear in a Web browser window inside the development environment or in an external window.
4. In the **At Startup** list, choose what you want to appear when you start Visual Studio .NET.

Viewing the Start Page

You can view the Start Page at any time when you are working in the development environment.

► **To view the Start Page**

- On the **Help** menu, click **Show Start Page**.

What Is an Application Template?

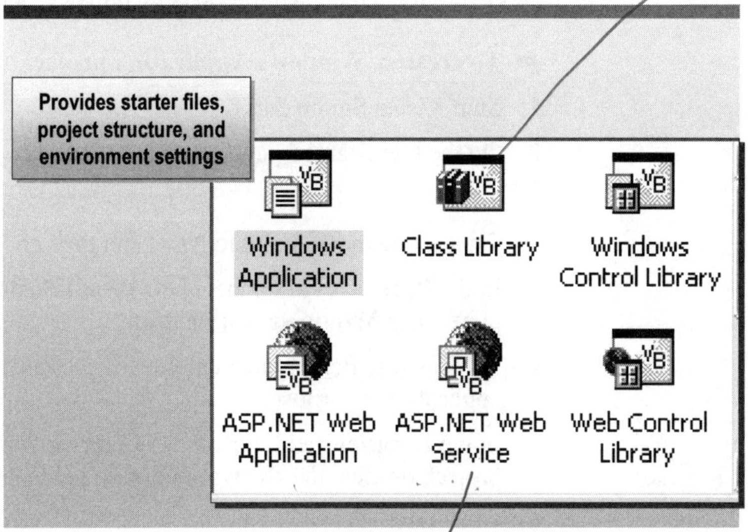

Introduction

Visual Studio .NET offers several application templates to support the development of different kinds of applications and components. Before you start a new project, you need to choose the type of template that you want to use.

Definition

An *application template* provides starter files and a project structure and contains the basic project objects and environment settings you need to create the type of application you want to build.

Examples of application templates

Two of the most commonly used templates are the Windows Application and the ASP.NET Web Application templates.

- Windows Application template

  This template provides the tools, structure, and starter code for a standard Windows-based application. It automatically adds the essential project references and files to use as a starting point for your application.

- ASP.NET Web Application template

  This template is used to create an ASP.NET Web application on a computer that has Internet Information Services (IIS) version 5.0 or later installed. To help you start designing your application, the template creates the basic files needed on the server.

Choosing a template

When starting a new Visual Basic .NET project, one of the first steps is to choose an application template. In this module, you will only use the Windows Application template to complete the practices and the labs.

► To create a Windows Application project in Visual Basic .NET

1. Start Visual Studio .NET.
2. On the **Get Started** pane, click **New Project**.

   – Or –

   On the **File** menu, point to **New**, and then click **Project**.
3. In the **Project Types** pane, click **Visual Basic Projects**. In the **Templates** pane, click **Windows Application**.
4. In the **Name** field, type a unique project name that will indicate the application's purpose.
5. In the **Location** field, type the directory in which you want to save your project, or click the **Browse** button to navigate to it.
6. Click **OK**.

   The Windows Forms Designer opens, showing Form1 of the project you created.

How to Use Solution Explorer

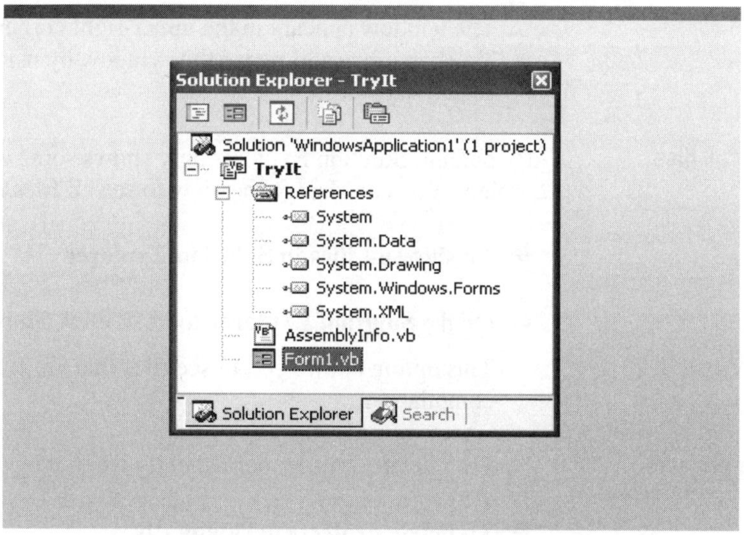

Introduction

Solution Explorer allows you to view files and perform file management tasks in a solution or a project. A single Visual Basic–based .NET solution and its projects appear in a hierarchical list that provides updated information about the status of your solution, projects, and files.

Terms and definitions

A *solution* is a container for the projects and solution items that can be built into an application. A solution usually contains one or more related projects.

A *project* is a container within a solution that is used to logically manage, build, and debug the project items that make up your application.

Project and solution files

Visual Studio .NET supports many file types and their associated file extensions. The following table describes some common file types that are specific to Visual Basic .NET–based solutions.

Extension	Name	Description
.sln	Visual Studio solution	Organizes projects, project items, and solution items in the solution by providing the environment with references to their locations on disk.
.suo	Solution user options	Records all of the options that you might associate with your solution so that each time you open the solution it includes customizations that you have made.
.vb	Visual Basic project	Represents forms, user controls, classes, and module files that belong to a single-project solution. Any files that are not based on a programming language have their own extension. For example, a Crystal Report file has the extension .rpt, and a text file has the extension .txt.
.vbproj	Visual Basic projects	Represents forms, user controls, classes, and module files that belong to a multiple-project solution. This extension allows you to differentiate between files written in Visual Basic .NET and other .NET-compatible languages. (Visual C# uses .csproj.)
.aspx .asmx .asax	Web project items	Web project items include Web-specific files such as .aspx for Web Forms, .asmx for XML Web services, and .asax for global application classes. Web projects also use the .vb file extension for classes and modules.

Opening Solution Explorer

► To open Solution Explorer

- On the **View** menu, click **Solution Explorer**.

  The window appears in the upper-right corner of your development area. You can move and resize this window by using standard drag-and-drop functionality.

Showing all files

By default, Solution Explorer only shows some of the files that are stored in the project. You can change the view to see all files in a solution.

► To show all files in Solution Explorer

- On the **Solution Explorer** toolbar, click **Show All Files**. 

  This option allows you to see files that are created manually or during compilation.

Deleting projects

You can delete projects permanently when they are no longer needed.

► To delete projects permanently

- In Windows Explorer, right-click the folder that contains the solution that you want to delete, and then click **Delete**.

Practice: Working with a Visual Basic .NET Project

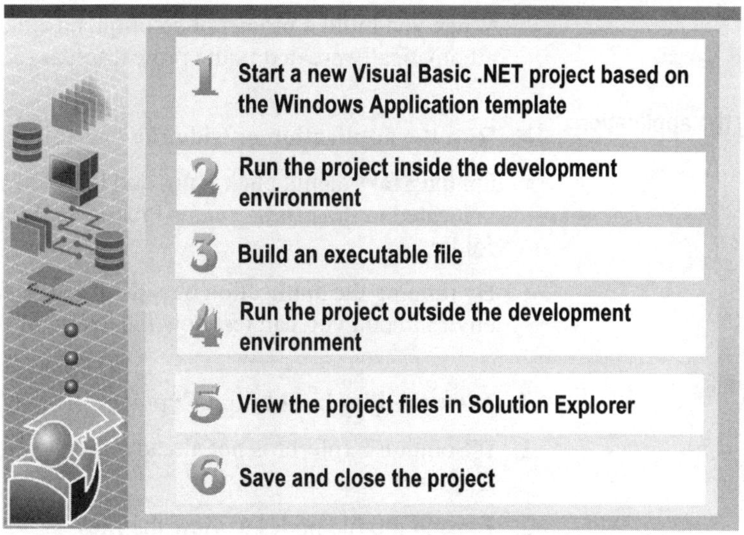

Introduction

In this practice, you will start a new Visual Basic .NET project and work with it in the development environment.

Starting the project

► **Start a new Visual Basic .NET project**

1. Start Visual Studio .NET.
2. On the **File** menu, point to **New**, and then click **Project**.
3. In the **Project Types** pane, click **Visual Basic Projects**. In the **Templates** pane, click **Windows Application**.
4. In the **Name** box, type **NewWindowsProj**.
5. Click **Browse**, navigate to *install_folder*\Practices\Mod01, and then click **Open**. Click **OK**.

Running the project in the IDE

► **Run the project inside the development environment**

1. Click the **Start** button ▸ on the standard toolbar. You can also press F5 to run the project.

   Because you have not made any changes to the starter code for the project, a blank form appears when the project is run.
2. Close the blank form to go back to the programming environment.

Building the project

▶ **Build an executable file for the project**

- On the **Build** menu, click **Build NewWindowsProj**.

  When you build a project or solution, an executable (.exe) file is automatically created in the project folder, in a subfolder named bin.

Running the application

▶ **Run the application outside the development environment**

- On the **Start** menu, click **Run**, and then browse to the .exe file. The .exe file is located in the *install_folder*\Practices\Mod01\NewWindowsProj\bin folder.

  By running the application outside of the Visual Studio .NET development environment, you can test how the user will experience the application.

Viewing files

▶ **View the files in Solution Explorer**

1. If Solution Explorer is not already open, on the **View** menu, click **Solution Explorer**.
2. Expand the file nodes to view the files.

   Notice the solution, project, AssemblyInfo.vb, and Form1.vb files. These files are included in every Windows Forms project.

Saving and closing the project

▶ **Close the project and quit Visual Studio .NET**

1. On the **File** menu, click **Exit**.
2. If prompted to save changes, click **Yes**.

Lesson: Exploring the Development Environment

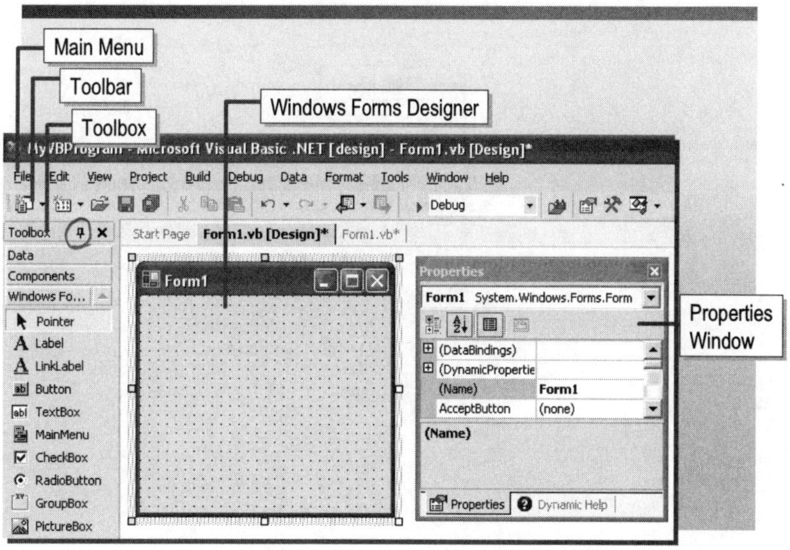

Solution Explorer
Holds more than one Project

Introduction

This lesson introduces the main features in the development environment that you use to create and modify applications, such as the Windows Forms Designer and the controls Toolbox.

Lesson agenda

This lesson includes the following topics and activities:

- Menus and Toolbars
- The Toolbox
- Windows Forms Designer
- Code Editor
- Properties Window
- Other Programming Windows
- Online Help System
- Practice: Working in the Development Environment

Lesson objectives

After completing this lesson, you will be able to:

- Use the main menu and standard toolbar to open, build (debug and release modes), run, save, and close an existing Visual Basic .NET–based application.
- View user interface forms in the Windows Forms Designer or the Code Editor.
- Use the Toolbox to add a button and a label to a form.
- Use the Properties window to view and set properties.
- Open, close, and reopen programming tools and windows.
- Use the online Help system to get more information.

Menus and Toolbars

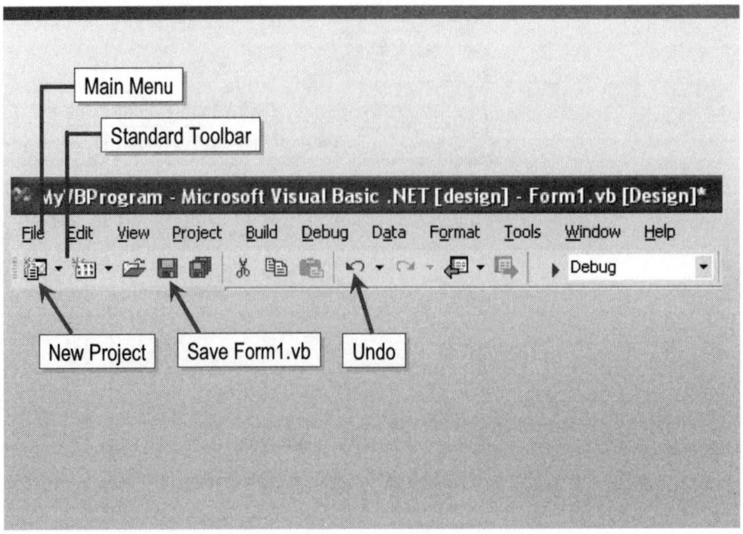

Introduction

When you start a Visual Basic .NET project and select an application template, the visual development environment appears. The main menu and standard toolbar provide access to most of the commands that control the Visual Studio .NET programming environment.

Main menu

Commands on the main menu work as they do in all Windows-based applications, and you can access them by using the keyboard or the mouse.

Standard toolbar

The standard toolbar provides buttons that serve as shortcuts for most of the common commands, such as **Open**, **Save**, **Start**, **Add New Item**, **Navigate Backward**, and **Navigate Forward**. It also contains buttons that open Solution Explorer, the Properties window, the Toolbox, and other key elements in the development environment.

Debug toolbar

The **Debug** toolbar provides shortcuts for the debugging features, such as stepping through code and setting breakpoints.

Docking features

Toolbars can either be docked (attached) or undocked (floating). By default, most toolbars are docked; however, you can undock or dock a toolbar at any time.

► **To undock a toolbar**

- Click anywhere on the toolbar except on a button, and drag the toolbar away from its docked position.

► **To dock a toolbar**

- Drag the toolbar to any edge of the main window.

The Toolbox

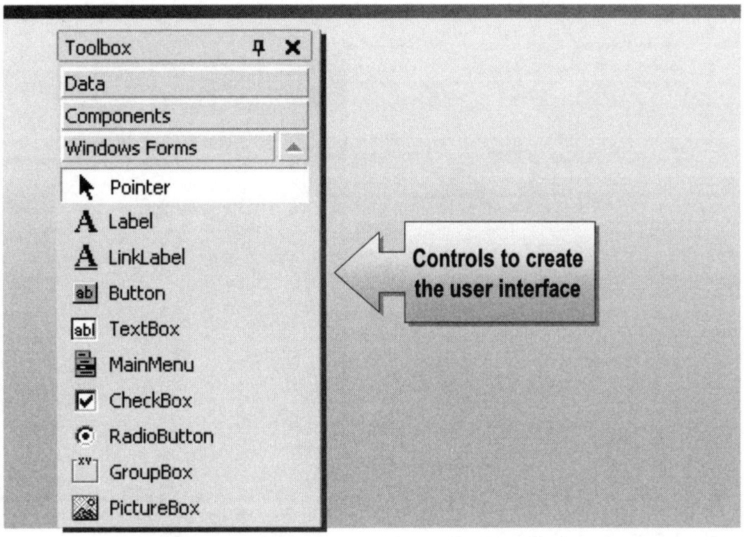

Introduction

You create the user interface objects for your application by adding controls from the Toolbox to a form. The Toolbox is initially located on the left side of the development environment. There are several tabs for different categories of controls, such as **Windows Forms** and **Data**.

How the Toolbox works

The Toolbox contains a variety of controls that you can use to add artwork, labels, buttons, list boxes, scroll bars, menus, and geometric shapes to a user interface. Each control you add to a form becomes a programmable user interface object in your application. These objects are visible to users when the application runs and operate like the standard objects in any Windows-based application.

Closing and opening the Toolbox

► **To close and open the Toolbox**

1. To close the Toolbox, click the **Close** button (**x**) in the upper-right corner of the Toolbox.
2. To open the Toolbox, on the **View** menu, click **Toolbox**.
3. To make the Toolbox stay open, click the pushpin on the Toolbox title bar.

Hiding and reopening the Toolbox

► **To hide and reopen the Toolbox**

1. To hide the Toolbox, click the pushpin on the Toolbox title bar.
2. To reopen the Toolbox when it is hidden, on the **View** menu, click **Toolbox**.

Moving the Toolbox

► **To move the Toolbox**

1. Right-click the Toolbox title bar, and then click **Floating**.
2. Drag the Toolbox to the desired location.

Windows Forms Designer

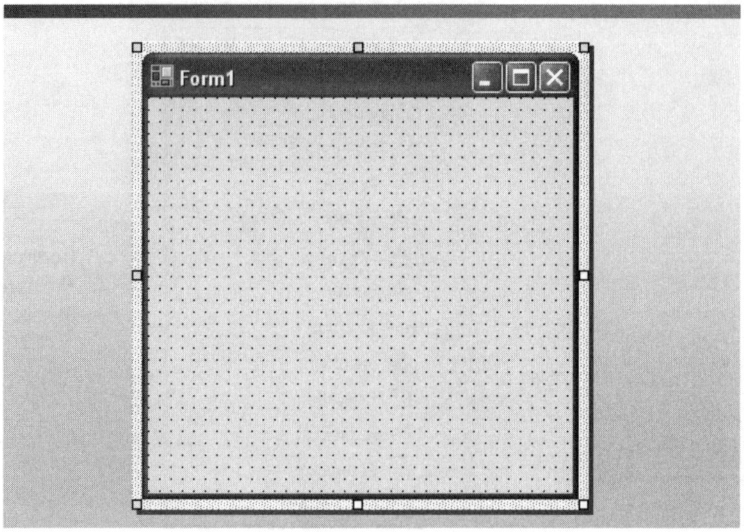

Introduction

When you start a project in Visual Basic .NET, the Windows Forms Designer opens in Design view, showing Form1 of the project. You place controls from the Toolbox on the form to create the user interface for a window used in your application.

Elements of a form

The default form contains the minimum elements used by most forms: a title bar, a control box, and **Minimize**, **Maximize**, and **Close** buttons.

Viewing a form

► **To view a form in Design view**

- In Solution Explorer, double-click the form.

  – Or –

  In Solution Explorer, select the form and click the **View Designer**  button on the toolbar.

Code Editor

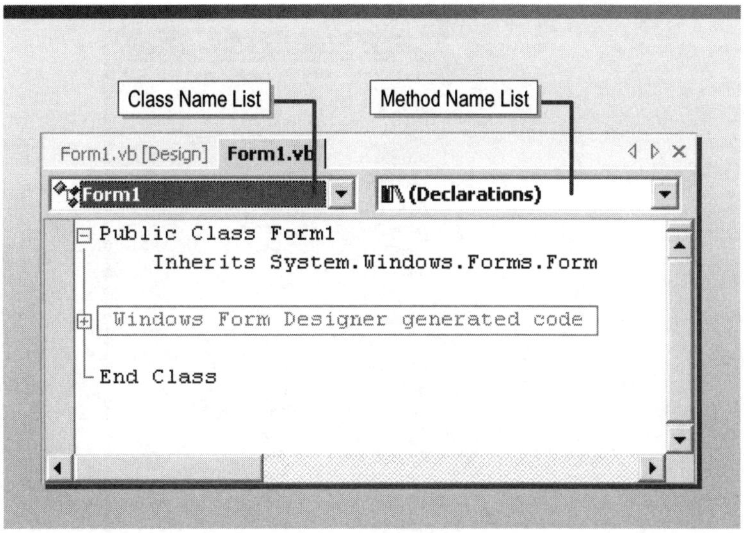

Introduction

Visual Studio .NET provides a Code Editor in which you write and maintain the code for your project. You can associate code directly with a form in your project or place it in a separate code module. A separate Code Editor is displayed for each form or module in your project, making it easy to organize, view, and move through the code.

How the Code Editor works

The Code Editor contains two drop-down lists at the top of the window: the **Class Name** list on the left and the **Method Name** list on the right. The **Class Name** list shows all the controls on the associated form. If you click a control name in the list, the **Method Name** list shows all of the events for that control. (Events are actions that the control can perform and that can be interpreted by your application.) By using the **Class Name** and **Method Name** lists together, you can quickly locate and edit the code in your application.

Opening the Code Editor

► **To open the Code Editor for a form**

1. In Solution Explorer, click the form for which you want to view code.
2. On the **Solution Explorer** toolbar, click the **View Code** button.

   – Or –

   On the **View** menu, click **Code**.

Properties Window

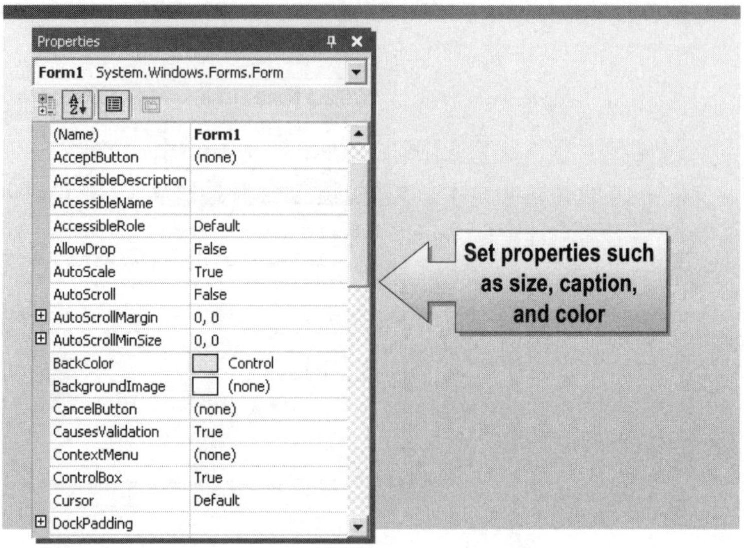

Introduction

The Properties window lists the property settings for the selected form or control that you can modify while you are creating or editing the application. A property describes a characteristic of an object, such as size, caption, or color.

Opening the Properties window

► **To open the Properties window**

- If the Properties window is not visible, click **Properties Window** on the **View** menu, or press F4.

Viewing properties

Some controls, documents, and forms display a large number of properties in the Properties window. This can make it difficult to locate the property you want to set. The Properties window allows you to view the properties for a form or control in a categorized view instead of an alphabetic view.

► **To view properties**

1. To view the properties by category, click the **Categorized** button in the Properties window.

   The properties for the selected form or control will be separated into categories defined by the control.

2. To view the properties in a category, expand the category node. To hide the properties in a category, collapse the category node.

3. To view the properties alphabetically, click the **Alphabetic** button in the Properties window.

Other Programming Windows

Programming Window	Purpose
Task List	Helps you to organize and manage the work of building your application
Output	Displays status messages for various features in the development environment
Class View	Allows you to examine the code behind classes and navigate to symbols in your solution
Command	Allows you to issue commands or evaluate expressions in the development environment
Object Browser	Allows you to view objects and their members

Introduction

There are several other programming windows in the development environment that you might find useful.

Task List window

The Task List window helps you to organize and manage the work of building your application.

► **To display the Task List window**

- On the **View** menu, point to **Other Windows**, and then click **Task List**.

Output window

The Output window displays status messages for various features in the development environment.

► **To access the Output window**

- On the **View** menu, point to **Other Windows**, and then click **Output**.

Class View window

Class View allows you to examine code and navigate to symbols which represent programming elements in your solution. The symbols, which are organized by project, appear in a hierarchical tree view, indicating the containment relationships between them.

► **To open the Class View window**

- On the **View** menu, click **Class View**.

Command window

The Command window is used to either issue commands or to debug and evaluate expressions in the development environment.

► **To open the Command window**

- On the **View** menu, point to **Other Windows**, and then click **Command Window**.

Object Browser window

The Object Browser allows you to examine and discover objects, such as namespaces and classes, that are part of your solution.

► **To open the Object Browser**

- On the **View** menu, point to **Other Windows**, and then click **Object Browser**.

Online Help System

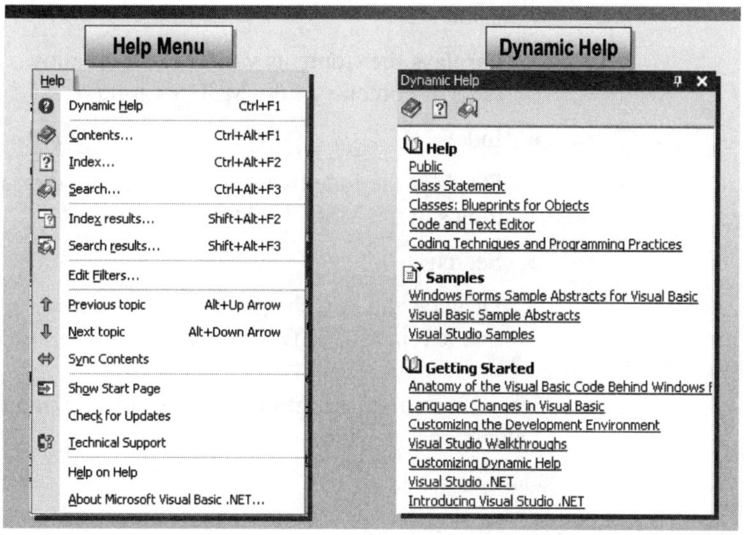

Introduction

Help in Visual Studio .NET is well integrated with the development environment. It provides the information you need based on the task you are currently performing. To increase your efficiency in using the development environment, consider the general situations in which Help might benefit you and where you might find Help in each situation.

Strategies for using Help

There are two primary ways to access Help in the development environment: the Dynamic Help window and the **Help** menu.

Dynamic Help window

The Dynamic Help window provides pointers to information specific to the current area you are using or the task you are trying to complete within the development environment. The development environment tracks the selections you make, the placement of the pointer, and the items that have focus while you interact with the product. The Dynamic Help window then filters through the topics available in Microsoft Developer Network (MSDN) to display relevant information. If no relevant information can be found, the window displays the text "No links are available for the current selection."

► **To open the Dynamic Help window**

- On the **Help** menu, click **Dynamic Help**.

Help menu

You can use the **Help** menu to navigate through Help documents and to access many categories of Help, including the following:

- Contents

  Displays the Contents window, which allows you to browse through the table of contents of the MSDN Library.

- Index

  Displays the Index window, which allows you to type keywords to locate topics in the MSDN Library.

- Search

  Displays the Search window, which allows you to type text and search for that text in the MSDN Library.

You can also access these categories by clicking the toolbar buttons in the Dynamic Help window.

Practice: Working in the Development Environment

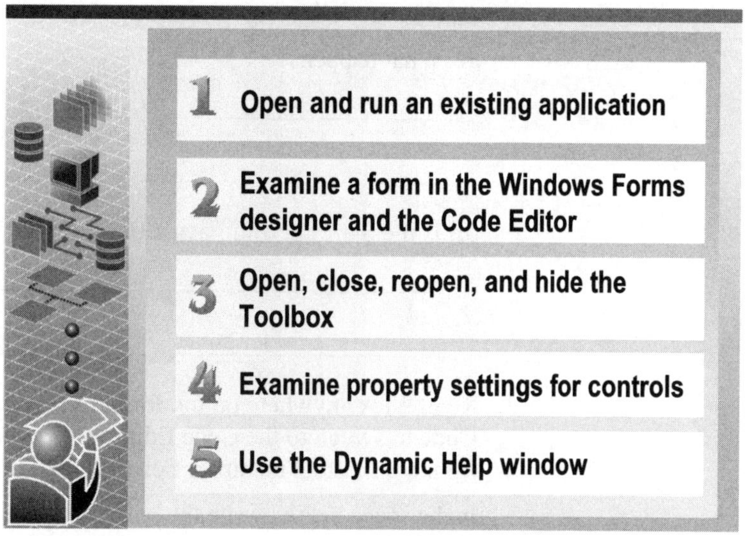

Introduction

In this practice, you will learn how to use the programming tools in the Visual Studio .NET development environment.

Opening a project

► **Open and run an existing application in Visual Basic .NET**

1. Start Visual Studio .NET.

   If Visual Studio.NET is already open, on the **File** menu, click **Close Solution** to close any open solutions.

2. On the **File** menu, point to **Open**, and then click **Project**.
3. Open the ApplicationToExplore.sln solution, which is in the *install_folder*\Practices\Mod01 folder.
4. On the standard toolbar, click the **Start** button or press F5.
5. Click the buttons on the form to see how the application works.
6. Quit the running application.

Examining form views

► **Examine a form in the Windows Forms Designer and the Code Editor**

1. In Solution Explorer, right-click **Form1.vb**, and then click **View Designer**. Answer the following questions:

   a. What happens?

   ____

   ____

   b. Is the Start Page still available?

   ____

   ____

2. Right-click anywhere on the form (except the title bar), and then click **View Code** to switch to the Code Editor. (Note that **View Code** is also available from the shortcut menu for Form1.vb in Solution Explorer.)

3. In the space below, write the names of the event handlers displayed in the Code Editor.

   Private Sub ____________________ & Private Sub ____________________

   ____

   ____

4. Click the **Form1.vb[Design]** tab to return to Design view.

Using the Toolbox

► **Open, close, reopen, and hide the Toolbox**

1. Point to the Toolbox icon on the left edge of the environment window. The Toolbox will open.

2. Click the pushpin icon in the Toolbox title bar. What happens?

   ____

   ____

3. Close the Toolbox.

4. To reopen the Toolbox, on the **View** menu, click **Toolbox**.

   Note that the pushpin icon has changed. Click the pushpin icon in the Toolbox title bar again. What happens?

   ____

   ____

Tip If you accidentally click a control, simply press ESC twice.

Examining properties

► **Examine property settings for controls**

1. In Design view, click **Button1**. Examine the settings for the **Name** and **TabIndex** properties.
2. Click on the form anywhere but on a control. What happens in the Properties window?

   ____

   ____

3. Examine the **Name** and **BackgroundImage** properties of the form.

Using Help

► **Use the Dynamic Help window**

1. Verify that Form1.vb is displayed in the design window. Click the form, click **Button1**, and then click the **BackColor** property for Button1.
2. Click the **Dynamic Help** tab at the bottom of the Properties window. If the tab is not visible, on the **Help** menu, click **Dynamic Help**.

   Notice that the suggested articles are related to the items selected in the Properties window.
3. From the list of articles under the **Help** heading, click **Properties Window** and view the related Help topic.
4. On the **Help** menu, click **Contents**.
5. In the Contents window, click **Visual Basic and Related** in the **Filtered by** box.
6. Click the **Sync Contents** ⇔ button on the toolbar to view this topic's location in the Help contents.
7. Quit Visual Studio .NET.

Lesson: Creating a Visual Basic .NET Project

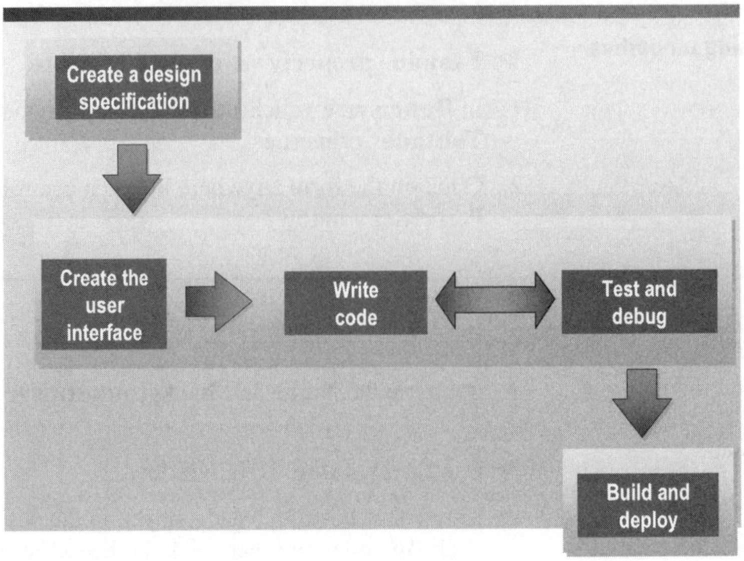

Introduction

This lesson explains how to create a simple application in Visual Basic .NET. The purpose of this lesson is to introduce you to the overall programming process, not to provide the details of language syntax or implementation.

Lesson agenda

This lesson includes the following topics and activities:

- The Development Process
- How to Create the User Interface
- How to Set Control Properties
- How to Add Code for Controls
- How to Save, Run, and Build the Application

Lesson objectives

After completing this lesson, you will be able to:

- Describe the process of creating an application in Visual Basic .NET.
- Start a new project and create the user interface objects.
- Set properties for the controls.
- Write event code to add functionality to an application.
- Save, run, and create a release build of an application.

The Development Process

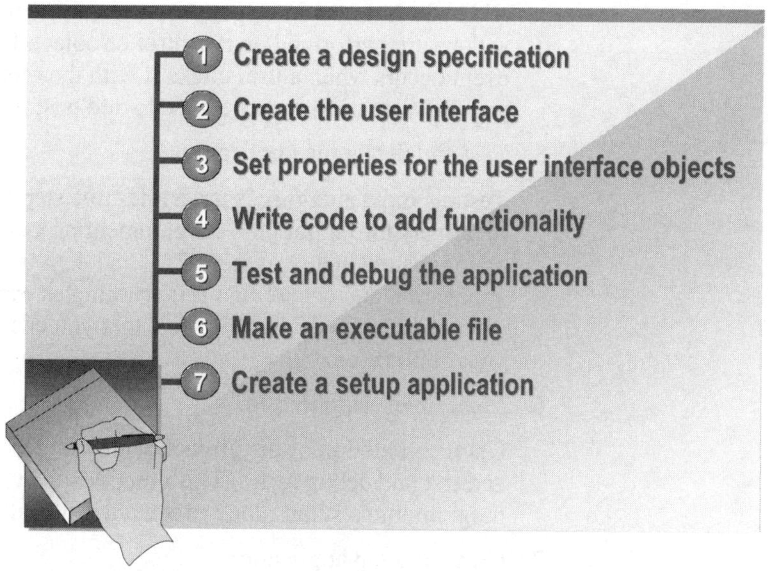

Visual Basic .NET contains everything you need to build your own applications for Windows, from start to finish. To create the user interface, you place controls from the Toolbox on a form, then you customize the controls by setting properties. After that, you define what your program should do by writing code. Finally, you can save, run, and compile your program so others can use it too.

Basic steps

Creating an application in Visual Basic .NET involves seven basic steps:

1. Create a design specification.

   The design specification is the blueprint you use when creating an application. Take time before writing any code to design the application you will be creating. Although Visual Basic .NET provides tools to help you quickly develop a solution, having a clear understanding of the user needs and initial feature set will help you be more efficient in your development efforts. This will also help you save time by minimizing the potential for rewriting code because of a poor or nonexistent design specification.

2. Create the user interface.

   To create the interface for your application, first place controls and objects on a form by drawing or painting them in the Windows Forms Designer. You can look at other applications, such as Microsoft Excel or Microsoft Word, for ideas on how to design the interface. For information about interface design, see *Microsoft Windows User Experience,* published by Microsoft Press®.

3. Set properties for the user interface objects.

   After you have added objects to a form, you can set their properties in the Properties window or in the Code Editor.

4. Write code to add functionality.

   After you have set the initial properties for the form and its objects, you can add code that runs in response to events. Events occur when different actions are performed on a control or object. For example, a button's **Click** event occurs when a user clicks it with the mouse. For most applications, you will also need to write code to add business logic and to access data.

5. Test and debug the application.

   Testing and debugging is not a one-time step but something that you do iteratively throughout the development process. Each time you make a major change in any of steps 2, 3, and 4, you will run a debug build of the application and ensure that it is working as expected. Visual Basic .NET offers numerous debugging tools that you can use to find and fix errors in your application.

6. Make an executable file.

   Upon completion of the project, you will create a release build of the project and test and debug again. This compiles the various files making up the program into a stand-alone executable file called an *assembly*.

7. Create a setup application.

   To run your application, the user usually needs other files, such as any dynamic-link library (DLL) files that you used to create your application. Visual Basic .NET provides the Setup Wizard, which automates the creation of the setup program and ensures that the user has all of the necessary files.

How to Create the User Interface

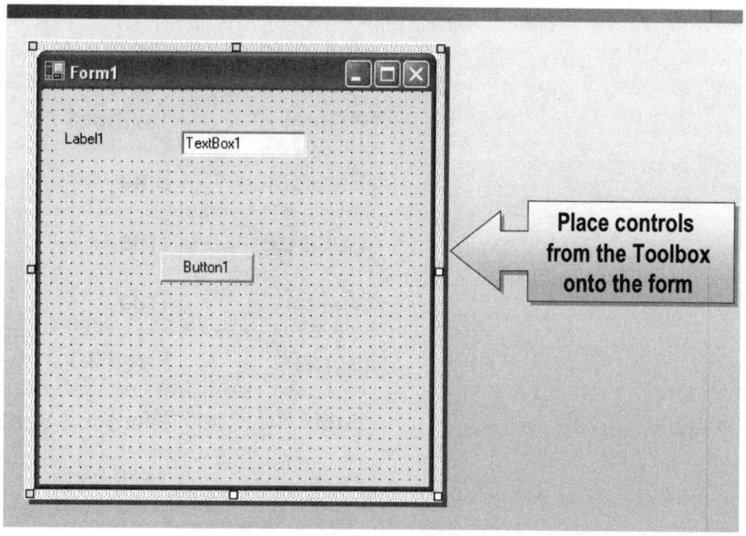

Introduction

When creating a new application, the first step is to create the user interface. In Visual Basic .NET, you can quickly create the user interface by adding controls from the Toolbox to a form.

Adding controls to a form

▶ **To add controls to a form**

1. If the Toolbox is not open, on the **View** menu, click **Toolbox**.
2. In the Toolbox, click the control that you want to add to the form and drag it to the desired location on the form.

Moving and sizing controls

▶ **To move and size controls**

1. To reposition the control, click the control to select it, and then drag the control to the desired position on the form.
2. To resize the control, click the control to select it, drag one of the sizing handles until the control is the desired size, and then release the mouse button.

How to Set Control Properties

Properties	Settings
(Name)	Textbox1
BackColor	Blue
Autosize	True
Visible	True
Border	Fixed 3D
Font	Microsoft SanSerif, 8.2 pt
Text	Textbox1

Introduction

You can change properties by selecting objects on the form and changing their settings in the Properties window.

Setting control properties

► **To set properties in the Properties window**

1. If the Properties window is not open, on the **View** menu, click **Properties Window**.
2. Click the control for which you want to set a property.
3. In the Properties window, select the property and set it to the desired value.

How to Add Code for Controls

- In the Class Name list, click the control
- In the Method Name list, click the event
- Add code between Private Sub and End Sub

```
Private Sub Button1_Click(. . .)Handles Button1.Click
    'Your code goes here
End Sub
```

Introduction

After you have set the initial properties for user interface objects, you can add code that runs in response to events. Events occur when different actions are performed on a control or object. For example, a button's **Click** event occurs when the user clicks it with the mouse.

Writing code

► **To write code for a control event**

1. In Solution Explorer, select the form for which you want to write code.
2. On the **View** menu, click **Code** to open the Code Editor.
3. In the **Class Name** list, click the control for which you want to write code.
4. In the **Method Name** list, click the desired event to open its event handler in the Code Editor.

   The Code Editor displays programming statements that mark the beginning and end of this particular event procedure.
5. Write your code between the starting and ending points in the body of the procedure.

Hot key
F8
toggles through
compile errors

How to Save, Run, and Build the Application

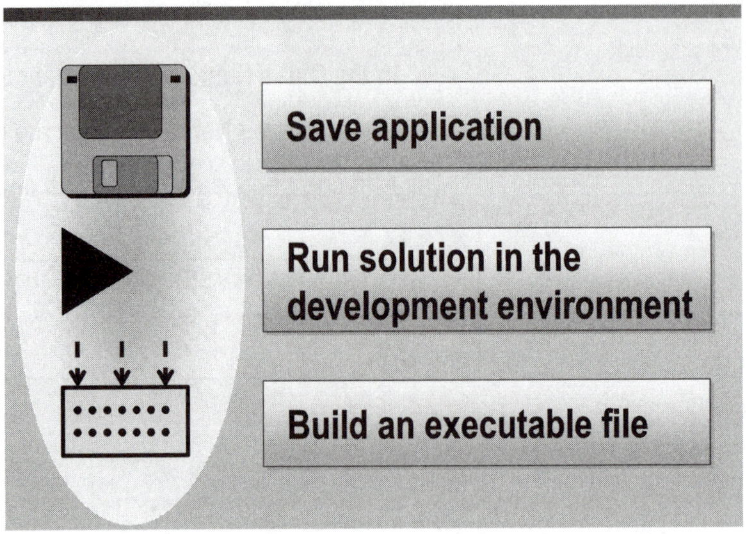

Introduction

After you have finished creating your application, you save it and run it inside the development environment to ensure that it is working properly. This build of the application is called the *debug build.* You can then build an executable file for the application so it can run outside the development environment. This build of the application is called the *release build.*

Saving the application

▶ **To save the application**

- On the **File** menu, click **Save All**.

Running the project

▶ **To run the project inside the development environment**

1. On the standard toolbar, click the **Start** ▶ button to create a debug build of the application.

   If the application runs without errors, a working version of the form appears.

2. Close the form to go back to the programming environment.

Building the project

▶ **To build an executable file for the project**

1. On the **Build** menu, click **Build Solution**.

   When you build a project or solution, an executable (.exe) file is automatically created in the *project_folder*\bin folder. If Debug is selected in the **Solution Configurations** list on the toolbar, a second .exe file is created in the *project_folder*\obj\Debug folder. If Release is chosen, the second .exe file is created in the *project_folder*\obj\Release folder.

2. To run this project in Windows, use the **Run** command on the **Start** menu or double-click the file name in Windows Explorer.

Review

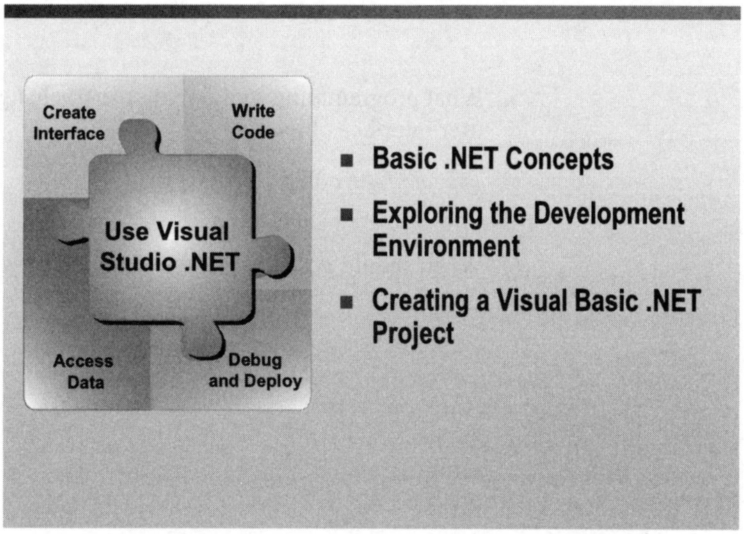

1. How do you open the Code Editor for a form? Give an example of why you would want to do so.

2. How can the common language runtime manage execution for applications written in many different programming languages?

3. After you create the design specification for your application, how do you create the user interface objects?

4. While you are creating an application in Visual Basic .NET, how can you ensure that it is working correctly after you make a major change?

5. What programming tool do you use to change the color and caption of a user interface object?

Property window

6. When should you create a release build of your application?

after testing
Release non debug

Build configuration Manager
Release

Lab 1.1: Creating Your First Application

Objectives

After completing this lab, you will be able to:

- Use the Visual Studio .NET development environment.
- Create the user interface for a simple Visual Basic .NET project.
- Add controls and limited functionality to a form.
- Build and run an executable application file.

Note This lab focuses on the concepts in this module and as a result may not comply with Microsoft security recommendations.

Scenario

In this lab, you will create a simple Windows-based application and add controls to a form. You will also create a release build of the application so that you can run it outside of the development environment. The finished form will look similar to the following screen shot in the Windows Forms Designer:

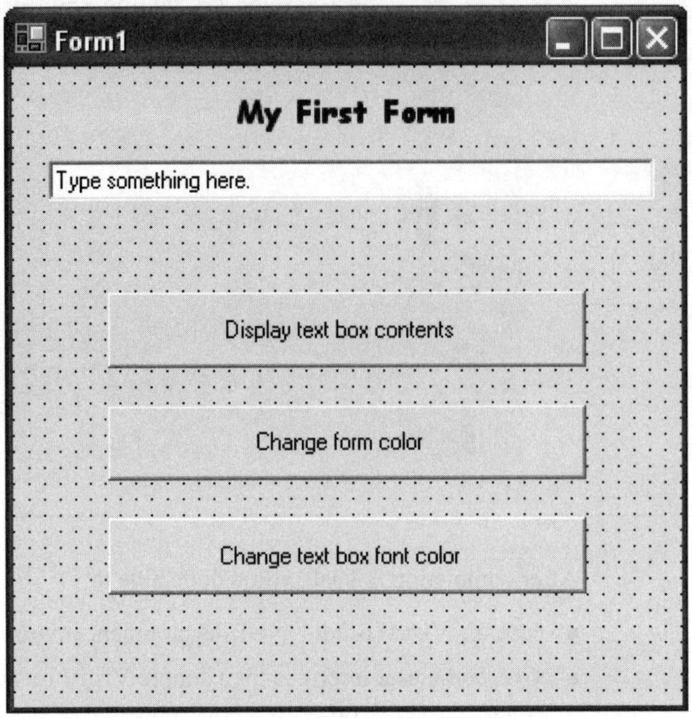

Design notes

1. When the user clicks **Display text box contents**, a message box displaying the contents of the text box will appear.
2. When the user clicks **Change form color**, the background color of the form will change.

Note As a general rule, accessibility guidelines suggest that developers should not change the background color on forms. If the background color is not changed, the form incorporates the Windows settings. In some instances, however, you might need to change background colors because of design requirements.

3. When the user clicks **Change text box font color**, the color of the text in the text box will change.

Solution files

The solution files for this lab are in the *install_folder*\Labfiles\Lab011\Ex01\Solution folder.

Estimated time to complete this lab: 30 minutes

Exercise 1
Creating Your First Application in Visual Basic .NET

In this exercise, you will start a new Windows-based application, add several controls to the automatically generated form, set properties for the controls, and add code to provide functionality for the controls.

► **Start a new application in Visual Basic .NET**

1. Start Visual Studio .NET (if it is not already open).
2. On the **File** menu, point to **New**, and then click **Project**.
3. In the **New Project** dialog box, click **Visual Basic Projects**, and then click **Windows Application**. Set the project name to **MyFirstProject** and the folder location to *install_folder*\Labfiles\Lab011\Ex01, and then click **OK**.

► **Add controls to the form**

1. Add one **Label** control to the form.

   To add a control in a specific location on the form, click the desired control and then click the chosen location on the form. The control will be added to the location you click on the form.
2. Add one **TextBox** control to the form.
3. Add three **Button** controls to the form.
4. Move and size the form and the controls so that the form looks like the following screen shot:

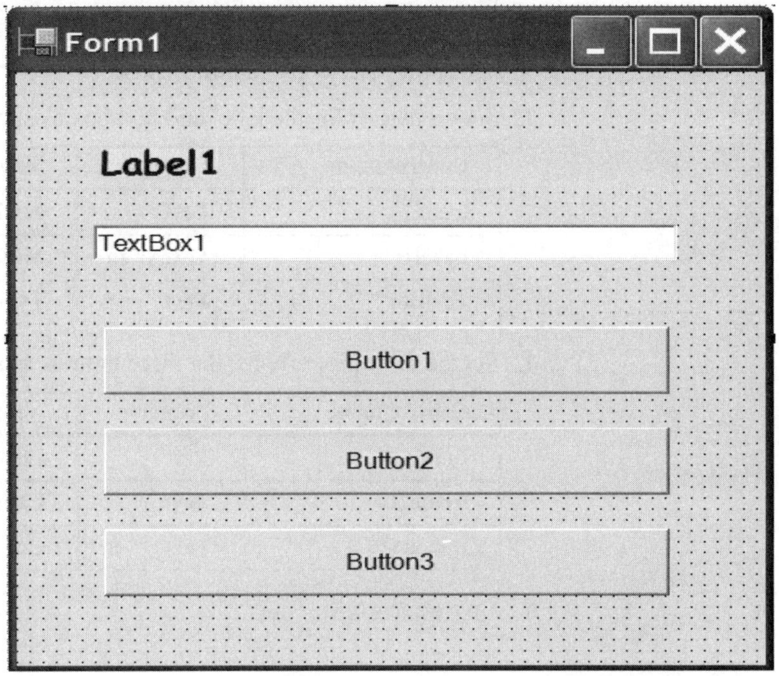

5. Save your work.

► **Set properties for the controls**

1. Click **Label1** on the form to display its properties in the Properties window.

   If the Properties window is not visible, on the **View** menu, click **Properties Window**.

2. In the Properties window, click the **Font** property, and then click the ellipsis ... button to display the **Font** dialog box. Change the font settings as shown in the following illustration, and then click **OK**.

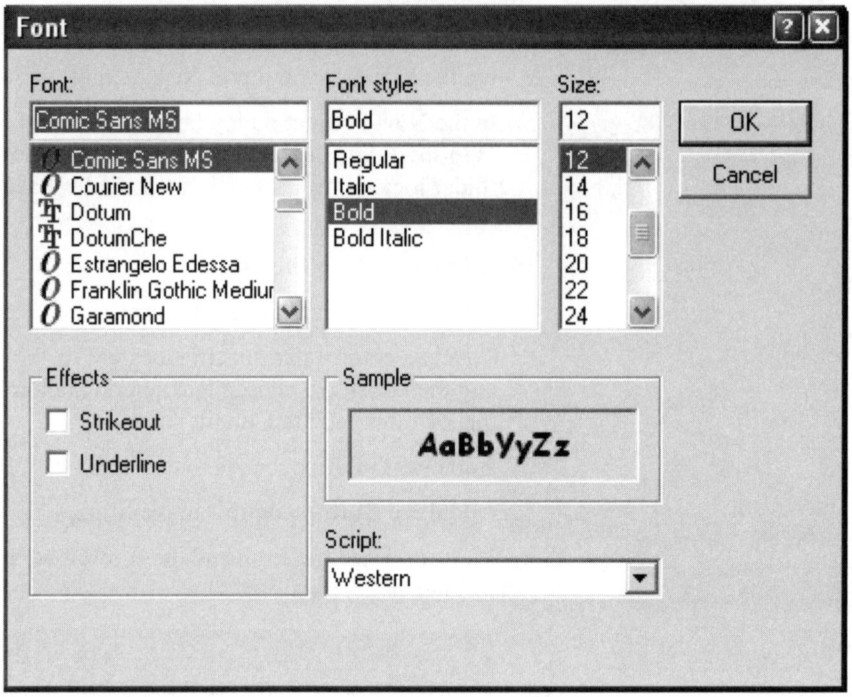

3. Set properties for the label and text box as shown in the following table.

Control name	Property	New value
Label1	**Text**	**My First Form**
Label1	**TextAlign**	**MiddleCenter**
TextBox1	**Text**	**Type something here**

4. Set the **Text** property for the three buttons as shown in the following table.

Control name	Property	New value
Button1	**Text**	**Display text box contents**
Button2	**Text**	**Change form color**
Button3	**Text**	**Change text box font color**

5. Save your work.

Note In the next three procedures, you will use the Code Editor for Form1.vb to add several lines of code to your application so that it can respond to user input. The purpose of this procedure is to learn how to add code to your application and not how to write code, so do not be concerned if you are not familiar with the event handler code and syntax.

► Add code to the Click event handler of the Display text box contents button

1. Double-click the **Display text box contents** button on the form. This opens the Code Editor for Form1.vb with the following code already inserted:

```
Private Sub Button1_Click (...)

End Sub
```

Tip The form has two views: Design view (Form1.vb[Design]) and Code view (Form1.vb). You can switch back and forth between these views by clicking the tabs at the top of the form.

2. Type the following line of code in the **Button1_Click** event handler:

```
MessageBox.Show(TextBox1.Text)
```

Your code should look like the following:

```
Private Sub Button1_Click (...)
   MessageBox.Show(TextBox1.Text)
End Sub
```

► Add code to change the color of the button and form background

1. Switch to the Design view of the form.
2. Double-click the **Change form color** button to open the Code Editor.
3. Type the following line of code in the **Button2_Click** event handler:

```
Me.BackColor = Color.CadetBlue
```

Your code should look like the following:

```
Private Sub Button2_Click (...)
   Me.BackColor = Color.CadetBlue
End Sub
```

► Add code to change the font color of the text box

1. Switch to the Design view for the form.
2. Double-click the **Change text box font color** button on the form to open the Code Editor.
3. Type the following line of code in the **Button3_Click** event handler:

```
TextBox1.ForeColor = Color.Red
```

Your code should look like the following:

```
Private Sub Button3_Click (...)
  TextBox1.ForeColor = Color.Red
End Sub
```

► Run and test your application in the design environment

1. Click the **Start** button on the standard toolbar.
2. Click all of the buttons on the running form to ensure that they work correctly.
3. Change the text in the text box, and then click **Display text box contents**.
4. Quit the application.

► Save and build an executable file for your application

1. To save your solution, click the **Save All** button on the standard toolbar.
2. On the standard toolbar, in the **Solution Configurations** list, change the solution configuration from **Debug** to **Release**.
3. On the **Build** menu, click **Build Solution** to create a release build of your application.
4. Quit Visual Studio .NET.
5. In Windows Explorer, locate your executable file in the *install_folder*\Labfiles\Lab011\Ex01\MyFirstProject\obj\Release folder.
6. Double-click the executable file to run it, and test all of the functionality outside the IDE. Then close the application.

msdn® training

Module 2: Working with Forms and Controls

Contents

Microsoft®

Overview

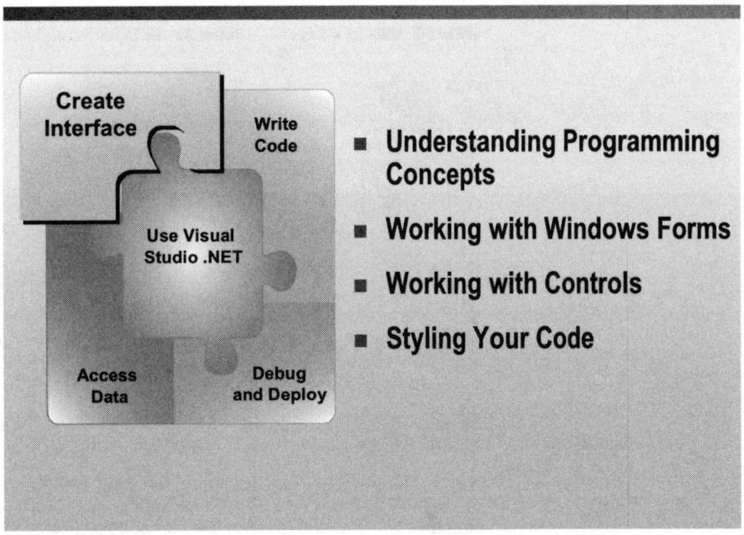

Introduction

In this module, you will learn about classes, objects, properties, methods, and events. You will explore the basics of using Microsoft® Visual Basic® .NET forms, controls, and code to create an application. You will learn code statements to manage multiple forms in an application. Finally, you will learn about Visual Basic naming conventions and how to format and document your code.

Objectives

After completing this module, you will be able to:

- Explain fundamental programming concepts, including event-driven programming, classes, objects, properties, methods, and events.
- Use forms and controls to create a user interface.
- Create and manage multiple forms in a simple application.
- Interact with a user by using the **MessageBox** function.
- Use Visual Basic standards for naming the elements you create and for formatting and documenting your code.

Multimedia: What Are Objects, Properties, Methods, and Events?

Introduction

This animation introduces you to fundamental elements that you will be using in Visual Basic .NET and learning about throughout this module: objects, properties, methods, and events.

Animation script

To write applications in Visual Basic .NET, you will work with objects, methods, properties, and events.

Objects are the building blocks of a Visual Basic–based application—the programmable elements that you use to create the application. For example, the form that you use to create a window and the button and text box that you add to the form are all examples of objects. To interact with an object, you use properties, methods, and events. To understand what properties, methods, and events are, consider an analogy between a physical object—an alarm clock—and a Visual Basic object—a form.

Properties are the characteristics of an object. For example, the properties of the alarm clock include its height, width, and color. The properties of the form also include its height, width, and color.

Methods are the things that an object can do. For example, two methods of an alarm clock include **SetHours** and **SetMinutes**. The methods of the form are things it can do, like **Hide** or **Show**.

Events are actions that an object can respond to. For example, when a user sets the alarm, the alarm clock can respond to the **Alarm** event by making a sound. When a user closes a form, the form responds to the **Closed** event and executes the code for the event.

So objects are programmable elements. Properties are characteristics, methods are actions, and events are things an object can respond to.

Lesson: Understanding Programming Concepts

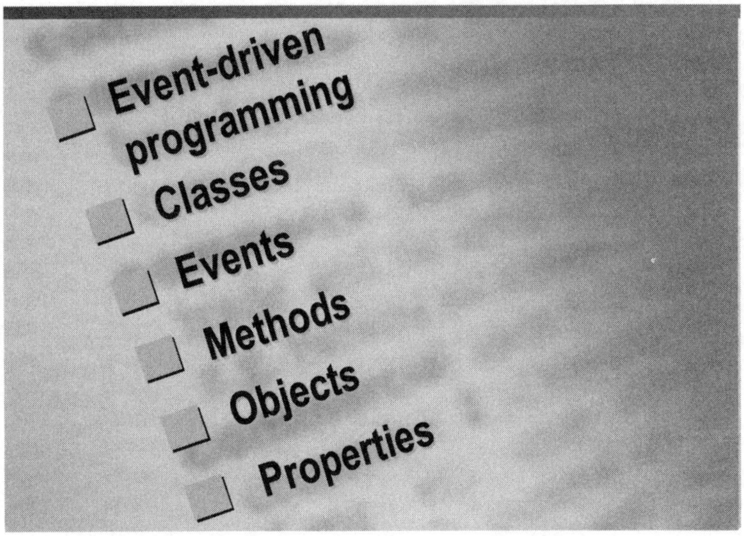

Introduction

This lesson describes fundamental programming concepts that you need to understand before writing code in Visual Basic .NET.

Lesson agenda

This lesson includes the following topics and activities:

- What Is Event-Driven Programming?
- Classes: Blueprints for Objects
- What Are Properties, Methods, and Events?
- Practice: Properties, Methods, and Events

Lesson objectives

After completing this lesson, you will be able to:

- Explain the difference between event-driven programming and procedural programming.
- Distinguish between classes and objects.
- Describe properties, methods, and events.

What Is Event-Driven Programming?

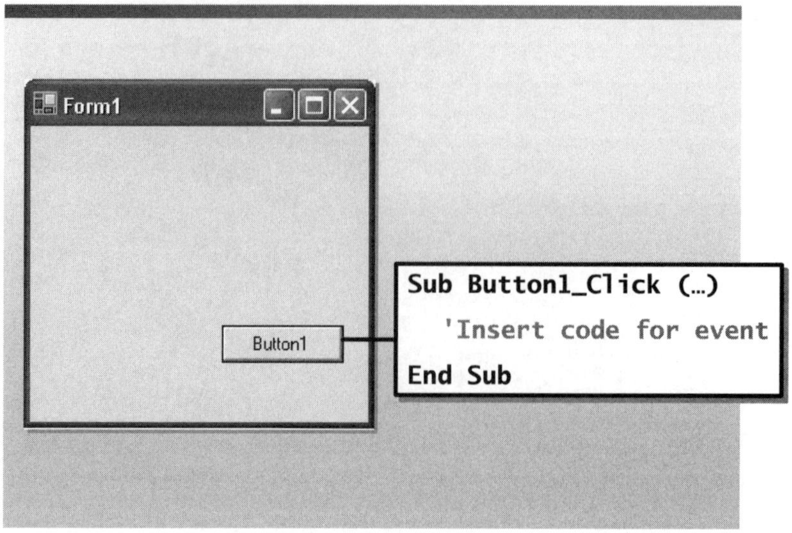

Introduction

Applications written in Visual Basic are *event driven*. Event-driven programming can best be understood by contrasting it to procedural programming.

Procedural programming

Applications written in procedural languages run by proceeding logically through the program code, one line at a time. Logic flow can be temporarily transferred to other parts of the program by means of various code statements, directing the program from beginning to end.

Example of procedural programming

In a procedural program, the main program controls how the user enters information.

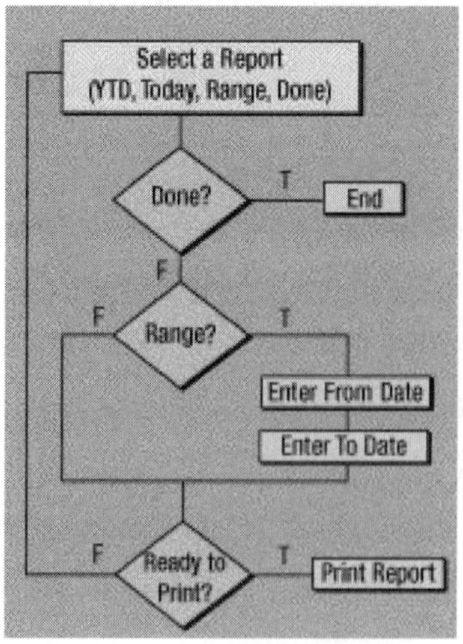

Event-driven programming

Program statements in an event-driven application execute only when a specific event calls a section of code assigned to that event. Events can be triggered by keyboard input, mouse actions, the operating system, or code in the application. An event-driven program constantly evaluates and responds to sets of events. If an event occurs, and the associated event procedure contains code, Visual Basic invokes that code.

Example of event-driven programming

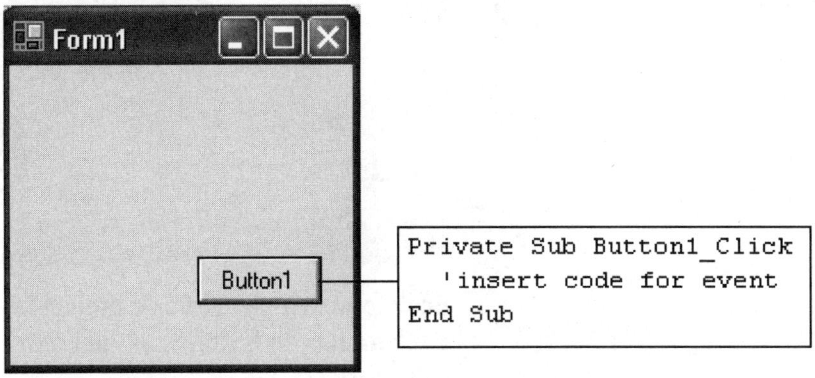

Consider what happens when a user clicks a button named **Button1** on a form. The mouse click is an event. When the **Click** event occurs, Visual Basic runs the code in the **Sub** procedure named **Button1_Click**. When the code has finished running, Visual Basic waits for the next event.

Note The purpose of this example is to familiarize you with the basic approach used in event-driven programming. Do not be concerned if the code syntax is unfamiliar.

Classes: Blueprints for Objects

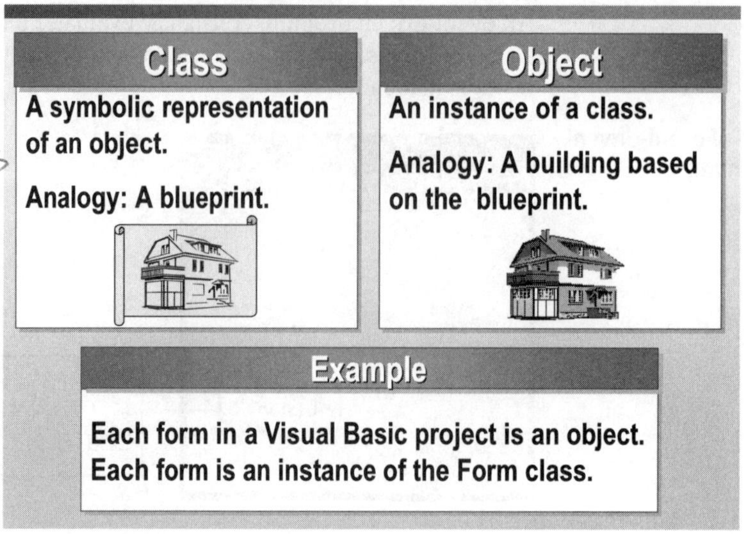

Introduction

The terms *class* and *object* are sometimes used interchangeably, but, in fact, classes describe the *structure* of objects, while objects are *instances* of classes. Classes and objects are closely related. You cannot talk about an object without regard to its class.

Definitions

A *class* is a symbolic representation of an object. A class describes the attributes and operations that characterize any member, or object, of the class, in the same way that a blueprint of a house describes the items that make up the house, such as doors, windows, and walls.

An *object* is an instance of a class. You use a class as a basis to create many individual objects, in the same way that you can use the blueprint of a house to create many individual houses. Each object is an exact yet distinct copy of its class.

Because an object is an *instance* of a class, the act of creating an object is called *instantiation*.

Visual Basic examples

In Visual Basic, the **Form** class defines forms as being rectangular, having a caption, having the ability to be clicked, and so on. Each form you use in a Visual Basic project is a separate object—an instance of the **Form** class.

The controls in the Toolbox in Visual Basic .NET also represent classes. When you drag a **Button** control from the Toolbox to a form, you are actually creating an instance of the **Button** class—a **Button** object.

What Are Properties, Methods, and Events?

Properties	Size Text	Volume Bass
Methods	Close Hide	Tune
Events	Click	Low Battery

Introduction

Classes describe the properties, methods, and events that make up the objects that are members of the class. To control an object, you use its properties, methods, and events.

Properties

Properties are characteristics of an object, such as size, color, and text.

Methods

Methods are actions that an object can perform. **Close** and **Hide** are common examples of methods for a form.

Events

Events are actions, often generated by a user, that are recognized by an object, for example, key presses, button clicks, or mouse movements. Each form or control has its own set of events that it recognizes. Events are triggered when some aspect of the object is changed. For example, clicking a mouse triggers the **Click** event.

Analogy to a physical object

To understand the relationship between objects, properties, and methods, consider a stereo radio. The radio is an object and has a number of properties, such as volume, bass, and treble. The radio's volume is a property that you can change. You can also change the radio station, another property, by using the radio's "tune" method.

Each of these properties and methods performs a specific purpose, and is used to attain a given goal or objective, such as tuning the radio. As a radio owner, you learn how to use these objects, but, for the most part, you do not learn how to install, maintain, or repair them. You only need to know how to operate them and what to expect.

In the same way, with Visual Basic, you can use objects—forms and controls—to create applications. For the most part, you can use objects without having a detailed understanding of how they work.

Practice: Properties, Methods, and Events

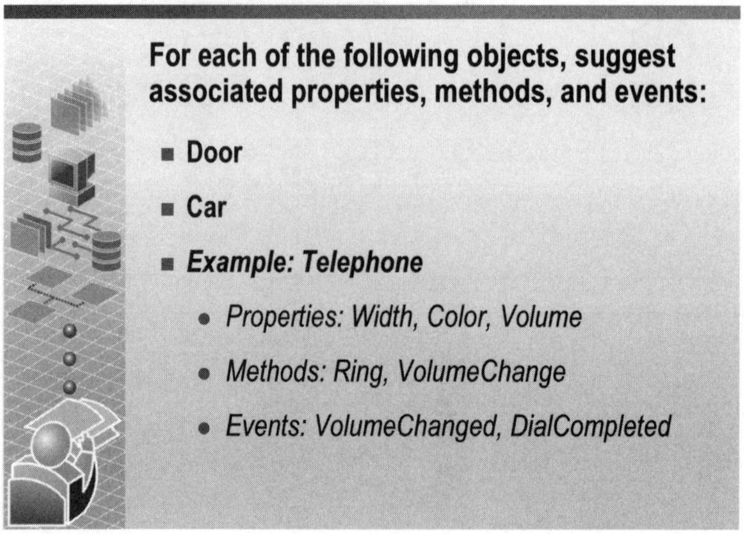

For each of the following objects, suggest associated properties, methods, and events.

Object	Properties	Methods	Events
Example: **Telephone**	**Width, Color, Volume**	**Ring, VolumeChange**	**VolumeChanged, DialCompleted** (in response to a user dialing)
Door			
Car			

Lesson: Working with Windows Forms

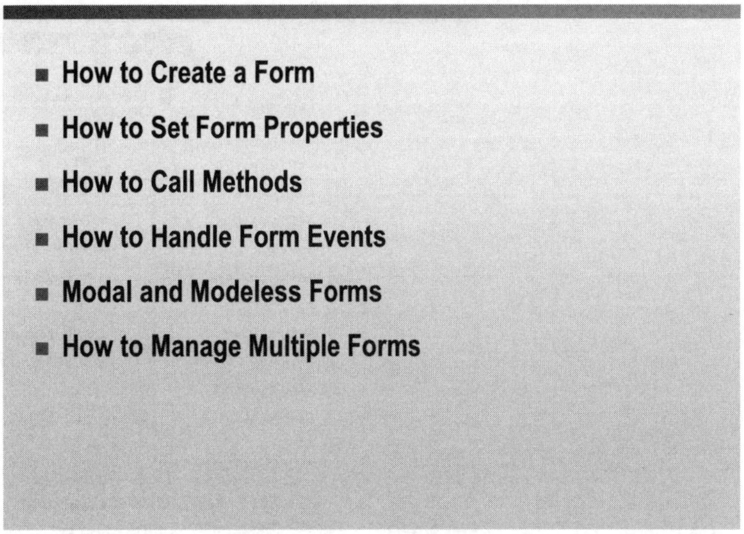

Introduction

The starting point for a Microsoft Windows® application is a form. In this lesson, you will learn how to create a form, set its properties, call form methods, and write code to handle form events. You will also learn how to work with multiple forms, including showing, hiding, and closing modal and modeless forms.

Lesson agenda

This lesson includes the following topics and activities:

- How to Create a Form
- How to Set Form Properties
- How to Call Methods
- How to Handle Form Events
- Practice: Writing Code for Form Events
- Multimedia Demonstration: Managing Forms
- Modal and Modeless Forms
- How to Manage Multiple Forms

Lesson objectives

After completing this lesson, you will be able to:

- Add forms to a project.
- Set form properties at design time.
- Call methods.
- Write code for form events.
- Designate a form as modal or modeless.
- Hide, show, and close forms.

How to Create a Form

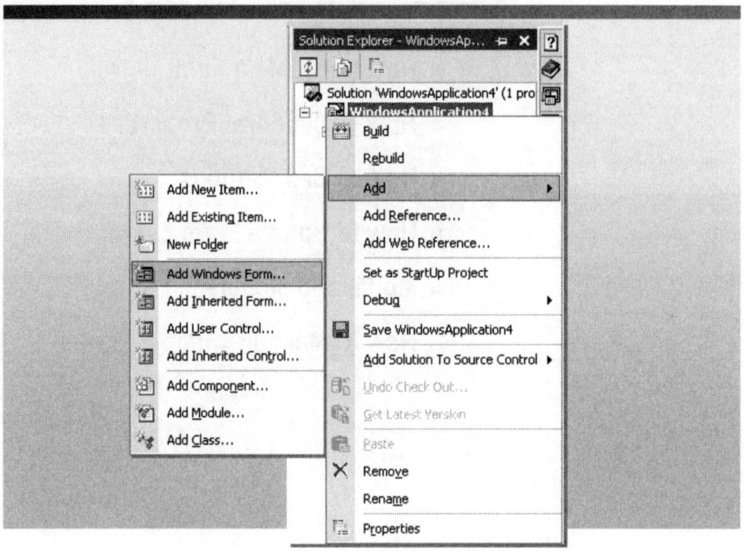

Introduction

In Visual Basic, a form is a window used in your application. When you create a new Windows Application project, Visual Basic provides a design window that contains a form. The default form contains the minimum elements used by most forms: a title bar, a control box, and **Minimize**, **Maximize**, and **Close** buttons.

Adding forms

Most applications require more than one window. You need to add a form to your project for every window that your application requires.

► **To add forms to your project**

1. If Solution Explorer is not open, on the **View** menu, click **Solution Explorer**.
2. In Solution Explorer, right click the project name, point to **Add**, and then click **Add Windows Form**.
3. In the **Add New Item** dialog box, set an appropriate name for the form, and then click **Open**.

How to Set Form Properties

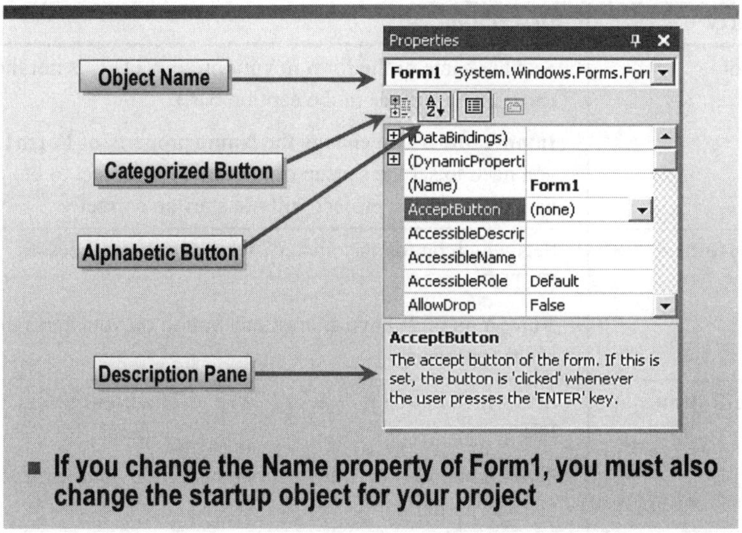

Introduction

While you are building the user interface of a Visual Basic–based application, you must set the properties for the objects you create.

Setting form properties

You can set form properties either by writing code or by using the Properties window. Any property settings you establish at *design time*—when you are designing the application—are used as the initial settings each time your application runs.

► **To set form properties at design time**

1. If the Properties window is not open, on the **View** menu, click **Properties Window**.
2. In Design view, click the form for which you want to set a property. The name of the form appears in the **Object** drop-down list at the top of the Properties window.
3. Use the **Alphabetic**  and **Categorized**  buttons in the Properties window to choose whether to view the form properties alphabetically or by category.
4. In the Properties window, click the property you want to set.

Note When you click a property, a description of the property appears at the bottom of the Properties window, in the Description pane.

5. Type or select the property setting you want.
6. To view how the new property setting affects the form, you can run your application by clicking the **Start** button  on the standard toolbar.

Common form properties

The following table describes some common form properties that you typically set at design time.

Property	Description	Default setting
(Name)	Sets the name of the form in your project. (This is not the name that users see in the caption bar.) **Important:** If you change the **Name** property of **Form1**, you need to set the startup object for your project to the new name, or the project will not start up correctly.	**Form1 (Form2, Form3,** and so on)
AcceptButton	Sets which button is "clicked" whenever a user presses ENTER. **Note:** You must have at least one button on your form to use this property.	**(none)**
CancelButton	Sets which button is "clicked" whenever a user presses ESC. **Note:** You must have at least one button on your form to use this property.	**(none)**
ControlBox	Determines whether a form displays a control box in the caption bar.	**True**
FormBorderStyle	Controls the appearance of the border for the form. This will also affect how the caption bar appears, and what buttons are allowed to appear on it.	**Sizable**
MaximizeBox	Determines whether a form has a **Maximize** button in the upper right corner of its caption bar.	**True**
MinimizeBox	Determines whether a form has a **Minimize** button in the upper right corner of its caption bar.	**True**
StartPosition	Determines the position of a form on the screen when it first appears.	**WindowsDefaultLocation**
Text	Sets the text displayed in the caption bar of the control.	**Form1 (Form2, Form3,** and so on)

Changing the startup object

When you start a new project, Visual Basic lists **Form1** as the default startup object for your project. If you change the **Name** property of **Form1**, you need to set the new name as the startup object, or your project will not start up correctly.

► To change the startup object for your project

1. If Solution Explorer is not open, on the **View** menu, click **Solution Explorer**.
2. In Solution Explorer, right click the project name, and then click **Properties**.
3. In the **Startup object** box, click the new startup object for your project.

Practice (optional)

In this optional practice, you will change two form properties and observe the resulting changes to the form. The practice should take no more than 10 minutes.

► **Set form properties**

1. Open a new Windows application in Visual Basic .NET. Set the project name to **FormProperties** and the location to *install_folder*\Practices\Mod02.
2. Open the Properties window for **Form1**.
3. Set a new value for the **Cursor** property.
4. Run the application, and rest the mouse pointer over the form to view the change.
5. Return to design mode by quitting the application. To quit the application, you can click the **Close** box on the form.
6. Click the **Opacity** property for **Form1**, and type a value between 10 percent and 90 percent.
7. Run the application to view the change.
8. Return to design mode by quitting the application.

How to Call Methods

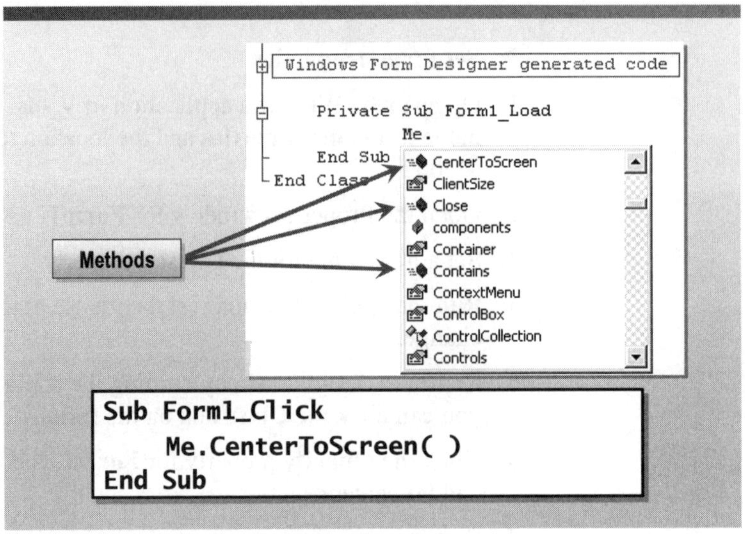

Introduction

Forms provide unique *methods*, or actions that they can perform. You call a method of a form to cause the form to perform an action.

Common form methods

The following table describes some form methods that you will use frequently.

Method	Description
CenterToScreen	Causes the form to center itself on the screen when the form opens.
Close	Causes the form to close.
Hide	Causes the form to become invisible, but to remain in memory.
Show	Causes the form to become visible.

Syntax

Use the following syntax to call a method of a form from within the form code:

```
Me.Method( )
```

- "Me" refers to the instance of the form.
- *Method* is the form method you are calling.
- You must include the parentheses ( ) in this code. The parentheses can be used to pass additional information, called parameters, in the program.

Example of calling a method

The following code makes the form appear in the center of the screen by calling the form's **CenterToScreen** method:

```
Me.CenterToScreen( )
```

Using IntelliSense

Visual Basic .NET offers a feature called Microsoft IntelliSense®, which makes language reference information easily available in pop-up windows and drop-down lists. You can use IntelliSense to view and select the available properties, methods, and events of objects.

► To use IntelliSense to view and select available form methods

1. Double-click the form in the design window.

   Double-clicking the form opens the Code Editor and sets the insertion point in a block of code. In this example, you will use IntelliSense to write code for the **Form1_Load** event.

2. Type **Me**

   After you type the period, IntelliSense will display a list of available properties and methods for the form.

   The  icon represents a method.

   The  icon represents a property.

3. Double-click the method you want to call.

   The method you choose appears in your code, and the IntelliSense window closes.

How to Handle Form Events

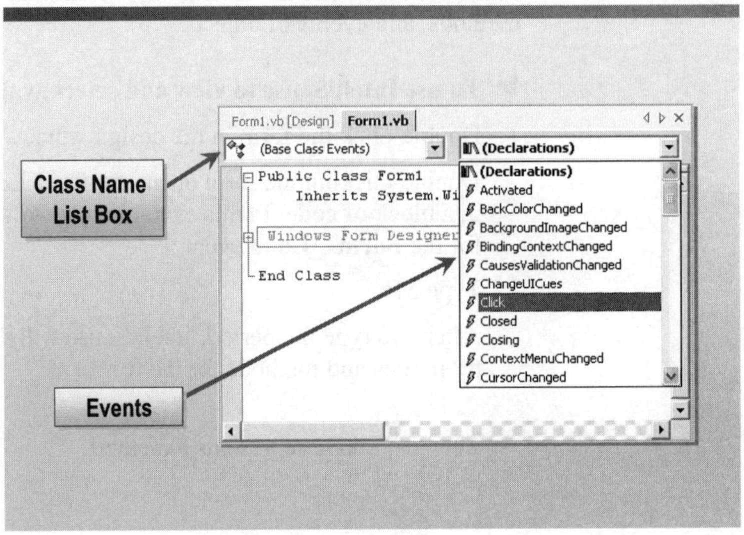

Introduction

To respond to actions performed on an object, you write code in the event handler, or code block, associated with the object's event. This code runs when the event occurs.

Common form events

The following table describes some form events for which you will frequently write code.

Event	Description
Activated	Occurs when the form is activated in code or by a user.
Click	Occurs when the form is clicked.
Closed	Occurs after the form is closed by a user or by the **Close** method of the form.
Closing	Occurs while the form is being closed. (Occurs before the **Closed** event.)
Deactivate	Occurs when the form loses focus and is not the active form.
GotFocus	Occurs when the form receives focus.
Load	Occurs before a form appears for the first time.

Event handlers

An *event handler* is a segment of code that is called when a corresponding event occurs. For example, you can write code in an event handler for the **Activated** event of a form to perform operations such as updating the data displayed in the controls of the form when the form is activated. Event handlers are a type of **Sub** procedure.

Note Form events occur in a specified order. For example, the **Load** event occurs before the **Activated** event can occur. It is important to know this order because the order of events affects the order in which your code runs.

Visual Basic uses a standard naming convention for event handlers. The convention is to combine the name of the object which sends the event, an underscore, and the name of the event. For example, the **Click** event of a form named Form1 would be named **Sub Form1_Click**.

Adding an event handler

► **To add an event handler**

1. Open the Code Editor for the form for which you want to add an event handler.
2. In the **Class Name** list box, click **(Base Class Events)**. The following illustration shows the **Class Name** list box with **(Base Class Events)** selected.

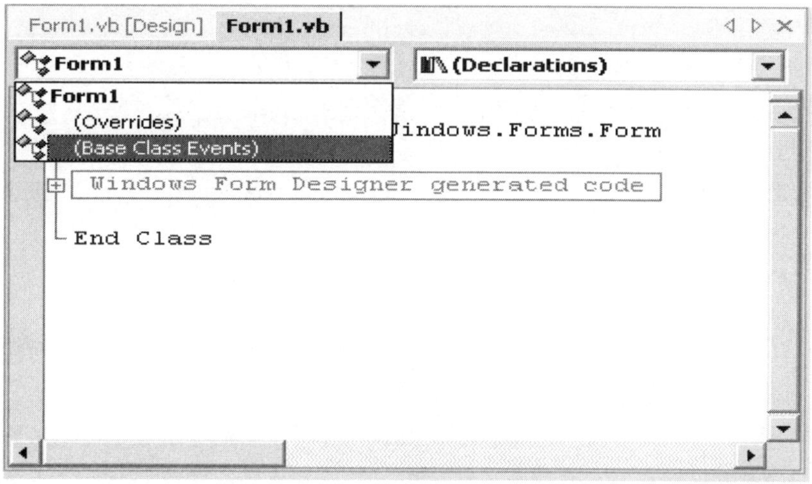

3. Click the drop-down arrow for the **Method Name** list box to view events available for the form. The following illustration shows the **Method Name** list box with form events listed and the **Click** event selected. Note that the lightning bolt icon to the left of the event name indicates that it is an event.

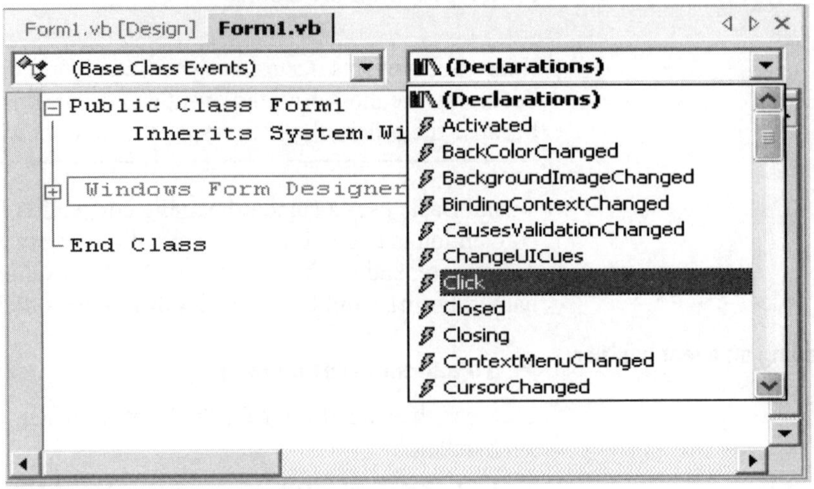

4. Click the event to add the event handler.

Practice: Writing Code for Form Events

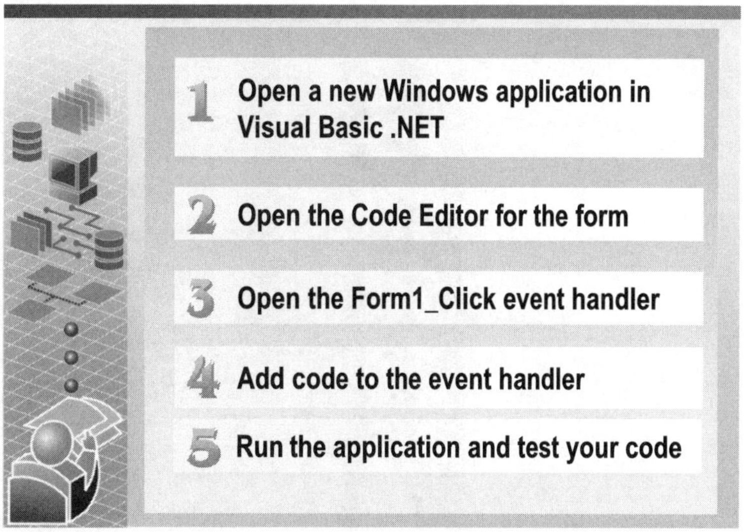

In this practice, you will write code for the **Click** event of a form. When the form is clicked, a beep will sound, and then the form will close.

► **Write code for the Click event handler**

1. Open a new Windows application in Visual Basic .NET. Name the project **WritingCode** and set the folder location to *install_folder*\Practices\Mod02.
2. Open the Code Editor for the form.
3. Create the **Form1_Click** event handler by clicking **(Base Class Events)** in the **Class Name** list box and clicking **Click** in the **Method Name** list box.
4. In the event handler, type the following code:

```
Beep( )
Me.Close( )
```

   This code causes a beep to sound, and then closes the form by calling the **Close** method of the form.

5. Run your application by clicking the **Start** button  on the standard toolbar.
6. Click the form to verify that the code works.

Multimedia: Managing Forms

In this demonstration, you will learn the difference between a modal and a modeless form. You will learn how to manage multiple forms, determining which forms users see and which forms are open or closed by using the **Show**, **Hide**, and **Close** methods of the form.

Modal and Modeless Forms

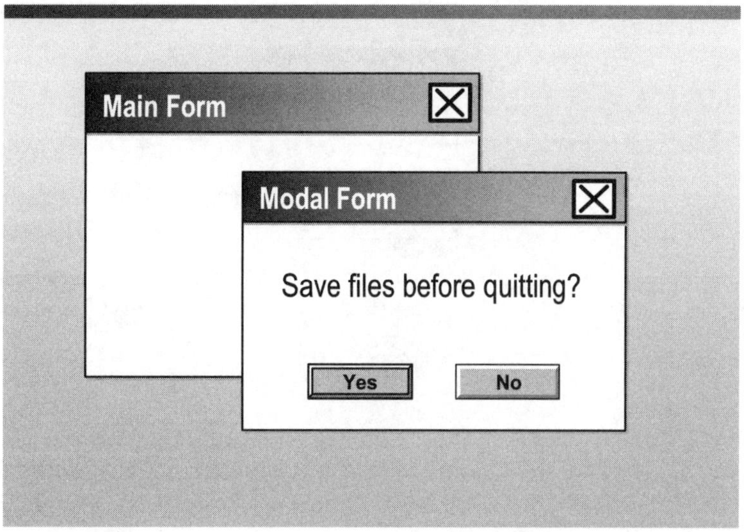

Introduction

If your application uses more than one form, you need to determine whether the forms in the application should be modal or modeless.

Modeless forms

Modeless forms allow the user to switch to another form or dialog box without interacting with the modeless form. For example, if you have more than one modeless window open, you can move a window out of the way and interact with another window without closing the first window.

Modal forms

Modal forms do not allow the user to interact with other forms in the application until the modal form has been unloaded. The program must hide or close a modal form (usually in response to some user action) before input to another form can occur. For example, a message box is modal. The user must respond before interacting with other forms in the application.

By default, forms you create in Visual Basic .NET are modeless. To make a form modal, you call the form's **ShowDialog** method.

User considerations

Modal interactions force users to complete one task before continuing on with a different task. Modeless interactions allow users to move freely between one task and another without fully completing one of them.

Although limiting the amount of user control sometimes benefits the user, as a general rule, your applications should minimize modal interactions. Long processes should run in the background, keeping the foreground interactive. For example, when something is printing, users should be able to minimize the window even if the document cannot be altered.

Modal interaction takes control away from the user. Modeless interaction gives control back to the user. Design your software to give the user maximum control by minimizing modal interactions.

How to Manage Multiple Forms

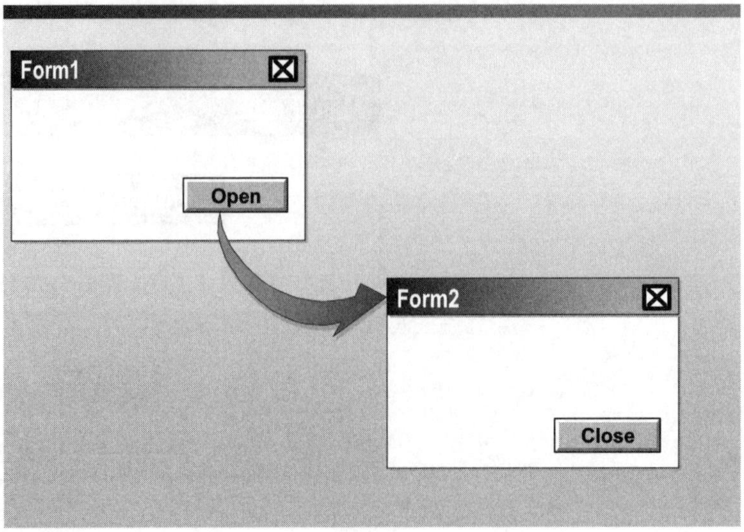

Introduction

In most applications, the user interface is composed of multiple windows or dialog boxes. To show or hide forms, you use the **Show** method or the **Hide** method of the form. To close a form, you use the **Close** method.

Syntax to show forms

The **Show** method displays a form object. To use the **Show** method to display a second form from an existing open form, use the following syntax:

```
FormName.Show( )
```

Note An instance of the *FormName* form must exist before you can call the form's **Show** method.

Syntax to hide forms

The **Hide** method makes a form object invisible but does not close it. This means that the form will disappear, but all of its contained objects and variables will still be loaded in memory.

To use the **Hide** method to hide a second form from an existing open form, use the following syntax:

```
FormName.Hide( )
```

To hide the form that is currently running, use the **Me** keyword to call the **Hide** method of the form.

```
Me.Hide( )
```

Example

Consider a scenario in which the user will click a button on one form to display a second form in the application. When the second form opens, the user no longer needs the first form, so you want it to disappear. However, you need access to variables or elements in that form, so you do not want to close it.

To implement this scenario, you would add a button to the first form and enter the following code for the button's **Click** event:

```
Sub OpenButton_Click(...)
' This code runs when the user clicks a
' button named OpenButton.

  Dim CalculationForm as new Form2( )
  CalculationForm.Show( )
  ' Declares an instance of a second form and then
  ' calls the Show method of the second form. This
  ' makes the second form visible.

  Me.Hide
  ' Calls the Hide method of the current form. This
  ' makes the current form invisible.

End Sub
' The end of this block of code.
```

Important In the preceding example, the **Hide** method hides the first form instead of closing it.

Syntax to close forms

The **Close** method closes a form object. When you close a form, all resources created within the object are closed and the form is disposed of. To use the **Close** method to close a second form from an existing open form, use the following syntax:

```
FormName.Close( )
```

To close the form that is currently running, use the **Me** keyword to call the **Close** method from the running form, as shown in the following example:

```
Me.Close( )
```

Note Multiple-document interface (MDI) applications allow you to display multiple documents at the same time, with each document displayed in its own window. MDI applications often have a **Window** menu with commands for switching between windows or documents.

This discussion is beyond the scope of this course. For more information about Windows Forms development in Visual Basic .NET, see Course 2565, *Developing Microsoft .NET Applications for Windows (Visual Basic .NET)*.

Lesson: Working with Controls

- How to Add Controls to a Form
- How to Set Control Properties
- How to Add Code to Control Events
- How to Use the MessageBox Function

Introduction

In this lesson, you will learn how to create a user interface by adding basic controls to a form, setting properties for the controls, and writing code for control events. You will also learn how to create message boxes to interact with the user.

Lesson agenda

This lesson includes the following topics and activities:

- How to Add Controls to a Form
- How to Set Control Properties
- Multimedia Demonstration: Form and Control Events
- How to Add Code to Control Events
- How to Use the **MessageBox** Function
- Practice: Creating a Message Box

Lesson objectives

After completing this lesson, you will be able to:

- Add controls to a form.
- Set control properties.
- Add code to control events.
- Use a message box to interact with users.

How to Add Controls to a Form

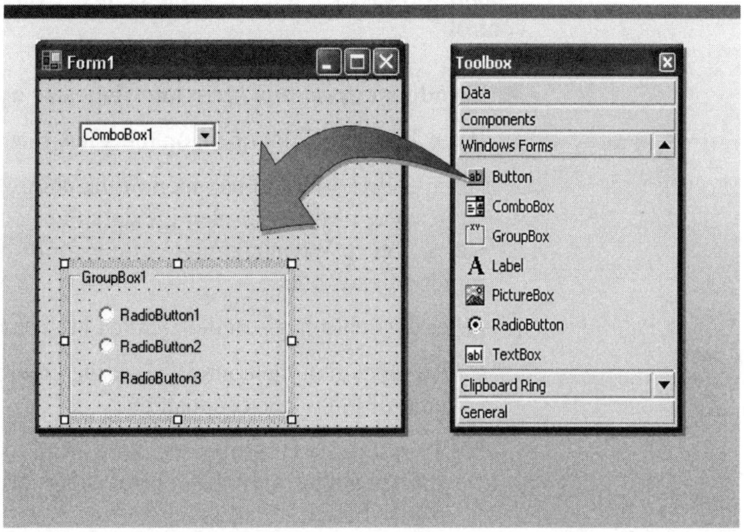

Introduction

Almost every application you write in Visual Basic uses controls on a form. *Controls* are objects that are contained within form objects. Buttons, text boxes, and labels are examples of controls.

Basic controls

The table below describes four more complex controls that you will use frequently.

Control	Description
ComboBox	Allows you to display a list of suggested choices to a user. Combo boxes can save space on a form because the list can be displayed in a drop-down menu.
GroupBox	Allows you to group other controls in a subdivision of the form. For example, you can use a group box to group several radio buttons.
PictureBox	Allows you to display a graphic on your form in bitmap, Graphics Interchange Format (GIF), Joint Photographic Experts Group (JPEG), metafile, or icon format.
RadioButton	Allows users to select one item from a short, predefined list. Although you add radio buttons to the form one at a time, you typically use two or more together. When grouped together, only one radio button can be checked at a time.

Adding controls to a form

There are two ways to add controls to a form. The first way allows you to add several controls quickly, and then size and position them one by one. The second way gives you more initial control over the size and position of the control.

► To add controls to a form and then size and position them

1. If the Toolbox is not open, on the **View** menu, click **Toolbox**.
2. Double-click the Toolbox icon of the control you want to add. This places an instance of the control at the default size in the upper left corner of the active object. When adding multiple controls in this manner, they are placed on top of each other.
3. After the controls are added, you can reposition and resize them.
   a. To reposition the control, click the control to select it, and then drag the control to the correct position.
   b. To resize the control, click the control to select it, drag one of the eight sizing handles until the control is properly sized, and then release the mouse button.

► To size and position controls while you add them to a form

1. If the Toolbox is not open, on the **View** menu, click **Toolbox**.
2. Click the Toolbox icon for the control you want to add.
3. Move the mouse pointer over the form. The pointer changes to a cross hair.
4. Position the cross hair where you want the upper left corner of the control to be.
5. Click and drag the cross hair toward the lower right corner. A rectangle is drawn on the screen, indicating the control's size and location.
6. When the control is correctly sized, release the mouse button. The sized control appears in the correct location on the form.
7. You can reposition or resize the control after you have released the mouse button.
   a. To reposition the control, click the control to select it, and then drag the control to the correct position.
   b. To resize the control, click the control to select it, drag one of the eight sizing handles until the control is properly sized, and then release the mouse button.

How to Set Control Properties

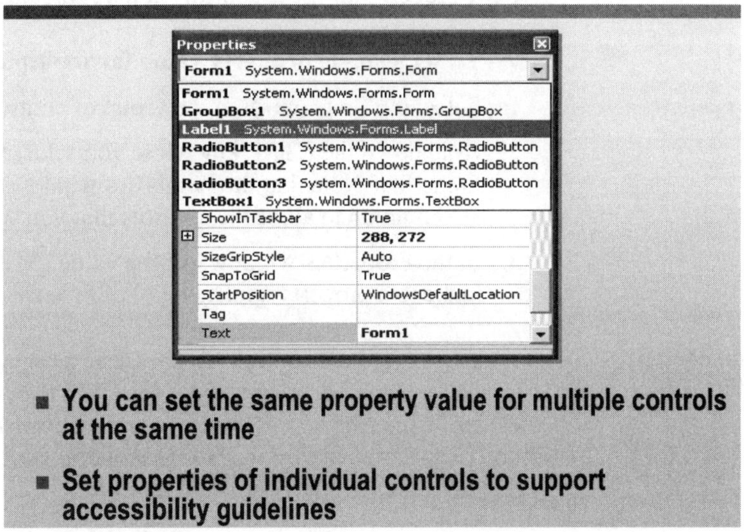

Introduction

Most graphical controls contain properties that can be changed to define their appearance. Controls can have properties that specify how they will interact with the user. You can also use control properties to make your application more accessible to people with disabilities.

Setting control properties

► **To set control properties by using the Properties window**

1. If the Properties window is not open, on the **View** menu, click **Properties Window**.
2. Choose the control for which you want to set a property.

   To do this, you can either click the control, or click the name of the control in the **Object** drop-down list at the top of the Properties window.
3. Choose whether to view the control properties alphabetically or by category by using the **Alphabetic**  and **Categorized**  buttons in the Properties window.
4. In the Properties window, click the property you want to set.

Note When you click a property, a description of the property appears in the Description pane at the bottom of the Properties window.

5. Type or select the property setting you want.

Setting properties for multiple controls

You can also set the same property value for multiple controls at the same time. For example, if you want several controls to use the same font, you can set the **Font** property for these controls at the same time.

► **To set a single property value for multiple controls**

1. Select the first control in the group of controls that you want to modify.
2. Hold down the CTRL key while you select the other controls that you want to modify. Note that the Properties window displays only the properties that are common to all of the controls that you select.
3. In the Properties window, set the value for the property. Any change you make to a property applies to all of the selected controls.

Common control properties

When you create a control, Visual Basic assigns it a default name indicating the type of control, and it appends a unique integer to the end of the name. For example, the first new **Button** object is **Button1**, the second is **Button2**, and so on. You should change the **Name** property of each control you use to a name that describes the purpose of the object.

Note A control's **Name** property must start with a letter and can include numbers and the underscore character (_), but it cannot include punctuation or spaces.

The following table describes the key properties of the **ComboBox**, **GroupBox**, **PictureBox**, and **RadioButton** controls.

Control	Property	Property description
ComboBox	**Items**	Lists the items that appear in the combo box.
GroupBox	**Text**	Sets the caption for the group box.
PictureBox	**Background Image**	Sets the background image used for the control.
	Image	Determines the image displayed in the control.
RadioButton	**CheckAlign**	Determines the location of the check box relative to the control's text.
	Checked	Indicates whether the item is checked or not when the program first runs.

Accessibility considerations

Accessibility has important business implications for software developers. Many governments have accessibility regulations for software purchase. An estimated 30 million residents of the U.S. alone are affected by the accessibility of software.

Controls in the standard toolbox for Windows Forms support many accessibility guidelines. In addition, the following table shows how the properties of individual controls can be set to support accessibility guidelines.

Control property	Considerations for accessibility
AccessibleDescription	Contains a description that is reported to accessibility aids. Accessibility aids are specialized programs or devices, such as screen readers, that help people with disabilities use computers more effectively.
AccessibleName	Contains the name that will be reported to an accessibility aid.
AccessibleRole	Describes the role of the element in the user interface.
TabIndex	Creates a sensible navigational path through the form. It is important for controls without intrinsic labels, such as text boxes, to have their associated label immediately precede them in the tab order.
Text	Use the "&" character to create access keys. For example, if you set **&Open** as the text property for a button, the button name is displayed as **Open**, with the letter O established as the access key for this button.
Font Size	If the font size is not adjustable, then it should be set to 10 points or larger. Once the form's font size is set, all the controls added to the form thereafter will have the same size.
ForeColor	If this property is set to the default, then the user's color preferences will be used on the form.
BackColor	If this property is set to the default, then the user's color preferences will be used on the form.
BackgroundImage	Leave this property blank to make text more readable.

Note For more information about improving the accessibility of your Windows-based application, see "Walkthrough: Creating an Accessible Windows Application" in the Microsoft Visual Studio® .NET documentation.

Multimedia: Form and Control Events

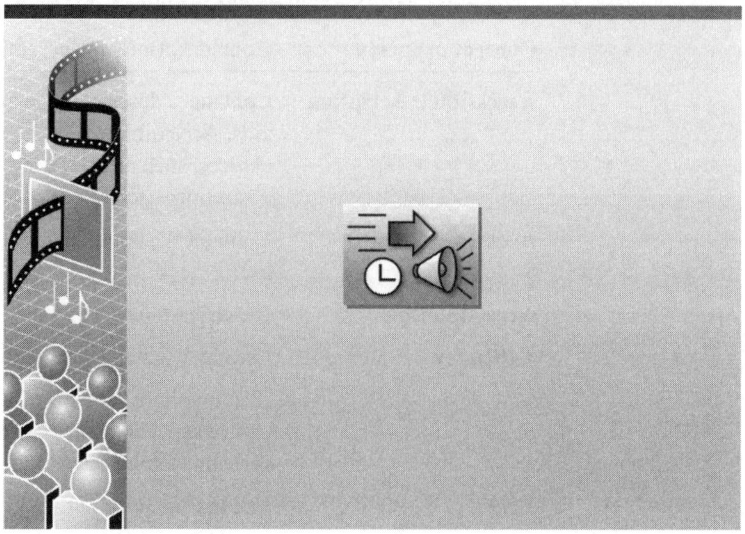

In this demonstration, you will learn several of the events that can occur as a result of user action. You will also learn how to trap certain events in your code by writing code for event handlers.

How to Add Code to Control Events

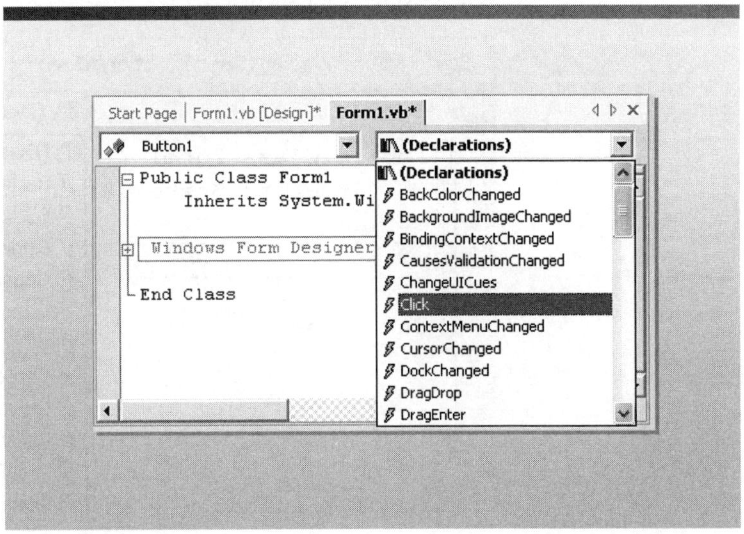

Introduction

Control events allow you to respond to actions performed on the control. You can write code in the code block, or event handler, associated with the control event. This code executes when the event occurs.

Adding code

► **To open an event handler for a control event**

1. On the **View** menu, click **Code** to open the Code Editor for the form you are working with.
2. In the **Class Name** list, click the control for which you want to write code. The following illustration shows the **Class Name** list with **Button1** selected:

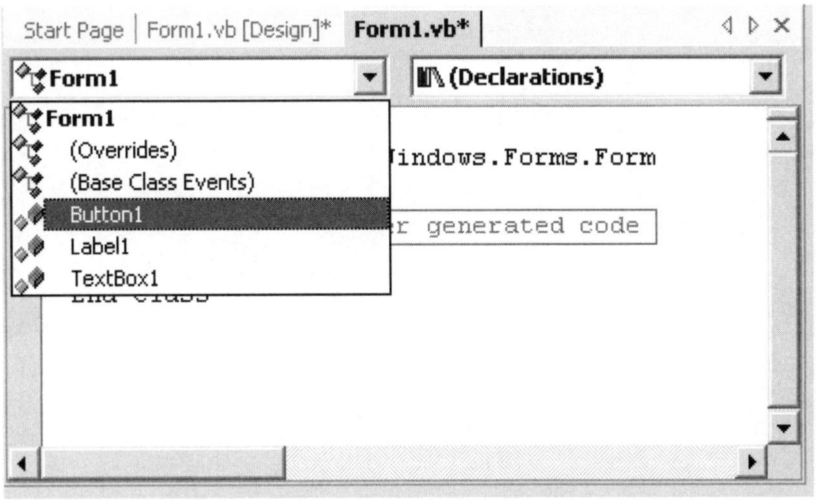

3. Open the **Method Name** list to view events available for the control. The following illustration shows a partial list of control events for **Button1**. The **Click** event is selected.

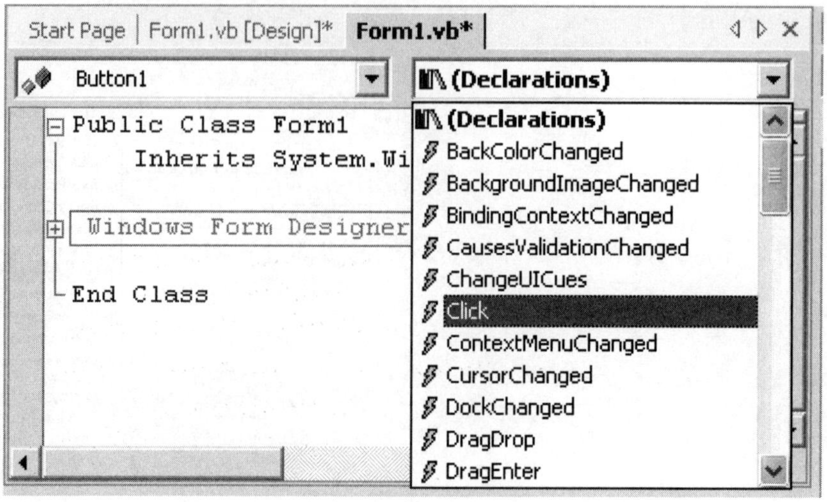

4. Click the event to open the event handler for the event.

How to Use the MessageBox Function

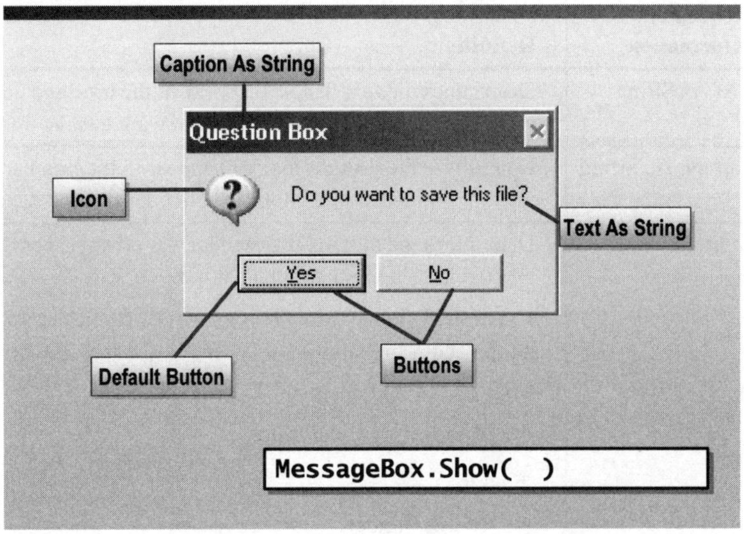

Introduction

A message box is a predefined dialog box that can be used to display information to the user or to query the user for simple information.

Syntax

Use the following syntax to call the **MessageBox** function and create a message box:

```
MessageBox.Show( )
```

Creating a message box

► **To create a message box**

1. Navigate to the code block in which you would like to add the code for the message box. For example, create a form with a button on it, and open the **Button1_Click** event handler.
2. Add the following code to your code block.

   ```
   MessageBox.Show(
   ```

3. Choose the message box option you will use for the message box.

   Visual Basic .NET offers twelve default options for creating a message box. These options are displayed in a window after you type the code listed in step 2. For each option, the window describes the required elements you need to enter between the parentheses for the **MessageBox.Show** function.

   Use the UP ARROW and DOWN ARROW buttons on your keyboard to review the options.

4. Enter the required elements in the order requested.
   a. You must separate each element with a comma.
   b. The group of elements must be contained within a set of parentheses ( ).

The table below explains the information that you need to enter for the first of the twelve message box options (option 1 of the 12 in the window).

	Requested information	Definition
1	text As String	Determines the text that will appear in the message box. The string must be contained in quotation marks. **Example:** "Do you want to save this file?"
2	caption As String	Determines the caption that will appear in the title bar of the message box. The string must be contained in quotation marks. **Example:** "Question Box"
3	buttons	Determines the buttons that will appear on your message box. You choose these buttons by double-clicking them in a list box. **Example:** Double-click **MessageBoxButtons.YesNo** if you want two buttons—a **Yes** button and a **No** button—to appear on the message box. Your options include the following: • Abort, Retry, & Ignore • OK • OK & Cancel • Retry & Cancel • Yes & No • Yes, No, & Cancel
4	Icon	Determines the icon that will appear on your message box to tell the user something about the content of the message box. You choose the icon by double-clicking it in a list box. **Example:** Double-click **MessageBoxIcon.Question** to display a question mark icon in the message box.
5	defaultButton	Determines which of the buttons on your form will be selected as the default button. You choose the default button by double-clicking it in a list box. **Example:** If you chose to display the **Yes** and **No** buttons on your message box, double-click **MessageBoxDefaultButton.Button1** to select **Yes** as the default.
6	options	Determines the display and association options that you will use for the message box. You choose these options by double-clicking them in a list box. **Example:** Double-click **MessageBoxOptions.DefaultDesktopOnly** to display the message box on the active desktop. For information about each of the display and association options, see "MessageBoxOptions Enumeration" in the Visual Studio .NET documentation.

Example of a message box

If you were to select the examples suggested in the table above, the resulting message box would look like the following screen shot.

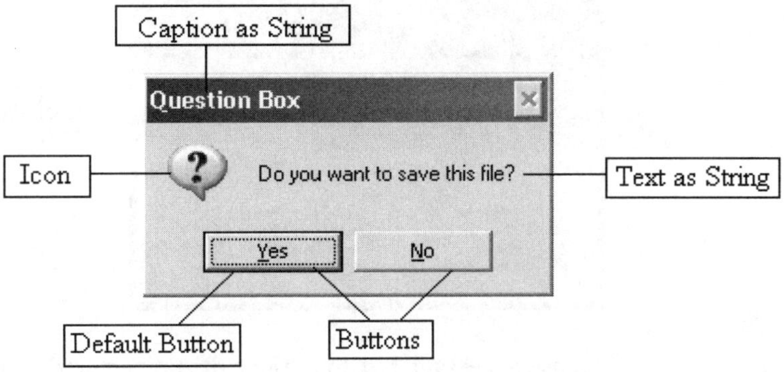

Your code would look as follows:

```
Private Sub Button1_Click(. . .)
  MessageBox.Show("Do you want to save this file?", _
   "Question Box", MessageBoxButtons.YesNo, _
   MessageBoxIcon.Question, MessageBoxDefaultButton.Button1, _
   MessageBoxOptions.DefaultDesktopOnly)
End Sub
```

Retrieving text from a text box

You can also use the **MessageBox** function in conjunction with a text box to retrieve the text entered into the text box either by default or by the user. To retrieve text box text by using a message box, use the following syntax, where *TextBoxName* is the value entered in the **Name** property for the **TextBox** control.

```
  MessageBox.Show(TextBoxName.Text)
```

Example of retrieved text

For example, consider the following form, on which a text box named ColorTextBox is provided for users to enter their favorite color.

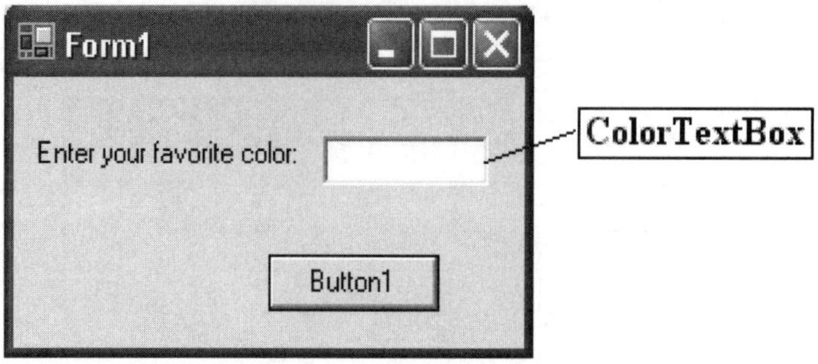

To use a message box to retrieve the text entered by the user, you can use the following code:

```
MessageBox.Show(ColorTextBox.Text)
```

If you added this code to the **Button1_Click** event, the following message box would appear when you click the button on the form. (In this example, the user has entered "Green" in the text box.)

Practice: Creating a Message Box

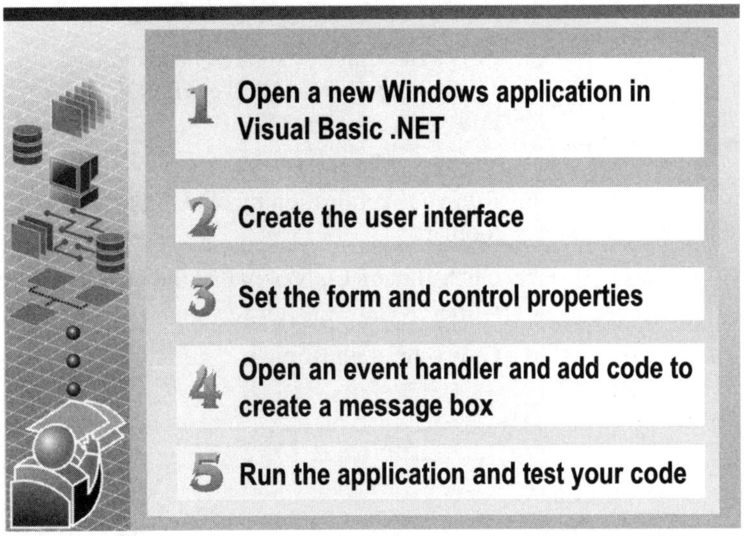

In this practice, you will create a form and then add a **TextBox** control and a **Button** control to the form. You will write code for the **Click** event of the button. When the button is clicked, a message box will appear. The message box will display the text that is in the text box.

► **Write code to create a message box from a control event**

1. Open a new Windows application in Visual Basic .NET. Set the project name to **MessageBoxProject** and the location to *install_folder*\Practices\Mod02.
2. Add two controls to the default form: a **TextBox** and a **Button**. Your form should look something like the following screen shot:

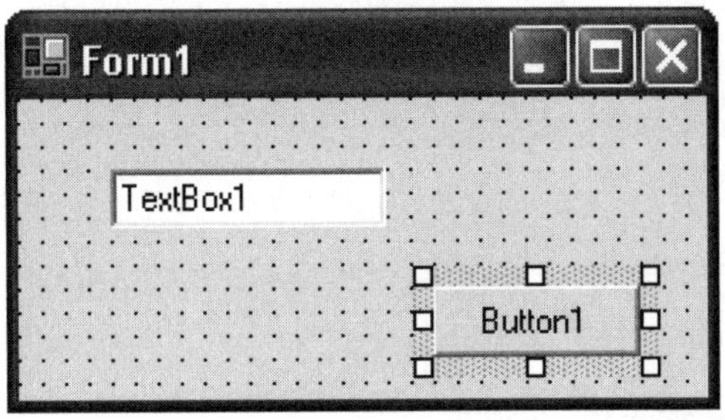

3. Set the **Text** property of the TextBox1 control to: **Please enter your name here**.

   The text "Please enter your name here" should now appear in the text box on your form.
4. Double-click the button to create the **Button1_Click** event handler.

5. In the **Button1_Click** event handler, write the code to retrieve the text from TextBox1 and display it in a message box.

   Your code should look as follows:

```
Private Sub Button1_Click(...)
   MessageBox.Show(TextBox1.Text)
End Sub
```

6. Run your application by clicking the **Start** button on the standard toolbar.

7. Click **Button1** to verify that the code in the **Button1_Click** event handler works as you expect it to.

8. Quit your application.

Lesson: Styling Your Code

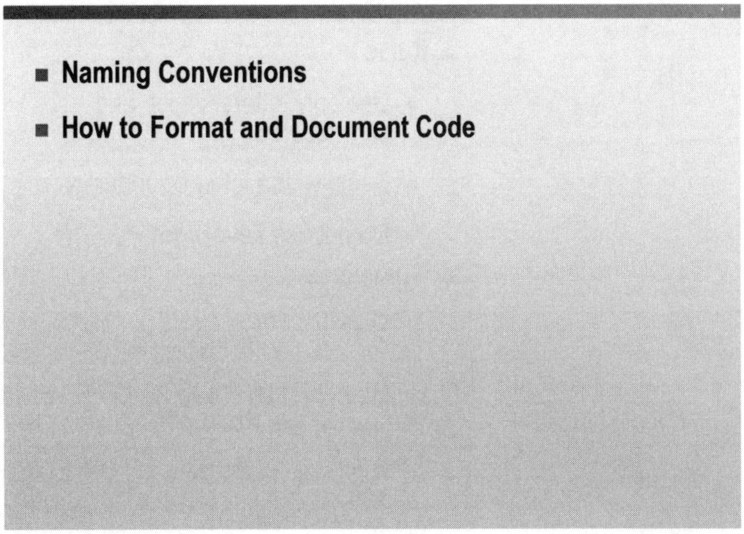

Introduction

You can make your code easier to read and maintain by using standard naming conventions and by formatting and documenting your code properly.

Lesson agenda

This lesson includes the following topics and activities:

- Naming Conventions
- How to Format and Document Code

Lesson objectives

After completing this lesson, you will be able to:

- Use standard naming conventions to name elements that you create.
- Format and document your code by using indenting, the line-continuation character, concatenation, and commenting.

Naming Conventions

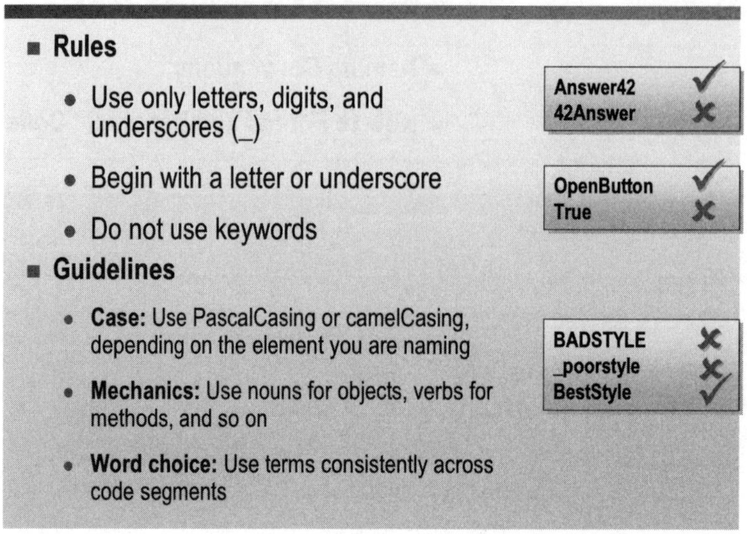

Introduction

If you consistently follow naming guidelines, your code will be easier to read and maintain. There are also rules for naming that you must follow for your program to run correctly.

Naming rules

There are four key rules you must follow when you name an element in Visual Basic. If you do not follow these rules, you program will not run; it will generate an error.

1. Every name must begin with an alphabetic character or an underscore (_).
2. Every name must contain only alphabetic characters, decimal digits, and underscores.
3. Every name must contain at least one alphabetic character or decimal digit if it begins with an underscore.
4. No name can be the same as a restricted keyword.

Naming guidelines

You can assign any name to an object, but it is a good idea to adopt a naming convention and use it consistently throughout your programs. There are three elements of naming guidelines:

1. Case: There are two capitalization styles that are standard in Visual Studio .NET. The choice of style depends on the element you are naming. For information about when to use which style, see the note that follows.
   - PascalCasing

     This convention is to capitalize the first character of each word. For example, use **OpenButton** rather than **Openbutton** or **Open_Button**.
   - camelCasing

     This convention is to capitalize the first character of each word except for the first word. For example, use **backColor** rather than **back_color** or **backcolor**.
2. Mechanics: Use nouns for objects, verbs for methods, and so on.
3. Word choice: Use terms consistently across code segments.

Note Visual Studio .NET provides extensive documentation on naming guidelines. For more information about naming guidelines, see "Design Guidelines for Class Library Developers" in the Visual Studio .NET documentation.

How to Format and Document Code

- Indenting

```
Sub Button1_Click
    Me.Close
End Sub
```

- Line continuation and concatenation

```
MessageBox.Show("User Name = " & UserName.Text & _
    ", Password = " & Password.Text)
```

- Adding comments

```
'Make CalculationForm visible
   Dim CalculationForm as new Form2( )
   CalculationForm.Show( )
```

- Add comments to your code to make it more readable and easier to maintain

Introduction

You can make your code easier to read and maintain by using proper formatting and documenting techniques. These techniques include indenting segments of code, breaking and combining lines of code, and adding comments to your code.

Indenting code

Use indenting to differentiate segments of code, such as loops and conditional statements. To indent a line of code, use the TAB key on your keyboard, or use the **Increase Indent** button on the **Text Editor** toolbar.

► **To view the default settings for code indentation**

1. On the **Tools** menu, click **Options**.
2. Click the **Text Editor** folder, and then click the **Basic** folder.
3. Click **Tabs** to view or change the default tab and indent settings and to verify that Smart Indenting is turned on.

Line-continuation character

You can use line breaks to ensure that you can read all of your code in the Code Editor without using the horizontal scroll bar. In Visual Basic, you break a line of code by using the line-continuation character, which is an underscore (_) preceded by a space.

For example, line breaks have been used in the following code so that the entire string can be viewed in the Code Editor without having to scroll to the right.

```
MessageBox.Show("User Name = " & UserName.Text & _
    ", Password = " & Password.Text)
```

Note that the line following the line break is indented. This creates the visual cue that the indented text is a part of the text that comes before the line break.

Concatenation

If you must divide a string into two or more strings, place a line-continuation character between the strings, and then concatenate them, or link them, by using an ampersand (&).

It is important to preserve all spaces in the string when it is concatenated.

Code	How it will display
Incorrect:	
`MessageBox.Show("User Name =" & UserName.Text)`	User Name =*username.*
Correct:	
`MessageBox.Show("User Name = " & UserName.Text)`	User Name = *username*

Commenting code

To comment your code, use a single quotation mark ('). Visual Basic ignores anything following a single quotation mark, so comments can be placed on their own line or at the end of a line of code.

You can add or remove comment symbols for a block of code by selecting two or more lines of code and choosing the **Comment Selection** and **Uncomment Selection** buttons on the **Text Editor** toolbar.

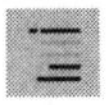 This is the **Comment Selection** button.

 This is the **Uncomment Selection** button.

The following are two examples of commented code:

- Comment placed at the end of a line of code:

```
CalculationForm.Show( ) ' Make CalculationForm visible
```

- Comment placed on its own line:

```
' Create the message box for the Button1_Click event

  Private Sub Button1_Click ...

  MessageBox.Show("Do you want to save this file?", _
      "Question Box", MessageBoxButtons.YesNo, _
      MessageBoxDefaultButton.Button1)

  End Sub
```

When to comment your code

As you write more complicated code, use comments to make your code more readable and easier to maintain. You should use comments to explain the purpose of a section of code in natural language, especially when the purpose might not be obvious or clear. For example, a comment above a calculation function might say "Calculate the user's projected monthly payment by using the input from the user."

The following list provides some guidelines regarding when you should comment your code:

- Begin procedures with a comment block. This block should include information such as the purpose of the procedure, the value returned by a function, the arguments used by the procedure, and so on.
- In longer procedures, use comments to break up units of work within the procedure.
- When you declare variables, use a comment to indicate how the variable will be used.
- When you write a decision structure, use a comment to indicate how the decision is made and what it implies.

Review

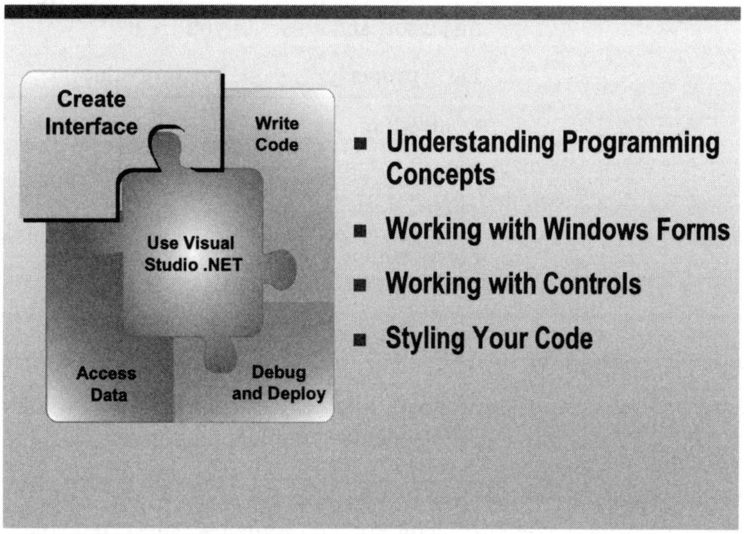

1. What is the relationship between classes and objects?

2. Identify each of the following elements as a property, method, or event.

a. **Click**	e. **Size**
b. **Close** method	f. **Resize**
c. **Text**	g. **Show**
d. **KeyPress**	h. **Closing** event

3. You are creating a new application and change the properties for Form1, as listed in the table below. When you try to run the application, you get an error message notifying you of build errors. What is the probable cause of this error, and how can you fix it?

Form property	New value
ControlBox	**False**
Name	**LogonForm**
Text	**Logon Form**
StartPosition	**CenterScreen**

4. Evaluate whether each of the following statements is true or false. For any false statement, explain why it is false.

   a. When you call the **Hide** method of a form, the form closes.

   b. You use the following syntax to display a form:

      *FormName.*Show( )

   c. You should give users maximum control by minimizing the modal interactions in your applications.

5. You are writing a program and need to place the contents of the **FirstNameTextBox** into a message box. Write the code that would create this message box.

6. The following code is listed in the Code Editor for Form1, which has one button named **ClickMeButton**. Add a comment to this code that explains what it does. Be sure to use the correct character for indicating a comment.

```
Private Sub ClickMeButton_Click(...)
   Me.CenterToScreen( )
   MessageBox.Show("Hi")
End Sub
```

Lab 2.1: Creating the User Interface

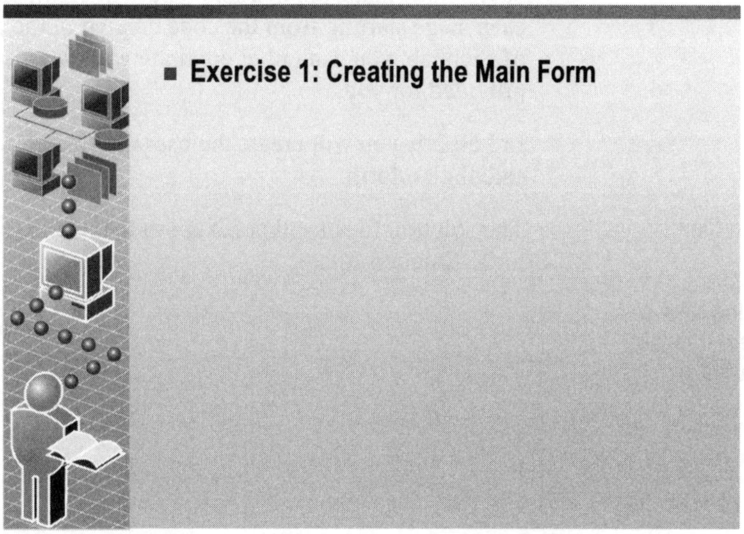

Objectives

After completing this lab, you will be able to:

- Create forms and add controls to create a user interface.
- Set and change form and control properties.
- Write code to handle form and control events.
- Change the startup object of a project.

Note This lab focuses on the concepts in this module and as a result may not comply with Microsoft security recommendations.

Prerequisites

Before working on this lab, you must have:

- Experience with adding controls to a form.
- Experience with the Visual Studio .NET development environment.
- Familiarity with how to write code to handle events.
- Knowledge of form and control properties.

Scenario

In the labs for Modules 2, 4, 5, 6, and 12 of Course 2559B, *Introduction to Visual Basic .NET Programming with Microsoft .NET,* you will create a loan payment estimate application. You will create the full application in stages, each stage starting from the code created in the previous lab. At the beginning of each lab, you can either continue with your own files or start with the files provided for you.

In Lab 2.1, you will create the user interface for this application, a loan calculation form.

Solution files

The solution files for this lab are in the *install_folder*\Labfiles\Lab021\Ex01\Solution folder.

Estimated time to complete this lab: 45 minutes

Exercise 1
Creating the Main Form

In this exercise, you will create a main form for a loan payment estimate application. You will start a new project, rename the form, place controls on the form, set properties for the controls, and change the startup object for your project.

► Create a new project

1. Start Visual Studio .NET.
2. On the **File** menu, point to **New**, and then click **Project**.
3. In the **New Project** dialog box, click **Visual Basic Projects**, and then click **Windows Application**. Set the project name to **LoanApplication** and the folder location to *install_folder*\Labfiles\Lab021\Ex01\Starter. Click **OK**.
4. In Solution Explorer, click **Form1.vb**.
5. In the Properties window, change the **File Name** property to **Main.vb**.

► Add controls to the main form

1. Add two **Label** controls to the form.
2. Add one **TextBox** control to the form.
3. Add one **ComboBox** control to the form.
4. Add a **GroupBox** control to the form, and then add three **RadioButton** controls inside the **GroupBox** control.
5. Add a **Button** control to the form.

   Your form should look similar to the following screen shot.

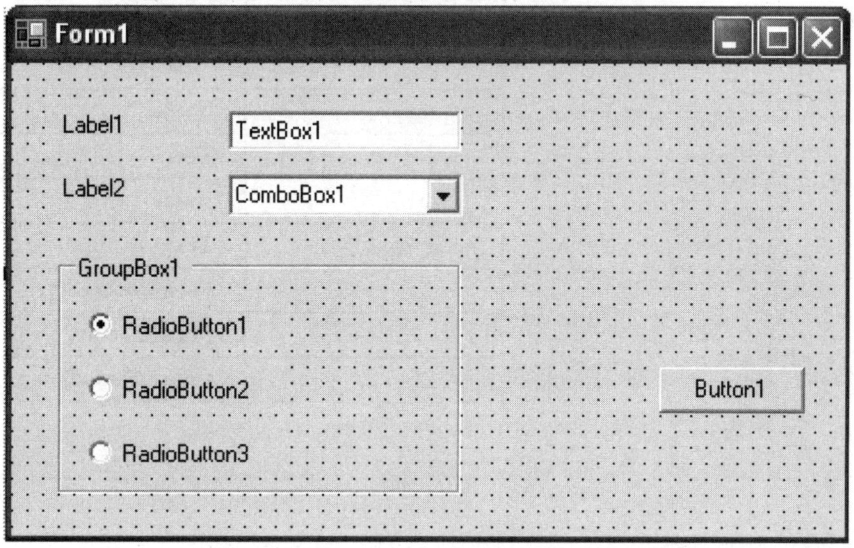

6. Set the properties for the controls as listed in the following table.

Control name	Property	Property value
Label1	**Name**	**LoanLabel**
	Text	**Loan Amount**
Label2	**Name**	**RateLabel**
	Text	**Interest Rate**
TextBox1	**Name**	**LoanTextBox**
	Text	*blank*
ComboBox1	**Name**	**RateComboBox**
	Text	*blank*
	Items	**4.5** **6.25** **7.0** **8.325** **9.0** **10.0**
GroupBox1	**Name**	**TermGroupBox**
	Text	**Loan Term**
RadioButton1	**Name**	**Length5RadioButton**
	Text	**5 Years**
	Checked	**True**
RadioButton2	**Name**	**Length15RadioButton**
	Text	**15 Years**
RadioButton3	**Name**	**Length30RadioButton**
	Text	**30 Years**
Button1	**Name**	**DoneButton**
	Text	**&Done**
Form1	**Name**	**MainForm**
	Text	**Loan Payment Estimate**
	FormBorderStyle	**FixedSingle**
	MaximizeBox	**False**
	CancelButton	**DoneButton**

Your form should now look similar to the following screen shot.

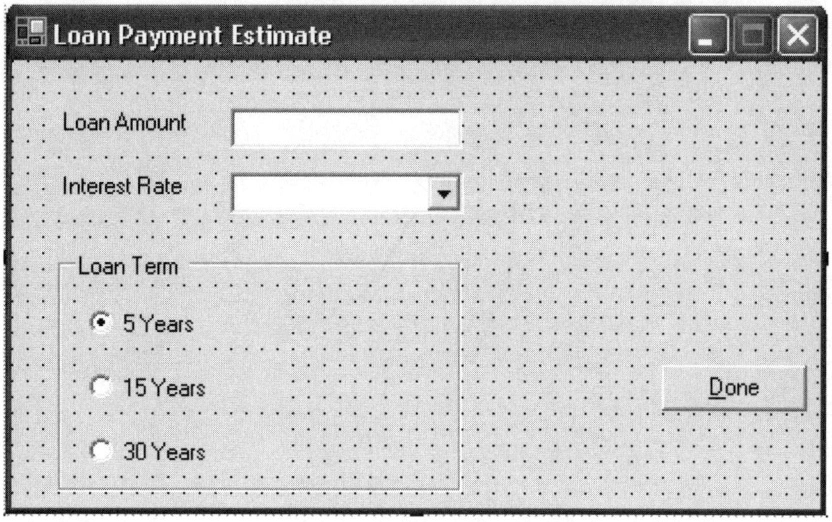

► Add an event handler

- To quit the loan application, create an event handler for the **Click** event of the **Done** button. Call the **Me.Close** method when a user clicks the **Done** button.

► Change the startup object

- In Solution Explorer, right-click **LoanApplication** project and then click **Properties**. In the **Startup object** box, change the startup object to **MainForm**, and then click **OK**.

► Test the application

1. On the **Debug** menu, click **Start**. Type a loan amount and select an interest rate.
2. Click the **Done** button to quit the application.
3. Run the application again.
4. Press ESC.

   What happens? Why?

   ____

   ____

msdn® training

Module 3: Using Variables and Arrays

Contents

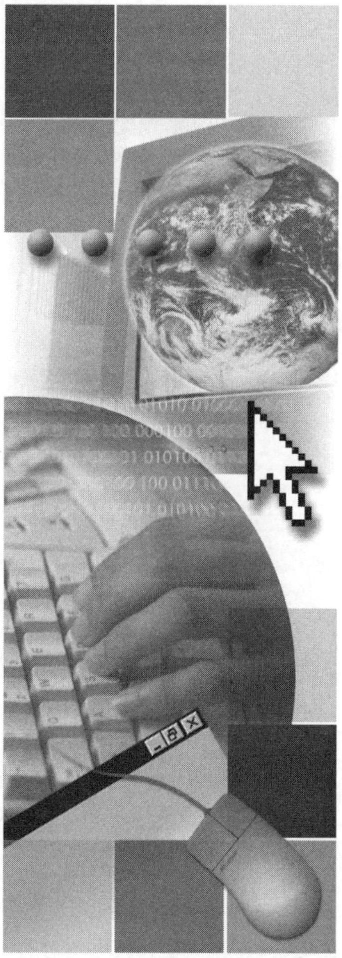

Microsoft®

Overview

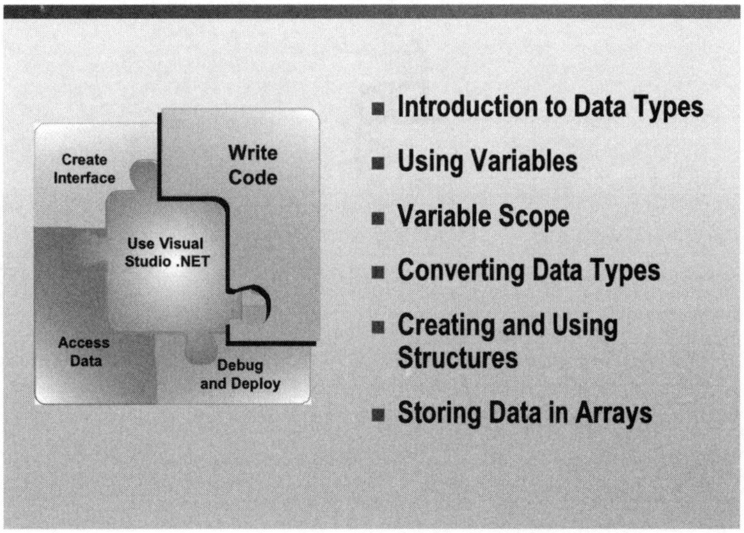

Introduction

When your application is running, it uses variables to store values in temporary locations in memory so it can process data and perform calculations. This module explains how to name, declare, assign values to, and use variables. It also describes how to store data in an array.

Objectives

After completing this module, you will be able to:

- Describe the various data types that you can use to declare variables.
- Name, declare, initialize, and use variables and constants.
- Declare variables with different levels of scope.
- Create user-defined data structures.
- Convert variable values from one data type to another.
- Store data in arrays.

Multimedia: What Are Variables?

Introduction

This multimedia animation explains what variables are and how applications use them to process data and calculate values.

Animation script

As your code runs, it needs to store various kinds of data in memory for use by other parts of your application. For example, you might need to store data entered on one form for use by another form. Or you might need to store information from your form before saving it to a database. Or you might need to perform a mathematical calculation.

In Microsoft® Visual Basic®, as with most programming languages, you use variables to store values that can change when your application is running. Variables make it possible to process almost any kind of data.

Suppose you have a form on which users can enter numbers in two textboxes and then click a button to display the total. You can use variables to store the **TextBox** properties so that Visual Basic can manipulate the data. Here, they are used to perform the addition calculation.

Think of your computer's memory as a warehouse where you will store your variables. When storing items in a warehouse, you need to know three things:

- How much space do you need for a particular item?
- What type of item are you storing?
- How do you locate the item after you store it?

Look at the syntax for declaring a variable. Now examine the declaration for an integer variable to see how it handles size, type, and location. The **Dim** statement reserves the space in memory, the variable name *Number1* is assigned to that space, **As** is a keyword that indicates that a data type is to follow, and the **Integer** data type defines the amount of space and categorizes this variable as a number. When variables are declared as integers, Visual Basic can apply the correct functionality for integers.

Visual Basic provides many data types that you can use to define your variables, including **Integer**, **Double**, **String**, and **Form**. In this module, you will learn how to use these data types to store and process data in your applications.

Lesson: Introduction to Data Types

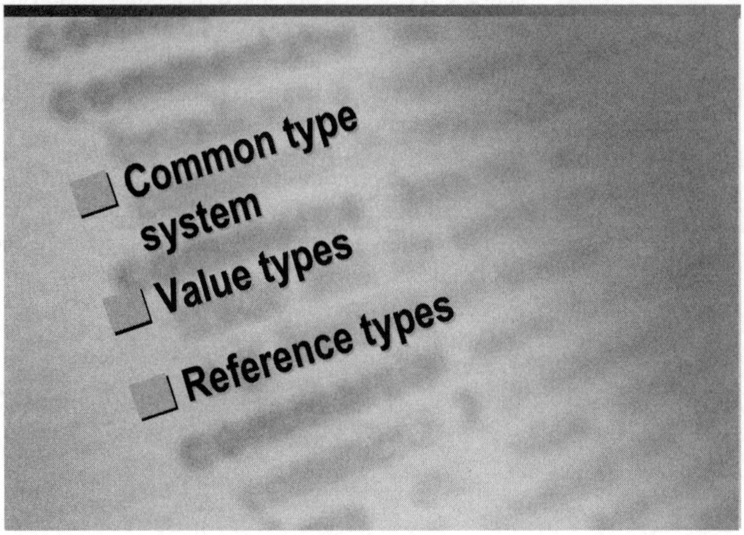

Introduction

The *data type* of a programming element refers to the kind of data it can hold and how that data is stored. The common type system defines the data types that are supported by the common language runtime. Visual Basic .NET uses data types that correspond directly to the data types in the common type system.

This lesson describes the common type system, explains how Visual Basic .NET implements the common types, and explains how to choose the appropriate data type for a given variable.

Lesson agenda

This lesson includes the following topics and activities:

- What Is the Common Type System?
- Data Types
- How to Choose a Data Type
- Practice: Choosing Data Types

Lesson objectives

After completing this lesson, you will be able to:

- Describe the types available in the common type system.
- Explain the difference between value-type and reference-type variables.
- List some of the commonly used data types available in Visual Basic .NET.
- Choose the appropriate data type for a variable.

What Is the Common Type System?

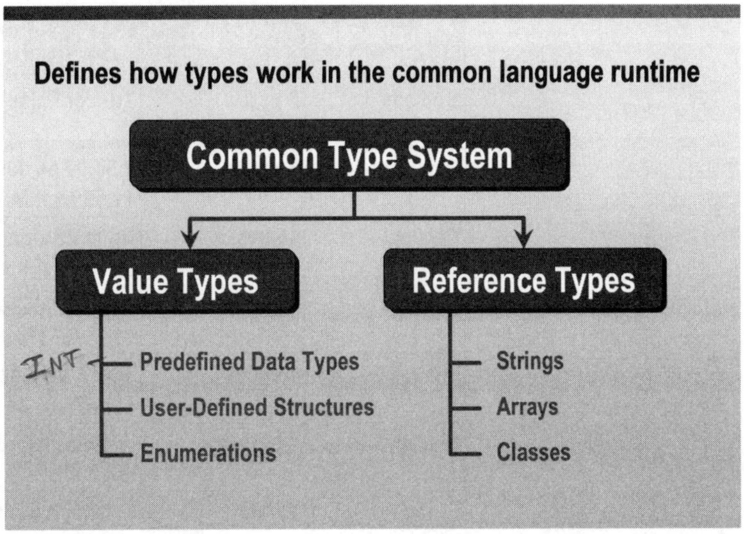

Introduction

The common type system defines how types are declared, used, and managed in the common language runtime. Each of the data types used in Visual Basic .NET correspond directly to a type defined in the common type system.

Advantages of the common type system

The common type system is of fundamental importance in creating applications for the Microsoft .NET platform. It makes it possible for one developer to create a project in Visual Basic .NET and then integrate it with a component created by another developer in Microsoft Visual C#™ and a function written by yet another developer in another .NET-compatible language. All of these pieces can be integrated into a single solution. The compilers and tools in Microsoft Visual Studio® .NET and the common language runtime all rely on the common type system to provide:

- Cross-language integration.
- Type-safe code, meaning that types are only accessed in well-defined, allowable ways.
- The tools that manage and enable high-performance code execution.

Value types vs. reference types

The common type system supports two general categories of types: *value types* and *reference types*.

A value-type variable directly contains its data. Each value-type variable has its own copy of data, so operations on one value-type variable cannot affect another variable.

A reference-type variable contains a reference or pointer to the value of an object. Two reference-type variables can reference the same object, so operations on one reference-type variable can affect the object referenced by another reference-type variable.

Data Types

Visual Basic .NET type	Storage size	Range of values
Boolean	2 bytes	True or False
Date	8 bytes	0:00:00 on January 1, 0001 to 11:59:59 P.M. on December 31, 9999
Decimal	16 bytes	Up to 29 significant digits, with values up to 7.9228 x 10^{28} (signed)
Double	8 bytes	-4.94065645841246544E-324 to +1.79769313486231570E+308 (signed)
Integer	4 bytes	-2,147,483,648 to +2,147,483,647 (signed)
Single	4 bytes	-3.4028235E+38 to 1.401298E-45 (signed)
String	Varies	0 to approximately 2 billion Unicode characters

Introduction

The preceding illustration lists some of the commonly used types in Visual Basic .NET. The term *signed* means that the numbers can be positive or negative, as in +48 or -48.

Note For a complete list of Visual Basic .NET data types and their descriptions, search titles only for "Data Type Summary" in the Visual Basic .NET documentation.

How to Choose a Data Type

Select data type…	To handle…	CTS type	Example
Boolean	True or false conditions	Value	True
Short, Integer, Long, Byte	Whole integers	Value	23 (Integer)
Single, Double, Decimal	Numbers with integers and fractional parts	Value	9456.72 (Decimal)
Date	Date and time values	Value	02/12/2003 12:30:42 A.M.
String	Printable and displayable characters	Reference	"House"
Object	A pointer to the value of an object	Reference	myClass myPerson

Introduction

Visual Basic does not require you to explicitly select a data type when you declare a variable. Nevertheless, it is a good idea to do so because it will make your applications more reliable, and they will require less memory. The data type determines the allowable values for a variable, which, in turn, determine the operations that can be performed on that variable.

Selecting a data type

You can follow the general guidelines shown in the preceding illustration to select the appropriate data type for a variable.

Strong typing

If you declare variables without a data type, they are given the **Object** data type by default. This makes it easy to write programs quickly, but it can cause them to run more slowly. Specifying data types for all your variables is known as *strong typing*. Using strong typing is recommended because it:

- Minimizes the amount of memory used by the application.
- Allows the compiler to perform type checking. This catches statements that can fail at run time because of mismatched variables and values.
- Results in faster execution of your code.
- Enables Microsoft IntelliSense® support for your variables. This technology allows you to see their properties and other members as you type the code.

Practice: Choosing Data Types

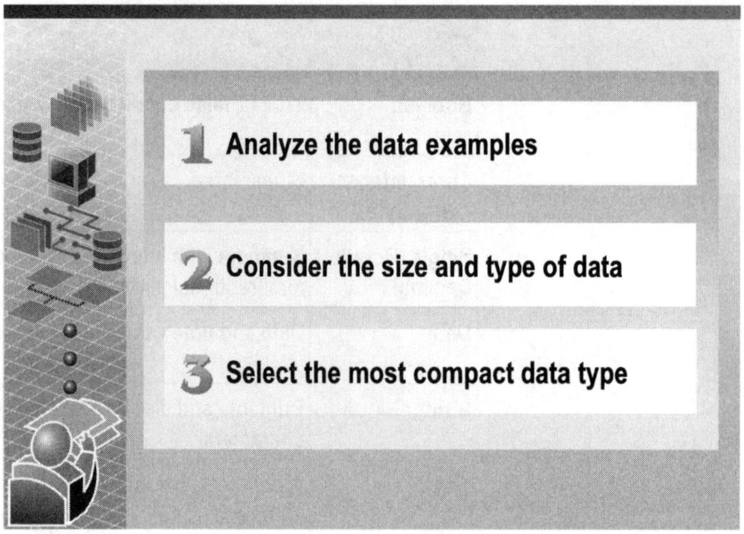

Introduction

Work in pairs to analyze the example data and choose the appropriate data type.

Instructions

Choose the most compact data type for each of the following examples of data:

- Street address

  ____

  ____

- Loan amount

  ____

  ____

- Phone number

  ____

  ____

- Interest rate

  ____

  ____

- Birthday

  ____

  ____

- Personal identification number

  ____

  ____

Lesson: Using Variables

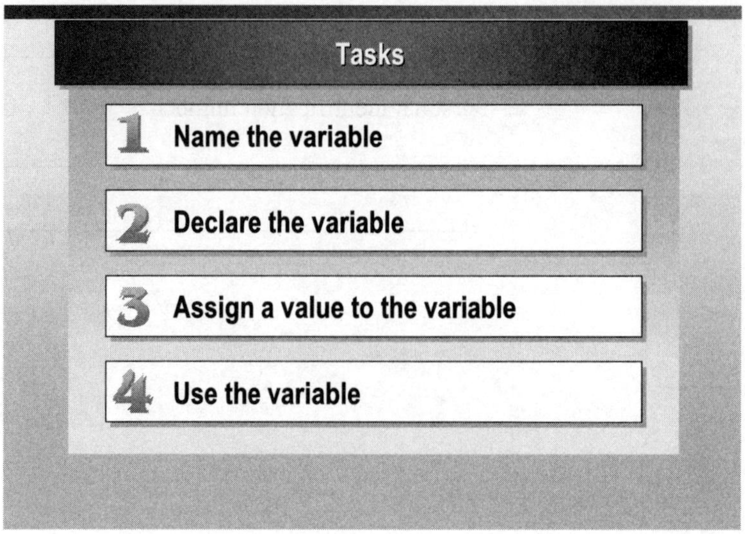

Introduction

Before you can use a variable in your application, you need to name and declare the variable and assign a value to it. This lesson explains how to create and use variables and constants.

Lesson agenda

This lesson includes the following topics and activities:

- What Are Variables?
- How to Name Variables
- How to Declare Variables
- How **Option Explicit** Affects Variables
- How to Assign Values to Variables
- How to Use Variables
- Variables vs. Constants
- Practice: Find the Bugs

Lesson objectives

After completing this lesson, you will be able to:

- Explain the purpose of variables.
- Follow established rules and guidelines for naming variables.
- Declare value-type and reference-type variables.
- Assign values to variables.
- Use variables in an application.
- Describe the difference between variables and constants.

What Are Variables?

- **Variables store values that can change when an application is running**
- **Variables have six basic elements:**

Element	Description
Name	The word that identifies the variable in code
Address	The memory location at which the value is stored
Data type	The type and starting size of data the variable can store
Value	The value at the variable's address
Scope	The set of all code that can access and use the variable
Lifetime	The period of time for which a variable is valid

Introduction

You often need to store values temporarily when performing calculations in Visual Basic. For example, you might want to calculate several values, compare them, and perform different operations on them depending on the result of the comparison.

Definition

You use variables to store values that can change when an application is running.

Variable elements

A variable has the following six elements:

Element	Description
Name	The word that you use to refer to the variable in code.
Address	The memory location at which the value of the variable is stored.
Data type	The type and starting size of data the variable can store.
Value	The value at the variable's address.
Scope	The set of all code that can access and use the variable.
Lifetime	The period of time during which a variable is valid and available for use. Its value can change over its lifetime, but it always holds some value when it exists in memory.

Examples of variables

A variable can be used in many ways, including the following:

- As a counter that stores the number of times an event is triggered
- As temporary storage for property values
- As a location to hold a value returned from a function
- As a location to store directory or file names

How to Name Variables

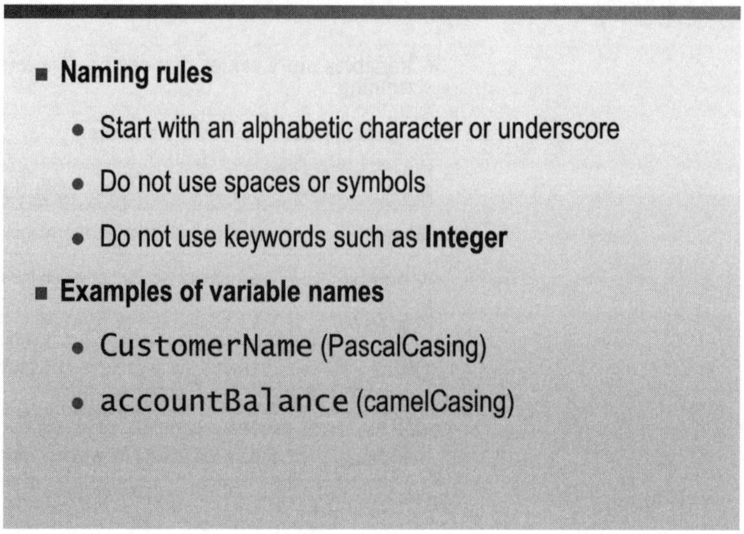

Introduction

When you declare a variable, it is important to develop a naming strategy. Both clarity and consistency are important, especially when others will need to read or maintain your code.

Rules

When you name a variable in Visual Basic .NET, you must observe the following rules:

- Start each variable name with an alphabetic character or an underscore (_).
- Do not use spaces or symbols.
- Do not use keywords such as **Integer** or **Date**.

Recommendations

It is recommended that you observe the following guidelines when naming variables:

- Provide meaningful, descriptive names, such as *accountNumber*.

  Although typing a long variable name can be tedious when writing code, it will make your code more readable and easier to maintain.
- Begin each separate word in the name for a public variable with a capital letter, as in *CustomerName*. This is called *PascalCasing*.
- Avoid using abbreviations.

  Although you can use a variable name such as *acctno*, it is much easier to read your code if you use the name *accountNumber*. If you must use abbreviations, make sure they are consistent throughout the entire application.
- Use a unique name within the scope of the variable. *Scope* refers to the set of all code that recognizes the variable.
- When declaring local and private variables, start the first word with a lowercase character, as in *newCustomer*. This is called *camelCasing*.

How to Declare Variables

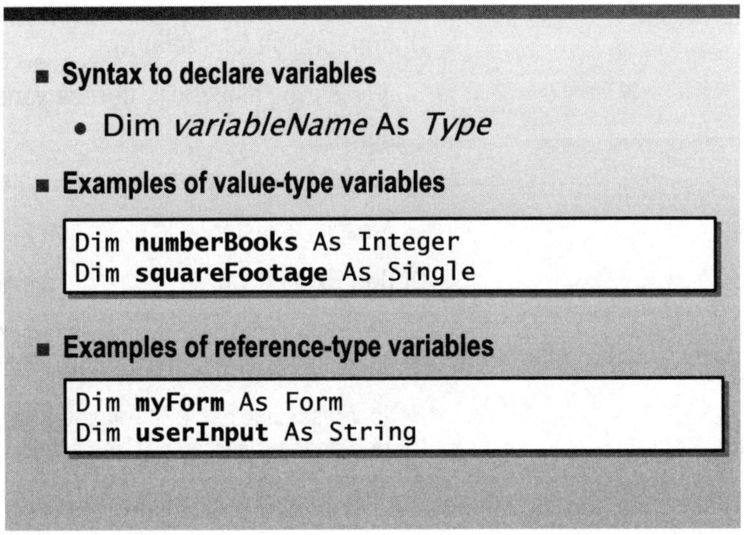

Introduction

You declare a variable to specify its name and characteristics. The declaration statement for both value-type and reference-type variables is the **Dim** statement. The declaration's location and contents determine the variable's characteristics.

Syntax

To declare a variable, use the following syntax:

```
Dim variableName As Type
```

You use the **Dim** statement to declare and allocate storage space for variables in blocks, procedures, modules, structures, and classes. You use the **As** clause in the **Dim** statement to specify the variable's data type.

Note The keyword **Dim** is an abbreviation of the word *dimension*.

Examples of value types

The following examples show how to declare variables with predefined value types:

```
Dim numberBooks As Integer
Dim squareFootage As Single
```

Examples of reference types

The following examples show how to declare variables with reference types:

```
Dim myForm As Form
Dim userInput As String
```

Although you use similar declaration syntax to declare both value-type and reference-type variables, the runtime handles them differently. A reference-type variable always contains either a pointer to a value of that type or a null reference. A value-type variable contains the variable's actual value.

How Option Explicit Affects Variables

- **Option Explicit On (default)**
  - Forces you to explicitly declare variables before using them
  - Reduces logic errors and makes code easier to maintain
  - Results in faster code execution
- **Option Explicit Off**
  - Allows you to implicitly use variables without declaring them
  - Increases likelihood of naming conflicts and unexpected behavior caused by spelling errors
  - Results in slower code execution

Introduction

In general, you should explicitly declare variables in your application before you use them. This reduces the likelihood of logic errors and makes your code easier to maintain. Although it is not recommended, you can use variables in your application without first declaring them. This is called *implicit* declaration.

How Option Explicit works

When **Option Explicit** is **On** (this is the default), you must explicitly declare variables before you can use them, or the compiler will generate an error.

When **Option Explicit** is **Off**, you can implicitly declare a variable by simply using it in your code. It will be created as an object type. Although it might be convenient to declare variables implicitly, it increases the likelihood of naming conflicts and unexpected behavior caused by spelling errors. It is also an inefficient use of memory storage.

Example of an advantage of Option Explicit

For example, assume that the variable *currentSalary* holds an employee's annual salary. A procedure uses this variable in a formula that calculates the employee's bonus. Assume that the *currentSalary* variable was typed incorrectly, as shown in the following example:

```
Dim currentSalary As Integer
currentBonus = currentSalry * .10
```

With **Option Explicit** set to **Off**, this calculation will result in a bonus of $0.00 because the variable *currentSalry* will be implicitly declared as a new object variable and will be initialized to empty. When *currentSalry* is used in the calculation, Visual Basic will automatically convert it to 0. If this calculation is performed multiple times within a looping structure, your application will run noticeably slower because it takes time for Visual Basic to create, initialize, and convert the variable each time.

Setting Option Explicit

You can set **Option Explicit** to **On** or **Off** at the project level in the development environment.

► **To set Option Explicit**

1. In Solution Explorer, click the project name for which you want to set **Option Explicit**.
2. On the **View** menu, click **Property Pages**.
3. Expand the **Common Properties** folder, and then click the **Build** folder.
4. Under **Compiler Defaults**, click **Off** or **On** as desired in the **Option Explicit** list, and then click **OK**.

You can also set **Option Explicit** to **On** or **Off** by placing the appropriate statement at the beginning of your code:

```
' This turns Option Explicit On
Option Explicit On
' This turns Option Explicit Off
Option Explicit Off
```

How to Assign Values to Variables

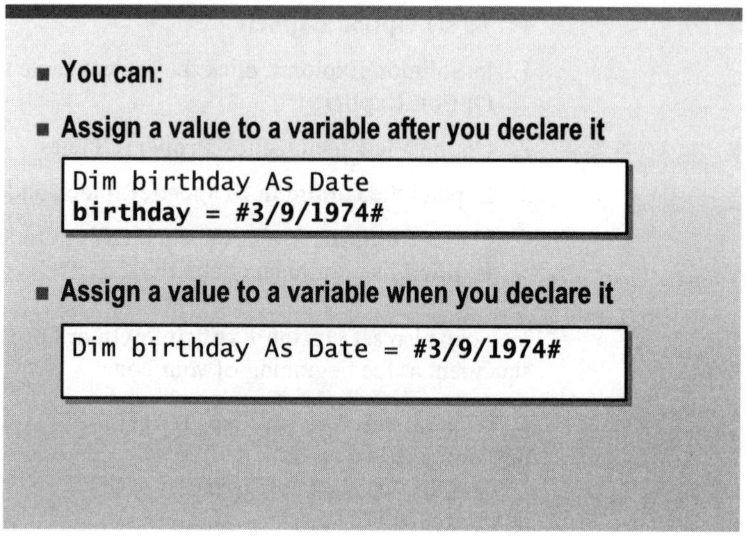

Introduction

Before you can use variables in your application, you need to assign values to them. You can assign a value to a variable after you declare it or when you declare it.

Syntax

To assign a value to a variable, use the assignment operator (=), as shown in the following expression:

VariableName = *Value*

The value on the right side of the expression is assigned to the variable on the left side of the expression.

Assigning a value after declaration

You can assign values to variables after you declare them, as shown in the following example:

```
Dim birthday As Date
birthday = #3/9/1974#
```

When you create a variable with the **Dim** statement, Visual Basic automatically initializes numeric variables to 0, text strings to empty (""), and date variables to January 1, 0001.

Assigning values when declaring

Alternatively, you can assign a value to a variable when you declare it, as shown in the following examples:

```
Dim birthday As Date = #3/9/1974#
Dim goodNews As String = "Your check is in the mail."
Dim testCondition As Boolean = True
```

Note **Date** values must be enclosed in number symbols (##), and **String** values must be enclosed in quotation marks ("").

How to Use Variables

You can use variables to:

- **Store values from expressions**
- **Store user input**
- **Store objects**
- **Store property values**
- **Return values**
- **Display output**

Introduction

After you name and declare variables and assign them values, you can start using them in your application. Variables can maintain the same value throughout an application or they can change values several times, depending on how you use them.

Examples

You can use variables to store data that originated from an expression, as shown in the following examples:

```
newMessage = "You have new Mail!"
unreadMail = totalMail - readMail
```

You can use variables to store information input by the user, as shown in the following examples:

```
userName = nameTextBox.Text
applicationDate = appDateTextBox.Text
```

You can use variables to store objects, as shown in the following example:

```
myForm = mainForm
```

Variables vs. Constants

Variables	Constants
Declare with **Dim**	Declare with **Const**
Values **change** while application is running	Values **stay the same** while application is running
Use **more** memory than constants	Use **less** memory than variables

Syntax to declare a constant:

```
Const constantName As Type
```

Introduction

If a variable in your program contains a value that never changes, consider storing the value as a constant instead of as a variable. Constants provide a way to use meaningful names in place of a value that does not change (such as π, a fixed mathematical quantity).

How constants work

Constants store values that, as the name implies, remain constant throughout the execution of an application. Advantages of using constants include the following:

- They make code easier to read.
- They use less memory than variables.
- They make application-wide changes easier to accomplish.

Syntax

To declare a constant, use the **Const** statement with the following syntax:

```
Const constantName As Type
```

You name and specify scope levels for constants by following the same rules as those used for variables.

Example

The following example shows how to declare and use a constant:

```
Dim area, radius, circumference As Double
Const Pi As Double = 3.1415
area = Pi * radius ^ 2
circumference = 2 * Pi * radius
```

Practice: Find the Bugs

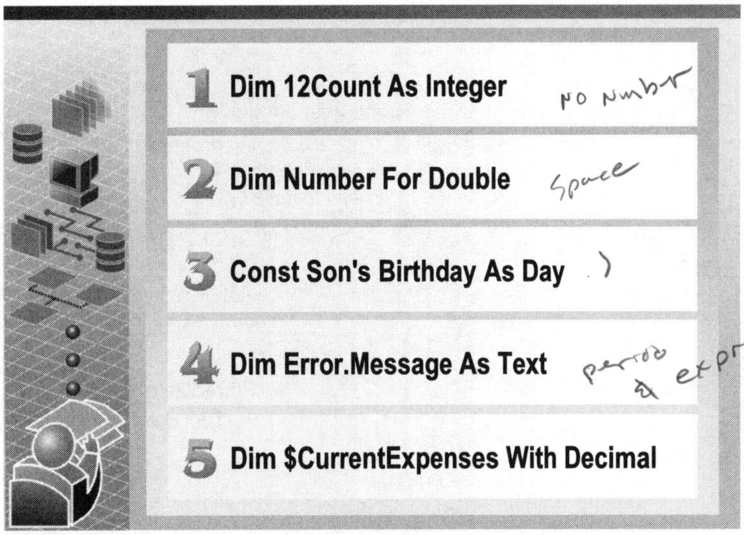

Introduction

Work in pairs to find and fix the bugs on the slide.

Instructions

Rewrite the following declaration statements to fix the errors. Follow the naming rules and recommendations for local variables.

```
Dim 12Count As Integer
Dim Number For Double
Const Son's Birthday As Day
Dim Error.Message As Text
Dim $CurrentExpenses With Decimal
```

Lesson: Variable Scope

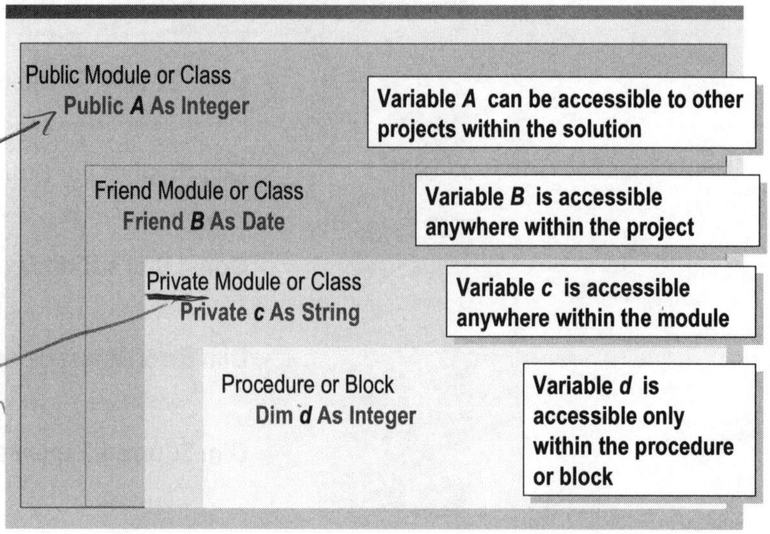

Introduction

When using variables, you need to ensure that they are accessible to all areas of code that refer to them. Alternatively, you might need to restrict access to certain variables. The set of all code that can refer to a variable by its name is referred to as the *scope* of the variable. This lesson describes the different scope levels that apply to variables and explains how to ensure that each variable in your application has the appropriate scope.

Lesson agenda

This lesson includes the following topics and activities:

- What Is Scope?
- How to Declare Local Variables
- How to Declare Static Variables
- How to Declare Module Variables
- Multimedia Demonstration: How to Set Access Levels for Variables
- Practice: Setting Access Levels for Variables

Lesson objectives

After completing this lesson, you will be able to:

- Explain the different scope levels for variables.
- Choose the appropriate access level for a variable, based on how it is used in an application.
- Declare local variables in blocks and procedures.
- Declare static local variables.
- Declare module variables for use in standard modules, classes, projects, solutions, and namespaces.

What Is Scope?

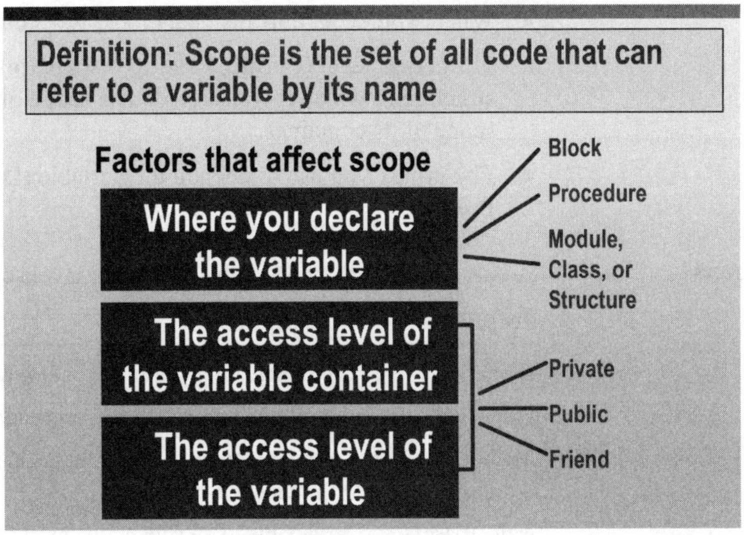

Introduction

When declaring variables, one of the first things you will likely consider is scope. If you use a variable outside its scope, the compiler will generate an error.

Definitions

To learn how scope works with variables, you need to be familiar with the terms and definitions in the following table.

Term	Definition
Variable scope	The set of all code that can refer to a variable by its assigned name without qualifiers.
Block	A code block that starts with a condition such as **If** or **While** and ends with an **End**, **Loop**, or **Next** statement.
Procedure	A code block that starts with a declaration statement such as **Sub** and ends with an **End** statement.
Module	A file that groups common procedures and global data to make them accessible for use throughout one or more projects.
Assembly	A stand-alone executable file into which the various files are compiled when you build a solution.
Access modifier	A keyword such as **Public** or **Friend** that you use to specify the access level of a variable or its container (module, class, or structure).

Factors that affect scope

You assign the scope of a variable when you declare it. There are three primary factors that affect the scope of a variable:

- Where you declare it: Inside a block, procedure, module, class, or structure.
- The access level (**Public**, **Friend**, or **Private**) of the module, class, or structure in which it is declared. The scope of a variable cannot exceed the scope of its container.
- The syntax you use to declare the variable (**Dim**, **Private**, **Friend**, or **Public**).

Scope levels

A variable can have one of the following levels of scope:

Scope level	Description
Block	Available only within the code block in which it is declared
Procedure	Available only within the procedure in which it is declared
Module	Available to all code within the module, class, or structure in which it is declared
Namespace	Available to all code in the namespace

You can further define the scope of a module variable by declaring an access modifier—**Private**, **Public**, or **Friend**—when you declare it. You will learn more about access modifiers in the topic How to Declare Module Variables, in this lesson.

Note To learn more about scope, see the Visual Basic .NET documentation.

How to Declare Local Variables

Where to declare	Keyword	Access modifier	Scope
In block	Dim	None	Block level
In procedure	Dim	None	Procedure level

Example of local variable: block level

```
If x < > 0 Then
     Dim blockNumber As Integer
     blockNumber = x + 1
End If
```

Example of local variable: procedure level

```
Sub ShowMessage_Click( )
     Dim myVariable As String
     ' Insert code to add functionality
End Sub
```

Introduction

When you declare variables in a block or procedure, they are referred to as *local* variables, meaning that their scope is limited to the block or procedure in which they are declared. When considering scope, remember that local variables are a good choice for any kind of temporary calculation. They use memory only when their procedure is running, and their names are not susceptible to naming conflicts.

Syntax

To declare a local variable, use the **Dim** statement with the following syntax:

```
Dim variableName As Type
```

Example of block-level scope

The following example shows how to declare a local variable named *blockNumber* with block-level scope:

```
If x <> 0 Then
     Dim blockNumber As Integer
     blockNumber = 1 / x
End If
```

Note In general, when declaring any variable, it is good programming practice to keep the scope as narrow as possible. (Block scope is the narrowest.) Keeping scope narrow helps conserve memory and minimizes the chances of your code referring to the wrong variable.

Example of procedure-level scope

The following example shows how to declare a local variable *name* with procedure-level scope:

```
Sub ShowMessage_Click( )
     Dim name As String
     name = NameTextBox.Text
     MessageBox.Show("Welcome Back, " & name & "!")
End Sub
```

In this example, the contents of the **Name** text box are placed into the variable *name,* and then the variable is used as part of the prompt in a message box.

How to Declare Static Variables

- **Where: Declare inside a block or procedure**
- **Syntax: Use Static keyword (no access modifier)**
  - Static *variableName* As *Type*
- **Example**

```
Sub AddItem_Click( )
   Static items As Integer
   'Add 1 to the counter
   items += 1
   MessageBox.Show ("The count is now " & items)
End Sub
```

Introduction

The lifetime of a local variable starts when a procedure calls it and ends when the procedure finishes. Once the lifetime of a local variable ends, the instance of the variable is destroyed and its value is lost. There are times when you might want the lifetime of a local variable to extend beyond the lifetime of the procedure. For example, you might want a procedure to perform a specific action the first time it is called and then do nothing in subsequent calls. You can declare a static variable to achieve this functionality.

Definition

A *static variable* survives as long as your application continues running. Static variables remain in existence and retain their latest values between calls to the procedure in which they are declared. However, they cannot be accessed by code in other procedures.

Syntax

To declare a local static variable, use the following syntax:

```
Static variableName As Type
```

Example

Static variables are useful for maintaining counters that are used only within a procedure. The following example shows how to declare a static variable that keeps track of how many times the **AddItem** procedure executes. Each time the procedure runs, the value stored in *items* is incremented by 1.

```
Sub AddItem_Click( )
    Static items As Integer

    ' Add 1 to the counter
    items += 1

    ' Use the ampersand(&) to combine a string and a variable
    Messagebox.Show("The count is now " & items)
End Sub
```

Note You can achieve the same results as in the previous code by declaring *items* as a module variable. However, other procedures would have access to the variable and would also be able to change it. Unless module-level scope is desired, it is recommended that you use a static variable.

How to Declare Module Variables

- **Declare in module, class, or structure**

Use access modifier ...	Scope
Private	Module
Friend	Project
Public	Solution

- **Examples**

```
Private myModuleMessage As String
Friend myProjectMessage As String
Public mySolutionMessage As String
```

Introduction

When you declare variables in a module, class, or structure but not inside any procedure, they are referred to as *module variables*. After you declare a module variable, you can assign a value to it, assign its scope by using an access modifier, and use it within that scope.

Syntax

To declare a module variable, use the following syntax:

```
AccessModifier variableName As Type
```

You can use any of several access modifiers, including the ones described in the following table.

Access modifier	Scope	Description
Private	Module	Accessible from anywhere within the module, class, or structure in which it is declared. If you declare a module variable with the **Dim** keyword, it defaults to **Private** access.
Friend	Project	Accessible from anywhere within the project but not outside the project.
Public	Solution	Accessible from anywhere within the solution. There are no restrictions on the use of **Public** variables.

Note The scope of a module variable is determined not only by the access modifier that you use to declare it but also by the access level of the module, class, or structure in which you declare it. The scope of the variable cannot be greater than the scope of its container. For more information about accessibility and a complete list of access modifiers, see the Visual Basic .NET documentation.

Example of module-level scope

The following example shows how to declare and use a variable with module-level scope:

```
' Put the following declaration at module level
' (not in any procedure)
Private myModuleMessage As String
' ...
Sub InitializeModuleVariable( )
  myModuleMessage = "This variable has module-level scope."
End Sub
' ...
Sub UseModuleVariable( )
  MessageBox.Show(myModuleMessage)
End Sub
```

Example of project-level scope

The following example shows how to declare and use a variable with project-level scope:

```
' Put the following declaration at module level
' (not in any procedure)
Friend MyProjectMessage As String
' ...
Sub InitializeProjectVariable( )
  MyProjectMessage = "This variable has project-level scope."
End Sub
' ...
Sub UseProjectVariable( )
  MessageBox.Show(MyProjectMessage)
End Sub
```

Example of solution-level scope

The following example shows how to declare and use a variable with solution-level scope:

```
' Put the following declaration at module level
' (not in any procedure)
Public MySolutionMessage As String
' ...
Sub InitializeSolutionVariable( )
  MySolutionMessage = _
      "This variable has solution-level scope."
End Sub
' ...
Sub UseSolutionVariable( )
  MessageBox.Show(MySolutionMessage)
End Sub
```

Multimedia: How to Set Access Levels for Variables

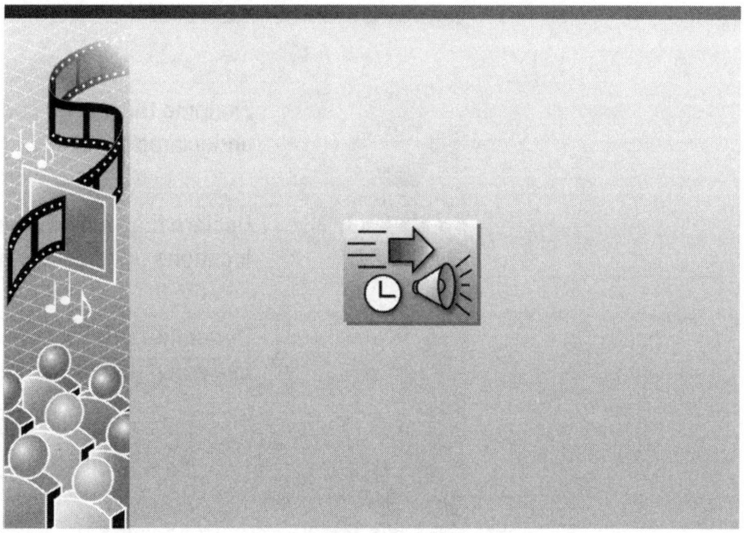

Introduction

This multimedia demonstration shows how to declare a variable with different levels of scope. You will see where to declare variables and how to specify the appropriate access modifiers to assign several different levels of scope.

Practice: Setting Access Levels for Variables

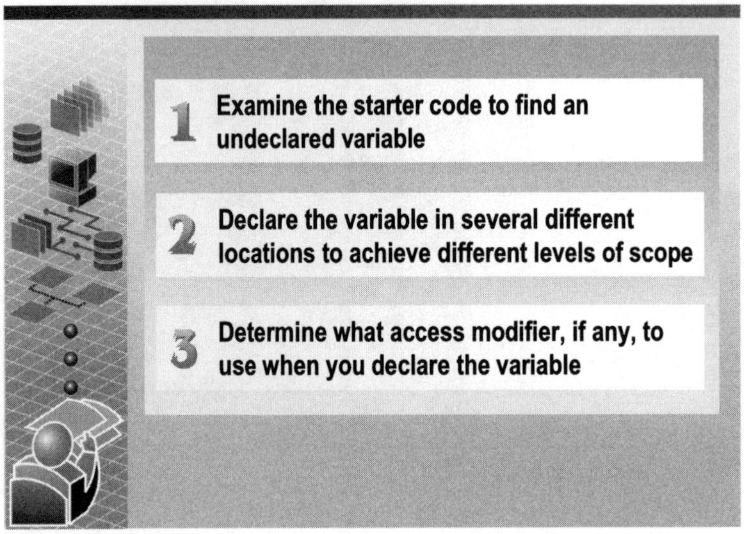

Introduction

In this practice, you will examine the starter code to find a variable that has not been declared. You will determine where to declare the variable and what access modifier to use to assign different levels of scope to the variable.

Instructions

► **Open the starter code for the practice**

1. Start Visual Studio .NET.
2. Open the Scope.sln file, which is in the *install_folder*\Practices\Mod03\Scope\Starter folder.

► **Set access levels for the variable**

1. Open the Code Editor for Form1.vb.
2. Find the undeclared variable *myVariable* in the starter code.
3. Declare *myVariable* as a local variable with procedure-level scope.

> **Tip** The development environment highlights errors in code by using a blue underline. If you see an error, rest the mouse pointer on the code containing the error, and a ToolTip will appear to help you fix the error.

4. Declare *myVariable* as a module variable that is available anywhere in the **Form1** class.
5. Declare *myVariable* as a module variable that is available anywhere in the project.
6. Declare *myVariable* as a module variable that is available anywhere in the solution.

Solution files

The solution files for this practice are located in the *install_folder*\Practices\Mod03\Scope\Solution folder.

Lesson: Converting Data Types

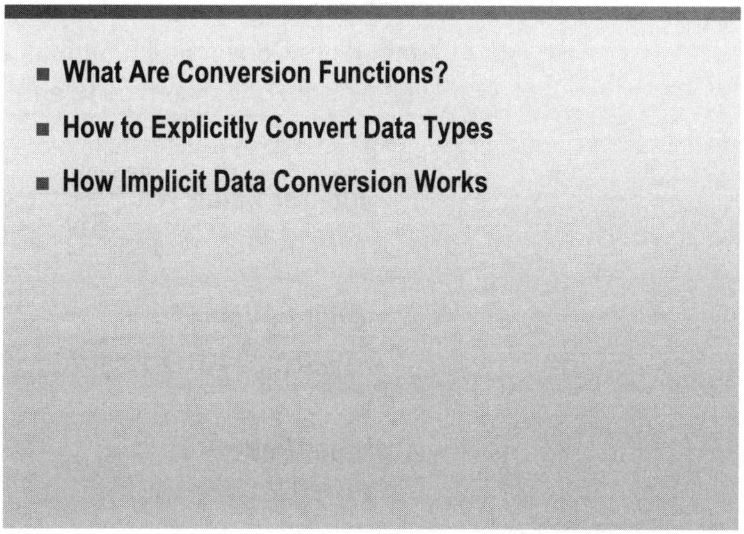

Introduction

The process of converting a value of one data type to another is called *conversion* or *casting*. You can explicitly convert values from one type to another before they are used, thus avoiding bugs in your code and making your code run faster. Visual Basic .NET can also perform some data type conversions automatically or implicitly, such as converting some strings to integers. However, implicit conversions can yield unexpected results.

In this lesson, you will learn about the differences between the explicit and implicit conversion. You will also learn how to use the conversion functions in Visual Basic .NET to explicitly convert data types.

Lesson agenda

This lesson includes the following topics:

- What Are Conversion Functions?
- How to Explicitly Convert Data Types
- How Implicit Data Conversion Works

Lesson objectives

After completing this lesson, you will be able to:

- Describe some common conversion functions.
- Convert variables explicitly from one data type to another.
- Explain how implicit data conversion works and when not to use it.

What Are Conversion Functions?

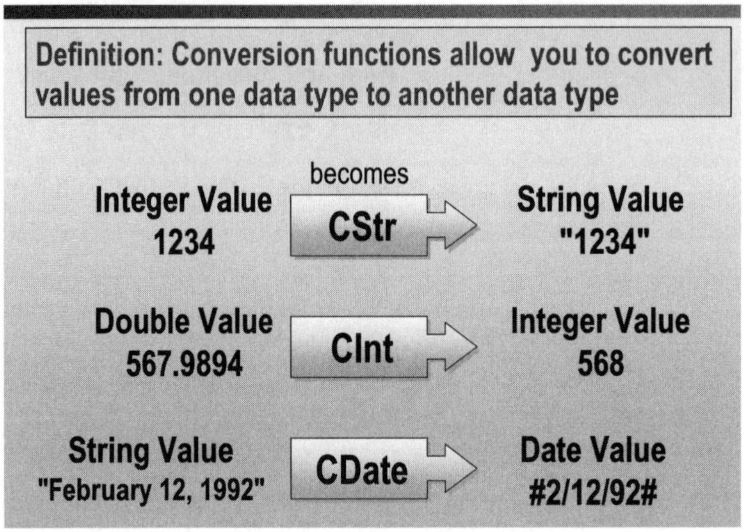

Introduction

You can use conversion functions to force the result of an operation to a particular data type rather than the default data type. For example, you could convert a string value to an integer value.

Definition

Conversion functions allow you to explicitly convert a value from one data type to another.

Examples of conversion functions

Visual Basic offers an extensive list of conversion functions, including the ones described in the following table.

Conversion function	Converts to data type	Allowable data types for conversion
CStr	**String**	Any numeric type, **Boolean**, **Char**, **Date**, **Object**
CInt	**Integer**	Any numeric type, **Boolean**, **String**, **Object**
CDbl	**Double**	Any numeric type, **Boolean**, **String**, **Object**
CDate	**Date**	**String**, **Object**
CType	Type specified	Same type as allowed for the corresponding conversion function

The following code shows how to use several conversion functions:

```
Private Sub Button1_Click(...)
  ' Use string conversion on Integer

  Dim myVariable As Integer
  myVariable = 1234
  MessageBox.Show(myVariable)
  MessageBox.Show(CStr(myVariable) & "1")

End Sub

Private Sub Button2_Click(...)
  ' Use integer conversion on Double

  Dim myVariable As Double
  myVariable = 567.9894
  MessageBox.Show(myVariable)
  MessageBox.Show(CInt(myVariable))

End Sub

Private Sub Button3_Click(...)
  ' Use date conversion on String

  Dim myVariable As String
  myVariable = "February 12, 1992"
  MessageBox.Show(myVariable)
  MessageBox.Show(CDate(myVariable))

End Sub
```

How to Explicitly Convert Data Types

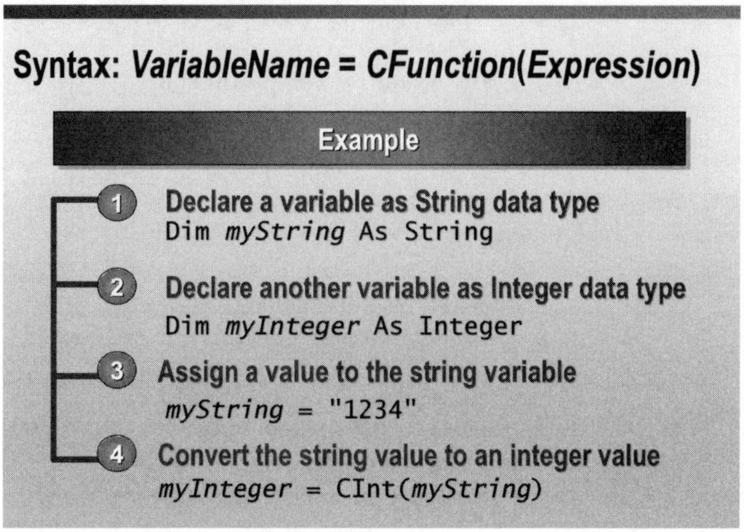

Introduction

It is recommended that you use conversion functions to explicitly convert values before they are used. Explicit conversions run faster than implicit conversions because there is no call to a procedure to accomplish the conversion. An *implicit conversion* is an automatic conversion of a value from one data type to another.

Syntax

To use a conversion function, you place it on the right side of an assignment statement, using the following syntax:

```
VariableName = CFunction(Expression)
```

The *expression* parameter can be any valid expression, such as a variable, a result of a function, or a constant value.

Widening vs. narrowing conversions

A *widening conversion* changes a value to a data type that can accommodate any possible value of the original data, such as converting an **Integer** to a **Long**. A *narrowing conversion* changes a value to a data type that might not be able to hold some of the possible values, such as changing a **String** to an **Integer**, or a **Long** to an **Integer**.

Example

The following example shows how to use the **CStr** and **CDbl** conversion functions to write code that converts feet and inches to meters.

```
Private Sub Calculate_Click(...)
    Dim feet As Double, inches As Double
    Dim millimeters As Double, meters As Double

    'First, extract feet and inches from the text boxes.
    'The Text property returns a string, but we need a double,
    'so CDbl( ) is used to perform the conversion.
    feet = CDbl(FeetTextBox.Text)
    inches = CDbl(InchesTextBox.Text)

    'Next, convert feet and inches to millimeters.
    millimeters = (inches * MillimetersPerInch) + _
        (feet * MillimetersPerInch * InchesPerFoot)

    'Convert millimeters to meters.
    meters = millimeters / 1000

    'Display the result in a label. Because the Text property
    'is a string, use CStr( ) to convert the double.
    MeterResult.Text = CStr(meters)
End Sub
```

In this example, you can assume that the constant values MillimetersPerInch and InchesPerFoot were declared and assigned appropriate values at the module level.

Example of CInt

The following example shows how to use the **CInt** function to convert a **Double** value to an **Integer**:

```
Dim myDouble As Double
Dim myInt As Integer
myDouble = 2345.5678
' Set myInt to 2346
myInt = CInt(myDouble)
```

Example of CDate

The following example shows how to use the **CDate** function to convert strings to **Date** values. In general, hard-coding dates and times as strings (as shown in this example) is not recommended. Use date literals and time literals, such as #Feb 12, 1969# and #4:45:23 PM#, instead.

```
Dim myDateString, myTimeString As String
Dim myDate, myTime As Date
myDateString = "February 12, 1969"
myTimeString = "4:35:47 PM"
' ...
' Convert to Date data type
myDate = CDate(myDateString)
myTime = CDate(myTimeString)
```

How Implicit Data Conversion Works

- **Data types are automatically converted**
- **No special syntax is required in code**
- **Example of implicit data conversion:**

```
Dim sequence As String
Dim number As Integer
' ...
sequence = "1234"
number = sequence
' The value in sequence is implicitly converted
  to an Integer
```

- **Disadvantages of implicit data conversion:**
  - Can yield unexpected results
  - Code runs slower
- **Option Strict disallows any implicit narrowing type conversions**

Introduction

Visual Basic can perform some data type conversions implicitly. An *implicit conversion* is when a value is converted automatically from one data type to another as required by the code in which the data type is used. It does not require any special syntax in the source code.

Examples

If you place the string "1234" in an **Integer** variable, Visual Basic will automatically convert the string to an integer. Or, if a string such as "100" is added to a numeric value in the formula "100" + 10, Visual Basic implicitly converts the string to the integer value 100 and adds it to 10.

Disadvantages

There are disadvantages to relying on Visual Basic to perform implicit conversions. Implicit conversions can yield unexpected results. For example, when two strings are added together, Visual Basic concatenates the strings regardless of their contents; so "100" + "10" = "10010." If a narrowing conversion is required, data can be truncated. Moreover, when Visual Basic must perform implicit conversions, the code runs slower because of the extra work that Visual Basic must perform.

How Option Strict affects data conversions

With **Option Strict** set to **Off** (the default), all widening and narrowing conversions can be done implicitly. With **Option Strict** set to **On**, only widening conversions are permitted implicitly, and narrowing conversions must be explicit or the compiler will generate an error.

Note For more information about the **Option Strict** compiler switch, see the Visual Basic .NET documentation.

Lab 3.1: Creating and Using Variables

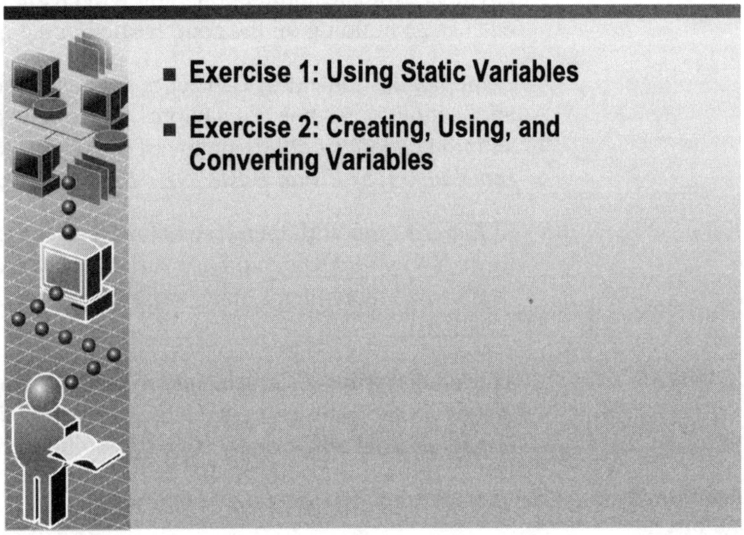

Objectives

After completing this lab, you will be able to:

- Declare and use variables.
- Use data conversion functions.

Prerequisites

Before working on this lab, you must:

- Be familiar with the Visual Studio .NET development environment.
- Have experience with creating, opening, and modifying forms and controls.
- Have experience with writing code for form events.

Note This lab focuses on the concepts in this module and as a result may not comply with Microsoft security recommendations.

Scenario

In the labs for Modules 2, 4, 5, 6, and 12 of Course 2559B, *Introduction to Visual Basic .NET Programming with Microsoft .NET,* you will create a loan payment estimate application. You will create the full application in stages, each stage building on the code created in the previous lab.

Although the context of Lab 3.1 is similar to the loan payment estimate application, this lab is not a part of that application. You will not use the solution code for Lab 3.1 in any of the related labs in Course 2559B, *Introduction to Visual Basic .NET Programming with Microsoft .NET.*

In Lab 3.1, you will open an existing Visual Studio solution that provides a form. You will declare and use variables needed for a loan application. You will declare and increment a static variable. You will also use data type conversion functions.

Solution files

The solution files for this lab are in the *install_folder*\Labfiles\Lab031\Ex01\Solution and *install_folder*\Labfiles\Lab031\Ex02\Solution folders.

Estimated time to complete this lab: 45 minutes

Exercise 1
Using Static Variables

In this exercise, you will declare a static variable to count the number of times users click a **Confirm Choices** button on a form, increment the variable each time users click the button, and display the variable's value in a message box.

► Open the loan variables project

1. Start Visual Studio .NET.
2. Open the LoanVariables.sln project, which is in the *install_folder*\Labfiles\Lab031\Ex01\Starter folder.
3. Open the Main form in both Design view and the Code Editor to familiarize yourself with the existing controls and code.

Important The completed lab for this module will not be used as a starter file for other modules in Course 2559B, *Introduction to Visual Basic .NET Programming with Microsoft .NET*. However, the variables you create will be the same as those in the starter code for Lab 4.1, Creating and Using Procedures, in Course 2559B, *Introduction to Visual Basic .NET Programming with Microsoft .NET*.

► Add a static variable to count the number of times the user clicks Confirm Choices

1. Open the Code Editor for the Main.vb form.
2. In the **ConfirmButton_Click** event handler, add a static **Integer** variable named *viewChoices*.
3. Increment the value of the *viewChoices* variable by 1 each time the user clicks **Confirm Choices**. This variable will allow you to count the number of times the user clicks **Confirm Choices**.
4. Display the number of clicks on **Confirm Choices** to the user by using the **MessageBox** function, as follows:

```
MessageBox.Show("Number of times loan choices viewed: " _
   & viewChoices)
```

5. Your completed code should look as follows:

```
Private Sub ConfirmButton_Click(...)
   Static viewChoices As Integer
   viewChoices += 1

MessageBox.Show("Number of times loan choices viewed: " _
   & viewChoices)
End Sub
```

▶ Run and test the application

1. To run the application, click the **Start** ▶ button.
2. Click **Confirm Choices** several times.

   What happens? The message box should accurately display the number of times you have clicked **Confirm Choices**.
3. Quit the application.

Exercise 2
Creating, Using, and Converting Variables

In this exercise, you will add variables and constants to the Main form to accept and process the data that the user types into the text box and the combo box. You will modify the **ConfirmButton_Click** event handler to allow data to be converted to the correct data type and to display it.

► Add variables to handle user input and calculate interest

1. Open the Code Editor for the Main.vb file.

   If you did not complete Exercise 1, use the LoanVariables.sln file in the *install_folder*\Labfiles\Lab031\Ex02\Starter folder.

2. Add form-level variables to store the loan amount, annual interest rate, monthly interest rate, and total payments, as shown in the following table.

Variable name	Data type
loanAmount	**Double**
interestRate	**Double**
monthRate	**Double**
numberOfPayments	**Integer**

   Your code should look as follows:

```
Dim loanAmount As Double
Dim interestRate As Double
Dim monthRate As Double
Dim numberOfPayments As Integer
```

► Add constant variables for payment period and payment term

- Add two form-level constants to store the number of months in a year and a loan term of 5 years. Your code should look as follows:

```
Private Const conversionPeriod As Integer = 12
Private Const loanLength As Integer = 5
```

Important You are hard coding the value of the *loanLength* variable to 5 years for the purposes of this lab only. When you continue to develop the loan application in other labs, you will assign the value of *loanLength* according to the user's choice in a group box.

► Assign values to the variables and display the values for confirmation

1. In the **ConfirmButton_Click** event handler, write code to assign the values that the user enters in the text boxes to the *loanAmount* and *interestRate* variables, as shown in the following table.

Variable name	Corresponding text box
loanAmount	LoanTextBox
interestRate	RateComboBox

In the assignment statements, use the **CDbl** conversion function to convert the text box data to the **Double** data type for use in calculation. Your code should look as follows:

```
loanAmount = CDbl(LoanTextBox.Text)
interestRate = CDbl(RateComboBox.Text)
```

2. Divide the annual interest rate by the conversion period to calculate a monthly interest rate, and assign the result of the calculation to the *monthRate* variable, as follows:

```
monthRate = interestRate / conversionPeriod
```

3. Calculate the total number of payments by multiplying the loan term by the conversion period, and assign the result to the *numberOfPayments* variable, as follows:

```
numberOfPayments = loanLength * conversionPeriod
```

► Create message boxes to allow the user to confirm the data entered

- In the **ConfirmButton_Click** event handler, just before the existing message box, add message boxes to create confirmation messages for the loan amount, annual interest rate, monthly interest rate, and total number of payments. Your code should look as follows:

```
MessageBox.Show("Loan amount: " & loanAmount)
MessageBox.Show("Annual interest rate: " & interestRate)
MessageBox.Show("Monthly interest rate: " & monthRate)
MessageBox.Show("Total number of payments: " & _
   numberOfPayments)
```

► Run and test your application

1. To run the application, on the standard toolbar, click the **Start** ▶ button.
2. Type or select appropriate information in the Main form, click **Confirm Choices**, and then click **OK** in the message boxes that appear. You can leave 5 years selected in the **Loan Term** box because the term is hard coded for this lab.
3. Is the information displayed correctly?

   For example, if you use 200,000 as the loan amount and 4.5 as the interest rate, the monthly interest rate should be 0.375 and the total number of payments should be 60.
4. When finished testing, quit the solution, and then quit Visual Studio.

Lesson: Creating and Using Structures

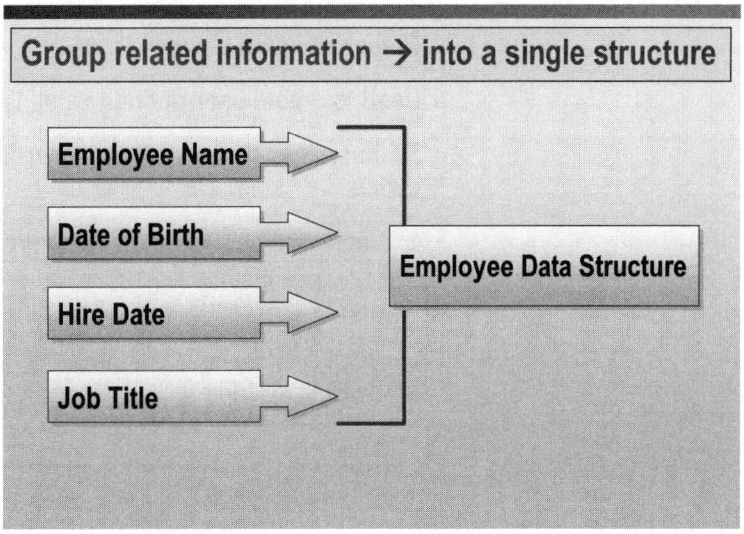

Introduction

In Visual Basic .NET, you can combine variables of several different data types to create a user-defined type known as a structure. Structures are useful when you want to create a single variable that groups together several related pieces of information. This lesson explains how to create and use structures.

Lesson agenda

This lesson includes the following topics and activities:

- What Are Structures?
- How to Declare Structures
- How to Use Structures
- Practice: Creating and Using Structures

Lesson objectives

After completing this lesson, you will be able to:

- Describe a structure and its elements.
- Declare and use structures.

What Are Structures?

- **Composite data types**
- **Used to create user-defined value types**
- **Members can be variables, properties, methods, or events**
- **Example of a user-defined structure:**

```
Public Structure Employee
   Public FirstName As String
   Public LastName As String
   Public HireDate As Date
   Public JobTitle As String
   Private Salary As Decimal
End Structure
```

- **Examples of predefined structures: *Point, Size, Color***

Introduction

You can combine data items of different types to create a single composite data type called a structure. Structures are useful when you want a single variable to hold several related pieces of information. After you declare a structure, you can declare variables of that type.

Definition

A *structure* is a composite data type that is created by combining other data types. Structures are value types—that is, a variable of a structure type contains the structure's data, rather than containing a reference to the data as a reference type does. Structures can have data, properties, methods, and procedures, and can raise and handle events.

Example

The simplest and most common use of structures is to encapsulate related variables, creating a user-defined data type. For example, you might want to keep an employee's name, hire date, job title, and salary together. You could use several variables for this information, or you could define a structure and use it for a single employee variable. The advantage of the structure becomes apparent when you have many employees and therefore many instances of the variable.

The following example shows a simple *Employee* structure:

```
Public Structure Employee
   Public FirstName As String
   Public LastName As String
   Public HireDate As Date
   Public JobTitle As String
   Private Salary As Decimal
End Structure
```

Note The preceding example uses the *Employee* structure to handle a simple list of attributes. The *Employee* structure could also have members such as a **Hire** method and a **Promoted** event. However, if your application design would benefit from using *Employee* as a template for another programming element, such as a *Manager* or a *StaffMember*, creating *Employee* as a class would be a better choice. Classes can be used as templates, and are more extensible than structures.

For more information about classes, see Module 7, "Object-Oriented Programming in Visual Basic .NET," in Course 2559B, *Introduction to Visual Basic .NET Programming with Microsoft .NET.*

Visual Basic .NET–provided structures

Visual Basic .NET also provides many predefined structures for you to use. For example, the following list describes several existing structures that support graphics in the .NET platform. These structures are part of the **System.Drawing** namespace.

- The *Point* structure represents an ordered pair of integer x and y coordinates that defines a point in a two-dimensional plane. You might use the *Point* structure to capture the location of the mouse when the user clicks in your application.
- The *Size* structure represents the size of a rectangular region by using an ordered pair of width and height. You use the *Size* structure when you modify the **Size** property of a form.
- The *Color* structure represents an ARGB (alpha, red, green, blue) color. You use the *Color* structure when you modify the color of a form or control.

How to Declare Structures

- **Inside a module, file, or class (not in a procedure)**
- **Syntax to declare structures:**

```
AccessModifier Structure StructureName
    ' Declare structure members here
End Structure
```

- **Where access modifier is:**
  - **Public** for unrestricted access
  - **Protected** for access only within its own class
  - **Friend** for access anywhere in the application or assembly
  - **Private** for access only within its declaration context
- **Do not assign values to data members in the declaration**

Introduction

The first step in creating a structure is to declare it. You can declare structures in a source file or inside a module or class, but not inside a procedure.

Syntax

You begin a structure declaration with the **Structure** statement, and you end it with the **End Structure** statement. Between these two statements, you must declare at least one member. The members can be of any data type. Use the following syntax to declare a structure:

```
AccessModifier Structure StructureName
  ' Declare structure members here
End Structure
```

Structure members

You must declare every data member of a structure and specify an access level for it. This means that every statement in the variable declaration section of the structure must use **Dim**, **Friend**, **Private**, or **Public**. If **Option Explicit** is **On**, it is a good idea to include the **As** clause in every statement. Members declared with **Dim** default to **Public** access, and members declared without the **As** clause default to the **Object** data type.

You cannot initialize any of the data members in the structure declaration. When you declare a variable to be of a structure type, you assign values to the members by accessing them through the variable.

Access levels

Structures can be accessed from anywhere within the file, module, or class in which they are declared. A structure in a file is **Friend** by default. You can specify the access level of a structure by using the **Public**, **Protected**, **Friend**, or **Private** access modifier as described in the following table.

Access modifier	Access level
Public	Accessible from anywhere in the solution or from anywhere that references the project
Protected	Accessible only from within its own class
Friend	Accessible from within the application in which it is declared or from anywhere else in the assembly
Private	Accessible only from within the module, file, or other programming element in which it is declared, including from members of any nested types, such as procedures

Example

The following example shows how to declare an *Employee* structure to define a set of related data for an employee. It shows how to use the **Public**, **Friend**, and **Private** access modifiers to reflect the sensitivity of the data items.

```
Public Structure Employee
   ' Public members, accessible throughout declaration region
   Public FirstName As String
   Public MiddleName As String
   Public LastName As String
   ' Friend members, accessible anywhere in the same assembly
   Friend EmployeeNumber As Integer
   Friend BusinessPhone As Long
   ' Private members, accessible only in the structure itself
   Private HomePhone As Long
   Private Salary As Double
   Private Bonus As Double
End Structure
```

How to Use Structures

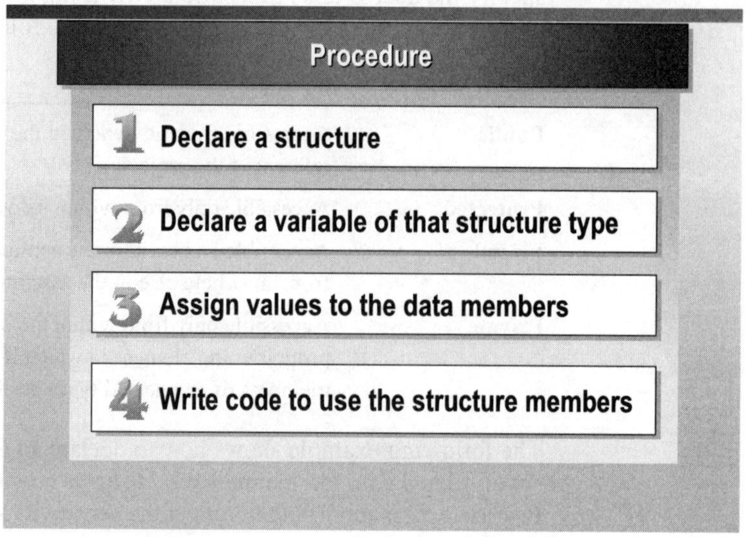

Introduction

Once you have created a structure, you can declare procedure-level and module-level variables as that structure type. You can then assign values to the data members of the variable structure and write code to use the structure members.

Procedure

Generally, the steps for using structures are as follows:

1. Declare a structure.

   For example, you can create a structure that records information about a computer system, as follows:

```
Private Structure computerInfo
   Public processor As String
   Public memory As Long
   Public purchaseDate As Date
End Structure
```

2. Declare a variable of the declared structure type.

   Now that you have declared a structure, you can create a variable of that structure type, as follows:

```
Dim mySystem As computerInfo
```

3. Assign values to the data members.

   To assign and retrieve values from the elements of a structure variable, you use the variable name you created along with the item in the structure block. Separate the name from the item with a period. For example, you can access and initialize the variables declared in the *computerInfo* structure as follows:

```
mySystem.processor = "x86"
mySystem.purchaseDate = #1/1/2003#
mySystem.memory = TextBox1.Text
```

4. Write code to use the structure members.

   After you assign values to the data members, you can write code to use them from anywhere in your code that is within their scope. In this example, the data members are only accessible from within the file where the structure is declared. For example, you can check to see if the computer has adequate memory to install a given application:

```
If mySystem.memory < 64000 Then NotEnoughMemory = True
```

Note A structure can contain any of the data types defined in Visual Basic .NET, including arrays, objects, and other structures. For more information about creating structures, see "Structures and Other Programming Elements" in the Visual Basic .NET documentation.

Practice: Creating and Using Structures

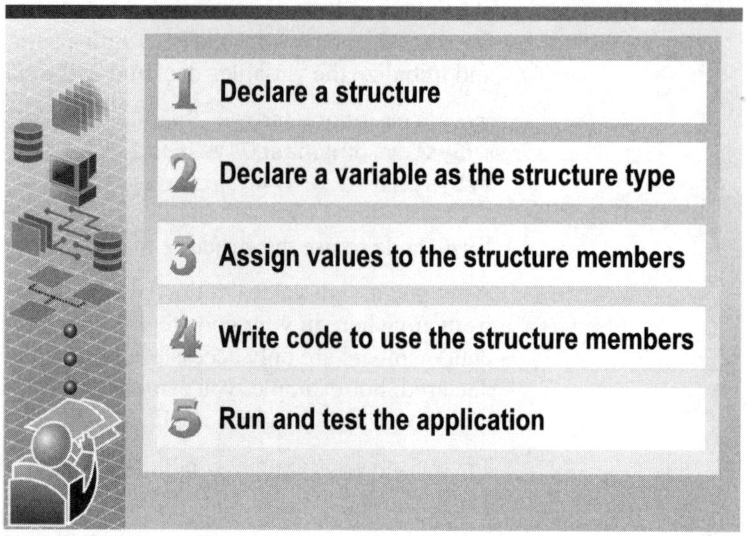

Introduction

In this practice, you will create a structure, use the structure, and test the application in which the structure is used to ensure that it works.

Scenario

Consider a scenario in which an application needs to manipulate data about a fleet of cars in order to manage lease information and maintain repair records. You might want to encapsulate the details for each car in a structure that can be used by developers creating the different parts of the application. The details involved will be limited to vehicle make, model, purchase price, and date of purchase.

Instructions

► **Open the starter code for the practice**

1. Start Visual Studio .NET.
2. Open the Structures.sln file, which is in the *install_folder*\Practices\Mod03\Structure\Starter folder.

► **Create a structure to store information about cars**

- Declare a public structure called *CarInfo* in the declarations section of Form1. Include the members shown in the following table.

Member name	Access modifier	Data type
Make	**Dim**	**String**
Model	**Dim**	**String**
PurchasePrice	**Dim**	**Single**
PurchaseDate	**Dim**	**Date**

▶ **Declare a variable of type *CarInfo* and assign values to it**

1. In the **Button1_Click** event, declare a variable called *myCar* of structure type *CarInfo*. Your code should look as follows:

```
Dim myCar As CarInfo
```

2. Assign values to the structure members. You can use the following values or choose your own values.

```
myCar.Make = "Jeep"
myCar.Model = "Cherokee"
myCar.PurchasePrice = 27999
myCar.PurchaseDate = #06/23/2000#
```

▶ **Display the car information in text boxes**

- Set the **TextBox** properties to display the *CarInfo* structure in text boxes on the form. Your code should look as follows:

```
TextBox1.Text = myCar.Make
TextBox2.Text = myCar.Model
TextBox3.Text = myCar.PurchasePrice
TextBox4.Text = myCar.PurchaseDate
```

▶ **Run and test the application**

- Run the application and click **Display Car Structure**. The running form should look as follows:

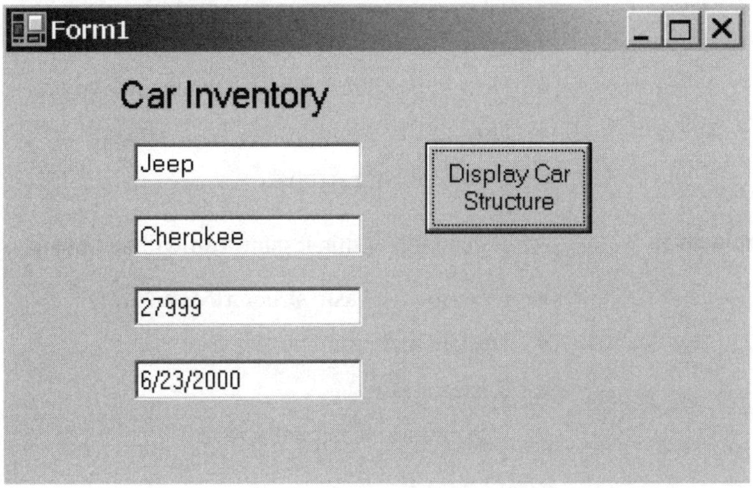

Solution files

The solution files for this practice are located in the *install_folder*\Practices\Mod03\Structure\Solution folder.

Lesson: Storing Data in Arrays

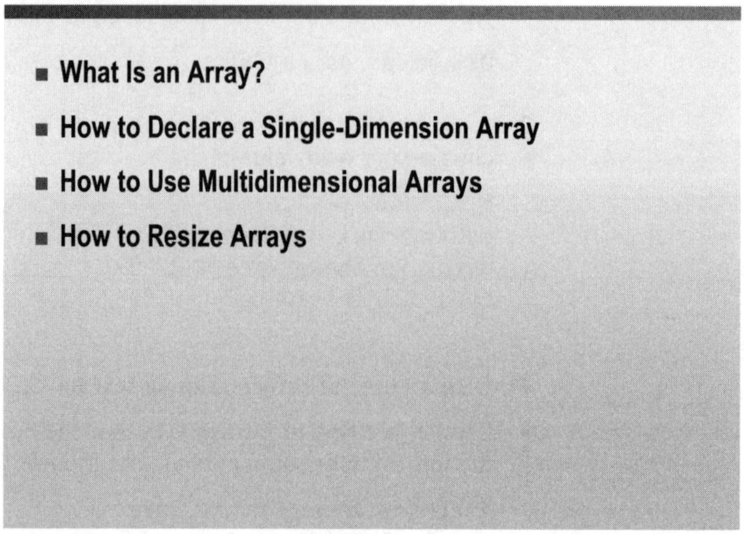

Introduction

By using arrays, you can store a group of elements that have the same data type under one variable name. You use a number (or *index*) to refer to a specific element in the series. By using arrays, you can easily access, use, and store values of the same type. This lesson explains how to declare and use arrays.

Lesson agenda

This lesson includes the following topics:

- What Is an Array?
- How to Declare a Single-Dimension Array
- How to Use Multidimensional Arrays
- How to Resize Arrays

Lesson objectives

After completing this lesson, you will be able to:

- Describe the basic structure of an array.
- Declare and initialize arrays.
- Resize arrays.
- Use multidimensional arrays.

What Is an Array?

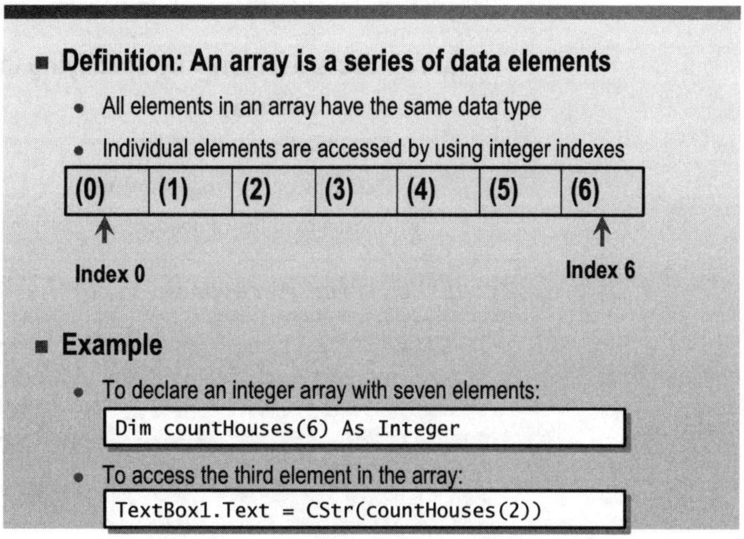

Introduction

An array is a fundamental data type in Visual Basic, as it is in most programming languages. You can use arrays to create shorter and simpler code in many situations because you can set up decision structures and loops to retrieve and modify any element in an array.

Definitions

An *array* is a sequence of data elements of the same type. You can access individual elements in an array by using the array name and an index or indexes (starting at 0) to specify the element's position in the array. An array has one or more dimensions with one or more elements in each dimension.

Analogy

Consider a neighborhood with one street and seven houses as an analogy for a single-dimension array. Think of the neighborhood as the array, the street as the dimension of the array, and the houses as the individual elements in the array. The data type of the array elements might be **Integer**.

Example

To declare the array described in the preceding analogy, you can use the following code:

```
Dim countHouses(6) As Integer
```

You can access the third house in the *countHouses* array as follows:

```
TextBox1.Text = CStr(countHouses(2))
```

How to Declare a Single-Dimension Array

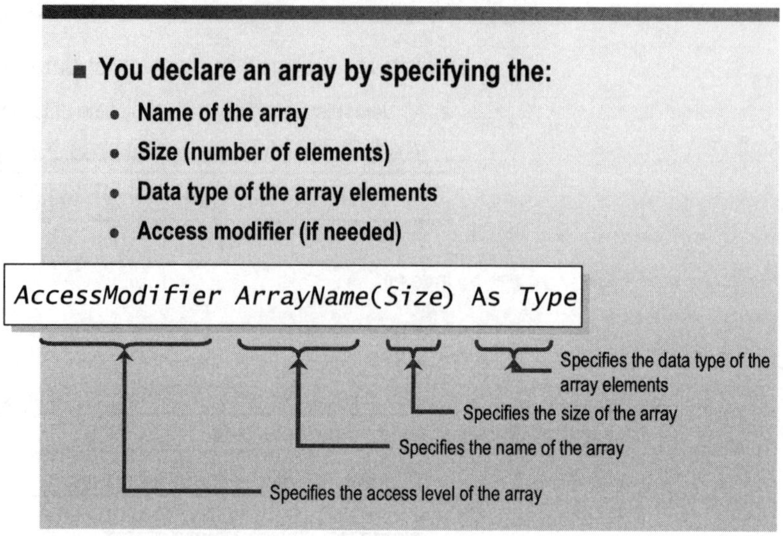

Introduction

You declare a single-dimension array by specifying its name, its size, the data type of the elements, and its access level.

Syntax

You create or declare arrays in code just as you declare other variables. You follow the same guidelines for naming, scope, and choosing data types. To declare arrays, use the following syntax:

```
AccessModifier ArrayName(Size) As Type
```

The **Size** argument specifies the initial number of elements in the array. Sometimes you do not need to specify an access modifier because the scope of the array is determined by where it is located in code. In that case, declare the array with the **Dim** keyword.

Examples of local arrays

You can declare local arrays by using the **Dim** statement and placing the declaration inside a procedure, as shown in the following example:

```
Sub InitializeArray( )
  ' Allocate 31 elements (0) to (30)
  Dim currentExpense(30) As Decimal
  Dim number As Integer
  For number = 0 to 30
      currentExpense(number) = 100
  Next number
End Sub
```

This example stores daily expenses for each day of the month in one 31-element array named *currentExpense*. Each element in the array contains one value, and you access the values by specifying the element's index. Each element of the array is assigned a value of 100.

Examples of public arrays

To create a public array, you use the **Public** keyword in place of **Dim**, as shown in the following example:

```
Public Counters(14) As Integer
Public Sums(20) As Double
```

The first declaration creates a single-dimensional array with 15 elements, with index numbers from 0 through 14. The second declaration creates an array with 21 elements, with index numbers from 0 through 20.

You can assign values to the elements of the array after you declare it, or you can initialize it when you declare it, by enclosing the values within braces, as shown in the following example:

```
Public Counters( ) As Integer = {1, 2, 3, 4, 5, 6, 7}
```

How to Use Multidimensional Arrays

- **Specify all dimensions and elements**
- **Total elements = product of all the sizes**
- **To declare a multidimensional array variable:**
  - Add one pair of parentheses after the variable name
  - Place commas inside the parentheses to separate the dimensions
  - Begin declaration with **Dim** statement or an access modifier
- **Example:**

```
Public ThreeDimensions(3,9,14) As Double
  ' Three-dimensional array
```

Introduction

An array can have more than one dimension. The *dimensionality*, or *rank*, corresponds to the number of subscripts used to identify an individual element in the array. You can specify up to 32 dimensions for an array; however, you will rarely need more than three dimensions.

Declaring variables in a multidimensional array

To declare a multidimensional array variable, add one pair of parentheses after the variable name and place commas inside the parentheses to separate the dimensions, as in the following example:

```
' Four-dimensional array
Dim My4DArray(2, 6, 4, 1) As Integer
```

For the keyword, use **Dim** for a local array, or specify an access modifier such as **Public** or **Friend** to provide a different level of scope.

Example of a two-dimensional array

You can think of a two-dimensional array as a grid. The following example shows how to declare a two-dimensional array with 4 rows and 3 columns.

```
Dim storageNumber(3, 2) As Double
```

To assign a value to a specific element in the array, refer to the index numbers of the element. For example, the following code shows how to assign a value to a specific element in the array declared in the previous code.

```
storageNumber(2, 1) = 24
```

The following illustration is a representation of the two-dimensional array created in this example:

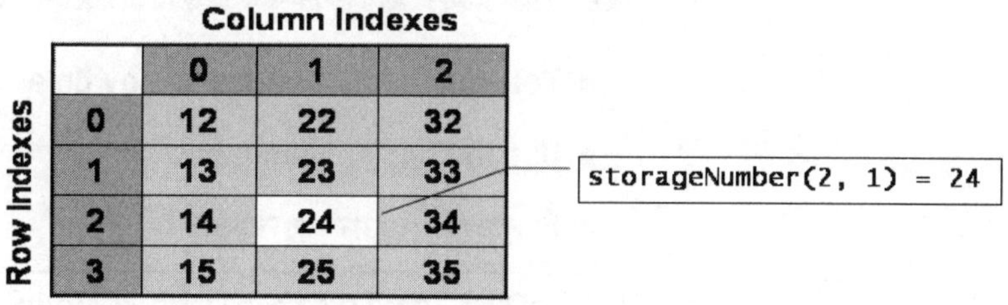

Example of a three-dimensional array

The following example shows how to create and access a public array that has three dimensions:

```
Public ThreeDimensions(3, 9, 14) As String
```

This declaration creates an array that has three dimensions with sizes of 4, 10, and 15. The total number of elements is the product of these three dimensions, or 600. You can think of a three-dimensional array as a cube.

The following code shows how to assign the value stored in a specific element of the preceding array to the **Text** property of a text box.

```
TextBox1.Text = ThreeDimensions(2,6,4)
```

Note When you add dimensions to an array, the total storage needed by the array increases dramatically. Therefore, you should avoid declaring an array that is larger than you need.

How to Resize Arrays

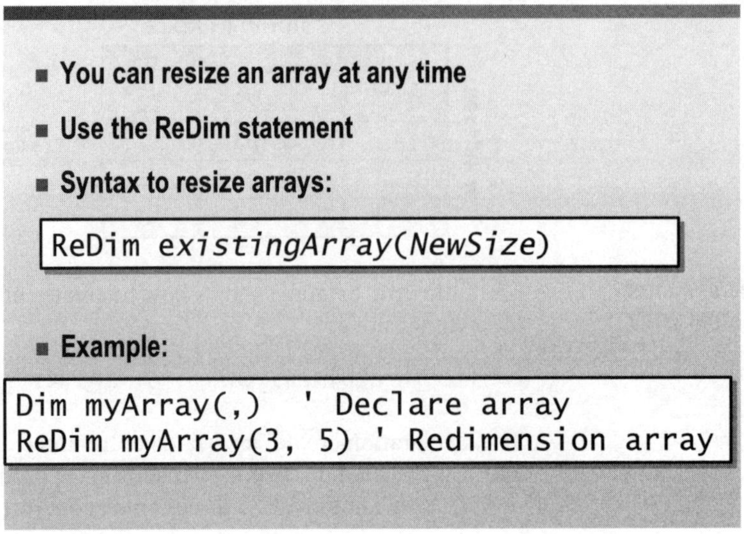

Introduction

In Visual Basic .NET, you can resize an array at any time by specifying new dimensions for it. You can even change the number of dimensions in the array. Resizing arrays helps you manage memory efficiently. For example, you can use a large array for a short time and then resize it to a smaller size. This frees up memory you no longer need.

Syntax

Use the following syntax to resize an existing single-dimensional array:

```
ReDim existingArray(NewSize)
```

If you are unsure of what size of array you need, you can declare the array without specifying the size of the dimensions, as shown in the preceding illustration.

Examples

The following example shows how to use the **ReDim** statement to allocate and reallocate storage space for array variables.

```
Dim number, myArray( ) As Integer
' Declare variable and array variable
' Allocate 6 elements
ReDim myArray(5)
For number = 0 to 5
' Initialize array
   myArray(number) = number
Next number
```

The following statement resizes the array without saving the contents of the elements.

```
' Resize to 11 elements
ReDim myArray(10)
For number = 0 To 10
' Initialize array
   myArray(number) = number
Next number
```

Preserving the original array values

When you **ReDim** an array, its existing values are normally lost. However, you can retain them by including the **Preserve** keyword in the **ReDim** statement. For example, the following statement allocates a new array, initializes its elements from the corresponding elements of the existing **myArray**, and assigns the new array to **myArray**.

```
ReDim Preserve myArray(10)
```

Review

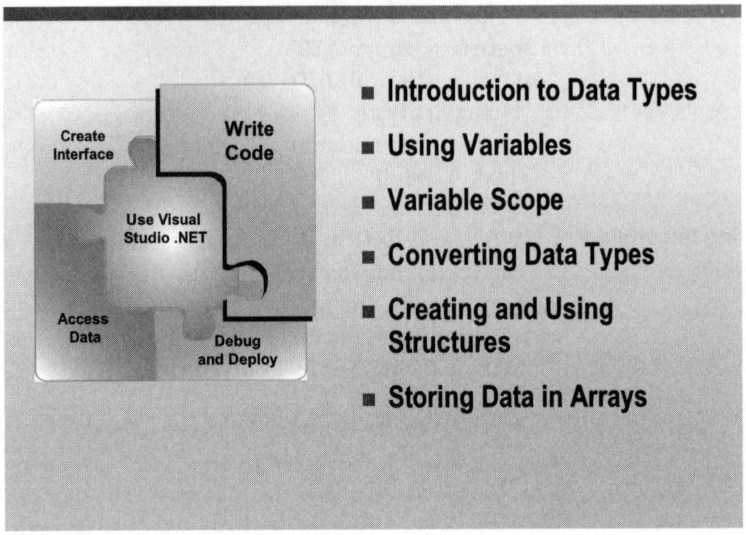

1. Which Visual Basic .NET data type do you use to store **True** or **False** values?

2. Declare a local variable called *myDayOff,* and assign to it a value of 12/25/2001. Write this code in two different ways.

Dim mydayoff as date = #12/25/2001#

Available through solution project

3. Review the following code.

```
Public Class BankAccount
. . .
    Public MyVariable As Integer
. . .
End Class
```

   a. What is the scope level of *MyVariable*?

   b. How can you rewrite the code so that *MyVariable* can only be accessed from within the project in which it is declared?

4. True or false: the value of a local variable is preserved between multiple procedure calls unless you explicitly destroy the instance of the variable.

   only for procedure

5. What is the value and data type of *myInteger* after the following code runs?

```
Dim myInteger As Integer
Dim myDouble As Double
myInteger = 5555
myDouble = CDbl(myInteger)
```

Return same value

Remains same

6. First, create a public structure named *CustomerInfo* with the following data members:

   - A *FirstName* variable that is accessible anywhere in the solution
   - A *LastName* variable that is accessible anywhere in the solution
   - An *AccountNumber* variable that is accessible anywhere in the project
   - A *HomePhone* variable that is accessible anywhere in the structure

   Second, declare a *FirstCustomer* variable of type *CustomerInfo*.

7. Write the code to assign a value of 100 to the fourth element in the second column of the following array. What is the total number of elements in the array?

```
Dim testArray(8,8) As Integer
```

TestArray (3,1) = 100

Total = 9x9

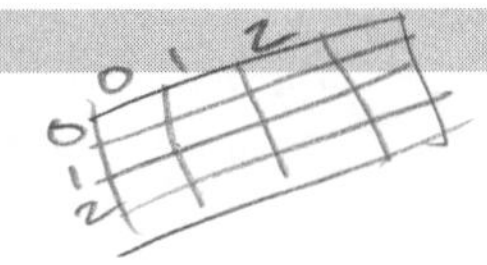

Public (scope) Structure custInfo

Public firstName as String

end structure

Lab 3.2: Using Structures and Arrays

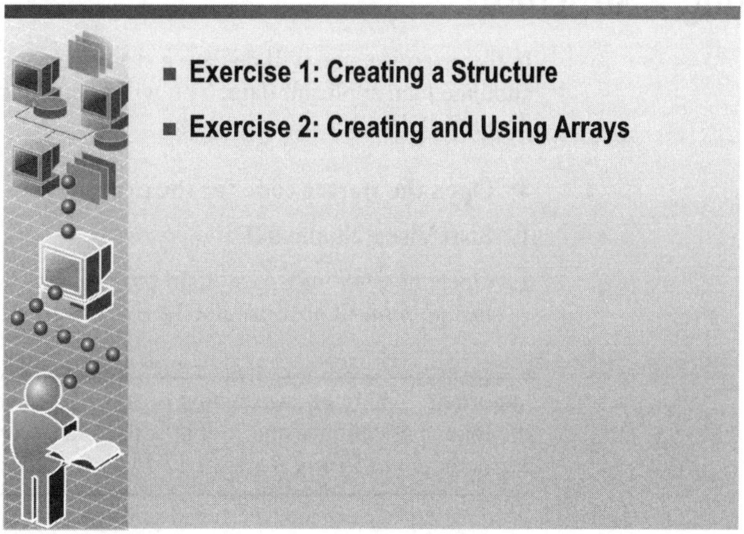

Objectives

After completing this lab, you will be able to:

- Declare and use a structure.
- Declare and use an array.

Note This lab focuses on the concepts in this module and as a result may not comply with Microsoft security recommendations.

Prerequisites

Before working on this lab, you must:

- Be familiar with the Visual Studio .NET development environment.
- Be able to declare variables.
- Be able to modify forms and controls.

Note For more information about structures, see "Structures: Your Own Data Types," in the Visual Studio .NET documentation. For more information about arrays, search the Visual Basic .NET documentation.

Scenario

In this lab, you will create and use a structure in an existing application. You will also add an array to allow the structure to be used and displayed three times. Although the context of this lab is a loan application, it is not part of the loan application scenario that is used in other labs in Course 2559B, *Introduction to Visual Basic .NET Programming with Microsoft .NET.*

Solution files

The solution files for this lab are in the *install_folder*\Labfiles\Lab032\Ex01\Solution and *install_folder*\Labfiles\Lab032\Ex02\Solution folders.

Estimated time to complete this lab: 30 minutes

Exercise 1
Creating a Structure

In this exercise, you will declare a structure containing four members to simulate loan applicant data. You will assign data to the structure members and display all data in a message box.

► Open the starter code for the project

1. Start Visual Studio .NET.
2. Open the StructuresArrays.sln project, which is in the *install_folder*\Labfiles\Lab032\Ex01\Starter folder.

Important Although the context of this lab is a loan application, it is not part of the loan application scenario that is used in several other labs in Course 2559B, *Introduction to Visual Basic .NET Programming with Microsoft .NET.*

► Add a data structure

1. Open the Code Editor for Form1.vb.
2. Just above the commented **MessageBox** statement, create a *loanApplicant* structure with the following members and data types.

Member name	Data type
ApplicantNumber	**Integer**
Name	**String**
Salary	**Decimal**
LoanRequested	**Decimal**

Your code should look like the following:

```
Public Structure loanApplicant
   Dim ApplicantNumber As Integer
   Dim Name As String
   Dim Salary As Decimal
   Dim LoanRequested As Decimal
End Structure
```

3. Declare a module-level *applicant* variable as a *loanApplicant* structure. Your code should look like the following:

```
Dim applicant as loanApplicant
```

► Populate the structure members with data from the form

1. In the **AddButton_Click** event handler, assign a starting number to the *ApplicantNumber* member of the *loanApplicant* structure for use when displaying information. (Code to be added appears in bold in the following example.) Assigning this starting number will also help you keep track of the array items in Exercise 2.

```
Private Sub AddButton_Click(...)
   applicant.ApplicantNumber = 1
End Sub
```

2. In the **AddButton_Click** event handler, write code to assign text box property values to the structure members, as follows. (Code to be added appears in bold.)

```
Private Sub AddButton_Click(...)
   applicant.ApplicantNumber = 1
   applicant.Name = NameTextBox.Text
   applicant.Salary = CDec(SalaryTextBox.Text)
   applicant.LoanRequested = _
      CDec(LoanRequestedTextBox.Text)
End Sub
```

► Display structure information to the user

1. In the **DisplayButton_Click** event handler, uncomment and then examine the line of code provided in the starter code. This code displays each structure member on separate lines in a message box. The commented code is reproduced below.

```
MessageBox.Show("Loan Applicant No: " & _
applicant.ApplicantNumber & ControlChars.CrLf & _
"Loan Applicant Name: " & applicant.Name & _
ControlChars.CrLf & "Salary: " & _
applicant.Salary & ControlChars.CrLf _
& "Loan Requested: " & applicant.LoanRequested)
```

Note This code uses the **ControlChars.CrLf** constant to create line returns in the message box text. For more information about **ControlChars.CrLf**, see "Print and Display Constants" in the Visual Basic .NET documentation.

---

2. In the **DisplayButton_Click** event handler, create a second message box to inform the user that the application will close, and then write code to close the application. Your code should look as follows:

```
MessageBox.Show("Application will close now.")
Application.Exit( )
```

► **Run and test the application**

1. To run the application, on the standard toolbar, click the **Start** button. ▶
2. Type sample data in the **Name**, **Salary**, and **Loan Requested** boxes.
3. Click **Add to Structure**.

   When you click **Add to Structure**, nothing visible will happen.
4. Click **Display** and the structure elements will appear in a message box.
5. Click **OK** to close the message box, and then click **OK** again to quit the application.

Exercise 2
Creating and Using Arrays

In this exercise, you will add an array based on the *loanApplicant* structure. You will modify the **AddButton_Click** event handler to allow multiple applicants to be added to the array. You will also modify the **DisplayButton_Click** event handler to accommodate the new array.

► Create an array based on the *loanApplicant* structure

1. Open the StructuresArrays.sln file that you created in Lab 3.2, Exercise 1 (if it is not already open).

   If you did not complete Lab 3.2, Exercise 1, open the StructuresArrays.sln file in the *install_folder*\Labfiles\Lab032\Ex02\Starter folder.

2. Open the Code Editor for Form1.vb.
3. Locate the code that declares the *loanApplicant* variable. In its place, declare an array of *loanApplicant* type that has three elements, as follows:

```
Dim applicant(2) As loanApplicant
```

► Track the number of applicants

1. In the **AddButton_Click** event handler, write code to declare a static variable as a counter, and to initialize it to 1, as follows:

```
Static countClicks As Integer
```

2. In the **AddButton_Click** event handler, just after the declaration of the static variable, change the references to the *loanApplicant* variable to refer to the array by using *countClicks* to acquire the number of the current array element, as follows:

```
applicant(countClicks).ApplicantNumber = countClicks + 1
applicant(countClicks).Name = NameTextBox.Text
applicant(countClicks).Salary = CDec(SalaryTextBox.Text)
applicant(countClicks).LoanRequested = _
   CDec(LoanRequestedTextBox.Text)
```

3. In the **AddButton_Click** event handler, just after the code that sets each set of array properties, write code to increment *countClicks* each time the user clicks **Add**, and to trap the current values by incrementing the counter. Your code should look as follows:

```
countClicks +=1
```

► Get the text box ready for the next add sequence

- In the **AddButton_Click** event handler, just after the code that increments *countClicks*, write code to set the focus on the **NameTextBox** control and then select all text in it. Your code should look as follows:

```
NameTextBox.Focus( )
NameTextBox.SelectAll( )
```

▶ Write code to accommodate multiple loan applications

1. In the **DisplayButton_Click** event handler, edit the **MessageBox** statement to use the array by replacing the references to `applicant` with `applicant(0)`.
2. Open the MessageBoxCode.txt file located in the *install_folder*\Labfiles\Lab032\Ex02\Starter folder, cut the three lines of code, and then paste them into your code.

   Alternatively, you can copy the entire **MessageBox** statement, and then paste it two times after the initial **MessageBox** statement. If you choose this alternative method, increase the array reference numbers to `applicant(1)` in the second statement and to `applicant(2)` in the third statement.
3. Verify that the final two statements in the **DisplayButton_Click** event procedure are the **MessageBox** statement indicating that the application will close and the statement that closes the application.

   Your code for the entire **DisplayButton_Click** event procedure should look as follows:

```
Private Sub DisplayButton_Click(...)
   MessageBox.Show("Loan Applicant No: " & _
       applicant(0).ApplicantNumber & ControlChars.CrLf & _
       "Loan Applicant Name: " & applicant(0).Name & _
       ControlChars.CrLf & "Salary: " & _
       applicant(0).Salary & ControlChars.CrLf & _
       "Loan Requested: " & applicant(0).LoanRequested)

   MessageBox.Show("Loan Applicant No: " & _
       applicant(1).ApplicantNumber & ControlChars.CrLf & _
       "Loan Applicant Name: " & applicant(1).Name & _
       ControlChars.CrLf & "Salary: " & _
       applicant(1).Salary & ControlChars.CrLf & _
       "Loan Requested: " & applicant(1).LoanRequested)

   MessageBox.Show("Loan Applicant No: " & _
       applicant(2).ApplicantNumber & ControlChars.CrLf & _
       "Loan Applicant Name: " & applicant(2).Name & _
       ControlChars.CrLf & "Salary: " & _
       applicant(2).Salary & ControlChars.CrLf & _
       "Loan Requested: " & applicant(2).LoanRequested)

   MessageBox.Show("Application will close now.")
   Application.Exit( )

End Sub
```

► Run and test your application

1. To run the application, on the standard toolbar, click the **Start** button.
2. Enter sample data in the **Name**, **Salary**, and **Loan Requested** boxes.
3. Click **Add to Structure**.
4. Repeat steps 2 and 3 two more times for a total of three times.
5. Click **Display**, and then click **OK** in all message boxes.
6. Quit Visual Studio .NET.

Note When you click **Add to Structure**, nothing visible will happen on the form, and you will be returned to the first text box. However, the structure members are being populated in memory. Then, when you click **Display**, you will see each applicant's information appear in a separate message box. The application will cause an exception if you click **Add to Structure** more than three times. The correct structure to handle this is an **If. . .Then** structure or a loop. You will learn about these in Module 5, "Decision Structures and Loops," in Course 2559B, *Introduction to Visual Basic .NET Programming with Microsoft .NET.*

---

msdn® training

Module 4: Working with Procedures

Contents

Microsoft®

Overview

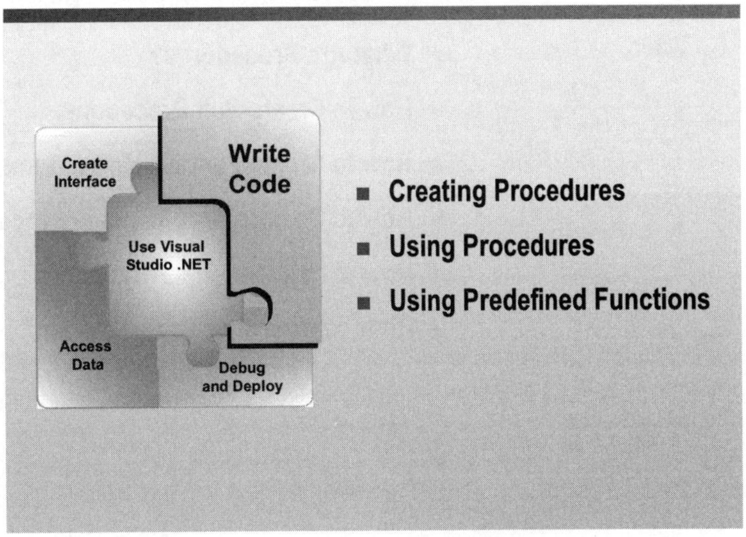

Introduction

Programming an application, especially a large project, is made easier by breaking it into smaller pieces. Using *procedures* can help you group your code into logical sections and condense repeated or shared tasks, such as frequently used calculations. In this module, you will learn how to create and use procedures.

Objectives

After completing this module, you will be able to:

- Differentiate between a **Sub** procedure and a **Function** procedure.
- Create and call **Sub** and **Function** procedures.
- Write procedures in modules to enable code reuse.
- Pass arguments by value and by reference.
- Use predefined functions in your application code.

Lesson: Creating Procedures

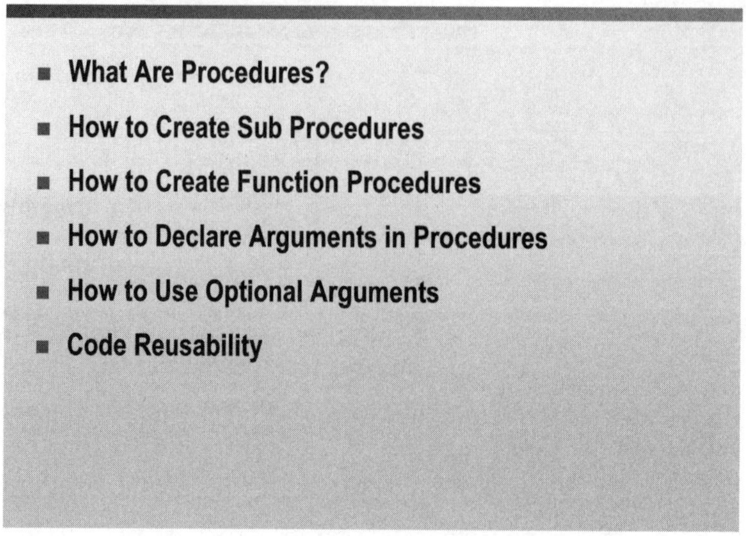

Introduction

This lesson explains how to create **Sub** and **Function** procedures, how to declare arguments in a procedure, and how to create procedures in a module.

Lesson agenda

This lesson includes the following topics and activities:

- What Are Procedures?
- How to Create **Sub** Procedures
- How to Create **Function** Procedures
- How to Declare Arguments in Procedures
- Multimedia: Passing Arguments
- How to Use Optional Arguments
- Multimedia: Writing Reusable Code
- Code Reusability
- Practice: Creating a Function in a Module

Lesson objectives

After completing this lesson, you will be able to:

- Describe and create a **Sub** procedure.
- Describe and create a **Function** procedure.
- Explain the difference between passing arguments to a procedure by value and passing arguments by reference.
- Declare arguments, including optional arguments, in a procedure.
- Create procedures in a module.

What Are Procedures?

- **Procedures are the executable code statements in a program, enclosed by a declaration statement and an End statement**
- **Three types:**
  - **Sub** procedures (including event **Sub** procedures)
  - **Function** procedures
  - **Property** procedures
- **Enable code reuse**
- **Declared as public by default**

Definition

Procedures are the executable code statements in a program. The statements in a procedure are enclosed by a declaration statement and an **End** statement.

Note You might find the terms *methods, procedures,* and *functions* used interchangeably in various references. This module adheres to the terminology found in the Microsoft® Visual Studio® .NET documentation.

Types of procedures

There are three types of procedures in Microsoft Visual Basic® .NET: **Sub** procedures, **Function** procedures, and **Property** procedures.

- **Sub** procedures perform actions but do not return a value to the calling procedure. Event handlers are **Sub** procedures that are executed in response to an event.
- **Function** procedures can return a value to the calling procedure. The **MessageBox.Show** statement is an example of a function.
- **Property** procedures return and assign values of properties of classes, structures, or modules.

Note For information about creating and using **Property** procedures, see Module 7, "Object-Oriented Programming in Visual Basic .NET," in Course 2559B, *Introduction to Visual Basic .NET Programming with Microsoft .NET.*

Using procedures

A procedure can be invoked, or *called*, from another procedure. When one procedure calls another procedure, control is transferred to the second procedure. When the code in the second procedure is finished running, it returns control to the procedure that called it.

Because of this functionality, procedures are useful for performing repeated or shared tasks. Instead of writing the same code more than once, you can write a procedure and call it from various points in your application or from other applications.

Procedure accessibility

You use an access modifier to define the *accessibility* of the procedures you write—that is, the permission for other code to call the procedure. If you do not specify an access modifier, procedures are declared as public by default.

The table below shows the accessibility options for declaring a procedure within a module.

Access modifier	Description
Public	No restrictions on access
Friend	Accessible from within the program that contains the declaration and from anywhere else in the same assembly
Private	Accessible only in the module that contains the declaration

Note The **Protected** access modifier can only be used on procedures declared within a class. For more information about declaring procedures in a class, see Module 7, "Object-Oriented Programming in Visual Basic .NET," in Course 2559B, *Introduction to Visual Basic .NET Programming with Microsoft .NET.*

How to Create Sub Procedures

Sub procedures perform actions but do not return a value to the calling procedure

```
[accessibility] Sub subname[(argumentlist)]
    ' Sub procedure statements
End Sub
```

Example:

```
Private Sub AboutHelp( )
   MessageBox.Show("MyProgram V1.0", "MyProgram Help")
End Sub
```

Definition

A **Sub** procedure is a series of Visual Basic statements enclosed by the **Sub** and **End Sub** statements. **Sub** procedures perform actions but do not return a value to the calling procedure.

Syntax to create a Sub procedure

Use the following syntax to create a **Sub** procedure:

```
[accessibility] Sub subname[(argumentlist)]
    ' Statements of the Sub procedure go here
End Sub
```

Example of a Sub procedure

The following code creates a **Sub** procedure **Sub AboutHelp** that uses a message box to display a product name and version number:

```
Private Sub AboutHelp( )
  MessageBox.Show("MyProgram V1.0", "MyProgram Help")
End Sub
```

How to Create Function Procedures

Function procedures perform actions and can return a value to the calling program

```
[accessibility] Function name[(argumentlist)] As datatype
  ' Function statements, including optional Return
  ' statement
End Function
```

Example:

```
Public Function DoubleTheValue(ByVal J As Double) As _
  Double
 . . .
  Return J*2
 . . .
End Function
```

Definition

A **Function** procedure is a series of Visual Basic statements enclosed by the **Function** and **End Function** statements. **Function** procedures are similar to **Sub** procedures, but functions can return a value to the calling program.

Syntax to create a Function procedure

Use the following syntax to create a **Function** procedure:

```
[accessibility] Function functionname[(argumentlist)] As _
  datatype
    ' Statements of the function go here, including optional
    ' Return statement
End Function
```

Example of a Function procedure

The following code creates a function named **Square** that returns the square of an integer:

```
Function Square(SquareValue As Integer) As Integer
  Square = SquareValue * SquareValue
End Function
```

Returning values

The value a **Function** procedure sends back to the calling program is called its *return value*. The function returns the value in one of two ways:

- It assigns a value to its own function name in one or more statements of the procedure. Control is not returned to the calling program until an **Exit Function** or **End Function** statement is executed.

  The **Exit Function** statement causes an immediate exit from a **Function** procedure. Any number of **Exit Function** statements can appear anywhere in the procedure.

- It uses a **Return** statement to specify the return value, and returns control immediately to the calling program.

The advantage of assigning the return value to the function name is that control does not return from the function until the program encounters an **Exit Function** or **End Function** statement. This allows you to assign a preliminary value and adjust it later, if necessary.

Example of assigning the return value

The following example assigns the return value to the function name **DoubleTheValue** and then uses the **Exit Function** statement to return to the calling procedure:

```
Function DoubleTheValue(ByVal j As Integer) As Double
   . . .
  DoubleTheValue = j*2
  ' Control remains within the function
   . . .
  Exit Function
  ' Control returns to the calling function
   . . .
End Function
```

If you exit the function without assigning a return value, the function returns the default value appropriate to the data type of the function. For example, it returns 0 for **Byte**, **Char**, **Decimal**, **Double**, **Integer**, **Long**, **Short**, and **Single**.

Example of using the Return statement

The **Return** statement simultaneously assigns the return value and exits the function, as shown in the following example:

```
Function DoubleTheValue(ByVal j As Integer) As Double
   . . .
   Return j*2
   ' Control is immediately returned to the calling function
   . . .
End Function
```

How to Declare Arguments in Procedures

- ***Arguments*** **are data passed to procedures**
- **You can pass arguments *ByVal* or *ByRef***
  - **ByVal:** The procedure cannot modify the value of the original variable
  - **ByRef:** The procedure can modify the value of the original variable
  - **Exception:** Nonvariable elements are never modified in calling code, even if passed by reference
- **ByVal is the default in Visual Basic .NET**
- **Syntax and example:**

```
([ByVal|ByRef] argumentname As datatype)
```

```
(ByVal Name As String)
```

Introduction

A procedure that performs repeated or shared tasks uses different information for each call. This information might consist of variables, constants, and expressions that are passed to the procedure by the calling procedure. Each value passed to a procedure is called an *argument.*

Parameters vs. arguments

When you define a procedure in Visual Basic .NET, you describe the data and data type that the procedure is designed to accept from a calling procedure. The elements defined in the procedure are referred to as *parameters.*

When you call the procedure, you substitute an actual value for each parameter. The values that you assign in place of parameters are called *arguments.*

Note Despite this subtle difference, the terms *argument* and *parameter* are often used interchangeably. This module adheres to the terminology found in the Visual Studio .NET documentation.

Passing ByVal and ByRef

When you define a procedure, you define how other procedures can pass arguments to the procedure. You can choose to pass arguments to it either by reference (**ByRef**) or by value (**ByVal**). In Visual Basic .NET, the default passing mechanism is by value. If you do not specify either **ByVal** or **ByRef** in your parameter definitions, **ByVal** is automatically added to the parameter definition for you.

Passing mechanism	Explanation	Implications	Advantage
By value Keyword: **ByVal**	The called procedure receives a copy of the data when it is called.	If the called procedure modifies the copy, the original value of the variable remains intact. When execution returns to the calling procedure, the variable contains the same value that it had before the value was passed.	Protects the variable from being changed by the called procedure.
By reference Keyword: **ByRef**	The called procedure receives a reference to the original data (the data's address in memory) when it is called.	The called procedure can modify the variable directly. When execution returns to the calling procedure, the variable contains the modified value.	The called procedure can use the argument to return a new value to the calling code.

Exceptions

The programming element underlying an argument can be either a variable element, capable of having its value changed, or a nonvariable element. Nonvariable arguments are never modified in the calling code, even if they are passed by reference. The called procedure might modify its copy of such an argument, but that modification does not affect the underlying element in the calling code.

The following table lists variable and nonvariable elements.

Variable elements (can be modified)	Nonvariable elements
Declared variables, including object variables	Constants
Fields (of classes)	Literals
Array elements	Enumerations
Structure elements	Expressions

Declaring arguments

You use the same syntax to declare the arguments for **Sub** procedures and **Function** procedures. You declare each argument for a procedure the same way you declare a variable, specifying the argument name and data type. You can also specify the passing mechanism and whether the argument is optional.

The syntax for each argument in the argument list for a procedure is as follows:

```
([ByVal|ByRef] [ParamArray] argumentname As datatype)
```

Note For more information about **ParamArray** syntax, see How to Pass Arrays to Procedures in this module.

If the argument is optional, you must also include the keyword **Optional** and supply a default value in the declaration, as follows:

```
Optional [ByVal|ByRef] argumentname As datatype = defaultvalue
```

Note For more information about optional arguments, see How to Use Optional Arguments in this module.

Example of declaring an argument

In the following example, the **Sub** procedure **Hello** is designed to take an argument **Name** of type **String** by value from a calling procedure.

```
Public Sub Hello(ByVal Name As String)
    MessageBox.Show("Hello, " & Name & "!")
End Sub
```

Note The argument names used when calling a procedure do not need to match the parameter names used to define the procedure.

Multimedia: Passing Arguments

Introduction

In this animation, you will learn about the difference between passing arguments to procedures *by value* and passing them *by reference*.

Animation script

When you pass an argument to a procedure, you can choose to pass the argument by reference or by value. In this animation, you will learn about the difference between passing *by value* and passing *by reference*.

First, consider passing the argument by value, because this is the default passing mechanism in Visual Basic .NET.

When you pass an argument by value, using **ByVal**, a copy of the value is created and passed to the procedure that you call. When you pass an argument **ByVal**, any changes made by the procedure are made only on the copy of the argument. The original argument is not changed.

To understand how this affects your code, consider the following example:

```
Sub Count(ByVal number As Integer)
  number = number + 1
End Sub

Sub Test( )
  Dim myNumber As Integer = 10
  Count(myNumber)
  MessageBox.Show(myNumber)
End Sub
```

The **Sub** procedure **Count** takes one parameter, **number**, by value. It adds one to this value.

In the calling procedure:

- The first line of code assigns a value of 10 to the variable *myNumber*.
- The second line of code passes *myNumber* to the **Sub** procedure **Count**.
- The third line of code displays the value of the variable *myNumber* in a message box.

Based on your understanding of passing by value, what do you expect the message box to display?

The answer is 10. Why?

When you make the call to the **Count** procedure, a copy of *myNumber* is passed to the procedure. The copy of *myNumber* is changed to 11, but this copy is destroyed when the **Count** procedure is finished executing code. It is not passed back to the calling procedure. The message box displays the original value of *myNumber*, or 10.

Now, consider passing a value by reference. When you pass a value by reference, using **ByRef**, the calling procedure passes a reference to the actual data, not a copy, to the called procedure. The called routine uses this reference to use and modify the value of the data.

To pass the value by reference, you need to make only one change to this code; change the word **ByVal** to **ByRef** in the procedure declaration. This is a small change in code, but it has important implications, as shown in the following code:

```
Sub Count(ByRef number As Integer)
  number = number + 1
End Sub

Sub Test( )
  Dim myNumber As Integer = 10
  Count(myNumber)
  MessageBox.Show(myNumber)
End Sub
```

The message box in the calling procedure would now display 11 as the value of *myNumber*. Why?

When you make the call to the **Count** procedure, a reference to the variable is passed to the procedure. The **Count** procedure changes the value of the variable to 11. When the message box in the calling procedure retrieves the value of *myNumber*, it retrieves the new value.

When you design procedures in your application, be sure that for each declared argument you consider whether the argument should be passed by value or by reference.

- The advantage of passing by reference is that the procedure can use the argument to return a value to the calling code.
- The advantage of passing by value is that it protects the variable from being changed by the called procedure.
- In Visual Basic .NET, the default passing mechanism is by value.

How to Use Optional Arguments

- **Rules for declaring optional arguments:**
  - You must specify a default value
  - The default value must be a constant expression
  - Arguments following an optional argument must also be optional
- **Syntax:**

```
(Optional [ByVal|ByRef] argumentname As datatype = defaultvalue)
```

- **Example:**

```
Function Add (ByVal value1 As Integer, ByVal value2 As _
   Integer, Optional ByVal value3 As Integer = 0) As Integer
```

Introduction

You can specify that a procedure argument is optional and does not need to be supplied when the procedure is called. This provides flexibility when your procedure is called by another procedure. The user can decide whether or not to provide an argument.

Declaring an optional argument

Optional arguments are indicated by the **Optional** keyword in the procedure definition. In addition, when you declare an optional argument, the following rules apply:

- You must specify a default value for all optional arguments.
- The default value for an optional argument must be a constant expression.
- Every argument following an optional argument in the procedure definition must also be optional.

The following code shows the syntax for declaring an optional argument:

```
Optional [ByVal|ByRef] argumentname As datatype = defaultvalue
```

Example of optional argument

The following example shows a procedure declaration with an optional argument:

```
Function Add(ByVal value1 As Integer, ByVal value2 As _
  Integer, Optional ByVal value3 As Integer = 0) As Integer
  ' The default value for the optional argument is 0
```

Incorrect example of optional argument

The following example contains an error; remember that arguments following an optional argument must also be optional.

```
Function Add(ByVal value1 As Integer, Optional ByVal _
  value2 As Integer = 0, ByVal value3 As Integer) As Integer
  ' Causes an error
```

Calling procedures with optional arguments

When you call a procedure with an optional argument, you can choose whether or not to supply the argument. If you do not supply the argument, the procedure uses the default value declared for that argument.

When you omit one or more optional arguments in the argument list, you use successive commas to separate the spaces marking their positions. The following call supplies the first and fourth arguments but not the second or third:

```
SubCount(arg1, , , arg4)
' Leaves out arg2 and arg3
```

Multimedia: Writing Reusable Code

This multimedia demonstration introduces you to the concept of procedures. Specifically, it shows how to structure code for increased reusability, how to create a procedure in a module, and how to pass arguments and return a value from a function.

Code Reusability

Use a...	For...	Examples
Structure	Objects that do not need to be extended	**Size** **Point**
Module	Utility functions and global data	**Temperature conversion**
Class	Extending objects or objects that need cleanup	**Forms** **Button**

- **Creating a module:**

```
[Public|Friend] Module ModuleName
   . . .
End Module
```

Introduction

One of the most important processes in creating a Visual Basic–based application is designing code for code reuse. How you write code affects the reusability of the code.

Writing code for reuse

You can write code intended for reuse, including procedures, in structures, modules, or classes. The following table provides an overview of the situations in which you would choose each of these options.

Use a...	for...	Example
Structure	Creating objects that do not need to be extended and that have a small instance size	**Size** and **Point** are structures that are available in the Microsoft .NET Framework class library
Module	Providing utility functions and global data for use by multiple modules or classes	Utility functions such as temperature conversion, area calculation, data access, and so on, needed by multiple modules
Class	Extending objects, or for objects that need resource cleanup	**Forms** class, **Button** class, and so on

Writing procedures in a structure

The following code shows how you can write a procedure in a structure. Assume that variables *x*, *y*, and *z* in the example have already been declared.

```
Structure TableDimensions
  Private legHeight, topWidth, topDepth As Integer
  Public Sub New(ByVal legHeight As Integer, _
      ByVal topWidth As Integer, ByVal topDepth as Integer)
      Me.legHeight = x
      Me.topWidth = y
      Me.topDepth = z
  End Sub
End Structure
```

Creating a module

To create a module, you first add a module to your project. You then write the code statements that define the data and procedures for your module.

► **To add a module to a project**

1. If Solution Explorer is not open, on the **View** menu, click **Solution Explorer**.
2. In Solution Explorer, right-click your project, point to **Add**, and then click **Add New Item**.
3. In the **Add New Item** dialog box, in the **Name** box, type a name for your module, select **Module** under **Templates**, and then click **Open**.

Syntax

The following syntax declares a module block:

```
[Public|Friend] Module modulename
  ' Add classes, properties, methods, fields, and events for
  ' the module
End Module
```

Accessibility of a module

As with procedures and variables, you use access modifiers to define the accessibility of a module. If you do not use an access modifier, modules are declared as **Friend** by default.

The following table defines available access modifiers for a module.

Access modifier	Definition
Public	No restrictions on access
Friend	Accessible within the program that contains the declaration and from anywhere else in the same assembly

Note For information about classes, see Module 7, "Object-Oriented Programming in Visual Basic .NET," in Course 2559B, *Introduction to Visual Basic .NET Programming with Microsoft .NET*.

Practice: Creating a Function in a Module

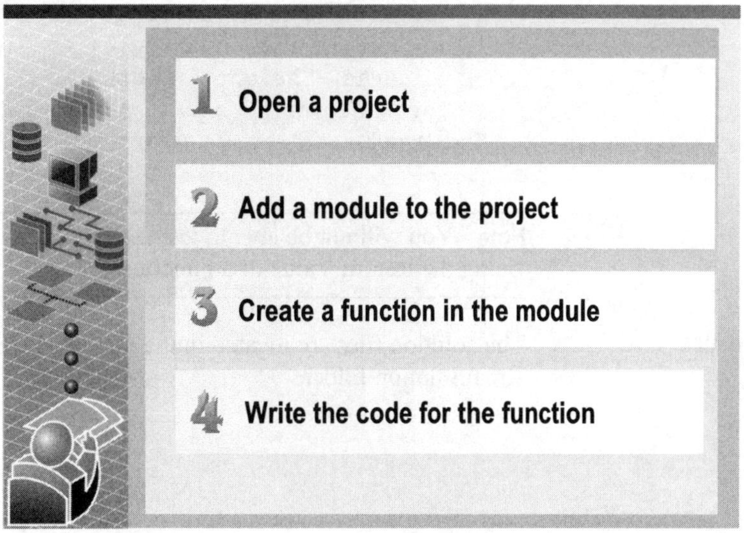

In this practice, you will add a module to a project and create a function in the module. The function will take **height** and **width** as arguments and return **Area**.

Note You will use the code you create in this practice as the starter code for the practice Using the Return Value of a Function, which is later in this module.

► **Create a function in a module**

1. Open a new project in Visual Basic .NET. Use the Windows Application template. Set the project name to **CalculateArea** and the location to *install_folder*\Practices\Mod04\Area, and then click **OK**.
2. Add a new module to the project. To do this, on the **Project** menu, click **Add New Item**. In the **Templates** pane, click **Module**, leave the name as the default, and then click **Open**.
3. In the module, create a new function named **Area** that returns a **Single** data type.
   a. The function should take two arguments named **height** and **width** by value. Declare each argument as **Single**.
   b. In the body of the function, write code to multiply **height** and **width** and to assign the return value to **Area**, as shown in the following code:

```
Area = height * width
```

4. Save your project. Your completed code should look as follows:

```
Module Module1
   Function Area(ByVal height As Single, _
       ByVal width As Single) As Single
       Area = height * width
   End Function
End Module
```

Note You will not be able to test the function until you complete the practice Using the Return Value of a Function.

Solution files

The solution files are located in the *install_folder*\Practices\Mod04\Area\Solution folder.

Lesson: Using Procedures

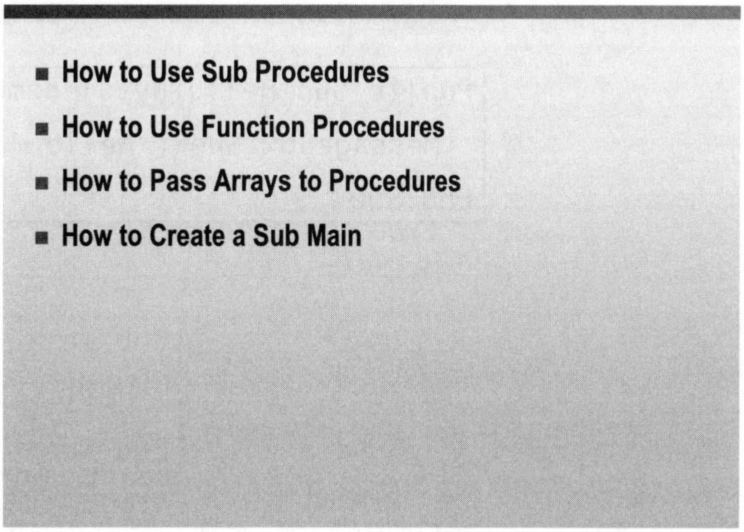

Introduction

One of the most important benefits of using procedures effectively is code reuse. The procedures you create for one program can be used throughout that program and in other projects, often with little or no modification. Procedures are useful for repeated or shared tasks, such as frequently used calculations.

This lesson describes how to use **Sub** and **Function** procedures, how to use **ParamArray** syntax to pass arguments, and how to modify application startup by creating a **Sub Main** procedure.

Lesson agenda

This lesson includes the following topics and activities:

- How to Use **Sub** Procedures
- How to Use **Function** Procedures
- Practice: Using the Return Value of a Function
- How to Pass Arrays to Procedures
- How to Create a **Sub Main**
- Practice: Creating a **Sub Main**

Lesson objectives

After completing this lesson, you will be able to:

- Call and pass arguments to a **Sub** procedure.
- Pass arguments to a function and use a return value.
- Use **ParamArray** to declare an array in a procedure argument.
- Modify application startup by creating a **Sub Main** procedure.

How to Use Sub Procedures

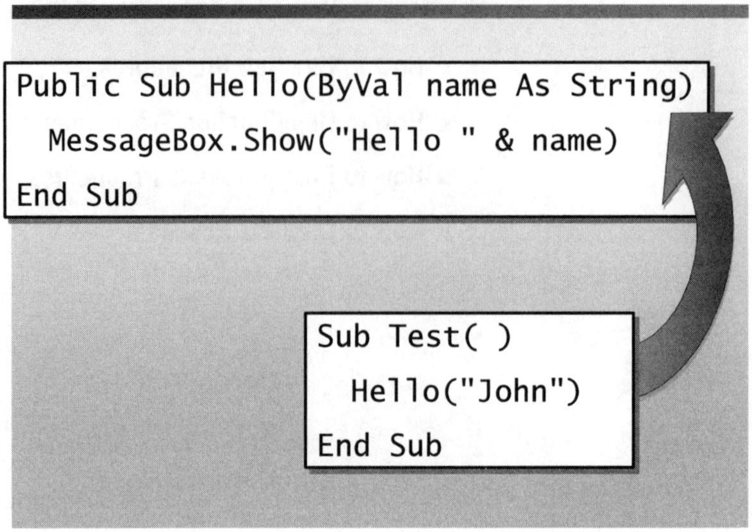

Introduction

To use a **Sub** procedure, you call it from another procedure.

Code flow

Each time a **Sub** procedure is called, its statements are executed, starting with the first executable statement after the **Sub** statement and ending with the first **End Sub**, **Exit Sub**, or **Return** statement encountered. After the **Sub** procedure executes its code, it returns program execution to the line of code following the line that called the **Sub** procedure.

Calling a Sub procedure

The syntax to call a **Sub** procedure is as follows:

```
[Call] Subname [(Argumentlist)]
```

- You must call the **Sub** procedure *on a line by itself* in your code—you cannot call it by using its name within an expression.
- The calling statement must provide values for all arguments that are not optional.
- You can optionally use the **Call** statement to call a **Sub** procedure. Using the **Call** statement can improve the readability of your program.

Note **Sub** procedures do not return a value to the calling statement. A **Sub** procedure can, however, pass information back to the calling code by modifying any arguments passed by reference.

Example of a simple call

The following code shows an event procedure that calls a **Sub** procedure called **SetData**:

```
Sub DataButton_Click(...)
  SetData( )
End Sub
```

Example using the Call statement

You can also use the following code to perform the same task:

```
Sub DataButton_Click(...)
  Call SetData( )
End Sub
```

Incorrect example of a simple call

The following call contains an error:

```
Sub DataButton_Click(...)
  MessageBox.Show(SetData( ))
End Sub

' Causes an error, because the Show method expects a String
' data type, not a procedure
```

Example of a call with arguments

Consider the following definition for the **Sub** procedure **SetData**:

```
Public Sub SetData(ByVal cars As Integer, ByVal trucks As _
  Integer, ByVal vans As Integer)
      ' Code for SetData Procedure
End Sub
```

The syntax to call this procedure includes the procedure name and the argument list in parenthesis, as shown in the following code:

```
Sub DataButton_Click(...)
  SetData(10, 20, 30)
End Sub
```

Incorrect example of a call with arguments

The following call to the **SetData** procedure defined in the example above contains an error.

```
Sub DataButton_Click( )
  SetData(10, 20)
End Sub

' Causes an error, because there is no value for the third
' parameter of the SetData procedure. The calling statement
' must provide values for all arguments that are not optional.
```

Practice (optional) Passing Arguments by Reference

In this practice, you will create two procedures. The first procedure will take an argument by reference. The second procedure will call the first procedure and pass a value by reference. You will observe the effect of calling a procedure and passing a value by reference.

► **Create the user interface**

1. Open a new project in Visual Basic .NET. Use the Windows Application template. Set the project name to **ByRefTest** and the location to *install_folder*\Practices\Mod04\ByRefTest and then click **OK**.
2. Open Form1 in Design view.
3. Open the Toolbox. Add one **TextBox** control and one **Button** control to your form. Arrange the controls so that your form looks something like the following screen shot:

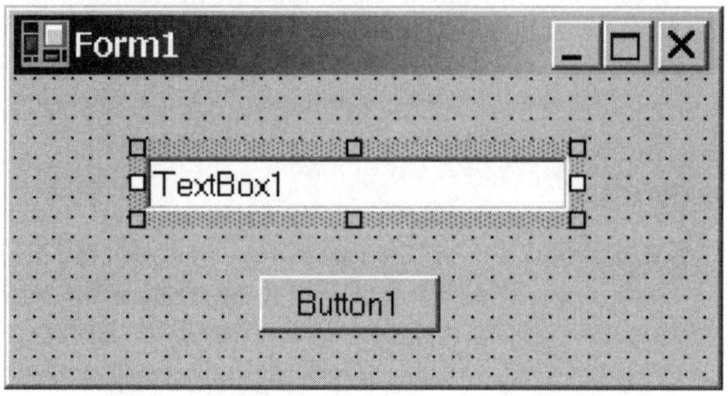

► **Create a procedure that takes an argument by reference**

1. Open the Code Editor for Form1.
2. Create a procedure named **Hello** that takes one **String** argument, *Name*, by reference. Your code should look like the following:

```
Public Sub Hello(ByRef Name As String)

End Sub
```

3. To view the effect of passing a variable by reference when you call a second procedure, add the following three lines of code to the **Hello** procedure:

   a. Display the current value of *Name* in a message box.

   b. Set the value of the *Name* variable to **Samantha**.

   c. Display the new value of *Name* in a message box.

   Your code should look similar to the following code:

```
Public Sub Hello(ByRef Name As String)
   MessageBox.Show("Hello, " & Name & "!")
   Name = "Samantha"
   MessageBox.Show("Hello, " & Name & "!")
End Sub
```

► Call a procedure and pass an argument

- Add an event handler for the **Button1_Click** event. In the event handler, call the **Hello** procedure, passing the **Text** property of TextBox1 as an argument.

  Your code should look as follows:

```
Private Sub Button1_Click(...) Handles Button1.Click
   Hello(TextBox1.Text)
End Sub
```

► Run the application and test the results

1. Run the application.
2. Type your name in TextBox1.
3. Click **Button1**, verify that your name appears, and then click **OK**.

   The second message box containing the name "Samantha" will immediately open.

4. Before you click **OK**, look at the text box. While you click **OK**, observe the change in the text box.

   The name "Samantha" will appear in the text box after the message box closes, even though no code specifically assigning a new value to the **TextBox1.Text** property has been written.

Solution files

The solution files for this practice are located in the *install_folder*\Practices\Mod04\ByRefTest\Solution folder.

How to Use Function Procedures

- **Calling a function**
  - Include the function name and arguments on the right side of an assignment statement

```
Dim celsiusTemperature As Single
celsiusTemperature = FtoC(80)
```

  - Use the function name in an expression

```
If  FtoC(userValue) < 0 Then
   ...
End If
```

Introduction

A **Function** procedure differs from a **Sub** procedure in that a **Function** procedure can return a value to the calling procedure.

Calling a function

You call a **Function** procedure by including its name and arguments either on the right side of an assignment statement or in an expression. Consider the following function, which converts a temperature in Fahrenheit to a temperature in Celsius.

```
Function FtoC(ByVal temperature As Single) As Single
    ' Convert Fahrenheit to Celsius
    FtoC = (temperature - 32.0) * (5 / 9)
End Function
```

The following sample calls illustrate how you might call this function:

```
Dim celsiusTemperature As Single
celsiusTemperature = FtoC(80)
  ' Call the procedure by including its name and arguments on
  ' the right side of an assignment statement. In this call,
  ' the value 80 is passed to the FtoC function, and the
  ' return value is assigned to celsiusTemperature.

If FtoC(userValue) < 0 Then . . .
  ' Call the procedure by using it in an expression. In this
  ' call, the FtoC function is used as part of an expression.
End If
```

Code flow

Each time the function is called, its statements are executed, starting with the first executable statement after the **Function** statement and ending with the first **End Function**, **Exit Function**, or **Return** statement encountered.

Practice: Using the Return Value of a Function

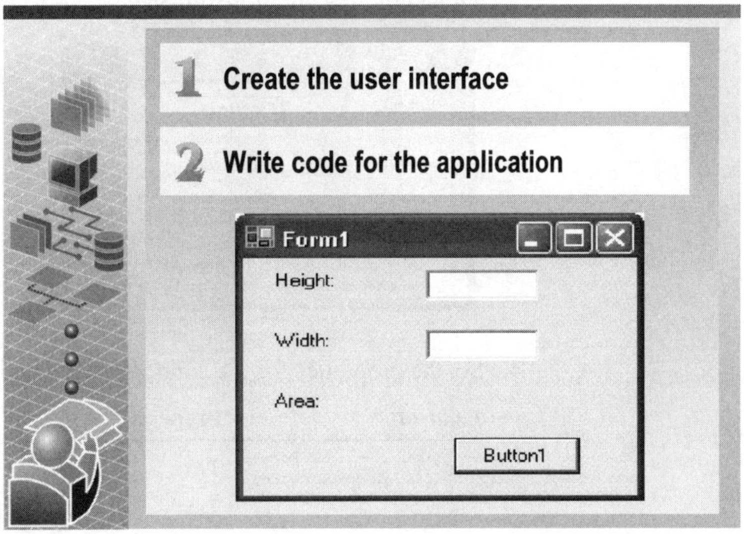

In this exercise, you will create a simple application that calculates the area of a rectangle, given its height and width.

First, you will create the user interface for the application. The user will type values for height and width into two text boxes on a form and then click a button to calculate the area of the rectangle with the given dimensions. The result will be displayed as a label on the form.

Next, you will write the code for the application. You will call the **Area** function that you created in the first practice in this module (Creating a Function in a Module), pass arguments to the function, and return a value.

► **Create the user interface**

1. Open the CalculateArea project that you created in the practice Creating a Function in a Module. This project should be located in the *install_folder*\Practices\Mod04\Area folder.

   If you did not complete this practice, open the CalculateArea.sln solution located in the *install_folder*\Practices\Mod04\FunctionReturnValue\Starter folder, and familiarize yourself with the form and module in the project.

2. Open Form1 in Design view.

3. Open the Toolbox. Add four **Label** controls, two **TextBox** controls, and a **Button** control to your form. Arrange the controls so that your form looks something like the following screen shot:

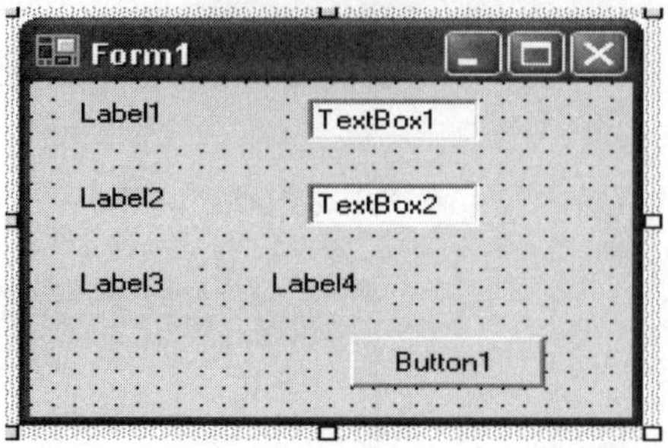

4. Set the properties for the controls as shown in the following table.

Control	Property	New value
Label1	**Text**	**Height**
Label2	**Text**	**Width**
Label3	**Text**	**Area**
Label4	**Text**	*blank*
TextBox1	**Text**	*blank*
TextBox2	**Text**	*blank*

▶ Write code for the application

1. Add an event handler for the **Button1_Click** event. In the event handler:
   a. Call the **Area** function.
   b. Pass the **Text** property of TextBox1 and TextBox2 as arguments.
   c. Assign the return value to the **Text** property of Label4.

   Your code should look as follows:

```
Private Sub Button1_Click(...)
   Label4.Text = Area(TextBox1.Text, TextBox2.Text)
End Sub
```

2. Run the application.
3. Type numeric values into the **Height** and **Width** text boxes.
4. Click **Button1**, and verify that the expected answer appears.
5. Quit the application.

Solution files

The solution files for this practice are located in the *install_folder*\Practices\Mod04\FunctionReturnValue\Solution folder.

How to Pass Arrays to Procedures

- **Pass an array as you pass other arguments:**

```
Sub PassArray(ByVal testScores As Integer( ))
   ...
End Sub

Dim scores( ) As Integer = {80, 92, 73}
PassArray(scores)
```

- **Declare a parameter array:**

```
Sub StudentScores(ByVal name As String, ByVal _
        ParamArray scores( ) As String)
   ' Statements for Sub procedure
End Sub
```

- **Call a procedure with a parameter array:**

```
StudentScores("Anne","10","26","32","15","22","16")
```

Introduction

You can pass arrays as arguments to a procedure as you pass other arguments. Visual Basic .NET also provides the **ParamArray** keyword to declare a parameter array in the parameter definition for a procedure.

Passing arrays

You can pass single dimensional or multi-dimensional arrays to procedures in the same way that you pass other arguments.

The following example shows how to pass a single-dimensional array to a procedure:

```
Sub PassArray(ByVal testScores As Integer( ))
  ...
End Sub

Dim scores( ) As Integer = {80, 92, 73}
PassArray(scores)
```

The following example shows how to pass a two-dimensional array to a procedure:

```
Sub Pass2DArray(ByVal rectangle As Integer(,))
  ...
End Sub

Dim rectangle(,) As Integer = {{12, 1}, {0, 12}}
Pass2DArray(rectangle)
```

Using ParamArray

Usually, you cannot call a procedure with more arguments than the procedure declaration specifies. When you need an indefinite number of arguments, you can declare a parameter array, which allows a procedure to accept an array of values for an argument. You do not need to know the number of elements in the parameter array when you define the procedure. The array size is determined individually by each call to the procedure.

You use the **ParamArray** keyword to denote a parameter array. This keyword indicates that a procedure argument is an optional array of elements of a specified type. The following rules apply:

- A procedure can have only one parameter array, and it must be the last argument in the procedure definition.
- The parameter array must be passed by value. It is good programming practice to explicitly include the **ByVal** keyword in the procedure definition.
- The code within the procedure must treat the parameter array as a single-dimensional array, each element of which is the same data type as the **ParamArray** data type.
- The parameter array is automatically optional. Its default value is an empty single-dimensional array of the parameter array's element type.
- All arguments preceding the parameter array must be required. The parameter array must be the only optional argument.

Calling a procedure with a parameter array argument

When you call a procedure with a parameter array argument, you can pass any of the following for the parameter array:

- Nothing. That is, you can omit the **ParamArray** argument. In this case, an empty array is passed to the procedure. You can also pass the **Nothing** keyword, with the same effect.
- A list of an indefinite number of arguments, separated by commas. The data type of each argument must be implicitly convertible to the **ParamArray** element type.
- An array with the same element type as the parameter array.

Example of ParamArray declaration

The following code shows how you can define a procedure with a parameter array:

```
Sub StudentScores(ByVal name As String, ByVal ParamArray _
  scores( ) As String)
    ' Statements for Sub procedure
End Sub
```

Examples of calls to a procedure with a parameter array

The following examples show possible calls to **StudentScores**.

```
StudentScores("Anne", "10", "26", "32", "15", "22", "16")

StudentScores("Mary", "High", "Low", "Average", "High")

Dim JohnScores( ) As String = {"35", "Absent", "21", "30"}
StudentScores("John", JohnScores)
```

How to Create a Sub Main

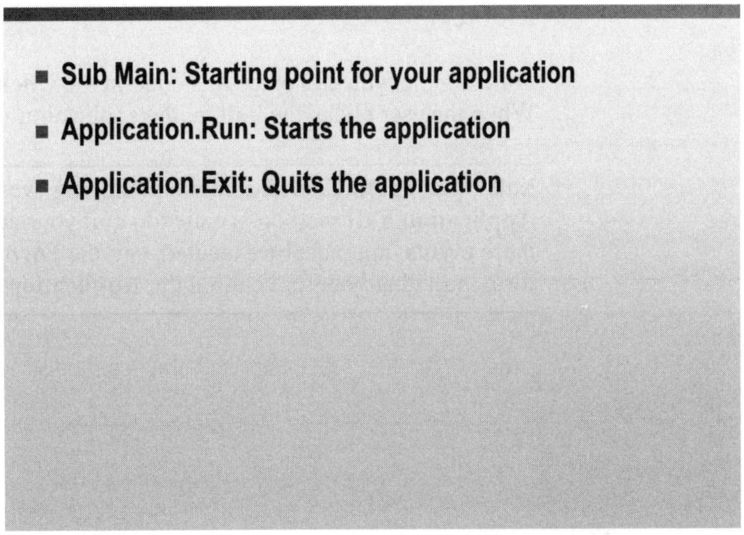

Introduction

To start and quit an application, the .NET Framework class library provides the **Application** class. The **Application** class provides methods (procedures) and properties to manage an application, including methods to start and quit an application, methods to process Microsoft Windows® messages, and properties to get information about an application.

The Sub Main procedure

When you create applications with the Windows Application template in Visual Basic .NET, Visual Basic automatically creates a hidden **Sub** procedure called **Sub Main** for the **Form** class. This procedure is used as the starting point for your application.

Creating a new Sub Main

In the **Sub Main** procedure, Visual Basic .NET calls the **Application.Run** method to start the application. You can change this behavior by creating your own **Sub Main** and making it the startup object. You can create the **Sub Main** in a module or in another class. After you create a **Sub Main**, you need to make this new procedure the startup object by using the Properties window.

► **To change the startup object to Sub Main**

1. If Solution Explorer is not open, on the **View** menu, click **Solution Explorer**.
2. In Solution Explorer, right-click the project name, and then click **Properties**.
3. In the left pane, under **Common Properties**, verify that **General** is selected.
4. In the **Startup object** list, click **Sub Main** to make this procedure the new startup object for your project.

Using Application.Exit

To quit an application, you call the **Application.Exit** method by using the following syntax:

```
Application.Exit( )
```

For example, you can place this code in the **Click** event handler for a button. When the user clicks the button, the application will quit.

Note The **Form.Closed** and **Form.Closing** events are not triggered when the **Application.Exit** method is called to quit your application. If you have code in these events that must be executed, call the **Form.Close** method for each open form individually before calling the **Application.Exit** method.

Practice: Creating a Sub Main

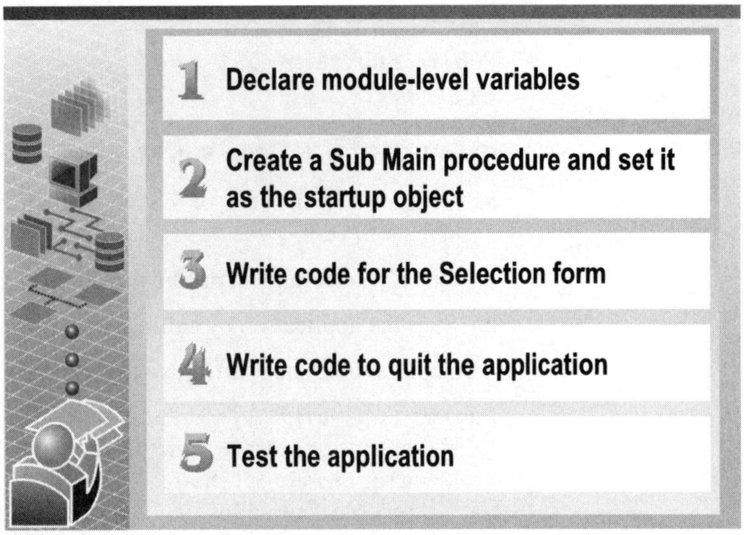

In this practice, you will write code for an application that consists of three forms, and create a **Sub Main** as the startup object for the project.

► Open the project

- Open the MultipleForms.sln project, which is in the *install_folder*\Practices\Mod04\Forms\Starter folder, and familiarize yourself with the forms and modules in the project.

► Declare variables

- Declare the following variables in the Starter module file.

Variable name	Access modifier	Data type
carLoanForm	**Friend**	**CarLoan**
homeLoanForm	**Friend**	**HomeLoan**
selectionForm	**Private**	**Selection**

Your code should look as follows:

```
Friend carLoanForm As CarLoan
Friend homeLoanForm As HomeLoan
Private selectionForm As Selection
```

► **Create a Sub Main procedure**

1. Declare a public **Sub Main** procedure in the Starter module. Your code should look as follows:

```
Public Sub Main( )
End Sub
```

2. Complete the body of the **Sub Main** procedure.

   a. Create a new instance of the Selection form and assign it to *selectionForm.*

   b. Call the **selectionForm.Show** method to display the form.

   c. Start the application by calling the **Application.Run** method.

   You code should look as follows:

```
Public Sub Main( )
     selectionForm = New Selection( )
     selectionForm.Show( )
     Application.Run( )
End Sub
```

3. Set the **Sub Main** as the startup object for the application.

► **Write code for the Selection form**

1. Open the Code Editor for the Selection form.
2. Add a **Click** event handler for the **Next** button.
3. Write code for the event handler.

   a. If the **CarLoanRadioButton** is selected, create a new instance of the CarLoan form. Your code should look as follows:

```
If CarLoanRadioButton.Checked Then
   carLoanForm = New CarLoan( )
```

Note You will learn more about **If...Then** statements later in Course 2559B, *Introduction to Visual Basic .NET Programming with Microsoft .NET.*

   b. Use the **Show** method to display the CarLoan form.

   c. Use the **Close** method to close the Selection form, as follows:

```
   carLoanForm.Show( )
   Me.Close( )
```

   d. If **HomeLoanRadioButton** is selected, create a new instance of the HomeLoan form. Your code should look as follows:

```
ElseIf HomeLoanRadioButton.Checked Then
   homeLoanForm = New HomeLoan( )
```

   e. Use the **Show** method to display the HomeLoan form.

f. Use the **Close** method to close the Selection form, as follows:

```
    homeLoanForm.Show( )
    Me.Close( )
```

g. If no option is selected, use a message box to prompt the user to make a selection. Your code should look as follows:

```
Else
    MessageBox.Show("Please select a loan type", _
         "Loan Type", MessageBoxButtons.OK, _
         MessageBoxIcon.Error)
End If
```

► **Write code to quit the application**

1. Create a **Click** event handler for the **Exit** button on the Selection form. Call **Application.Exit** to quit the application.
2. Create a **Click** event handler for the **Done** button on the HomeLoan form. Call **Application.Exit** to quit the application.
3. Create a **Closing** event handler for the HomeLoan form. Call **Application.Exit** to quit the application.
4. Create a **Click** event handler for the **Done** button on the CarLoan form. Call **Application.Exit** to quit the application.
5. Create a **Closing** event handler for the CarLoan form. Call **Application.Exit** to quit the application.

Note It is important to call **Application.Exit** at any point in the application that allows the user to close the application. If the appropriate closing code is not called, the application remains running, although the closed form is no longer accessible. In a more complex application, the closing code would be likely to include other code, such as code to save any changes, to close data connections, to confirm that the user wants to quit, and so on.

► **Test the application**

1. Run the application. Click **Car Loan** and click the **Next** button. Verify that the Car Loan Form opens.
2. Quit the application by clicking the **Close** button in the upper right corner of the form.
3. Run the application again. Click **Home Loan** and click the **Next** button. Verify that the Home Loan Form opens.
4. Quit the application by clicking the **Done** button.
5. Run the application again. Click the **Next** button without clicking a loan type. Verify that a message box prompts the user to choose a loan type.
6. Quit the application by using the **Exit** button on the Selection form.

Solution files

The solution files for this practice are located in the *install_folder*\Practices\Mod04\Forms\Solution folder.

Lesson: Using Predefined Functions

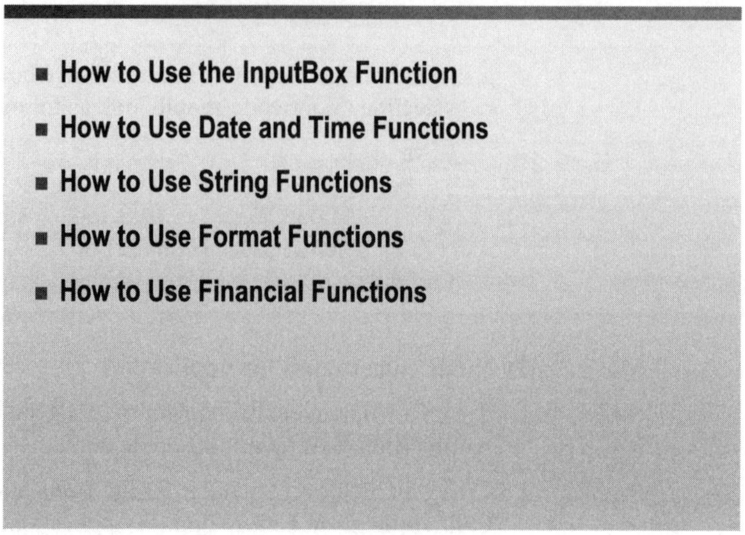

Introduction

The Visual Basic run-time library provides many predefined functions that you can use in your code. You call these functions in the same way that you call your own functions.

In this module, you will learn about the **InputBox** function, and sample date and time functions, string functions, format functions, and financial functions. For a complete list of predefined functions, see "Visual Basic Run-Time Library Members" in the Visual Studio .NET documentation.

Lesson agenda

This lesson includes the following topics and activities:

- How to Use the **InputBox** Function
- How to Use Date and Time Functions
- How to Use String Functions
- How to Use Format Functions
- How to Use Financial Functions
- Practice: Examining Predefined Functions

Lesson objective

After completing this lesson, you will be able to use predefined functions in your application code, including the **InputBox** function, date and time functions, string functions, format functions, and financial functions.

How to Use the InputBox Function

- **Displays a prompt in a dialog box, and returns the user input as a string**

```
Dim FileName As String
FileName = InputBox("Please enter file name","Search")
```

Introduction

The **InputBox** function is a predefined function that provides a simple way for you to interact with users. The **InputBox** function displays a prompt in a dialog box, waits for the user to enter text or click a button, and then returns a string containing the contents of the text box.

Parameters

The following function declaration shows the parameters for the **InputBox** function:

```
Public Function InputBox(ByVal Prompt As String, _
   Optional ByVal Title As String = "", _
   Optional ByVal DefaultResponse As String = "", _
   Optional ByVal XPos As Integer = -1, _
   Optional ByVal YPos As Integer = -1 ) As String
```

As you can see, the **Title**, **DefaultResponse**, **XPos**, and **YPos** arguments are optional. The following table explains the default values that apply if you choose not to pass one of these optional arguments to the **InputBox** function.

Parameter	Definition	Default value
Title	The text placed in the title bar	The application name
DefaultResponse	The value displayed in the text box as a default value if the user does not provide input	The displayed text box is empty
XPos	Specifies the distance of the left edge of the dialog box from the left edge of the screen	The dialog box is centered horizontally
YPos	Specifies the distance of the upper edge of the dialog box from the top of the screen	The dialog box is vertically positioned about one-third of the way down the screen

Example using the InputBox function

The following code creates an input box titled **Search**, which prompts the user to enter a file name and stores the user's response as a variable named *FileName*.

```
Dim FileName As String
FileName = InputBox("Please enter file name", "Search")
```

Result

The following screen shot shows the input box that is created by the preceding code.

Note For more information about the **InputBox** function, see "**InputBox** Function" in the Visual Studio .NET documentation.

How to Use Date and Time Functions

- **Perform calculations and operations involving dates and times**
- **Examples:**
  - **DateAdd**: Add or subtract a specific time interval from a date

```
DateAdd(DateInterval.Day, 10, billDate)
```

  - **DateDiff**: Determine how many specified time intervals exist between two date/time values

```
DateDiff(DateInterval.Day, Now, secondDate)
```

Introduction

Visual Basic provides many date and time functions that you can use in your applications. In this section, you will learn how to use two predefined functions to perform calculations and operations involving dates and times.

Using the DateAdd function

You can use the **DateAdd** function to add or subtract a specific time interval to or from a date. You pass the date and information about the interval to the function, and the **DateAdd** function returns a **Date** value containing the date and time value, to which a specified time interval has been added or subtracted.

Parameters

The **DateAdd** function has three parameters, none of which are optional, as shown in the following table.

Parameter	Definition
Interval	**DateInterval** enumeration value or string expression representing the time interval you want to add. For information about possible settings for the **Interval** argument, see "**DateAdd** Function" in the Visual Studio .NET documentation.
Number	Floating-point expression representing the number of intervals you want to add. **Number** can be positive (to get date/time values in the future) or negative (to get date/time values in the past).
DateValue	An expression representing the date and time to which the interval is to be added.

Example using the DateAdd function

The following code uses the **DateAdd** function to calculate the due date for a bill, given the billing date. In this scenario, the due date for the bill is 20 days after the billing date. Therefore, the **Interval** is **DateInterval.Day** and the **Number** is 20.

```
billDate = #12/31/2000#
DateAdd(DateInterval.Day, 20, billDate)
```

Using the DateDiff function

You can use the **DateDiff** function to determine how many specified time intervals exist between two date/time values. For example, you might use **DateDiff** to calculate the number of days between two dates or the number of weeks between today and the end of the year.

Parameters

The **DateDiff** function has five parameters, two of which are optional. These parameters are shown in the following table.

Parameter	Definition
Interval	**DateInterval** enumeration value or string expression representing the time interval you want to use as the unit of difference between **Date1** and **Date2**. For information on possible settings for the **Interval** argument, see "**DateDiff** Function" in the Visual Studio .NET documentation.
Date1, Date2	The two date/time values you want to use in the calculation. The value of **Date1** is subtracted from the value of **Date2** to produce the difference. Neither value is changed in the calling program.
DayOfWeek (Optional)	A value chosen from the **FirstDayOfWeek** enumeration that specifies the first day of the week. **FirstDayOfWeek.Sunday** is the default value.
WeekOfYear (Optional)	A value chosen from the **FirstWeekOfYear** enumeration that specifies the first week of the year. **FirstWeekOfYear.Jan1** is the default value.

Example using the DateDiff function

This example uses the **DateDiff** function to display the number of days between a given date and the current date.

```
Dim firstDate, msg As String
Dim secondDate As Date
  ' Declare variables
firstDate = InputBox("Enter a date")
  ' Get a given date from the user
secondDate = CDate(firstDate)
msg = "Days from today: " & DateDiff(DateInterval.Day, Now, _
  secondDate)
MessageBox.Show(msg)
  ' Create a message box which uses the DateDiff function and
  ' displays the number of days between a given date and the
  ' current date
```

Note For information about other date and time functions, see the **Microsoft.VisualBasic.DateandTime** section of "Visual Basic Run-Time Library Members" in the Visual Studio .NET documentation.

How to Use String Functions

- **Extract only a certain portion of a string**
- **Return information about a string**
- **Display information in a particular format**
- **Examples:**
  - **Trim**

    ```
    NewString = Trim(MyString)
    ```
  - **Len**

    ```
    Length = Len(customerName)
    ```
  - **Left**

    ```
    Microsoft.VisualBasic.Left(customerName, 5)
    ```

Introduction

In many cases, strings require some type of manipulation, formatting, or evaluation. For example, a person's name might be typed in with the last name appearing before the first name, or a file might contain fields that are separated by commas. The Visual Basic string functions can parse and manipulate strings in applications. These functions are used to return information about a string, extract only a certain portion of a string, or display information in a particular format.

Using the Trim function

You can use the **Trim** function to eliminate leading and trailing spaces in a specified string.

Example using Trim

The following example shows how to use the **Trim** function to return a string containing a copy of a specified string with no leading and trailing spaces:

```
Dim MyString, NewString As String
' Initialize string
MyString = "  1234 Street  "
' NewString = "1234 Street"
NewString = Trim(MyString)
```

Using the Len function

You can use the **Len** function to find the number of characters in a string or the number of bytes required to store a variable.

The following code shows the function declaration for the **Len** function. The parameter *Expression* in this declaration is any valid string expression or variable name.

```
Public Shared Function Len(ByVal Expression As datatype) As _
  Integer
```

Example using Len

In the following code, the **Len** function returns the number of characters in a string:

```
Dim customerName As string
Dim length As Integer
customerName = InputBox("What is your name?")
length = Len(customerName)
```

Using the Left function

You can use the **Left** function to return a specified number of characters from the left side of a string.

The following code shows the function declaration for the **Left** function. The parameter *Str* in this declaration is the string expression from which the leftmost characters will be returned by the function. The parameter *Length* is an integer indicating how many characters to return.

```
Public Shared Function Left(ByVal Str As String, _
  ByVal Length As Integer) As String
```

- If the value of *Length* is 0, a zero-length string (" ") is returned.
- If the value of *Length* is greater than or equal to the number of characters in *Str*, the entire string is returned.
- If you use this function in a Windows Form or any class that has a **Left** property, you must call the function by using its fully qualified name: **Microsoft.VisualBasic.Left**.

Example using Left

In the following code, the **Left** function returns five characters from the left side of a string:

```
Microsoft.VisualBasic.Left(customerName, 5)
```

Example using Len and Left

In the following code, the **Len** and **Left** functions are used together to remove the file name extension (the last four characters) from a file name:

```
fileName = Left(fileName, Len(fileName) - 4)
```

Note For information about other string functions, see the **Microsoft.VisualBasic.Strings** section of "Visual Basic Run-Time Library Members" in the Visual Studio .NET documentation.

How to Use Format Functions

- **Format numbers, dates, and times according to accepted standards**
- **Display regional formats without re-coding for nationalities or regions**
- **Examples:**
  - **FormatCurrency**

```
FormatCurrency(amountOwed, , , TriState.True,TriState.True)
```

  - **FormatDateTime**

```
FormatDateTime(myDate, DateFormat.LongDate)
```

Introduction

There are a number of universally accepted formats for numbers, dates, and times. Visual Basic provides a great deal of flexibility in displaying number formats in addition to date and time formats. An added benefit is that regional formats for numbers, dates, and times are easily displayed without re-coding for each nationality or region.

In this section, you will learn how to use two predefined functions for formatting.

Using the FormatCurrency function

You can use the **FormatCurrency** function to return an expression formatted as a currency value that uses the currency symbol defined in the computer's Control Panel. For example, you might use **FormatCurrency** to format the amount owed on a bill.

Parameters

The **FormatCurrency** function has five parameters, four of which are optional. When one or more of the optional arguments are omitted, the computer's matching regional-settings values are used as the default. The parameters for the **FormatCurrency** function are shown in the following table.

Parameter	Definition
Expression	Expression that needs to be formatted.
NumDigitsAfterDecimal (Optional)	Numeric value indicating how many places are displayed to the right of the decimal. Default value is –1, which indicates that the computer's regional settings are used.
IncludeLeadingDigit (Optional)	Indicates whether a leading zero is displayed for fractional values. Settings use Tristate Enumeration to set parameter as *true*, *false*, or *use default*, for example, **TriState.True**, **TriState.False**, or **TriState.UseDefault**.

(continued)

Parameter	Definition
UseParensForNegativeNumbers (Optional)	Indicates whether to place a negative value within parentheses. Settings use Tristate Enumeration to set parameter as *true*, *false*, or *use default*, for example, **TriState.True**, **TriState.False**, or **TriState.UseDefault**.
GroupDigits (Optional)	Indicates whether numbers are grouped using the group delimiter specified in the computer's regional settings, for example, using a comma to group every three digits to the left of a decimal point. Settings use Tristate Enumeration to set parameter as *true*, *false*, or *use default*, for example, **TriState.True**, **TriState.False**, or **TriState.UseDefault**.

Example using the FormatCurrency function

The following example uses the **FormatCurrency** function to format a string representing **amountOwed**:

```
Dim amountOwed As Double = 4456.43
Dim myString As String
myString = FormatCurrency(amountOwed, , , TriState.True, _
  TriState.True)

' Returns "$4,456.43" when regional settings are set to
' English (United States)
```

Using the FormatDateTime function

You can use the **FormatDateTime** function to format an expression as a date or time. For example, you might use **FormatDateTime** to change the expression **5/21/01** into the expression **Monday, May 21, 2001**.

Parameters

The **FormatDateTime** function has two parameters, as shown in the following table.

Parameter	Definition
Expression	Expression that needs to be formatted.
NamedFormat (Optional)	Indicates which format to use. If omitted, **GeneralDate** is used.

The following table shows the possible settings for the **NamedFormat** parameter.

Constant	Description
DateFormat.GeneralDate	Display a date and/or time. If there is a date, display it as a short date. If there is a time, display it as a long time. If present, both parts are displayed.
DateFormat.LongDate	Display a date in the long date format specified in the computer's regional settings.
DateFormat.ShortDate	Display a date in the short date format specified in the computer's regional settings.
DateFormat.LongTime	Display a time in the time format specified in the computer's regional settings.
DateFormat.ShortTime	Display a time in the 24-hour format (hh:mm).

Example using the FormatDateTime function

The following example uses the **FormatDateTime** function to format the expression **5/21/01**.

```
Dim myDate As DateTime = #5/21/01#
Dim myString As String
myString = FormatDateTime(myDate, DateFormat.LongDate)
  ' Returns "Monday, May 21, 2001" when regional settings are
  ' set to English (United States)
```

Note For information about other format functions, see the **Microsoft.VisualBasic.Strings** section in "Visual Basic Run-Time Library Members" in the Visual Studio .NET documentation.

How to Use Financial Functions

- **Perform calculations and operations involving finances; for example, interest rates**
- **Examples:**
  - **Pmt**

```
payment = Pmt(0.0083, 24, -5000, 0, DueDate.BegOfPeriod)
```

  - **Rate**

```
ratePerPeriod = Rate(24, 228, -5000, 0, DueDate.BegOfPeriod, _
  0.8)*100
```

Introduction

Visual Basic provides several financial functions that you can use in your applications. In this section, you will learn how to use two predefined functions to perform calculations and operations involving money.

Using the Pmt function

You can use the **Pmt** function to calculate the payment for an annuity based on periodic, fixed payments and a fixed interest rate. An *annuity* is a series of fixed cash payments made over a period of time, such as a mortgage on a home or a payment on a car loan.

Parameters

The **Pmt** function has five parameters, two of which are optional. For all arguments, cash paid out (such as deposits to savings) is represented by negative numbers. Cash received (such as dividend checks) is represented by positive numbers. The **Pmt** function's five parameters are shown in the following table.

Parameter	Definition
Rate	Interest rate per period, expressed as a **Double**. For example, if you get a car loan at an annual percentage rate (APR) of 10 percent and make monthly payments, the rate per period is 0.1/12, or 0.0083.
NPer	Total number of payment periods in the annuity, expressed as a **Double**. For example, if you make monthly payments on a two-year car loan, your loan has a total of 24 (or 2*12) payment periods. **NPer** must be calculated using payment periods expressed in the same units as the periods used in **Rate**. For example, if **Rate** is per month, **NPer** must be per month.
PV	Present value of a series of payments to be paid in the future, expressed as a **Double**. For example, when you buy a car, the loan amount is the present value of the monthly car payments you will make.

(continued)

Parameter	Definition
FV (Optional)	Future value, or cash balance, that you want after you have made the final payment, expressed as a **Double**. If you do not specify a value, the default is 0.
Due (Optional)	When the payments are due. Either end of the period (specified as **DueDate.EndOfPeriod**) or beginning of the period (specified as **DueDate.BegOfPeriod**). If you do not specify a value, the default is **DueDate.EndOfPeriod**.

Example using the Pmt function

The following code uses the **Pmt** function to calculate the monthly payment for a 24-month loan of $5,000 at an APR of 10 percent.

```
payment = Pmt(0.0083, 24, -5000, 0, DueDate.BegOfPeriod)
```

Using the Rate function

You can use the **Rate** function to calculate the interest rate per period on an annuity.

Parameters

The **Rate** function has the same parameters as the **Pmt** function, with the following exceptions:

- It takes a **Pmt** argument instead of a **Rate** argument. **Pmt** is a required argument representing the payment to be made each period and is expressed as a **Double**.
- It takes an optional **Guess** argument. This is the value that you estimate will be returned by **Rate**, expressed as a **Double**. If you do not specify a value, the default is 0.1 (10 percent).

Example using the Rate function

The following code uses the **Rate** function to calculate the interest rate per period on a 24-month loan of $5,000 with monthly payments of $228.

```
ratePerPeriod = Rate(24, 228, -5000, 0, DueDate.BegOfPeriod, _
 0.8)*100
```

Note For information about other financial functions, see the **Microsoft.VisualBasic.Financial** section in "Visual Basic Run-Time Library Members" in the Visual Studio .NET documentation.

Practice: Examining Predefined Functions

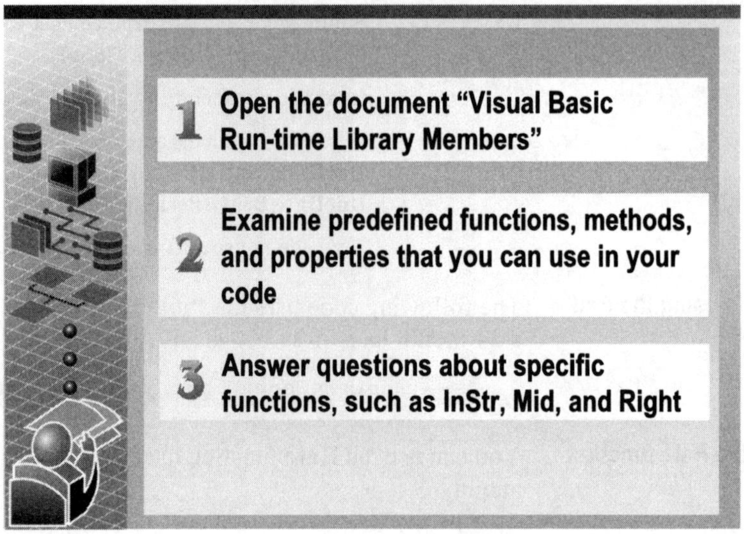

In this practice, you will use the Visual Studio documentation to learn about predefined functions and how to use them in your code.

► **Open the *Visual Basic Language Reference***

1. Click **Start**, point to **All Programs**, point to **Microsoft Visual Studio .NET**, and then click **Microsoft Visual Studio .NET Documentation**.
2. On the **Help** menu, click **Search**.
3. In the Search window, in the **Look for** box, type **run-time library members**. Verify that the search is filtered by **Visual Basic and Related,** select **Search in titles only**, and then click **Search**.
4. In the Search Results window, double-click **Visual Basic Run-Time Library Members**.
5. Without clicking any of the links on the page, examine the content of this library. Note that this page describes functions, methods, and properties that you can use in your code.

► Use the content of the library

Use the "Visual Basic Run-Time Library Members" document and the linked documents to answer the questions in the following list. To navigate back to the "Visual Basic Run-Time Library Members" document from other documents, you can use the **Web Navigate Back** button on the toolbar. ⇦

1. How is the content in the "Visual Basic Run-Time Library Members" document organized?

   ____

   ____

2. What is the purpose of the **InStr** function?

   ____

   ____

3. What value will the **InStr** function return if it cannot locate the second string?

   ____

   ____

4. What are the parameters of the **Mid** function? Note whether the parameters are required or optional.

   ____

   ____

5. Based on your answer to the previous question, what value would you expect the following code to assign to the *myAnswer* and *secondAnswer* variables?

```
Dim myString, myAnswer, secondAnswer As String
myString = "Using Mid Function"
myAnswer = Mid(myString, 7, 3)
secondAnswer = Mid(myString, 7)
```

   ____

   ____

6. In the line after the following code, add code that uses the **Right** function to return the string "Doe" from the string "John Doe".

```
Dim myString As String = "John Doe"
Dim subString As String
```

____

____

7. Is **Now** a predefined function?

____

____

8. List four topics that the *Visual Basic Language Reference* provides as links related to the reference topic that describes **Now**.

____

____

Review

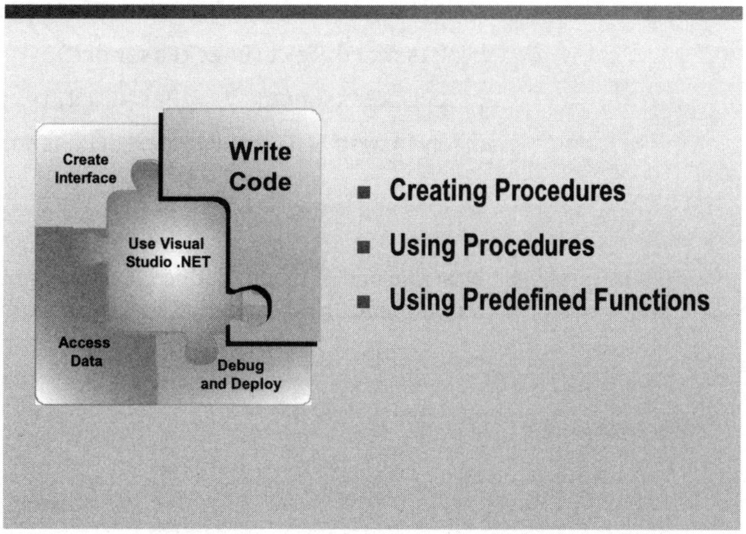

1. Explain the default values in Visual Basic .NET for the following elements:
   a. Accessibility for a procedure written in a module
   b. Passing mechanism for passing arguments to procedures
   c. Accessibility for a module

2. Given the following code, what value would the message box in the **Sub Test** procedure display? Why?

```
Sub Count(ByRef number As Integer)
   number = number + 1
End Sub

Sub Test( )
  Dim myNumber As Integer = 10
  Count(myNumber)
  MessageBox.Show(myNumber)
End Sub
```

3. Which of the following code statements calls the **CheckPassword** function and passes the contents of the **Password** text box?

   a. `myAnswer = CheckPassword.Text(Password)`

   b. `Password.Text(CheckPassword)`

   c. `CheckPassword( ) = Password.Text`

   d. `myAnswer = CheckPassword(Password.Text)`

4. Describe one of the predefined date and time functions provided by Visual Basic .NET, and give an example of when you might use it.

Lab 4.1: Creating and Using Procedures

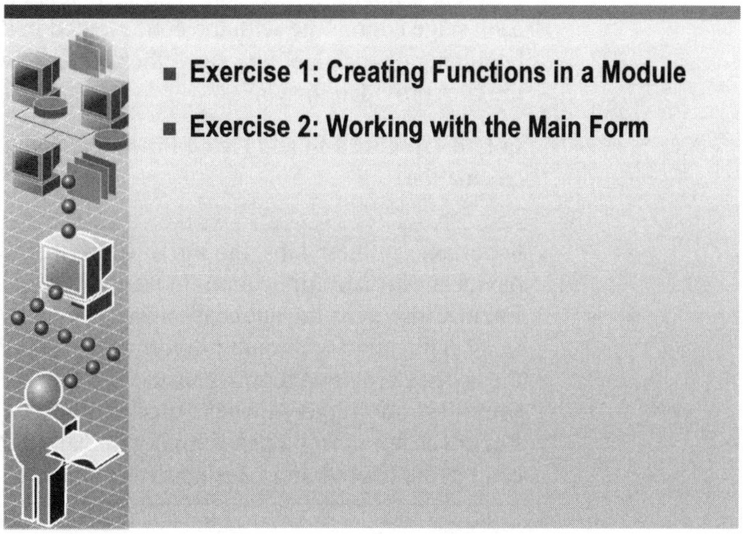

Objectives

After completing this lab, you will be able to:

- Create **Function** procedures in a module.
- Pass parameters to a procedure.
- Call procedures that are in a module.

Note This lab focuses on the concepts in this module and as a result may not comply with Microsoft security recommendations.

Prerequisites

Before working on this lab, you must:

- Have experience using variables and constants in Visual Basic .NET.
- Be familiar with creating and calling procedures in Visual Basic .NET.
- Have experience using controls and forms in Visual Basic .NET.

Scenario

In the labs for Modules 2, 4, 5, 6, and 12 of Course 2559B, *Introduction to Visual Basic .NET Programming with Microsoft .NET*, you will create a loan payment estimate application. You will create the full application in stages, each stage continuing with the code created in the previous lab. At the beginning of each lab, you can either continue with your own files or start with the files provided for you.

In Lab 4.1, Creating and Using Procedures, you will create procedures for loan calculation.

Important In these labs, the **Form.Close** method is used to close the loan payment estimate application. In an application with only one form, **Form.Close** quits the application and you do not need to call **Application.Exit**. In an application with multiple forms, you should call **Application.Exit** to quit the application. In addition, because the **Form.Closed** and **Form.Closing** events are not triggered when **Application.Exit** is called, you should call **Form.Close** for each open form before calling **Application.Exit** if you have code in the **Closed** and **Closing** events that must be executed.

Solution files

The solution files for this lab are in the *install_folder*\Labfiles\Lab041\Ex01\Solution and the *install_folder*\Labfiles\Lab041\Ex02\Solution folders.

Estimated time to complete this lab: 60 minutes

Exercise 1
Creating Functions in a Module

In this exercise, you will create utility functions in a module. These procedures will calculate the monthly payment and the total amount paid during the duration of the loan.

▶ Open the loan application project

- Open the loan application project from Lab 2.1, Creating the User Interface, in Module 2, "Working with Forms and Controls," in Course 2559B, *Introduction to Visual Basic .NET Programming with Microsoft .NET*. If you did not complete Lab 2.1, use the LoanApplication.sln project is in the *install_folder*\Labfiles\Lab041\Ex01\Starter folder.

▶ Add a new module to the project

1. On the **Project** menu, click **Add New Item**.
2. In the **Add New Item** dialog box, click **Module** in the **Templates** pane.
3. Change the module name to **Utility.vb**, and then click **Open**.
4. Declare a module-level constant to represent the number of months in a year. Your code should look as follows:

```
Private Const conversionPeriod As Integer = 12
```

▶ Calculate the monthly payment

1. Add the following public function to the module definition.

Function name	Parameters	Return value

MonthlyPayment	`loanAmount As Double,`
	`rate As Double,`
	`loanLength As Integer`
		Double

2. Complete the body of the function:

   a. Declare a **Double** variable named *interestRate* to hold the interest rate.

   b. Declare a **Double** variable named *monthRate* to hold the monthly interest rate.

   c. Declare an **Integer** variable named *numberOfPayments* to hold the number of payments.

   d. Calculate the interest rate by using the following line of code:

```
interestRate = rate / 100
```

   e. Calculate the monthly interest rate and save this value as *monthRate*, as shown in the following code:

```
monthRate = interestRate / conversionPeriod
```

f. Calculate the number of payments that will be made, and save this value as *numberOfPayments*, as shown in the following code:

```
numberOfPayments = loanLength * conversionPeriod
```

g. Use the Visual Basic **Pmt** function to calculate the monthly payment amount, and set this amount as the return value of the function, as shown in the following code:

```
MonthlyPayment = Pmt(monthRate, numberOfPayments, _
    -loanAmount)
```

► Calculate the total payment

1. Add the following public function to the module definition.

Function name	Parameters	Return value

TotalPaid	`loanAmount As Double,`
	`rate As Double,`
	`loanLength As Integer`
		Double

2. Complete the body of the function:

   a. Declare an **Integer** variable named *numberOfPayments* to hold the number of payments.

   b. Calculate the number of payments that will be made, and save this value as *numberOfPayments*, as shown in the following code:

```
numberOfPayments = loanLength * conversionPeriod
```

   c. Call the **MonthlyPayment** function to calculate the monthly payment. Multiply the value returned from the **MonthlyPayment** function by the total number of payments. Set this as the return value of the **TotalPaid** function. Your code should look as follows:

```
TotalPaid = MonthlyPayment(loanAmount, rate, _
    loanLength) * numberOfPayments
```

► Build the project

- Build the project and correct any errors.

Exercise 2
Working with the Main Form

In this exercise, you will add two buttons to the main form. These buttons will execute the code that calculates the monthly and total payments for the loan amount.

The following illustration shows the location of the new buttons that you will add to the form in the first procedure.

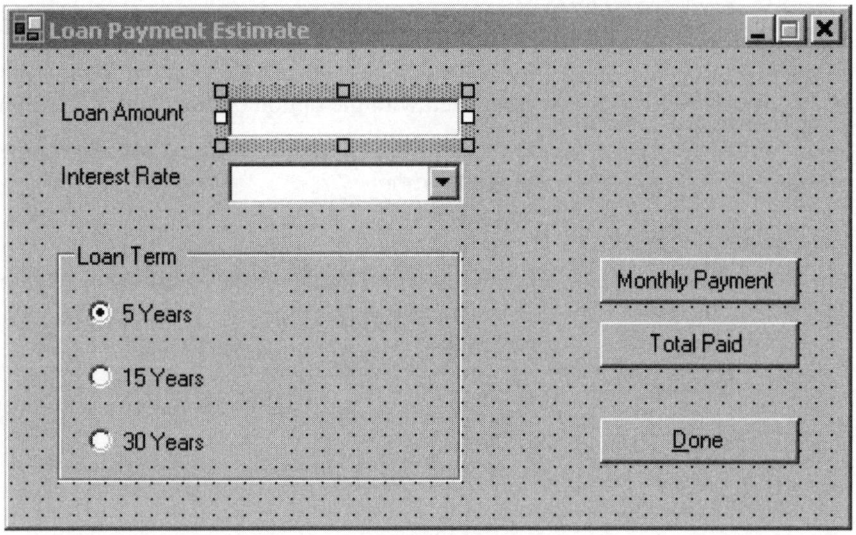

► **Add controls to the main form**

1. Open the **Main.vb** file in Design view. If you did not complete Exercise 1, use the project in the *install_folder*\Labfiles\Lab041\Ex02\Starter folder.
2. Add two **Button** controls to the form.
3. Set the properties for the controls as shown in the following table.

Current name	Property	New value
Button1	**Name**	**MonthlyPaymentButton**
	Text	**Monthly Payment**
Button2	**Name**	**TotalPaidButton**
	Text	**Total Paid**

► Store the loan term

1. In the **MainForm** class, declare a class-level private **Integer** variable named *loanTerm*. Initialize it to 5. Your code should look as follows:

```
Public Class MainForm
   Inherits System.Windows.Forms.Form

   Private loanTerm As Integer = 5

End Class
```

2. For each of the three option buttons, add a **CheckedChanged** event handler.
3. In each event handler, set the value of *loanTerm* to the appropriate value associated with the option button. Your code should look as follows:

```
Private Sub Length5RadioButton_CheckedChanged(...)
   loanTerm = 5
End Sub

Private Sub Length15RadioButton_CheckedChanged(...)
   loanTerm = 15
End Sub

Private Sub Length30RadioButton_CheckedChanged(...)
   loanTerm = 30
End Sub
```

► Add an event handler for MonthlyPaymentButton

- In the **MonthlyPaymentButton_Click** event handler, perform the following steps:

  a. Call the **MonthlyPayment** function that you created in Exercise 1.

  b. Use data type conversion function **CDbl** to convert the loan amount and loan rate data types before passing these values to the function.

  c. Use a message box to display the payment returned from the function.

  Your code should look as follows:

```
MessageBox.Show(MonthlyPayment(CDbl(LoanTextBox.Text), _
   CDbl(RateComboBox.Text), loanTerm)
```

► Add an event handler for TotalPaidButton

- In the **TotalPaidButton_Click** event handler, perform the following steps:

  a. Call the **TotalPaid** function that you created in Exercise 1.

  b. Use data type conversion function **CDbl** to convert the loan amount and loan rate data types before passing these values to the function.

  c. Use a message box to display the payment returned from the function.

  Your code should look as follows:

```
(MessageBox.Show(TotalPaid(CDbl(LoanTextBox.Text), _
   CDbl(RateComboBox.Text), loanTerm)
```

► Test the application

- Build, run, and test the application by entering loan amounts and then choosing interest rates and loan terms. Notice that the currency values are not formatted.

► Format the currency values

1. In the message box statements that call the **MonthlyPayment** function and the **TotalPaid** function, use the **FormatCurrency** function to format the monthly loan payment amount and total paid before displaying these values. Your code should now look as follows:

```
MessageBox.Show(FormatCurrency(MonthlyPayment(CDbl _
   (LoanTextBox.Text), CDbl(RateComboBox.Text), _
   loanTerm)))

MessageBox.Show(FormatCurrency(TotalPaid(CDbl _
   (LoanTextBox.Text), CDbl(RateComboBox.Text), _
   loanTerm)))
```

2. Test the application again and verify that the currency values are properly formatted.

msdn training

Module 5: Decision Structures and Loops

Contents

Microsoft

Overview

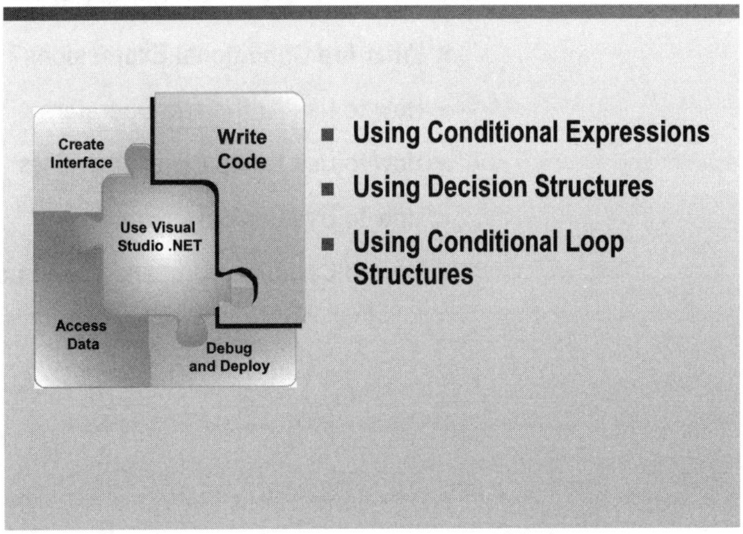

Introduction

Most computing in Microsoft® Visual Basic®–based applications is accomplished by creating procedures that are executed when a particular event occurs. For example, you write code for a **Button_Click** procedure that is executed when a user clicks the button.

You can extend this event-driven programming model by using decision structures and loops. You use decision structures to compare values and then execute a certain section of code based on the result. You use loop structures to execute a set of statements repeatedly until a condition is met. This module explains how to implement decision structures and loop structures to control program output and execution.

Objectives

After completing this module, you will be able to:

- Create formulas and conditional expressions by using arithmetic, comparison, and logical operators.
- Use **If…Then** statements to evaluate whether a condition is true or false and direct the program's flow accordingly.
- Use **Select Case** statements to test different values of the same expression and then run corresponding statements.
- Use **Do…Loop** statements to execute statements until or while a specific condition is met.
- Use **For…Next** statements to execute statements a set number of times.
- Choose the appropriate decision structure or loop based on the requirements of the application.

Lesson: Using Conditional Expressions

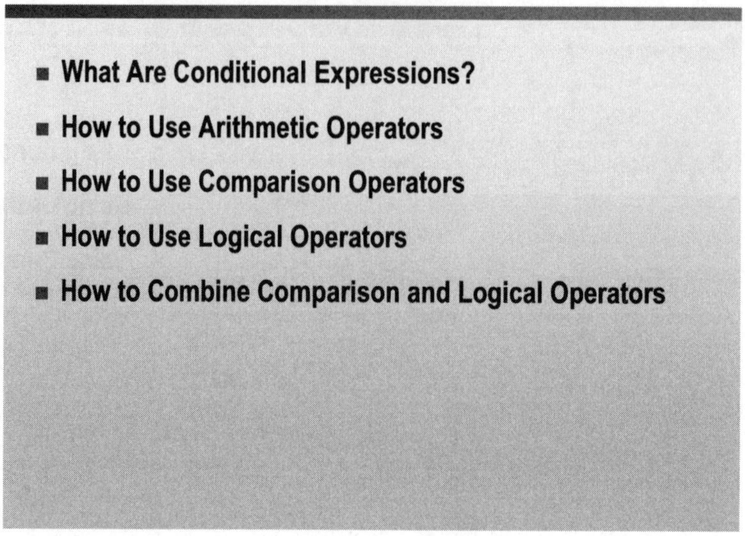

When you write applications in Microsoft Visual Basic .NET, you need to write expressions that the computer can evaluate. Expressions that evaluate to **True** or **False** are called *conditional expressions.* This lesson explains how to build conditional expressions by using basic arithmetic, comparison, and logical operators.

Lesson agenda

This lesson includes the following topics and activities:

- What Are Conditional Expressions?
- How to Use Arithmetic Operators
- How to Use Comparison Operators
- How to Use Logical Operators
- How to Combine Comparison and Logical Operators
- Practice: Evaluating Conditional Expressions

Lesson objectives

After completing this lesson, you will be able to:

- Describe mathematical, logical, and comparison operators.
- Use arithmetic, logical, and comparison operators to create formulas and evaluate conditions.

What Are Conditional Expressions?

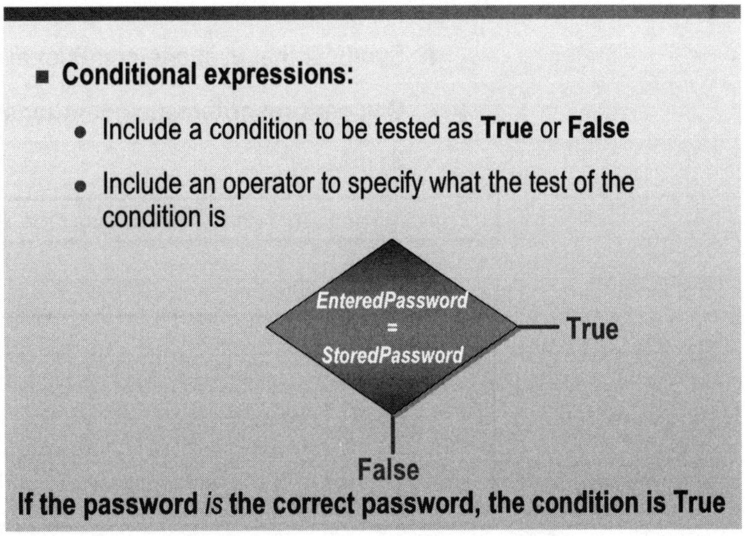

Conditional expressions allow you to develop your application to perform tasks selectively, based on values generated by your application or by values the user enters. Conditional expressions have many uses in programming, but they are commonly found in statements that control program execution.

Test conditions

Conditional expressions must return either **True** or **False**. The expression can be as simple as a variable defined as type Boolean (or a variable type that can be implicitly converted to Boolean), or it can be a combination of variables and literals joined by an operator that returns a Boolean result.

Examples of conditional expressions

The following table lists examples of conditional expressions and the values they return.

Conditional expression	Value the expression returns
5 > 2	Evaluates to **True**.
DateToday = #11/30/99#	Evaluates to **False** on the day you are reading this.
EnteredPassword = StoredPassword	Evaluates to **True** if *EnteredPassword* is the same as *StoredPassword*.
MyFirstName = "John"	Evaluates to **True** if you are named John. Evaluates to **False** if you are named anything else.

How to Use Arithmetic Operators

- Symbols that evaluate conditional expressions
- Can perform arithmetic operations
- Syntax:

```
expression1 arithmetic operator expression2
```

- Example:

```
Dim x As Integer
x = 52 * 17
x = 120 / 4
x = 67 + 34
x = 32 - 12
x = 23 ^ 3
```

Arithmetic operators are used to perform many of the familiar arithmetic operations that involve the calculation of numeric values represented by literals, variables, other expressions, function and property calls, and constants.

Arithmetic operators

The arithmetic operators that you will use most frequently in Visual Basic .NET are listed in the following table.

Arithmetic operator	Description
*	Multiplication
/	Division
+	Addition
-	Subtraction
^	Exponentiation

Syntax

The general syntax for arithmetic operators is as follows:

```
expression1 arithmetic operator expression2
```

Example of using arithmetic operators

The following example shows the most commonly used arithmetic operators:

```
Dim x As Integer
  x = 52 * 17
  x = 120 / 4
  x = 67 + 34
  x = 32 - 12
  x = 23 ^ 3
```

How to Use Comparison Operators

- **Symbols that evaluate conditional expressions and return a Boolean value**
- **Can compare numbers or strings**
- **Syntax:**

```
expression1 comparison operator expression2
```

- **Example:**

```
Dim Quantity As Integer
Dim LargeOrder As Boolean
LargeOrder = Quantity > 1000
```

A comparison operator performs an operation on two values and returns a Boolean result. Visual Basic .NET supports six comparison operators.

Boolean values

When Visual Basic .NET compares two expressions, it returns one of two values: **True** or **False**. These values are called *Boolean values*. When Boolean values are converted to numeric types, **False** becomes 0 and **True** becomes -1. Comparison operators return one of these Boolean values when they test a conditional expression.

Comparison operators

The six comparison operators you can use in Visual Basic .NET are as follows:

Operator	Description
<	Less than
<=	Less than or equal to
>	Greater than
>=	Greater than or equal to
=	Equal to
<>	Not equal to

Syntax

The general syntax for comparison operators is the following:

```
expression1 comparison operator expression2
```

Example of using comparison operators

For example, your sales order processing application will provide a discount on any order for which the quantity of the item being ordered is greater than 1000. The following code shows how you can reference this test more than once, so you decide to store the result of the test in a Boolean variable named *LargeOrder*.

```
Dim Quantity As Integer
Dim LargeOrder As Boolean
LargeOrder = Quantity > 1000
```

Example of comparing strings

When Visual Basic .NET compares the two strings, it compares each string character by character until the first mismatch occurs. One string equals another only if both strings are the same length and both contain exactly the same sequence of characters. Each character has a numerical value for comparison purposes.

String expressions	Result
"DOG" = "DOG"	**True**. Both strings are identical.
"DOG" = "dog"	**False**. Although both strings contain *dog*, one string is uppercase and the other is lowercase.

How to Use Logical Operators

- **Logical operators perform logical evaluation of expressions and return a Boolean value**
- **Syntax:**

```
expression1 logical operator expression2
```

- **Example:**

```
OrderedLastMonth And OrderDelivered
```

You use logical operators to evaluate one or more conditional expressions to return a single Boolean value of **True** or **False**. In Visual Basic .NET, you can use six logical operators.

Logical operators

The following table shows the six logical operators used in Visual Basic .NET. Notice that all the operators except **Not** work on two expressions, which are also called *operands*.

Operator	Function
And	Combines two expressions. Each expression must be **True** for the entire expression to be **True**. **True And True** = **True** **False And False** = **False** **True And False** = **False** **False And True** = **False**
Or	Combines two expressions. If either expression is **True**, the entire expression is **True**. **True Or True** = **True** **True Or False** = **True** **False Or True** = **True** **False Or False** = **False**
Not	Provides the logical negative of the input. **Not(True)** = **False** **Not(False)** = **True**
AndAlso	If the first expression in an **AndAlso** expression evaluates to **False**, the second expression is not evaluated and **False** is returned for the **AndAlso** expression.

(*continued*)

Operator	Function
OrElse	If the first expression in an **OrElse** expression evaluates to **True**, the second expression is not evaluated and **True** is returned for the **OrElse** expression.
Xor	Combines two expressions. The entire expression is considered **True** if the two expressions are not both **True** or both **False**. **True Xor True** = **False** **True Xor False** = **True** **False Xor True** = **True** **False Xor False** = **False**

Syntax

The general syntax for logical operators is as follows:

```
expression1 logical operator expression2
```

Examples of logical operators

The following table provides examples of the logical operators **And** and **Or**.

Code example	Result
OrderedLastMonth **And** OrderDelivered	Returns **True** if the last order was made during the previous month and the order was delivered. *OrderedLastMonth* and *OrderDelivered* are Boolean variables.
ChildMembership **Or** AdultMembership	Returns **True** if the member is either a child or an adult member.

How to Combine Comparison and Logical Operators

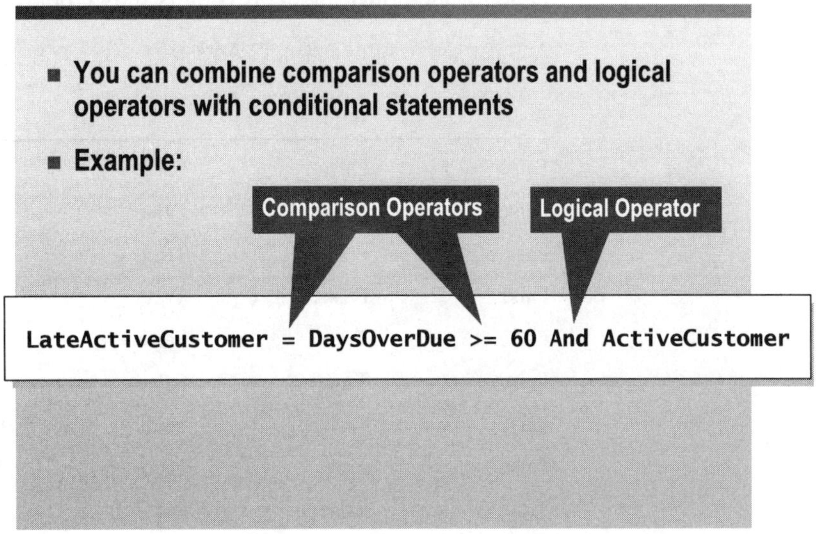

You might need to combine comparison operators and logical operators in your conditional expressions. When you combine operators, you need to know the order in which Visual Basic .NET resolves the operators. Visual Basic .NET resolves multiple operations in an expression according to a set of rules called *operator precedence.*

Example of combining operators

The following example combines comparison operators with a logical operator:

```
LateActiveCustomer = DaysOverDue >= 60 And ActiveCustomer
```

Operator precedence

When you combine comparison and logical operators in a single line of code, the comparison operators are evaluated after the arithmetic and concatenation operators but before the logical operators.

The result of the following example will be 130 because the multiplication operation has precedence:

x = 100 + 10 * 3

The logical operators are evaluated in the following order:

1. **Not**
2. **And**
3. **Or**
4. **Xor**

If you use the same comparison or logical operator multiple times in a single line of code, the operators are evaluated from left to right.

Forcing operator evaluation order

Operator precedence can often be the source of logic errors in a program. You can include parentheses to force the evaluation order. For example, the logic table for the following expression is shown below:

```
Answer = A And B Or C And D
```

A	B	C	D	Answer
False	False	False	False	False
False	False	False	True	False
False	False	True	False	False
False	False	True	True	True
False	True	False	False	False
False	True	False	True	False
False	True	True	False	False
False	True	True	True	True
True	False	False	False	False
True	False	False	True	False
True	False	True	False	False
True	False	True	True	True
True	True	False	False	True
True	True	False	True	True
True	True	True	False	True
True	True	True	True	True

Now examine the logic table when the evaluation order is changed. The answers that are different are formatted in bold:

```
Answer = A And (B Or C) And D
```

A	B	C	D	Answer
False	False	False	False	False
False	False	False	True	False
False	False	True	False	False
False	False	True	True	**False**
False	True	False	False	False
False	True	False	True	False
False	True	True	False	False
False	True	True	True	**False**
True	False	False	False	False
True	False	False	True	False
True	False	True	False	False
True	False	True	True	True
True	True	False	False	**False**
True	True	False	True	True
True	True	True	False	**False**
True	True	True	True	True

Practice: Evaluating Conditional Expressions

- Use the sample application to calculate the results of these expressions:

TestString = TestString	0 And 0
TestString = Teststring	-1 And 0
TestString < TestString	-1 And -1
Test < TestString	-1 Or -1
100 > 10	-1 Xor -1
10 < 10	-1 Xor 0
10 <= 10	0 Xor 0

► Start Microsoft Visual Studio® .NET and load the demonstration project

1. Click **Start**, point to **All Programs**, point to **Microsoft Visual Studio .NET**, and then click **Microsoft Visual Studio .NET**.
2. On the Start Page, click **Get Started**, and then click **Open Project**.

   In the **Open Project** dialog box, browse to *install_folder*\Practices\Mod05\ExpressionPractice, and then double-click **ExpressionPractice.sln**.

► Run the application

1. On the standard toolbar, click the **Start** button.
2. Calculate the answer to the expressions listed in the following table and use the application to check your calculations.

   a. To check the following expressions, pass the values as **String** values by leaving the **Treat Values As Numeric** check box clear.

Expression	Result (Write result from application below.)
TestString = TestString	
TestString = Teststring	
TestString < TestString	
Test < TestString	

b. To check the following expressions, pass the values as **Numeric** values by selecting **Treat Values As Numeric**. In the expressions that use logical operators, remember that -1 evaluates to **True** and 0 evaluates to **False**.

Expression	Result (Write result from application below.)
100 > 10	
10 < 10	
10 <= 10	
0 And 0	
-1 And 0	
-1 And -1	
-1 Or -1	
-1 Xor -1	
-1 Xor 0	
0 Xor 0	

► **Quit the application**

- Quit the application.

Lesson: Using Decision Structures

- **If...Then**

```
If Sales > 10000 Then
    Bonus = .10 * Sales
End If
```

- **If...Then...Else**

```
If Sales > 10000 Then
    Bonus = .10 * Sales
Else
    Bonus = 0
End If
```

- **If...Then...ElseIf**

```
If Sales > 10000 Then
    Bonus = .10 * Sales
ElseIf Sales > 5000 Then
    Bonus = .05 * Sales
Else
    Bonus = .02 * Sales
End If
```

- **Select Case**

```
Select Case Rank
    Case 1
        Bonus = 0
    Case 2,3
        Bonus = .05 * Sales
    Case 4 to 6
        Bonus = .10 * Sales
    Case Else
        Bonus = .15 * Sales
End Select
```

In your program, you will want to execute some sections of your code only when a particular condition is met. This is accomplished by using a decision structure. This lesson explains how to use **If...Then** and **Select Case** decision structures. You will learn how to incorporate conditional expressions in these structures.

Lesson agenda

This lesson includes the following topics and activities:

- How to Use **If...Then** Statements
- How to Use **If...Then...Else** Statements
- How to Use **If...Then...ElseIf** Statements
- How to Use **Select Case** Statements
- Guidelines for Choosing a Decision Structure

Lesson objectives

After completing this lesson, you will be able to:

- Use **If...Then** statements.
- Use **If...Then...Else** statements.
- Use **If...Then...ElseIf** statements.
- Use **Select Case** statements.
- Choose the appropriate decision structure for a given scenario.

How to Use If...Then Statements

- Use for a decision that is either True or False
- If the condition is True, the statements following the If statement are executed
- If the condition is False, the statements following the If statement are not executed

```
If Sales > 10000 Then
    Bonus = .10 * Sales
End If
```

In general, you use an **If...Then** statement when your program must evaluate whether a statement is true or false.

If...Then statements evaluate whether a condition is true or false and direct the program's flow accordingly.

Syntax

If...Then statements can use either single-line or block-form syntax. Notice that the single-line version does not require the use of an **End If** statement. The single-line **If...Then** statement is usually used to execute only one statement conditionally. In block-form **If...Then** statements, it is customary to indent the code between the **If** and the **End If** statements. This best practice is purely to aid readability.

You can use the following single-line syntax:

```
If condition Then clause
```

Alternatively, you can use the following block-form syntax:

```
If condition Then
     statements
End If
```

Example of If...Then statement

This example compares the value of an integer named *Sales* to 10,000. If *Sales* exceeds 10,000, a 10 percent bonus is computed. If the value of *Sales* does not exceed 10,000, the line of code after **Then** is ignored and the bonus is not computed.

```
If Sales > 10000 Then
  Bonus = .10 * Sales
End If
```

How to Use If...Then...Else Statements

- Use for a decision with at least two options
- Each If statement must have corresponding End If
- If the condition is True, the statements following the If statement are executed
- If the condition is False, the statements following the If statement are not executed

```
If Sales > 10000 Then
    Bonus = .10 * Sales
Else
    Bonus = 0
End If
```

Introduction

If...Then...Else statements are an extension on the **If...Then** concept. By using an **If...Then...Else** block, you can define two blocks of code and have your program execute one or the other depending upon the result of a condition. If more than one of the conditions in a conditional structure is true, only the code statements enclosed by the first true condition are executed.

Syntax

An **If...Then...Else** statement includes the following components:

- A condition that evaluates to **True** or **False**
- One or more statements that execute depending on the result of the test condition
- An **End If** statement in the case of a block

To use an **If...Then...Else** statement, use the following syntax:

```
If condition Then
  statements
Else
  statements
End If
```

Example of If...Then...Else statement

The following example compares the value of an integer named *Sales* to 10,000. If *Sales* exceeds 10,000, a 10 percent bonus is computed. If the value of *Sales* does not exceed 10,000, the bonus equals zero.

```
If Sales > 10000 Then
  Bonus = .10 * Sales
Else
  Bonus = 0
End If
```

Nesting If...Then statements

You can use as many **If...Then** statements as you need in an **If...Then** structure. Adding **If...Then** statements within an **If...Then** structure is called *nesting*.

Example of nesting

For example, the following code shows how to implement a sales bonus given to a part-time employee that is less than the corresponding bonus given to a full-time employee.

```
If Sales > 10000 Then
  If EmployeeType = "Full-Time" Then
      Bonus = .10 * Sales
  Else
      Bonus = .08 * Sales
  End If
Else
  Bonus = 0
End If
```

How to Use If...Then...ElseIf Statements

- Use to nest decision statements
- Each If statement must have corresponding End If
- ElseIf statements do not have their own End If
- ElseIf statements cannot appear after an Else
- If the condition is True, the statements following the If statement are executed

```
If Sales > 10000 Then
    Bonus = .10 * Sales
ElseIf Sales > 5000 Then
    Bonus = .05 * Sales
Else
    Bonus = .02 * Sales
End If
```

Introduction

If...Then...ElseIf statements are like **If...Then...Else** statements, except that they allow your program to choose from more than two alternatives.

Syntax

To use an **If...Then...ElseIf** statement, use the following syntax:

```
If condition Then
  statements
ElseIf condition2 Then
  statements
Else
  statements
End If
```

Example of If...Then...ElseIf statement

The following example first compares the value of an integer named *Sales* to 10,000, and then compares it to 5,000. If *Sales* exceeds 10,000, a 10 percent bonus is computed. If *Sales* exceeds 5,000, a 5 percent bonus is computed. If the value of *Sales* does not exceed 10,000 and the value of *Sales* does not exceed 5,000, a 2 percent bonus is computed.

```
If Sales > 10000 Then
  Bonus = .10 * Sales
ElseIf Sales > 5000 Then
  Bonus = .05 * Sales
Else
  Bonus = .02 * Sales
End If
```

How to Use Select Case Statements

- Select a block of code to execute based on a list of possible choices
- Use as an alternative to complex nested If...Then...Else statements
- If multiple Case statements are true, only the statements belonging to the first true Case statement are executed

```
Select Case Rank
    Case 1
          Bonus = 0
    Case 2,3
          Bonus = .05 * Sales
    Case 4 to 6
          Bonus = .10 * Sales
    Case Else
          Bonus = .15 * Sales
End Select
```

Introduction

The **Select Case** statement allows your application to execute one of several blocks of code depending upon the value of a test expression. The **Select Case** statement works like a complex nested **If…Then…Else** structure, but the **Select Case** statement is easier to maintain than a nested **If…Then…Else** structure.

Syntax

The syntax for the **Select Case** statement is as follows:

```
Select Case testexpression
  [Case expressionlist-n]
      [statements-n1] . . .
  [Case Else]
      [elsestatement]
End Select
```

Example of Select Case statement

The following example shows how to use the **Select Case** statement to evaluate the value of a bonus based on six different conditions. If none of the conditions is true, the bonus is set to 15 percent.

```
Dim Rank As Integer
 [Set Rank value]
...
Select Case Rank
  Case 1
      Bonus = 0
  Case 2, 3
      Bonus = .05 * Sales
  Case 4 to 6
      Bonus = .10 * Sales
  Case Else
      Bonus = .15 * Sales
End Select
```

Guidelines for Choosing a Decision Structure

- Use If...Then statements to control the execution of a single block of code
- Use If...Then...Else statements to control the execution of two mutually exclusive sections of code
- Use Select Case statements when you have a list of possible values

Introduction

You need to carefully choose which decision structure to use because Visual Basic .NET will exit your decision structure as soon as it encounters the first true statement. This means that any conditions after the first true statement will not be tested.

Guidelines

Use the following guidelines to determine which decision structure to use:

- Use **If...Then** statements to control the execution of a single block of code.
- Use **If...Then...Else** statements to control the execution of two mutually exclusive sections of code. More sections are possible if you use **ElseIf** statements. But if you have used multiple **ElseIf** statements, you might want to use a **Select Case** statement instead.
- Use **Select Case** statements when you have a list of possible values.

Lab 5.1: Using Decision Structures

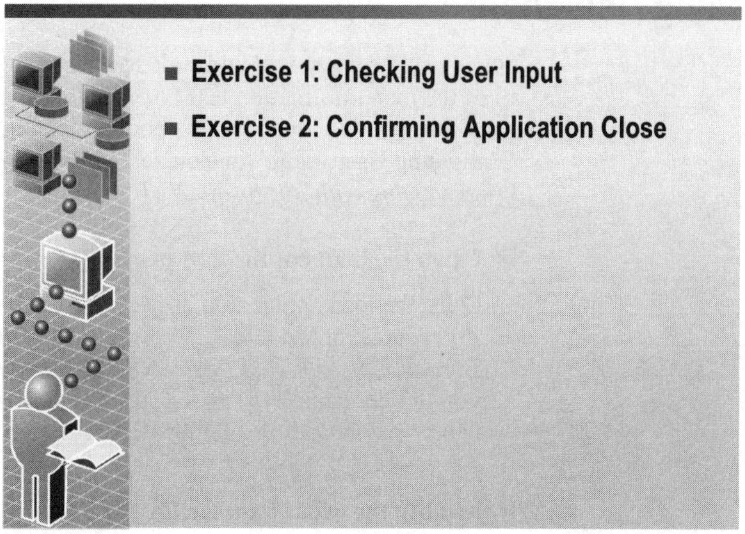

Objectives

After completing this lab, you will be able to:

- Construct conditional expressions.
- Use decision structures in a procedure.

Note This lab focuses on the concepts in this module and as a result may not comply with Microsoft security recommendations.

Prerequisites

Before working on this lab, you must have:

- Experience using variables and constants in Visual Basic .NET.
- Knowledge about procedures in Visual Basic .NET.
- Experience using controls and forms in Visual Basic .NET.

Scenario

In the labs for Modules 2, 4, 5, 6, and 12 of Course 2559B, *Introduction to Visual Basic .NET Programming with Microsoft .NET,* you will create a loan payment estimate application. You will create the full application in stages, each stage continuing with the code created in the previous lab. At the beginning of each lab, you can either continue with your own files, or start with the files provided for you.

In Lab 5.1, you will use conditional expressions and decision structures to check user input and to confirm the close of an application.

Solution files

The solution files for this lab are located in the *install_folder*\Labfiles\Lab051\Ex01\Solution folder.

Estimated time to complete this lab: 45 minutes

Exercise 1
Checking User Input

In this exercise, you will add code to verify that information has been typed into all of the loan information text boxes before calling the mortgage calculation functions. You will learn more about validating user input in Module 6, "Validating User Input," in Course 2559B, *Introduction to Visual Basic .NET Programming with Microsoft .NET.*

▶ Open the loan application project

- Open the loan application project from Lab 4.1, Creating and Using Procedures, in Module 4, "Working with Procedures," in Course 2559B, *Introduction to Visual Basic .NET Programming with Microsoft .NET.* If you did not complete Lab 4.1, use the LoanApplication.sln project in the *install_folder*\Labfiles\Lab051\Ex01\Starter folder.

▶ Modify the event handler for the MonthlyPayment button

- In the **MonthlyPaymentButton_Click** event handler, use an **If…Then…Else** statement to ensure that the user has entered the loan amount and selected an interest rate before calling the **MonthlyPayment** function. Your code should look as follows:

```
If (LoanTextBox.Text <> "" And _
   RateComboBox.Text <> "") Then

   MessageBox.Show(FormatCurrency(MonthlyPayment _
      (CDbl(LoanTextBox.Text), CDbl(RateComboBox.Text), _
      loanTerm)))
Else
   MessageBox.Show _
      ("Please enter loan amount and interest rate.", _
      "Invalid Data", MessageBoxButtons.OK, _
      MessageBoxIcon.Error)
End If
```

► Modify the event handler for the TotalPaid button

- In the **TotalPaidButton_Click event handler**, use an **If...Then...Else** statement to ensure that the user has entered the loan amount and selected the interest rate before calling the **TotalPaid** function. Your code should look as follows:

```
If (LoanTextBox.Text <> "" And _
   RateComboBox.Text <> "") Then
   MessageBox.Show(FormatCurrency(TotalPaid _
       (CDbl(LoanTextBox.Text), CDbl(RateComboBox.Text), _
       loanTerm)))
Else
   MessageBox.Show _
       ("Please enter loan amount and interest rate.", _
       "Invalid Data", MessageBoxButtons.OK, _
       MessageBoxIcon.Error)
End If
```

► Test the application

1. Run the application.
2. Click the buttons without entering any data.

   A message box should appear.
3. Type **20000** in the **Loan Amount** text box, select **10** in the **Interest Rate** box, and then click **Monthly Payment**.

   A message box displaying the amount $424.94 should appear.

Caution Do not enter non-numeric characters in either text box. If you do, the application will cause an exception. You will learn how to fix this problem in Module 6, "Validating User Input," in Course 2559B, *Introduction to Visual Basic .NET Programming with Microsoft .NET.*

Exercise 2
Confirming Application Close

In this exercise, you will prompt the user for confirmation before closing the application.

▶ **Modify the DoneButton_Click event handler**

- In the **DoneButton_Click** event handler, use a message box to prompt the user before the application is closed. If the user clicks the **OK** button in the message box, close the form (effectively closing the application since only one form exists). Otherwise, leave the application running. Your code should look as follows:

```
If (MessageBox.Show("Do you want to exit the application?", _
      "Close", MessageBoxButtons.YesNo, _
      MessageBoxIcon.Question) = DialogResult.Yes) Then
  Me.Close( )
End If
```

▶ **Test the application**

1. Run the application, and then click **Done**.
2. When presented with the message box asking if you want to quit, click **No**.

   You should be returned to the application.
3. Click **Done** again, and this time click **Yes** in the message box.

   The application should quit.

Lesson: Using Conditional Loop Structures

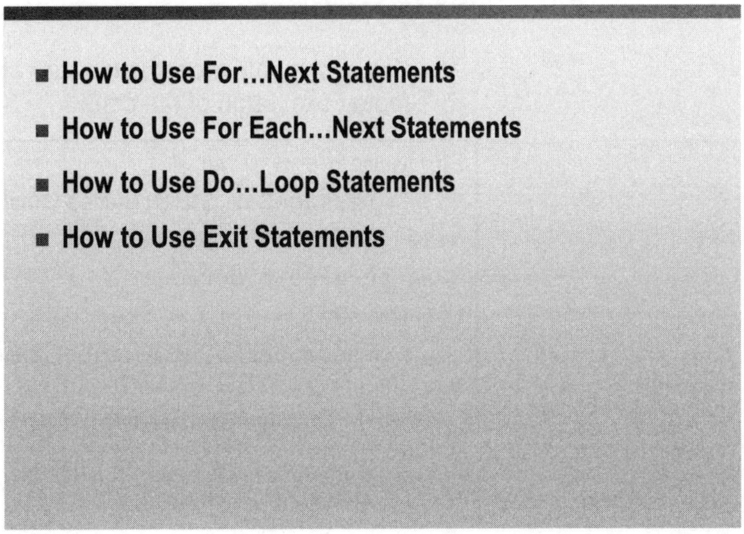

Introduction

It is likely that you will frequently need to repeat the execution of a block of code until a particular condition is met in the programs you develop. To repeat the execution of a block of code in Visual Basic .NET, you use conditional loop structures. This lesson describes how to use conditional loops to determine whether and when to execute code. This lesson also describes how to decide whether to use an **Exit** statement to exit a loop.

Lesson agenda

This lesson includes the following topics and activities:

- How to Use **For...Next** Statements
- How to Use **For Each...Next** Statements
- How to Use **Do...Loop** Statements
- How to Use **Exit** Statements
- Practice: Designing Loop Structures

Lesson objectives

After completing this lesson, you will be able to:

- Use **For...Next** statements to execute code a known number of times.
- Use **For Each...Next** statements to execute code for all the elements in a collection.
- Use **Do...Loop** statements to determine whether to execute a block of code depending upon a condition.
- Decide whether to use an **Exit** statement to immediately exit a loop.

How to Use For...Next Statements

- **Use when you know the number of times you want to repeat execution of the code**

```
For NamePos = 0 to 4
      MessageBox.Show(Names(NamePos))
Next
' In reverse order
For NamePos = 4 to 0 Step -1
      MessageBox.Show(Names(NamePos))
Next
```

Introduction

If you know the number of times a loop needs to execute, you can use a **For…Next** loop. A **For…Next** statement repeats a group of statements a specified number of times.

Syntax

A **For…Next** loop defines a loop that executes a given number of times as determined by a loop counter. The counter value in a **For…Next** loop can either increase or decrease depending on whether *step* is positive or negative.

The syntax of a **For…Next** statement is as follows:

```
For counter = start To end [Step step]
  [statements]
[Exit For]
Next [counter]
```

Example

In the following example, a **For...Next** statement is used to loop through the contents of a small array. A message box is used to display each name on the screen. The names are then displayed again, but in reverse order.

```
Dim NamePos as Integer
Dim Names(4) As String
Names(0) = "Bob"
Names(1) = "Tina"
Names(2) = "Robert"
Names(3) = "George"
Names(4) = "Greg"

For NamePos = 0 to 4
      MessageBox.Show(Names(NamePos))
Next
' In reverse order
For NamePos = 4 to 0 Step -1
      MessageBox.Show(Names(NamePos))
Next
```

Nesting For...Next statements

You can use as many **For...Next** statements as you need in a **For...Next** structure. Adding one or more **For...Next** statements within another **For...Next** statement is called *nesting*.

Consider a scenario in which you want to create multiple points with incremented X and Y coordinates for a computer game. You will then use those points to assign positions for graphics.

To create these points, you can use nested **For...Next** statements. The code in the following example creates three versions of *myPoint* with incremented X and Y values, and nine versions of *otherPoint* with incremented X and Y values.

```
Private Sub CreatePoints( )
  Dim x, y As Integer
  Dim myPoint(7) As Point
  Dim otherPoint(7) As Point
  For x = 1 To 3
      myPoint(x).X += 1
      myPoint(x).Y += 1
      MessageBox.Show(myPoint(x).ToString)

      For y = 1 To 3
          otherPoint(y).X += y + 1
          otherPoint(y).Y += y + 2
          MessageBox.Show(otherPoint(y).ToString)
      Next
  Next
End Sub
```

Note The message boxes in this code are provided as a way for you to view the values if you choose to try this code. They would not be necessary in the preceding computer game scenario.

How to Use For Each...Next Statements

- **A collection is a set of objects that are grouped together and referred to as a unit. For example:**
  - Items in a list box are part of an **Items** collection
  - Every form has a **Controls** collection that represents all the controls on that form
- **For Each ... Next statements are used to loop through elements in a collection**

```
Sub LightBlueBackground (. . .)
   Dim ThisControl As System.Windows.Forms.Control
    For Each ThisControl In ThisForm.Controls
      ThisControl.BackColor = System.Drawing.Color.LightBlue
    Next ThisControl
End Sub
```

Introduction

A **For Each...Next** statement executes a statement block for each element in a collection or an array.

Definition of collections

A *collection* is a set of objects that are grouped together and referred to as a unit.

Collections allow you to easily add, remove, and count items. By using an index number or key values, you can add items before or after other items. Collections are similar to arrays, but collections provide functionality that arrays do not have, including ease in adding, removing, and manipulating elements, and more functionality with objects.

You can create your own collections and add to them your own elements or existing elements. An element can be any data type, including objects or structures, and even other collection objects.

The Microsoft .NET Framework also provides many predefined collections. The following are some examples of predefined .NET Framework collections:

- When you add items to a **ListBox** you are using the **Items** collection. Each item you add is a member of the collection.
- Every form has a **Controls** collection that represents all the controls on that form. You can obtain a reference to a control in the collection by using its index, and loop through the members of the collection by using **For Each...Next** statements.
- Each Microsoft Excel worksheet is a part of the **Worksheet** collection of Excel. This means you can write code to loop through Excel worksheets and gather data into a new worksheet.

Syntax

The syntax for the **For Each…Next** statement is as follows:

```
For Each elementvariable In collection
      ' Statement block to be executed for each value
      '   of elementvariable
Next [elementvariable]
```

Example

In the following example, the **For Each…Next** statement is used to loop through a set of controls on a form and set the background color of every control on the form to light blue:

```
Sub LightBlueBackground (ByVal ThisForm As _
  System.Windows.Forms.Form)
   Dim ThisControl As System.Windows.Forms.Control
    For Each ThisControl In ThisForm.Controls
        ThisControl.BackColor = System.Drawing.Color.LightBlue
    Next ThisControl
End Sub
```

How to Use Do...Loop Statements

- **Do...Loop Until**
  - Runs the code in the loop and then evaluates the condition. Repeats until the condition evaluates as **True**.
- **Do Until...Loop**
  - Runs code in the loop only if the condition evaluates as **False,** and repeats until the test expression tests as **True**.
- **Do...Loop While**
  - Runs the code in the loop and then evaluates the condition. Repeats until the condition evaluates as **False**.
- **Do While...Loop**
  - Runs the code in the loop only if the condition evaluates as **True**, and repeats until the test expression tests as **False**.

Introduction

Do...Loop statements provide a way for your application to execute a block of code while a condition is true or until a condition is true. You can use **Do...Loop** statements when you know the condition that determines when execution of your code should stop.

Types of Do...Loop statements with Until keyword

When you add the **Until** keyword to a **Do...Loop** statement, you instruct your program to do something until a condition is true. In **Do...Loop** statements, an expression can be evaluated at the end of the loop or at the beginning of the loop. Looping structures that evaluate expressions at the end of a loop ensure that the code in the loop is executed at least one time. Looping structures that evaluate expressions at the beginning of a loop might be bypassed entirely, depending on the initial value of the expression.

If you want to check the condition you are testing before executing the code, and you want the code to execute until a condition is true, you can use the **Do Until...Loop** statement. This statement executes the code in the loop only if the condition evaluates as **False** and repeats until the test expression tests as **True**.

If you want to check the condition you are testing after executing the code, and you want the code to execute until a condition is true, you can use the **Do...Loop Until** statement. This statement executes and repeats execution until the expression tests as **True**.

Syntax

The **Do Until...Loop** syntax is as follows:

```
Do [Until condition]
  [statements]
[Exit Do]
Loop
```

The **Do...Loop Until** syntax is as follows:

```
Do
  [statements]
[Exit Do]
  [statements]
Loop [While condition]
```

Examples

In the following example of using **Do...Loop Until**, the code will loop until the user clicks **No** in a message box:

```
Dim LoopCount As Integer
Do
  LoopCount = LoopCount + 1
Loop Until MessageBox.Show("Loop?", "Do... Loop Until", _
  MessageBoxButtons.YesNo) = DialogResult.No
```

The following example of using **Do Until...Loop** finds all files in a directory that match a file specification. The example uses the **Dir** function to return the first file name that matches the specified path. The **Dir** function is called again to return any additional file names that match the path. When no more file names match the path the **Do Until...Loop** condition is evaluated as **True**, and the length of the string returned by **Dir** is equal to zero:

```
Dim Message As String
Dim Filespec As String
Dim Match As String

Message = "Enter a file specification."
' Get file extension
Filespec = InputBox(Message)
' Find first match
Match = Dir(Filespec)
Do Until Len(Match) = 0
    ' Display matching files
    MessageBox.Show(Match)
    ' Find next match
     Match = Dir( )
Loop
MessageBox.Show ("There are no more matching files.")
```

Using While instead of Until

You can use the **While** keyword instead of the **Until** keyword when the condition for the loop to continue is **True** instead of **False**. For example, the following two code blocks are functionally equivalent:

```
Dim EndOfLoop As Boolean
EndOfLoop = False
Do
' . . .
Loop Until EndOfLoop

Dim EndOfLoop As Boolean
EndOfLoop = False
Do
' . . .
Loop While Not(EndOfLoop)
```

How to Use Exit Statements

- **Use to leave Do loops or For loops early when a condition is met**

```
Do Until y=-1
    If x < 0 Then Exit Do
       x = Sqrt (x)
    If y > 0 Then Exit Do
       y = y + 3
    If z = 0 Then Exit Do
       z = x / y
Loop
```

Introduction

It is possible that during a loop structure you might want to leave the loop early if a particular condition is met. You can use **Exit** statements to exit a **Do** loop or **For** loop. The **Exit** statement allows you to exit directly from any decision structure, loop, or procedure. It immediately transfers execution to the statement following the last control statement.

Syntax

The syntax for the using the **Exit** statement in a **Do...Loop** statement is as follows:

```
Exit Do
```

The syntax for the using the **Exit** statement in a **For...Next** statement is as follows:

```
Exit For
```

Example

The following example shows multiple occurrences of the **Exit** statement inside a **Do...Loop** statement:

```
Do Until y = -1
  If x < 0 Then Exit Do
  x = Sqrt (x)
  If y > 0 Then Exit Do
  y = y + 3
  If z = 0 Then Exit Do
  z = x / y
Loop
```

Practice: Designing Loop Structures

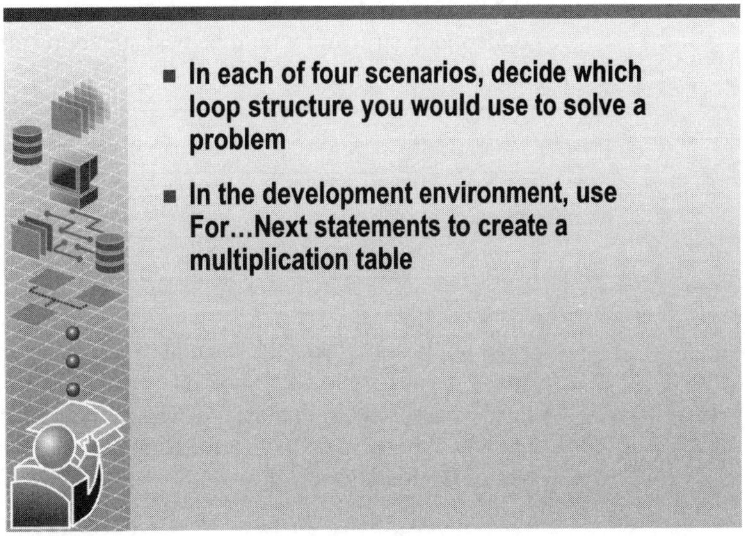

In this practice, you will decide which loop structures are appropriate for four different programming scenarios. You will then use **For...Next** statements to create a multiplication table.

Scenario 1

You have created a cash register application that stores the price of each item purchased in an array. When the user has finished purchasing items, the code needs to search the array and calculate the total of all items purchased. The size of the array will vary with the number of items purchased.

Which loop structure would be best suited to solve this problem?

____

____

____

Scenario 2

Your application contains the mathematical equation $y = x^3+3$. The application needs to calculate the result of this equation for values of x in the range -100 to 100 in steps of 10.

Which loop structure would be best suited to solve this problem?

Scenario 3

Your application takes the content of a log file on a computer's hard disk and displays this data in a text box on a form. The program sequentially reads the lines of data held in the log file. The number of lines of data held in the file is unknown, but you do have a function called **EOF** that returns **True** when the end of the file is reached.

Which loop structure would be best suited to solve this problem?

Scenario 4

Your application uses a **City** object to determine sales discount values on various retail items, depending on the city from which the items are purchased. You want to display the discounts associated with each city in a list box.

Which loop structure would be best suited to solve this problem?

____

____

____

____

Use a For...Next statement

► Use a For…Next statement

In this section of the practice, you will open a new project and use a **For...Next** statement to create a multiplication table on a form.

1. Open a new project in Visual Basic .NET. Use the Microsoft Windows® Application template. Set the project name to **MultiplicationTable** and the location to *install_folder*\Practices\Mod05\MultiplicationTable.
2. Add a label to the form, and resize the label so that the width is **255** and the height is **190**. Center the label on the form.
3. Set the **Font** property of the label to **Courier New**.
4. Create an event handler for the **Form1_Load** event, and add the following code:

```
Dim outerLoop, innerLoop As Integer
Dim result As String

   ' Outer For...Next loop
   For outerLoop = 1 To 10
      ' Inner For...Next loop
      For innerLoop = 1 To 10
         result = result & " " & (outerLoop * innerLoop)
      Next innerLoop
      result = result & vbCrLf
   Next outerLoop

' Display result in the label

Label1.Text = result
```

5. Answer the following questions before running the application:

   a. Which three lines of code define the inner loop?

   b. What will the values of *outerLoop* and *innerLoop* be the second time the inner loop runs?

   c. What do you expect the result in the label to look like after the code runs?

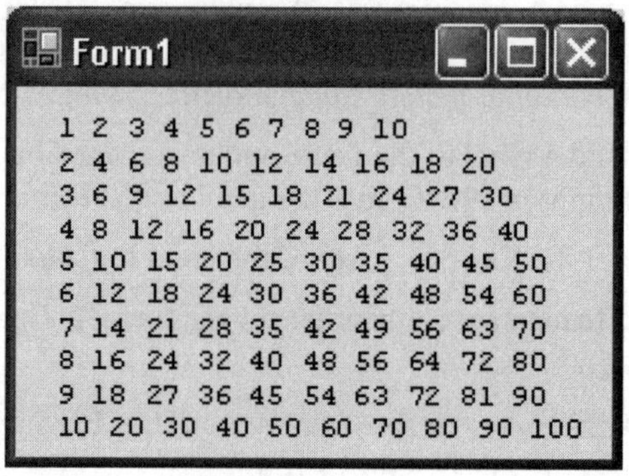

6. Run the application to verify your answer to question 5.c.

   A multiplication table will appear in the label on the form.

Solution files

The solution files for this practice are in the *install_folder*\Practices\Mod05\MultiplicationTable\Solution folder.

Review

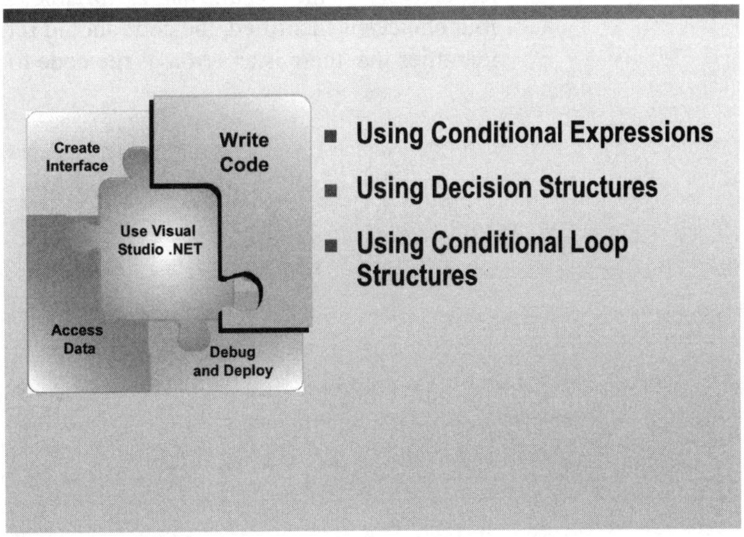

1. What is the result of the following conditional expression?

   "TinyDog" > "BigCat"

2. Write a decision statement to display a message box warning that the CPU is overheating if the CPU temperature is 125 degrees or higher.

3. What structure would be best for looping through a known number of questions?

4. What value should *x* contain for the following loop to end?

```
Do While x = True
   MessageBox.Show("Hello")
   ' Code to change the value of x
Loop
```

5. The *OceanName* variable will contain either Atlantic, Pacific, Indian, or Arctic. Your code needs to assign a number ranging from 1 to 4, respectively, to the *OceanNumber* variable. If a name that is not one of these four choices is identified, the code should return a message box that identifies that there is an error. Write code to perform this functionality.

msdn® training

Module 6: Validating User Input

Contents

Microsoft®

Overview

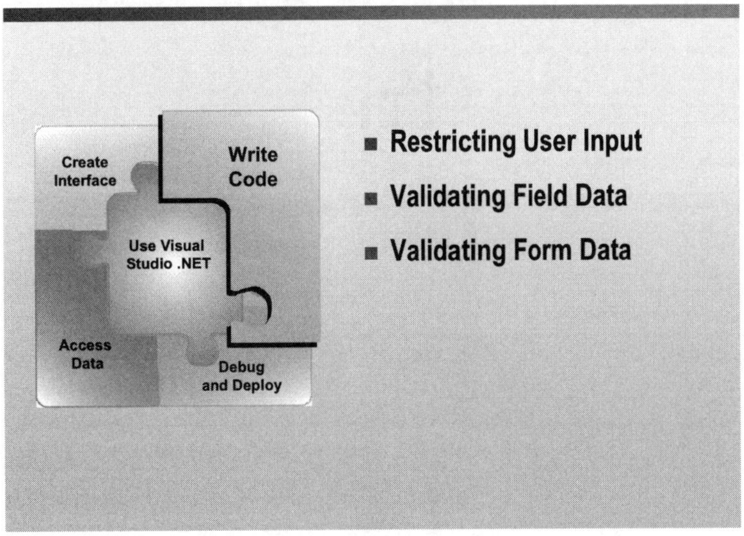

Introduction

In this module, you will learn how to validate user input at both the field level and the form level in the applications you create in Microsoft® Visual Basic® .NET. You will learn how to handle invalid input by providing error messages and guiding users through the process of finding and fixing errors. You will use control properties and methods to restrict and validate data entry.

Objectives

After completing this module, you will be able to:

- Restrict the type of data that can be entered in a field.
- Test user input at the field level to determine if it is valid, and display messages to help the user correct invalid data.
- Set control properties to specify the order of data entry, the type of data to enter, and how to display the data when the application is run.
- Validate user input at the form level, and guide users through the process of finding and fixing errors.

Multimedia: Validating User Input

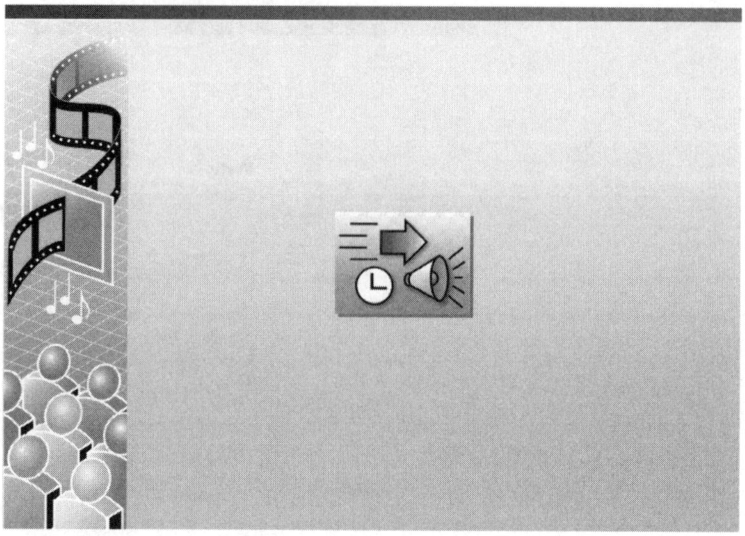

Introduction

This animation presents a scenario in which input validation is required and explains how to implement field-level and form-level validation.

Animation script

In most applications that you create, users enter information that needs to be processed or manipulated in some way. As the developer, you can write code that validates user input to ensure that your application will run correctly.

Suppose you have an order entry form that customers use to order items from an online catalog. Some fields on the order entry form are required, some fields are optional, and the Quantity field can only contain numbers. For this form, you need to provide two levels of input validation: field-level validation and form-level validation.

To provide field-level validation for the Quantity field, you write code behind the **TextBox** control to validate the user input and display an appropriate message to help the user enter valid data. If the user enters invalid data in the Quantity field, a message appears to help the user fix the error. You can call the validation code when the user attempts to move away from the field, as shown in this example.

To provide form-level validation, you write code behind the **Review Order** button to verify that all required fields have been filled in and display an appropriate message if data is missing.

The validation code behind this form might:

- Verify that the Item Number and Quantity fields are filled in.
- Verify that the Quantity field is numeric.
- Verify that a color has been selected in the **Color** combo box.
- Offer the user a chance to cancel the order.

If the user does not enter data in a required field and clicks **Review Order**, a message will appear to remind the user to provide the required data. After the user enters valid data in all required fields and clicks **Review Order**, the user can move to the next step in the order process.

When creating the user interface for your applications, you can write code to validate user input and display messages to help users correct invalid data.

Lesson: Restricting User Input

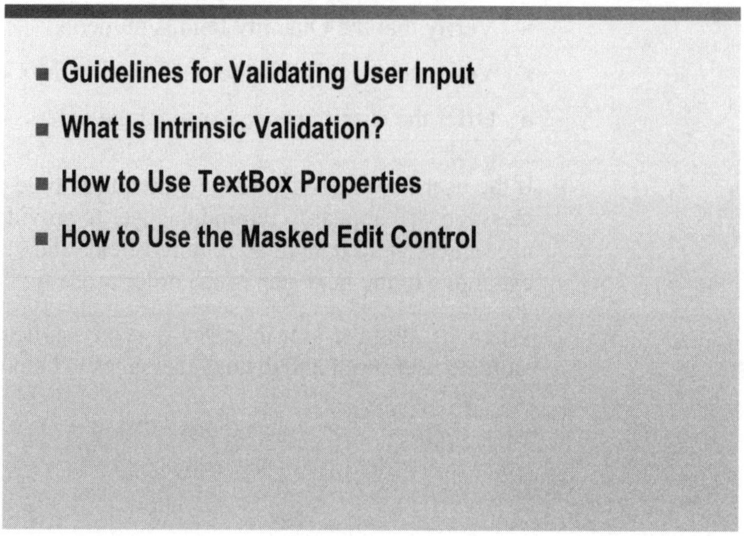

Introduction

This lesson describes how to restrict user input, set format parameters for displaying output, and display error messages that explain how to correct invalid data entries.

Lesson agenda

This lesson includes the following topics:

- Guidelines for Validating User Input
- What Is Intrinsic Validation?
- How to Use **TextBox** Properties
- How to Use the **Masked Edit** Control
- Practice: Using the **Masked Edit** Control

Lesson objectives

After completing this lesson, you will be able to:

- Use intrinsic validation for standard controls.
- Use the validation properties of the **TextBox** control.
- Restrict user input and format data by using edit masks in a **Masked Edit** control.
- Filter out mask characters in a **Masked Edit** control to prepare data for entry into a database.
- Control the order in which the user enters data in the fields on a form.

Guidelines for Validating User Input

Guidelines

- **Prevent users from entering invalid data whenever possible**
- **Guide users through the process of entering valid data**
- **Allow users flexibility in how and when they enter data**
- **Consider validation requirements when designing your application**
- **Place validation code in the appropriate location, depending on the requirements of your application**

Introduction

In most applications that you create, users will need to enter information that the application will process. For example, you could create an application that calculates the cost of goods sold based on income and expense values that a user enters. It is important for users to enter valid data so that the application will run correctly.

Guidelines

When writing your applications, consider the following guidelines for validating user input:

- Prevent users from entering invalid data whenever possible.

  One of the simplest ways to provide input validation is to restrict user entries to only valid data. For example, validation can be accomplished with the use of a control that does not allow users to enter anything except the required data. The **DateTimePicker**, for example, only allows users to enter dates.

- Guide users through the process of entering valid data.

  To avoid frustrating users with too many error messages, it is recommended that you design your validation code to run near the end of the form completion process. Write your validation code so that if an error is encountered, the user is directed to the field that holds the error and a message is displayed to help the user fix the error.

- Allow users flexibility in how and when they enter data.

  A well-written application guides users through correct data entry whenever possible, while still allowing them to interact with the fields on the form in the order they want, except when data in one field is absolutely required for another field.

- Consider validation requirements when designing your application.

  For each type of validation that you implement, you need to consider what validation technique to use. Some of the most common validation tasks include verifying that:

  - The data a user enters is numeric.
  - A number falls within a certain range of values.
  - A date is valid or falls within a range of dates.
  - All required fields have been filled in.
  - Credit card numbers or passwords match entries in a database.
  - A format or combination of conditions is present, such as the following part number format: HW-999-5678.

- Place validation code in the appropriate location.

  Generally, you will place your validation code near the end of the form completion process, but in some cases you might need to provide validation field by field. For example, if data is required in one field on an order form before data in other fields can be validated, you must validate that field when the data is entered.

Note It is also possible to validate data at the keystroke level. For more information about validating keystrokes, search for **KeyPress**, **KeyDown**, and **KeyUp** events in the Microsoft Visual Studio® .NET documentation.

What Is Intrinsic Validation?

- **Definition: The built-in control properties and methods that you can use to restrict and validate user input**
- **Common controls that provide intrinsic validation:**

Control	Validation technique
RadioButton	Restricts entry to On or Off
CheckBox	Restricts entry to Checked or Unchecked
CheckedListBox	Provides a list of valid entries
ListBox	Provides a list of valid entries (graphics and text)
DateTimePicker	Restricts entry to dates or times
MonthCalendar	Restricts entry to a range of dates
TextBox	Set properties to restrict or modify data entry

Introduction

For most typical data entry requirements, Visual Basic .NET controls exist that automatically restrict the data that users can enter. You can save time and effort if you become familiar with the properties and methods of these controls.

Definition

Intrinsic validation refers to a control's built-in properties and methods that you can use to restrict and validate user input. Most controls provide some form of intrinsic validation. For example, the **DateTimePicker** control allows the user to select only times and dates.

Controls with intrinsic validation properties

Some of the common controls that provide intrinsic validation are described in the following table.

Use this control...	For this type of data...	Intrinsic validation technique
DateTimePicker	Dates and times	Restricts entries to dates or times
MonthCalendar	Range of dates	Restricts entries to a range of dates
CheckedListBox **ComboBox** **DomainUpDown** **NumericUpDown**	Items in a list	Provides a list of valid entries
ListBox **ListView**	Items in a list with graphics and text	Provides a list of valid entries
CheckedListBox **CheckBox** **RadioButton** **TrackBar**	Range of values	Restricts values to a list, range, or predefined scale

(continued)

Use this control...	For this type of data...	Intrinsic validation technique
TextBox **RichTextBox** **LinkLabel**	Special text requirements	Restricts and modifies data entry in text boxes and labels
OpenFileDialog **SaveFileDialog** **PrintDialog**	Dialog boxes	Restricts entries to valid path names and file names

Example of DateTimePicker

You can use the **DateTimePicker** control to allow users to select a date. The **MinDate** and **MaxDate** properties allow you to define a range of acceptable dates. The following example shows how to access the date and the day of the week after the user has selected a date by using the control.

```
Private Sub Button1_Click(...)
  MessageBox.Show("The selected date is " & _
      DateTimePicker1.Value)
  MessageBox.Show("The day of the week is " & _
      DateTimePicker1.Value.DayOfWeek.ToString)
End Sub
```

Example of TrackBar

You can use the **TrackBar** control to allow users to set values on a scale by moving a pointer along a visual scale. Using this control allows users to avoid needing to choose a precise numerical value. The following example displays the value of a **TrackBar** control in a **MessageBox**. **Button** and **TrackBar** controls have been placed on the form.

```
Private Sub Button1_Click(...)
    MessageBox.Show(TrackBar1.Value)
End Sub
```

Example of using dialog boxes

You can use the **OpenFileDialog**, **SaveFileDialog**, and **PrintDialog** controls to restrict user input to valid path names and file names.

The following example creates an **OpenFileDialog**, sets several properties, and displays the dialog box by using the **ShowDialog** method. When run, the code first shows the user files in the C:\Company\Project Data directory; however, the user can navigate as usual in the dialog box. Assume that the directory shown exists, that the form has a **Button** control on it, and that the **System.IO** namespace has been added to the form. (The **System.IO** namespace allows reading of and writing to the stream object and files.)

```
Protected Sub Button1_Click(ByVal sender As Object, _
  ByVal e As System.EventArgs) Handles Button1.Click
  Dim myStream As Stream
  Dim openFileDialog1 As New OpenFileDialog( )

  openFileDialog1.InitialDirectory = _
     "c:\Company\Project Data"
  openFileDialog1.Filter = "txt files (*.txt)|*.txt" & _
     "|All files (*.*)|*.*"
  openFileDialog1.FilterIndex = 2
  openFileDialog1.RestoreDirectory = True

  If openFileDialog1.ShowDialog( ) = DialogResult.OK Then
     myStream = openFileDialog1.OpenFile( )
     If Not(myStream Is Nothing) Then
         ' Insert code to read the stream here
         myStream.Close( )
     End If
  End If
End Sub
```

How to Use TextBox Properties

- You can use the following properties to restrict or modify user input for TextBox controls:

Control	Validation technique
PasswordChar	Hides or masks characters entered into a text box
MaxLength	Sets the maximum number of characters that can be entered into a text box
ReadOnly	Provides a predetermined valid answer
CharacterCasing	Sets all characters in a text box to uppercase or lowercase

Introduction

You can use the intrinsic validation properties of the **TextBox** control to validate and restrict user input in text boxes. For example, you can mask or hide the characters entered in a text box or specify a maximum number of characters.

Validation properties of the TextBox control

You can set the following validation properties at design time in a **TextBox** control to restrict or validate user input:

- **PasswordChar**

  The **PasswordChar** property allows you to hide (or *mask*) characters that are entered into a text box. For example, if you set the **PasswordChar** property to asterisk (*), the user will only see asterisk characters in the text box. This technique is often used to hide passwords on logon dialog boxes.

  Although any character can be used, most Microsoft Windows®–based applications use the asterisk (*) character. The **PasswordChar** property does not affect the **Text** property; the **Text** property contains exactly what the developer types in the Properties window or sets in code.

- **MaxLength**

  The **MaxLength** property can be used to set a maximum number of characters that can be entered into a text box. The system beeps when the user tries to type more characters than the number specified in the **MaxLength** property.

- **ReadOnly**

  You can restrict all data entry in a **TextBox** control by setting the **ReadOnly** property to **True**. When this property is set to **True**, users can view the text in the text box, but they cannot edit the text.

- **CharacterCasing**

  You can use the **CharacterCasing** property to change the case of characters as required by your application. For example, you can change the case of all characters entered in a **TextBox** control used for password entry to uppercase or lowercase in order to enforce a policy for passwords.

Setting intrinsic validation properties

After you add a **TextBox** control to a form, you can set its validation properties at design time.

► **To set the TextBox control properties at design time**

- In the Properties window for the **TextBox** control, locate the desired validation properties and set their values.

Setting tab order

In Visual Basic .NET, you can set the tab order of controls visually.

► **To set the tab order of a control**

1. On the **View** menu, click **Tab Order**.

   This enables you to view the tab order of the form. A number representing the **TabIndex** property appears in the upper left corner of each control.

2. Click the controls sequentially to establish the correct tab order.

   You can set a control's position within the tab order to any value greater than or equal to zero.

3. When you finish setting the tab order, click **Tab Order** on the **View** menu to leave tab order mode.

Note Controls that cannot receive focus, in addition to disabled and invisible controls, do not have a **TabIndex** property and are not included in the tab order. When the user presses the TAB key, these controls are skipped.

How to Use the Masked Edit Control

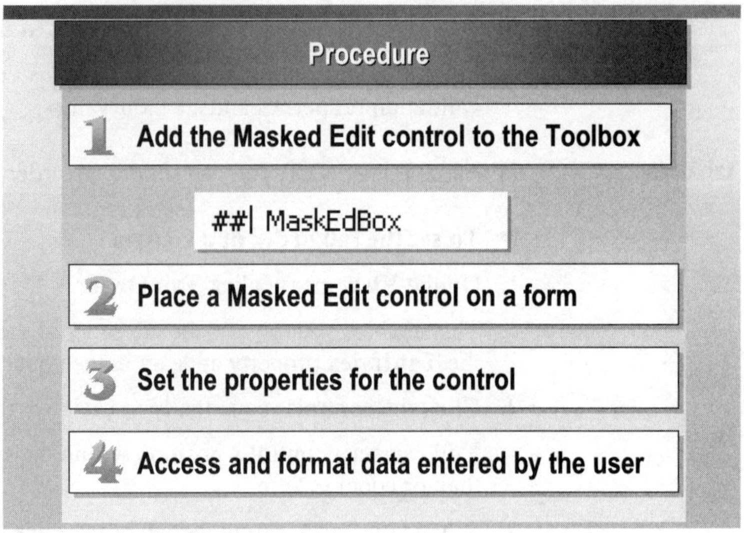

Introduction

You can use the **Masked Edit** control to ensure that users enter valid data and to format data output as required by your application. This control provides visual cues about the type of data being entered or displayed. For example, if the mask contains a # symbol, the user can only enter a number in that character position.

To use the **Masked Edit** control, you must perform the following steps:

1. Add the **Masked Edit** control to the Toolbox.
2. Place a **Masked Edit** control on a form.
3. Set the properties for the **Masked Edit** control.
4. Access and format the data entered by the user.

Adding the Masked Edit control to the Toolbox

► **To add the Masked Edit control to the Toolbox**

1. Open Visual Studio .NET.
2. On the **Tools** menu, click **Customize Toolbox**.

   The **Customize Toolbox** dialog box appears.
3. On the **COM Components** tab of the **Customize Toolbox** dialog box, check **Microsoft Masked Edit Control, version 6.0**, and then click **OK**.

   The **Masked Edit** control will appear at the bottom of the currently active tab in the Toolbox.

Adding a Masked Edit control to a form

The **Masked Edit** control generally behaves as a standard text box control with enhanced properties for masking input and formatting output. You can add the **Masked Edit** control to a form in the same way you add any other Toolbox control.

Setting properties

The properties that you can set to implement the functionality of the **Masked Edit** control include the following:

- **Mask** property

  You can define input masks at both design time and run time. The control can distinguish between numeric and alphabetical characters for validation, but it cannot check for valid content, such as the correct month or time of day.

  Some of the common characters you can use in an input mask are shown in the following table.

Character	Description
#	Digit placeholder (entry required).
9	Digit placeholder (entry optional).
?	Alphabetical character placeholder: a-z or A-Z (entry optional).
A	Alphanumeric character placeholder (entry required).
a	Alphanumeric character placeholder (entry optional).
\	Used in input mask to indicate that a literal follows. For example, to display a space in a mask, you would type a space after the \ character.

  The following are examples of input masks that you might want to use at design time.

Mask	Description
#####-9999	Nine-digit postal code. Example: 98765-1234, where the last four digits are optional.
(###)AAA-AAAA	Phone number with area code. Example: (123)555-0100, where the last seven characters are allowed in alphabetical or numeric characters and all are required.

  Note If you are writing an application that will be used internationally, be careful not to use mask formats that are specific to a certain country or geographic region, such as the U.S. postal code example in the preceding table.

- **TabIndex** property

  You use this property to set the order in which users enter data in multiple **Masked Edit** controls. A tab index can consist of any valid integer greater than or equal to zero. Lower numbers are earlier in the tab order.

- **Format** property

  The **Format** property defines the format you want to use for displaying and printing the contents of a control, such as numbers, dates, times, and text. You can choose from several standard formats in the Properties window for the **Masked Edit** control, or you can create your own custom format.

- **FormattedText** property

  The **FormattedText** property returns the data that the user has typed, along with the literal characters specified for the mask. This property is not available at design time and is read-only at run time.

- **ClipText** property

  The **ClipText** property returns the text in the **Masked Edit** control, excluding literal characters in the input mask. This is particularly important when implementing a **Masked Edit** control with a database. This property is not available at design time and is read-only at run time.

Example

The following code shows how to access the data entered by the user in a **Masked Edit** control and display it in both formatted and unformatted mode. A **Masked Edit** control named AxMaskEdBox1 has been placed on the form.

```
MessageBox.Show(AxMaskEdBox1.FormattedText)
MessageBox.Show(AxMaskEdBox1.ClipText)
```

Note "Ax" is used in naming to denote ActiveX® controls.

Practice: Using the Masked Edit Control

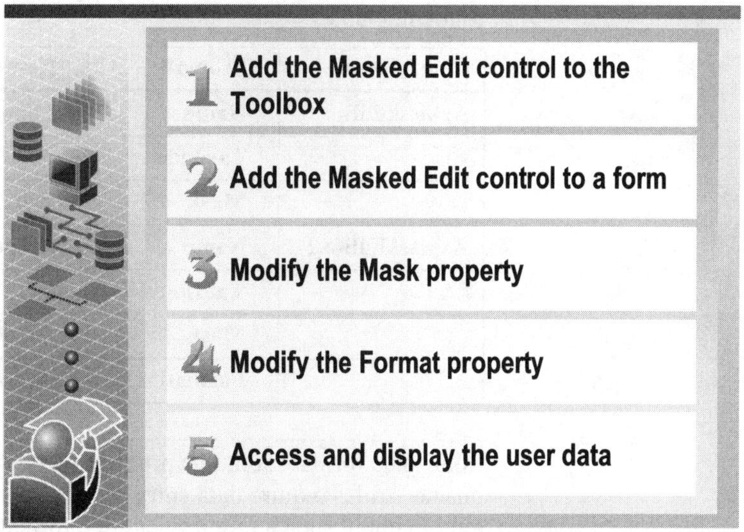

Introduction

In this practice, you will open an existing project and add two **Masked Edit** controls to a form. You will modify the mask properties to allow a user to enter a phone number in one control and a currency amount in the other control. You will then write code to access the data entered by the user in the **Masked Edit** controls and to display it in both formatted and unformatted mode.

Instructions

► **Open the starter code for the practice**

1. Open the MaskedEdit.sln file, which is in the *install_folder*\Practices\Mod06\MaskedEdit\Starter folder.
2. Notice that there are already two buttons on Form1.

► **Add the Masked Edit control to the Toolbox**

1. Ensure that the **Windows Forms** tab is selected on the Toolbox.
2. On **Tools** menu, click **Customize Toolbox**.
3. On the **COM Components** tab, check **Microsoft Masked Edit Control, version 6.0**, and then click **OK**.

   The **Masked Edit** control is added to the **Windows Forms** tab of the Toolbox, as shown in the following illustration:

► **Add two Masked Edit controls to Form1**

- Place two **MaskEdBox** controls on the form, one to the left of each existing button. Size the controls so that they are wide enough to contain a phone number (U.S. format).

► **Set the properties of the Masked Edit controls**

- In the Properties window, set the properties for the controls as shown in the following table.

Control name	Property	New value
AxMaskEdBox1	**Name**	**PhoneAxMaskedEdit**
	TabIndex	**0**
	Mask	**(###)AAA-AAAA**
AxMaskEdBox2	**Name**	**AmountAxMaskedEdit**
	TabIndex	**1**
	Mask	`$#,##0.00`
	Format	`$#,##0.00;($#,##0.00)`

Note The format set in this procedure, $#,##0.00, is appropriate when business rules require data entry rounded off to the nearest ten. For data entry without such a requirement, the format would be $##,###.##.

► **Display data entered in the Masked Edit controls**

1. In the **Button1_Click** event handler, add the following code to display the phone number the user enters, both as formatted and unformatted text:

```
MessageBox.Show(PhoneAxMaskedEdit.FormattedText)
MessageBox.Show(PhoneAxMaskedEdit.ClipText)
```

2. In the **Button2_Click** event handler, add the following code to display the currency amount the user enters, both as formatted and unformatted text:

```
MessageBox.Show(AmountAxMaskedEdit.FormattedText)
MessageBox.Show(AmountAxMaskedEdit.ClipText)
```

► **Test your work**

1. Run the application.
2. Type data into the **Phone Number** box. To see how the **Masked Edit** control works, try to type alphabetical characters into the first three placeholders in the mask.
3. Type invalid data into the **Amount** box, and then type numeric data into the **Amount** field.
4. Click **Button1** and notice the difference between the data displayed with the **FormattedText** property and the data displayed with the **ClipText** property.
5. Click **Button2** and examine the data that appears.
6. Quit Visual Studio .NET.

Solution files

The solution files for this practice are located in the *install_folder*\Practices\Mod06\MaskedEdit\Solution folder.

Lesson: Validating Field Data

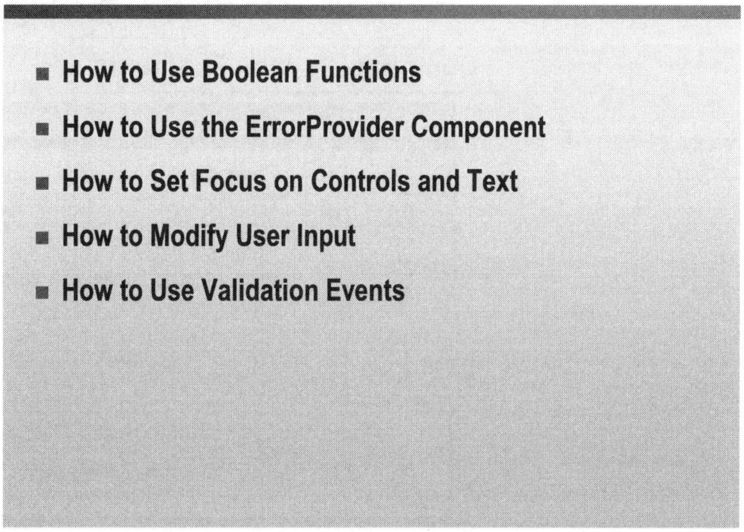

Introduction

In many cases, you will want to validate data as the user enters data in each field on a form. In this lesson, you will learn how to validate data in fields and provide messages that help the user to correct invalid data entries.

Lesson agenda

This lesson includes the following topics and activities:

- How to Use Boolean Functions
- How to Use the **ErrorProvider** Component
- How to Set Focus on Controls and Text
- How to Modify User Input
- How to Use Validation Events
- Practice: Validating Field Data

Lesson objectives

After completing this lesson, you will be able to:

- Use Boolean functions such as **IsNumeric** to validate user input.
- Use the **ErrorProvider** component to provide validation feedback for each control on a form.
- Set focus on a specific control or text so that a user can correct invalid data.
- Modify user input to prepare it for display or entry into a database.
- Use the **Validating** and **Validated** events to set field-level validation.

How to Use Boolean Functions

Common Boolean Functions

Function	Description
IsNumeric	Returns a Boolean value indicating whether an expression is recognized as a number
IsDate	Returns a Boolean value indicating whether an expression evaluates to a valid date

Example

```
If IsNumeric(TextBox1.Text) Then
  MessageBox.Show("The text box contains a number.")
End If
```

Introduction

Sometimes you need to test a variable to determine what type of data it holds and then take action based on the results. For example, you can use a Boolean function to test the data a user enters in a date field to determine whether it is a date or a string that can be converted to date.

Definition

A *Boolean function* evaluates an expression based on a given condition and returns a value of **True** or **False**.

Common Boolean functions

Visual Basic .NET provides many Boolean functions. Some of the most common functions are listed on the preceding illustration. Other Boolean functions that you can use include **IsError** and **IsNothing**.

Example

To test whether a user entered a numeric value, you can use the **IsNumeric** function. The **IsNumeric** function returns a value of **True** if the argument is numeric. If the argument is not numeric, the function returns **False**.

The following code shows how to use an **IsNumeric** function to test for a numeric value and display a message stating whether the value is numeric. There is a **TextBox** named **ValueTextBox** on the form in the example.

```
Private Sub EvaluateInput( )
    Dim InputValue As String
    InputValue = ValueTextBox.Text
    If IsNumeric(InputValue) Then
        MessageBox.Show(InputValue & " is a number.")
    Else
        MessageBox.Show(InputValue & " is not a number.")
    End If
End Sub
```

How to Use the ErrorProvider Component

- **Add the ErrorProvider component to a form**
  - Available on the **Windows Forms** tab of the Toolbox
- **Call the SetError method**
  - The first parameter specifies where the icon should appear, and the second parameter specifies error message to display:

```
ErrorProvider1.SetError (Textbox1, "Please enter a valid date.")
```

  - If the user enters invalid data, an error icon and message appear on the form:

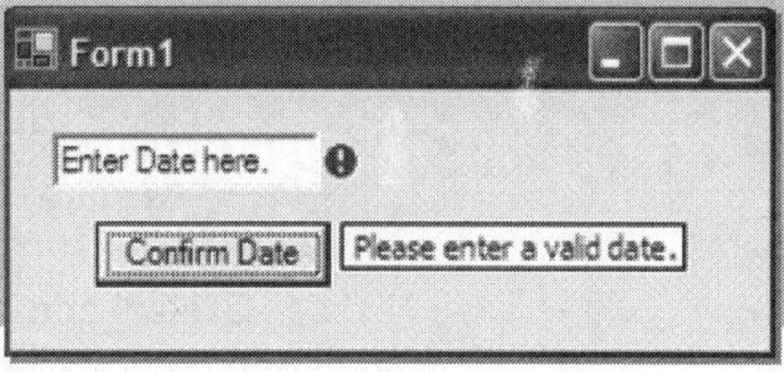

Introduction

The **ErrorProvider** component allows you to unobtrusively notify the user that something is wrong, and to communicate how to correct the problem. It has advantages over the message box in that it does not require the user to close a window before continuing, and in that once a message box is dismissed, the error message is no longer visible.

Adding an ErrorProvider to a form

The **ErrorProvider** component is available on the **Windows Forms** tab of the Toolbox. You can add an **ErrorProvider** to a form in the same way you add other controls from the Toolbox. After you add it to a form, you can use a single **ErrorProvider** component to handle validation messages for all controls on the form. The user simply rests the mouse pointer on the icon to reveal your error message.

SetError method

The key method of the **ErrorProvider** component is the **SetError** method, which specifies the error message string and where the error icon should appear.

Key properties

The **ErrorProvider** component's key properties are **ContainerControl** and **Icon**. You use the **ContainerControl** property to specify the appropriate container (usually the Windows Form) so that the **ErrorProvider** component can display an error icon on the form. When the component is added in the Windows Forms Designer, the **ContainerControl** property is automatically set to the containing form. If you add the component in code, you must set it yourself. You use the **Icon** property to specify a custom error icon, if desired, instead of the default.

Using ErrorProvider

You can use the **ErrorProvider** component to display an error icon when the user enters invalid data.

► **To display an error icon when the user enters invalid data**

1. Add an **ErrorProvider** component to the form that contains the controls to be validated.
2. Add code to the **Click** event handler of the control in which you want to provide validation feedback, in this case a button named **ConfirmDate**. The following code shows how to call the **SetError** method for a **TextBox** control named **HireDate**. The first argument of the **SetError** method specifies the control with which to associate the error icon if the user enters invalid data. The second argument specifies the error text to display.

```
Private Sub ConfirmDate_Click(...)
   If Not IsDate(HireDate.Text) Then
      ErrorProvider1.SetError(HireDate, _
         "Please enter a valid date.")
   Else
      ' Clear the error
      ErrorProvider1.SetError(HireDate, "")
   End If
End Sub
```

Note You must clear the error message from the **ErrorProvider** between each attempt by the user to fix the error and before the **ErrorProvider** can be used by another control.

How to Set Focus on Controls and Text

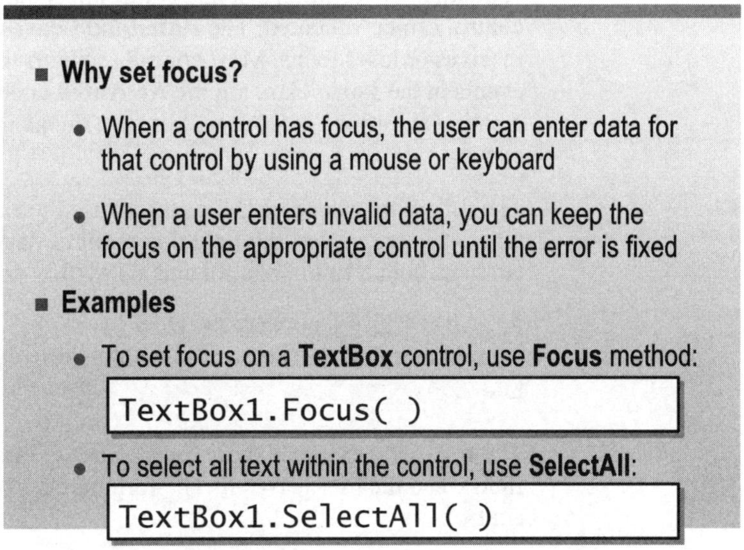

Introduction

When a control has focus, the user can enter data for that control by using a mouse or keyboard. For example, on a Visual Basic .NET form containing several text boxes, only the text box that has focus can receive input through the keyboard. If a user enters invalid data, you can programmatically keep the focus on the appropriate control until valid data is entered.

Methods

You use the **Focus** method to set focus on a control programmatically. You use the **SelectAll** method to select all text within the control.

Note Some controls, such as **Panel**, **GroupBox**, **PictureBox**, **ProgressBar**, **Splitter**, **Label**, and **LinkLabel**, cannot receive focus. Additionally, controls that are invisible at run time, such as the **Timer** control, cannot receive focus.

Example

The following code shows how to use the **Focus** and **SelectAll** methods to keep focus on a **TextBox** control until the user enters valid data. It also shows how to use the **ErrorProvider** component in conjunction with these methods to provide a message to help the user correct invalid data.

```
Private Sub ConfirmDate_Click(...)
   If Not IsDate(TextBox1.Text) Then
      ErrorProvider1.SetError(TextBox1, _
         "Please enter a valid date.")
      TextBox1.Focus( )
      TextBox1.SelectAll( )
   Else
      ' Clear the error
      ErrorProvider1.SetError(TextBox1, "")
   End If
End Sub
```

Enter and Leave events

You might need to validate data when the user does not click a button or other triggering control. You can use the **Enter** or **Leave** events for this type of validation, or for when a single control must have accurate data before another control can be validated. The **Enter** and **Leave** events occur when an object receives or loses focus. Most controls support these events. The equivalent events in the **Form** class are the **Activated** and **Deactivate** events. To avoid creating an infinite loop, do not use the **Focus** method in one or more **Leave** events.

Examples

The following example shows how to use the **Enter** event to provide guidance when the user moves to a field that requires data entry. The form in the example contains both a **Label** control and a **TextBox** control.

```
Private Sub FirstNameTextBox_Enter(...)
  GuidanceLabel.Text = "Please Enter your First Name."
End Sub
```

The following example shows how to use the **Leave** event to validate a single field when the user leaves it. The form in the example contains a **TextBox** control.

```
Private Sub FirstNameTextBox_Leave(...)
  If IsNumeric(FirstNameTextBox.Text) Then
      ' Code to continue goes here
  Else
      MessageBox.Show("Please use numeric characters.")
  End If
End Sub
```

How to Modify User Input

- You can modify user input by using the following functions:

Function	Description
UCase	Converts a specified string to uppercase
LCase	Converts a specified string to lowercase
Trim	Eliminates leading and trailing spaces in a specified string

- Example

```
Dim LowerCase, UpperCase As String
LowerCase = "Hello World 1234" ' String to convert
UpperCase = UCase(LowerCase) ' Returns "HELLO WORLD 1234"
```

Introduction

You can modify the data a user enters to ensure that it is displayed according to your format requirements or to prepare it for entry into a database. For example, you can convert a string of lowercase characters to uppercase characters, or vice versa. This might be useful for data that is not entered by means of a **TextBox** control, so you can convert characters to uppercase or lowercase at design time.

Functions

Visual Basic .NET provides several functions that you use to programmatically modify user input after it has been entered, including the **UCase** and **LCase** functions.

The **UCase** function returns a string or character containing the specified string converted to uppercase. Only lowercase letters are converted to uppercase; all uppercase letters and nonletter characters remain unchanged.

The **LCase** function returns a string or character containing the specified string converted to lowercase. Only uppercase letters are converted to lowercase; all lowercase letters and nonletter characters remain unchanged.

How to Use Validation Events

- Use the CausesValidation property to trigger the Validating event
- Validating event

```
Private Sub WarehouseTextbox_Validating(. . .)
    If WarehouseTextbox.Text = "" Then
      infoErrorProvider.SetError(WarehouseTextbox, _
          "Please enter a Warehouse name.")
      e.Cancel = True
    End If
End Sub
```

- Validated event

```
Private Sub WarehouseTextbox_Validated(. . .)
    infoErrorProvider.SetError(WarehouseTextbox, "")
End Sub
```

Introduction

Sometimes you will need to verify that a user has entered accurate data into a field before allowing the user to move to another field. All Windows Forms controls provide two validation events: the **Validating** event and the **Validated** event. You can use these events to ensure that specific fields in your application have accurate data before the user moves on to other fields.

CausesValidation property

You can use the **CausesValidation** property to trigger the **Validating** event for a control. The **CausesValidation** property is a Boolean property that is available on the Windows Forms controls provided by default in the Toolbox. When set to **True**, this property triggers the **Validating** event for the control that was active just prior to the current control. The property triggers this event when the user attempts to set focus on another control. When set to **False**, it cancels validation for any control requiring validation. The default value for this property is **True**.

Validating event

The **Validating** event is raised before a control loses focus, after the **Leave** event and before the **Validated** event. The **Validating** event handler can contain any validation code that you need for the specific control.

Example of using the Validating event

Consider the following form.

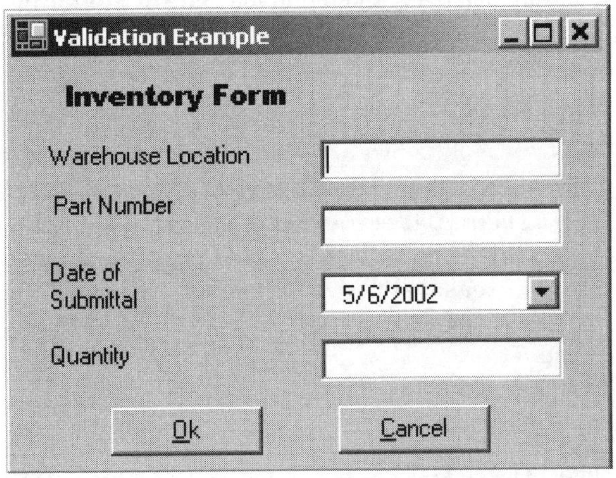

Imagine that the business requirements for the application specify that data must exist in each field before the user can move to the next field. If the **CausesValidation** property of the **Part Number** text box is set to **True**, and there is code in the **Validating** event of the **Warehouse Location** text box, this code will run as soon as the user tries to change focus from the **Warehouse Location** text box to the **Part Number** text box.

The following code uses the **Validating** event of the **WarehouseTextbox** control to verify that the user has entered data in the **Warehouse Location** text box. If the user has not entered data, the **ErrorProvider** provides an error message to the user.

```
Private Sub WarehouseTextbox_Validating(ByVal sender As _
  System.Object, ByVal e As _
  System.ComponentModel.CancelEventArgs) _
  Handles WarehouseTextbox.Validating

  If WarehouseTextbox.Text = "" Then
      infoErrorProvider.SetError(WarehouseTextbox, _
          "Please enter a Warehouse name.")
      e.Cancel = True
  End If
End Sub
```

The following example uses the **Value** property of the **DateTimePicker** control to ensure that dates entered in the **Date of Submittal** box are in the year 2002.

```
Private Sub submitDateTimePicker_Validating(ByVal sender As _
  Object, ByVal e As System.ComponentModel.CancelEventArgs) _
  Handles submitDateTimePicker.Validating

  If submitDateTimePicker.Value <= #1/1/2002# Or _
      submitDateTimePicker.Value >= #1/1/2003# Then
      infoErrorProvider.SetError(WarehouseTextbox, _
      "Please enter a date between 1/1/2002 and 1/1/2003.")
      e.Cancel = True
  End If
End Sub
```

Note The code that sets `e.Cancel` to **True** prevents focus from moving away from the text box as long as there is nothing in the text box. For more information about event cancel arguments, see "**CancelEventArgs.Cancel** Property" in the Visual Studio .NET documentation.

Validated event

The **Validated** event is triggered after the conditions in the **Validating** event have been met and before the **LostFocus** event occurs. In the previous example, the **Validated** event is triggered after the user enters valid data in the **NameTextbox** text box and moves to the next control.

In the **Validated** event handler, you can place code to manage controls whose content is dependent on the recently validated control. For example, if you have used an **ErrorProvider** to provide information about an error in the previous validation attempt, you can reset the **ErrorProvider** in the **Validated** event.

Example of using the Validated event

The following example uses the **Validated** event to reset the **ErrorProvider** control. The code for the **Validated** event is in bold text. The code for the **Validating** event is provided for clarity.

```
Private Sub WarehouseTextbox_Validating(ByVal sender As _
   Object, ByVal e As System.ComponentModel.CancelEventArgs) _
   Handles WarehouseTextbox.Validating
  If WarehouseTextbox.Text = "" Then
      infoErrorProvider.SetError(WarehouseTextbox, _
          "Please enter a warehouse name.")
      e.Cancel = True
  End If
End Sub

Private Sub WarehouseTextbox_Validated(ByVal sender _
  As System.Object, ByVal e As System.EventArgs) _
  Handles WarehouseTextbox.Validated
      infoErrorProvider.SetError(WarehouseTextbox, "")
End Sub
```

Practice: Validating Field Data

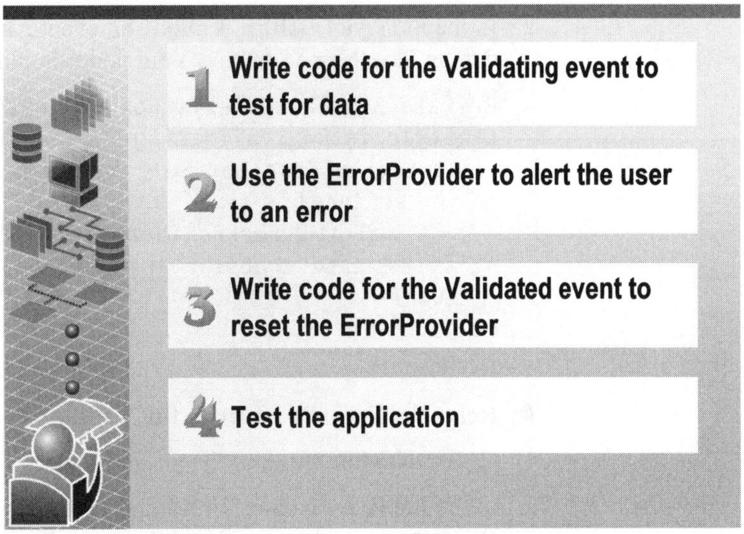

Introduction

In this practice, you will open an existing project and add code to validate the values entered in the fields on the form.

Instructions

► **Open the ValidationEvents project**

1. Open Visual Studio .NET.
2. Open the ValidationEvents.sln file, which is in the *install_folder*\Practices\Mod06\ValidationEvents\Starter folder.
3. Familiarize yourself with the controls and the code for this application.

► **Test for data in SkierNameTextbox**

1. Create a **Validating** event handler for the SkierNameTextbox control.
2. In the **SkierNameTextbox_Validating** event handler, write code to test for data in SkierNameTextbox. Your code should look as follows:

```
If SkierNameTextbox.Text = "" Then
   e.Cancel = True
   SkiFormErrorProvider.SetError(SkierNameTextbox, _
    "Please enter your name.")
End If
```

► **Reset the ErrorProvider in the Validated event for SkierNameTextbox**

1. Create a **Validated** event handler for the SkierNameTextbox control.
2. In the **SkierNameTextbox_Validated** event handler, write code to reset the **ErrorProvider** for SkierNameTextbox. Your code should look as follows:

```
Private Sub SkierNameTextbox_Validated(...) Handles _
   SkierNameTextbox.Validated
       SkiFormErrorProvider.SetError(SkierNameTextbox, "")
End Sub
```

► **Test for data in the SkiStyleListBox control**

1. Create a **Validating** event handler for the SkiStyleListBox control.
2. In the **SkiStyleListBox_Validating** event handler, write code to test for data in SkierNameTextbox. Your code should look as follows:

```
Private Sub SkiStyleListBox_Validating(...) Handles _
SkiStyleListBox.Validating
   If SkiStyleListBox.SelectedItems.Count = 0 Then
       e.Cancel = True
       SkiFormErrorProvider.SetError(SkiStyleListBox, _
       "Please choose a ski style.")
   End If
End Sub
```

► **Reset the ErrorProvider in the Validated event for SkiStyleListBox**

1. Create a **Validated** event handler for the SkiStyleListBox control.
2. In the **SkiStyleListBox_Validated** event handler, write code to reset the **ErrorProvider** for SkierNameTextbox. Your code should look as follows:

```
Private Sub SkiStyleListBox_Validated(...) Handles _
       SkiStyleListBox.Validated
   SkiFormErrorProvider.SetError(SkiStyleListBox, "")
End Sub
```

► **Test your work**

1. Run the application.
2. Attempt to tab through the **Skier Name** text box.

   An error icon should flash next to the **Skier Name** text box. Rest the mouse pointer on the icon to display the message "Please enter your name."
3. Type your name in the **Skier Name** text box and then press TAB.

   The error icon should disappear.
4. Attempt to tab through the **Ski Style** list.

   An error icon should flash next to the **Ski Style** list. Rest the mouse pointer on the icon to display the message "Please choose a ski style."
5. Click an item in the **Ski Style** list, and then press TAB.

   The error icon should disappear.
6. Click **OK**.

   A message box confirming your choices should appear.
7. Quit the application.

Solution files

The solution files for this practice are located in the *install_folder*\Practices\Mod06\ValidationEvents\Solution folder.

Lesson: Validating Form Data

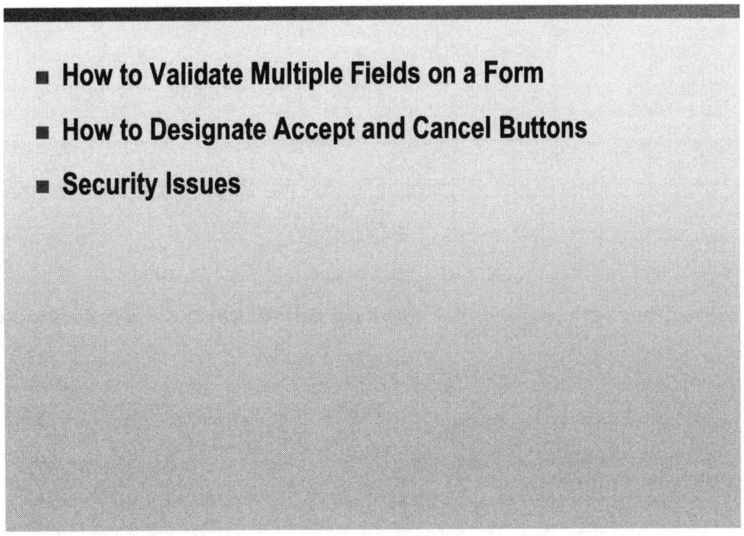

Introduction

In Visual Basic .NET, you can validate all fields on a form at one time. In most cases, you will want to perform data validation near the end of the form completion process. This limits the number of error messages and interruptions to which the user must respond.

Lesson agenda

This lesson includes the following topics and activities:

- How to Validate Multiple Fields on a Form
- How to Designate Accept and Cancel Buttons
- Security Issues

Lesson objectives

After completing this lesson, you will be able to:

- Validate multiple fields on a form at one time.
- Assign a form's **CancelButton** and **AcceptButton** properties to the desired buttons on the form.
- Access and display the identity of the currently logged-on Windows user.

How to Validate Multiple Fields on a Form

- **Provide visual cues to the user**
  - Example

    Disable the **OK** button until the user enters data in all required fields

- **Validate all the fields on the form at one time**
  - Example

    Put all the validation code in the **Click** event handler of the **OK** button

---

Introduction

There are several important aspects of form-level validation to consider. You can provide visual cues so the user knows when data has been entered in all required fields. You can write your validation code so that all fields on the form are validated at one time. If an error is discovered, you can set the focus on the control and on the text that needs to be corrected.

Providing visual cues to the user

When you implement form-level validation, it is important to provide visual cues to your users to enable them to determine which tasks they need to perform. For example, a form might contain fields for first name, last name, address, city, state, and postal code that need to be completely filled in before any further processing can take place.

A good way to communicate that the user has not filled in all of the required information is to disable a command such as an **OK** or **Submit** button. When the user has typed all required information, you can set the command button's **Enabled** property to **True**. This will inform users that they have successfully completed the task.

Example

One way to enable a command button when all fields have been completed is to loop through the **Controls** collection and validate each control. The **Controls** collection is a predefined collection provided by Visual Basic .NET that contains all controls on a form.

The following code shows how to use the **OK** button to give the user visual cues that required fields are still empty (**OK** button disabled) or that data has been entered in all required fields on a form (**OK** button enabled). The form in the example contains buttons named **ConfirmData** and **OK** and several text boxes.

```
Private Sub ConfirmData_Click(...) Handles ConfirmData.Click
  Dim controlVariable As Control

  For Each controlVariable In Me.Controls
      ' Check to see if the current control is a text box
      If TypeOf controlVariable Is TextBox Then
          ' Is there data in the text box?
          If Trim(controlVariable.Text) = "" Then
              ' If not, disable the OK button and exit
              OKButton.Enabled = False
              Exit Sub
          Else
              OKButton.Enabled = True
          End If
      End If
  Next

  ' Enable the OK command button
  OKButton.Enabled = True

End Sub
```

Validating all fields on a form at once

In some situations, you might want to validate all user input for a form in a single event handler. For example, you could have a form that requires customer information such as name, address, department name, and department number. For these fields, you can use text boxes to allow users to enter the information, and provide an **OK** button for users to click when they are ready to move to the next form or the next process in your application. You can then use the command button's **Click** event handler to validate data from each text box on the form, and direct the user to any field that might have invalid data by setting focus to that field.

Example

The following code shows how to validate all fields on a form at once. The following form has already been created, and an **ErrorProvider** component has been added to the form. If errors in data entry are found, users are directed to the appropriate fields to fix the errors.

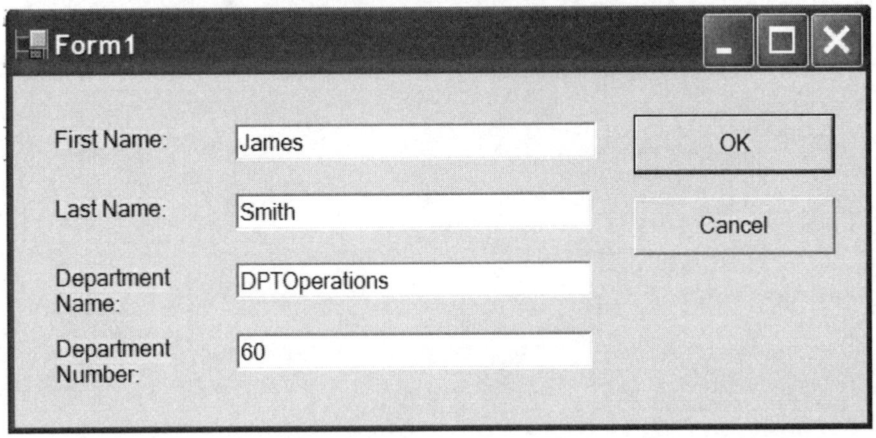

```
Private Sub OkButton_Click(ByVal sender As Object, _
   ByVal e As System.EventArgs) Handles OKButton.Click
   ' Clear error messages between each attempt by the user
   ' to fix an error
   ErrorProvider1.SetError(FirstNameTextBox, "")
   ErrorProvider1.SetError(LastNameTextBox, "")
   ErrorProvider1.SetError(DeptNameTextBox, "")
   ErrorProvider1.SetError(DeptNumberTextBox, "")

   ' Configure the ErrorProvider for each control and provide
   ' guidance to help users fix errors
   If FirstNameTextBox.Text = "" Then
       ErrorProvider1.SetError(FirstNameTextBox, _
           "You must provide a first name.")
       FirstNameTextBox.Focus( )
       Exit Sub
       ElseIf LastNameTextBox.Text = "" Then
           ErrorProvider1.SetError(LastNameTextBox, _
               "You must provide a last name.")
           LastNameTextBox.Focus( )
       Exit Sub
       ElseIf Microsoft.VisualBasic.Left(DeptNameTextBox.Text, 3) <> "DPT" Then
           ErrorProvider1.SetError(DeptNameTextBox, _
               "Your department number must start with DPT.")
           DeptNameTextBox.Focus( )
           DeptNameTextBox.SelectAll( )
       Exit Sub
       ElseIf Not IsNumeric(DeptNumberTextBox.Text) Then
           ErrorProvider1.SetError(DeptNumberTextBox, _
               "Your department number must be entered in numbers.")
           DeptNumberTextBox.Focus( )
           DeptNumberTextBox.SelectAll( )
           DeptNumberTextBox.ForeColor = Color.Red
       Exit Sub
       ElseIf CInt(DeptNumberTextBox.Text) < 50 Or _
           CInt(DeptNumberTextBox.Text) > 80 Then
           ErrorProvider1.SetError(DeptNumberTextBox, _
               "Your department number must be between 50 and 80.")
           DeptNumberTextBox.Focus( )
           DeptNumberTextBox.SelectAll( )
           DeptNumberTextBox.ForeColor = Color.Crimson
       Exit Sub
   Else
' User is successful and application continues to next process
           MessageBox.Show("Please continue.")
       End If
End Sub
```

How to Designate Accept and Cancel Buttons

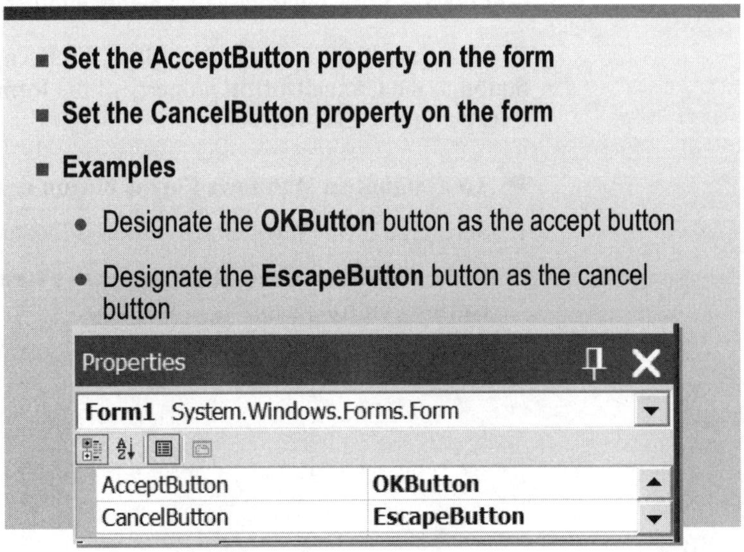

Introduction

In Windows-based applications, the ESC key enables the user to quickly exit an operation without committing to any action. The ENTER key allows the user to accept whatever data they have entered. You can assign ESC and ENTER key functionality to any buttons on a Windows Form to make it easier to use the form.

Designating a button as the accept button

On Windows Forms, you can designate any **Button** control to be the accept button, also known as the *default button*. Whenever the user presses ENTER, the default button is clicked regardless of which other control on the form has focus. An exception to this rule occurs when the control that has focus is another button—in that case, the button that has focus will be clicked.

In many applications, developers set the form's **AcceptButton** property to the **OK** button and place validation code in the **OK** button's **Click** event handler. If you follow this convention in your applications, when the user presses ENTER, your **OK** button code will run.

► **To designate a Windows Forms button as the accept button**

1. Select the form on which the button is located.
2. In the Properties window, set the form's **AcceptButton** property to the **Button** control's name.

Designating a button as the cancel button

On a Windows Form, you can designate any **Button** control to be the cancel button. The **Click** event code for the designated button will run whenever the user presses ESC, regardless of whether another control on the form has focus.

For example, if you write undo code in the **Escape** button, you can assign this button to the **CancelButton** property of the form. If the user presses ESC, your **Escape** button code will run.

► To designate a Windows Forms button as the cancel button

1. Select the form on which the button is located.
2. In the Properties window, set the form's **CancelButton** property to the **Button** control's name.

Security Issues

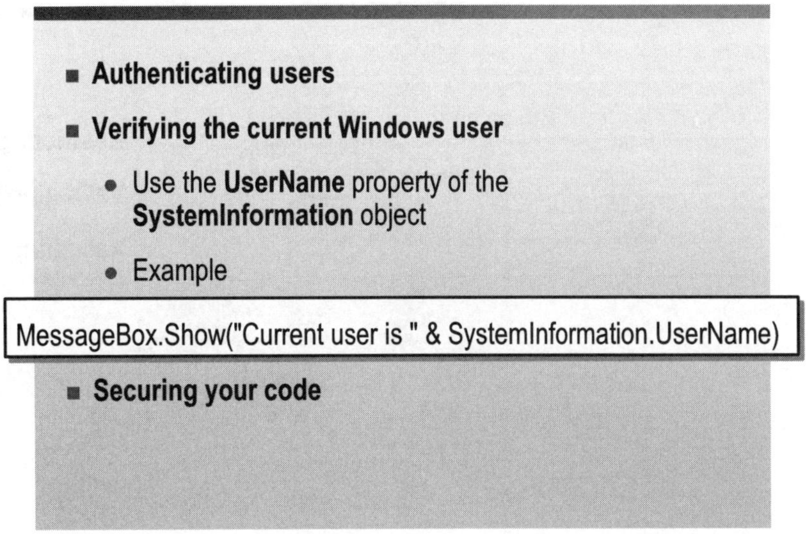

Introduction

The fundamental goal of any security technique is to control access to protected resources. There are several issues to consider when designing and implementing security for your application.

Authenticating users

Your Windows Forms application will make use of Windows XP Integrated Security. Users and client computers are set up within valid domains, and role-based permissions allow access to individual applications.

Verifying the current Windows user

To access and display the identity of the currently logged-on Windows user, you can use **SystemInformation**, as shown the following code:

```
Private Sub Button1_Click(...)
    MessageBox.Show("You are " & SystemInformation.UserName)
End Sub
```

Note For more information about **SystemInformation**, see the Visual Studio .NET documentation.

Securing your code

In the Microsoft .NET Framework, the security model is code based, meaning that security levels can be set for code, regardless of the user running the code. These security levels can define security for the browser, like the zone-based security available in Microsoft Internet Explorer, or for the operating system, like the policy- and permission-based security of the .NET Framework and Windows.

Note Though implementing security in your applications is very important, it is beyond the scope of this course. For more information, refer to Michael Howard and David LeBlanc's book *Writing Secure Code,* or see "Securing Applications" in the Visual Studio .NET documentation.

Review

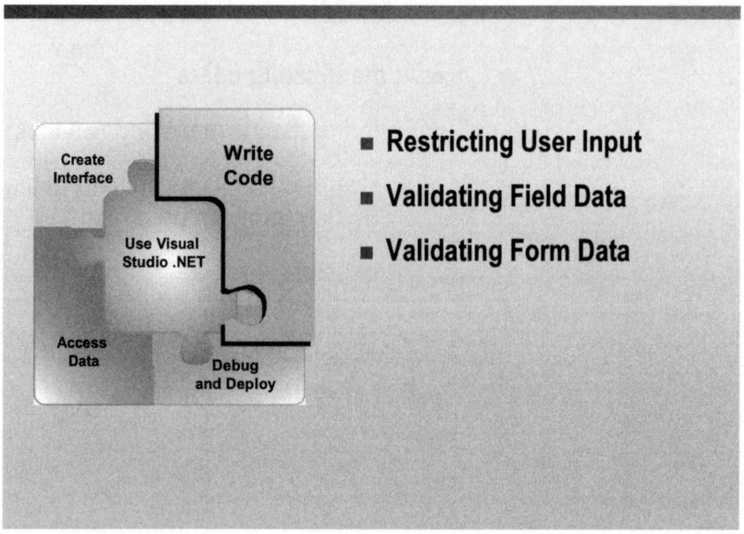

1. How do you make a **TextBox** read-only?

2. What occurs when a user enters an invalid character in a **Masked Edit** control?

3. How can you use intrinsic validation to restrict data entry to dates and times?

4. What happens when a user enters data in a **TextBox** in which the **PasswordChar** property is set to * (asterisk)?

5. Write the code to call the **SetError** method of ErrorProvider1 for TextBox1 and display the message "Please enter your first name."

6. What technique can you use to provide a visual cue to the user when all required fields on a form have been filled in?

7. If you want to provide validation feedback after the user has entered data in all required fields, where should you put your validation code?

Lab 6.1: Validating User Input

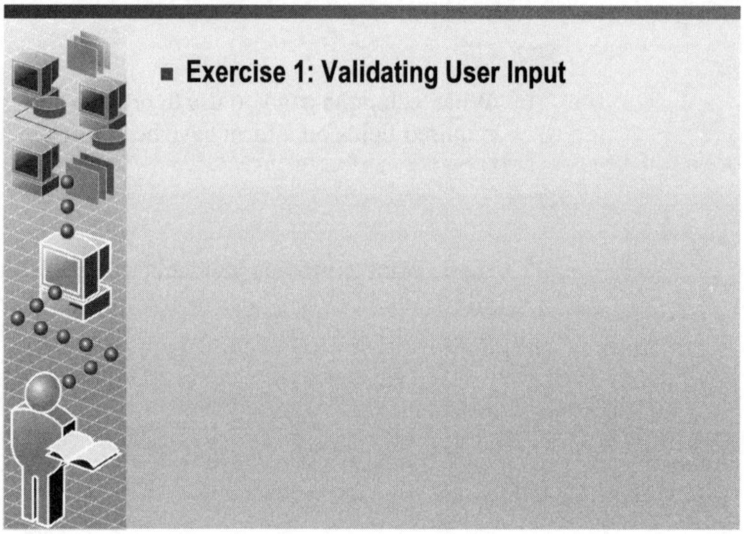

Objectives

After completing this lab, you will be able to:

- Use Boolean functions to validate the contents of a Windows Forms control.
- Use the **Validating** and **Validated** events to help users enter appropriate data.
- Use the **ErrorProvider** component to display error messages and to provide guidance for fixing data entries that are not valid.

Note This lab focuses on the concepts in this module and as a result may not comply with Microsoft security recommendations.

Prerequisites

Before working on this lab, you must be familiar with the following:

- Boolean functions
- The **Validating** and **Validated** events
- The **ErrorProvider** component

Scenario

In the labs for Modules 2, 4, 5, 6, and 12 of Course 2559B, *Introduction to Visual Basic .NET Programming with Microsoft .NET,* you will create a loan payment estimate application. You will create the full application in stages, each stage continuing from the code created in the previous lab. At the beginning of each lab, you can either continue with your own files or start with the files provided for you.

After Lab 5.1, Using Decision Structures in Module 5, "Decision Structures and Loops," in Course 2559B, *Introduction to Visual Basic .NET Programming with Microsoft .NET* has been completed, the form for the loan payment estimate application appears as follows:

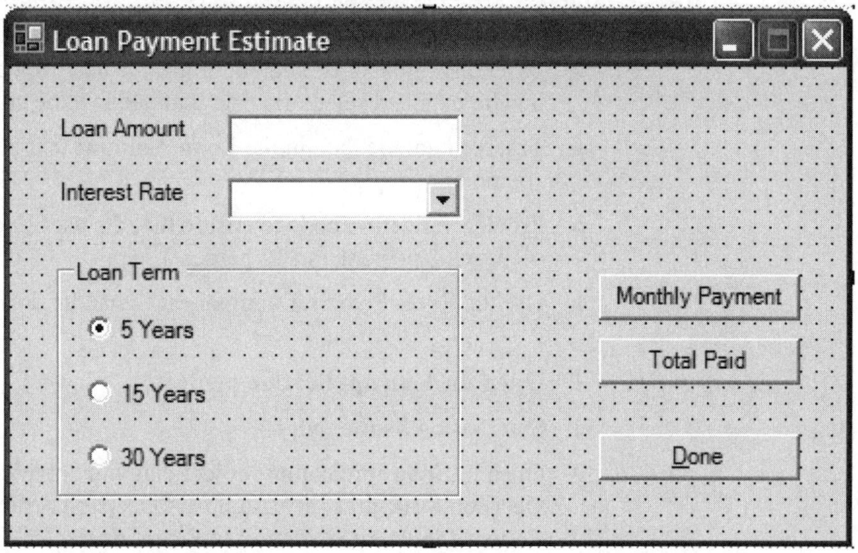

Solution files

The solution files for this lab are in the *install_folder*\Labfiles\Lab061\Ex01\Solution folder.

Estimated time to complete this lab: 45 minutes

Exercise 1
Validating User Input

In this exercise, you will:

- Set a default value for the **Interest Rate** combo box.
- Set the tab order for the controls to guide the user through the process of entering valid data in the form.
- Add and configure an **ErrorProvider** component to display a blinking error icon and provide guidance to enable users to fix invalid data entries in the **Loan Amount** text box.
- When invalid data is entered, return the user to the control containing invalid data and select the data that needs to be corrected.
- Test for numeric data in the **Loan Amount** text box and the **Interest Rate** combo box.
- Provide validation code to ensure that the user selects a valid interest rate (between 2 percent and 12 percent).
- Use the **ErrorProvider** component to handle data entries that are not valid.

▶ Open the loan application project

1. Start Visual Studio .NET.
2. Open the loan application project that you completed in Lab 5.1, Using Decision Structures, in Module 5, "Decision Structures and Loops," in Course 2559B, *Introduction to Visual Basic .NET Programming with Microsoft .NET.*

   If you did not complete Lab 5.1, open the LoanApplication.sln file in the *install_folder*\Labfiles\Lab061\Ex01\Starter folder.

▶ Set the tab order for the controls and specify a default value for the Interest Rate combo box

- Use the Properties window to set the properties for the controls as shown in the following table. Note that you can also click **Tab Order** on the **View** menu to set the **TabIndex** property of each control.

Control name	Property	New value
LoanTextBox	**TabIndex**	**0**
RateComboBox	**Text**	**4.5**
RateComboBox	**TabIndex**	**1**
MonthlyPaymentButton	**TabIndex**	**2**
TotalPaidButton	**TabIndex**	**3**
DoneButton	**TabIndex**	**4**

▶ Add an ErrorProvider component to the form

1. Add an **ErrorProvider** component to the MainForm form.
2. In the Properties window, change the name of ErrorProvider1 to **MainErrorProvider**.

▶ Add validation code to the LoanTextBox validating event

1. In the **LoanTextBox_Validating** event handler, write an **If...Then** statement that raises an error if the data in **LoanTextBox** is not numeric. Your code should look as follows:

```
If Not IsNumeric(LoanTextBox.Text) Then
   MainErrorProvider.SetError(LoanTextBox, _
   "Please enter a loan amount greater than 0 " & _
   "in numeric characters.")

   e.Cancel = True
Else
   e.Cancel = False
End If
```

Note The code that sets `e.Cancel` to **True** prevents focus from shifting away from the text box as long as there is nothing in the text box. It also selects the contents of the text box.

---

2. In the **LoanTextBox_Validating** event handler, add another conditional expression to test for zero or any occurrence of "0.0" as the first characters in LoanTextBox. (The test for zero or "0.0" prevents users from using variations of zero—for example "0.00" or "0.00000"—to circumvent your validation.) Your code should look as follows:

```
If Not IsNumeric(LoanTextBox.Text) Or _
   LoanTextBox.Text = "0" Or _
   Microsoft.VisualBasic.Left(LoanTextBox.Text, 3) _
   = "0.0" Then
   MainErrorProvider.SetError(LoanTextBox, _
      "Please enter a loan amount greater than 0 " & _
      "in numeric characters.")
   e.Cancel = True
Else
   e.Cancel = False
End If
```

3. At the beginning of the **LoanTextBox_Validating** event handler, clear the error message between each attempt to enter valid data. Your code should look as follows:

```
MainErrorProvider.SetError(LoanTextBox,"")
MainErrorProvider.SetError(RateComboBox,"")
```

▶ Add validation code to the RateComboBox validating event

1. In the **RateComboBox_Validating** event handler, add an **If...Then** statement that raises an error if the data in **RateComboBox** is not numeric. Your code should look as follows:

```
If Not IsNumeric(RateComboBox.Text) Then
   MainErrorProvider.SetError(RateComboBox, _
       "Please choose or enter an interest rate " & _
           "between 2 and 12 in numeric characters.")

   e.Cancel = True
Else
   e.Cancel = False

End If
```

2. In the **RateComboBox_Validating** event handler, add an **ElseIf** statement to test for rate amounts below 2 and greater than 12 in **RateComboBox**. Your code should look as follows:

```
If Not IsNumeric(RateComboBox.Text) Then
   MainErrorProvider.SetError(RateComboBox, _
       "Please choose or enter an interest rate " & _
           "between 2 and 12 in numeric characters.")
   e.Cancel = True
ElseIf RateComboBox.Text >= 2 And _
       RateComboBox.Text <= 12 Then
   e.Cancel = False
Else
   MainErrorProvider.SetError(RateComboBox, _
       "Please choose or enter an interest rate " & _
           "between 2 and 12 in numeric characters.")
   e.Cancel = True
End If
```

3. At the beginning of the **RateComboBox_Validating** event handler, clear the error message between each attempt to enter valid data. Your code should look as follows:

```
MainErrorProvider.SetError(LoanTextBox,"")
MainErrorProvider.SetError(RateComboBox,"")
```

▶ Use the error provider to provide validation feedback

1. In the **LoanTextBox_Validated** event handler, call the **SetError** method of **MainErrorProvider** to clear the validation message for the LoanTextBox control after the user has entered valid data. Your code should look as follows:

```
MainErrorProvider.SetError(LoanTextBox,"")
```

2. In the **RateComboBox_Validated** event handler, call the **SetError** method of **MainErrorProvider** to clear the validation message for the **RateComboBox** control after the user has entered valid data. Your code should look as follows:

```
MainErrorProvider.SetError(RateComboBox,"")
```

▶ Clear the error provider between calls

1. In the **MonthlyPaymentButton_Click** event handler, delete the current validation code so that only the **MessageBox** statement that calls the **MonthlyPayment** procedure remains. Your code should look as follows:

```
Private Sub MonthlyPaymentButton_Click(...)

  MessageBox.Show(FormatCurrency(MonthlyPayment(CDbl _
      (LoanTextBox.Text), CDbl(RateComboBox.Text), _
      loanTerm)))

End Sub
```

2. At the beginning of the **MonthlyPaymentButton_Click** event handler, clear the error message between calls to the **MonthlyPayment** function. Your code should look as follows:

```
MainErrorProvider.SetError(LoanTextBox,"")
MainErrorProvider.SetError(RateComboBox,"")
```

3. In the **TotalPaidButton_Click** event handler, delete the current validation code so that only the **MessageBox** statement that calls the **TotalPaid** procedure remains. Your code should look as follows:

```
Private Sub TotalPaidButton_Click(...)

  MessageBox.Show(FormatCurrency(TotalPaid(CDbl _
      (LoanTextBox.Text), CDbl(RateComboBox.Text), _
      loanTerm)))

End Sub
```

4. At the beginning of the **TotalPaidButton_Click** event handler, clear the error message between calls to the **TotalPaid** function. Your code should look as follows:

```
MainErrorProvider.SetError(LoanTextBox,"")
MainErrorProvider.SetError(RateComboBox,"")
```

▶ Test your work

1. Run the application.
2. Before entering any data, click **Monthly Payment**.

   A blinking error icon should appear next to the **Loan Amount** text box. To read the error message, rest the mouse pointer on the error icon. The message should be "Please enter a loan amount greater than 0 in numeric characters."
3. Type **twelve** in the **Loan Amount** text box, and then click **Monthly Payment**.

   A blinking error icon should appear next to the **Loan Amount** text box. To read the error message, rest the mouse pointer on the error icon. The message should be "Please enter a loan amount greater than 0 in numeric characters."
4. Type **500,000** in the **Loan Amount** text box, type **twelve** in the **Interest Rate** combo box, and then click **Monthly Payment**.

   A blinking error icon should appear next to the **Interest Rate** combo box. To read the error message, rest the mouse pointer on the error icon. The message should be "Please choose or enter an interest rate between 2 and 12 in numeric characters."
5. Enter **48** in the **Interest Rate** combo box, and then click **Monthly Payment**.

   A blinking error icon should appear next to the **Interest Rate** combo box. To read the error message, rest the mouse pointer on the error icon. The message should be "Please choose or enter an interest rate between 2 and 12 in numeric characters."
6. Enter **0** in the **Interest Rate** combo box, and then click **Monthly Payment**.

   A blinking error icon should appear next to the **Interest Rate** combo box. To read the error message, rest the mouse pointer on the error icon. The error message should be "Please choose or enter an interest rate between 2 and 12 in numeric characters."
7. Enter **3** in the **Interest Rate** combo box, and then click **Monthly Payment**.

   A message box displaying the monthly payment as $8,984.35 should appear.
8. Click **OK** in the message box.
9. Enter invalid data in either the **Loan Amount** text box or the **Interest Rate** combo box, and then click **Total Paid**.

   The blinking error icon and the same validation message that appeared for the **Monthly Payment** button should appear.
10. Type **500,000** in the **Loan Amount** text box, enter **3** in the **Interest Rate** combo box, and then click **Total Paid**.

    A message box displaying an amount of $539,060.72 should appear.
11. Click **OK** in the message box, and then quit the running application.

msdn training

Module 7: Object-Oriented Programming in Visual Basic .NET

Contents

Microsoft

Overview

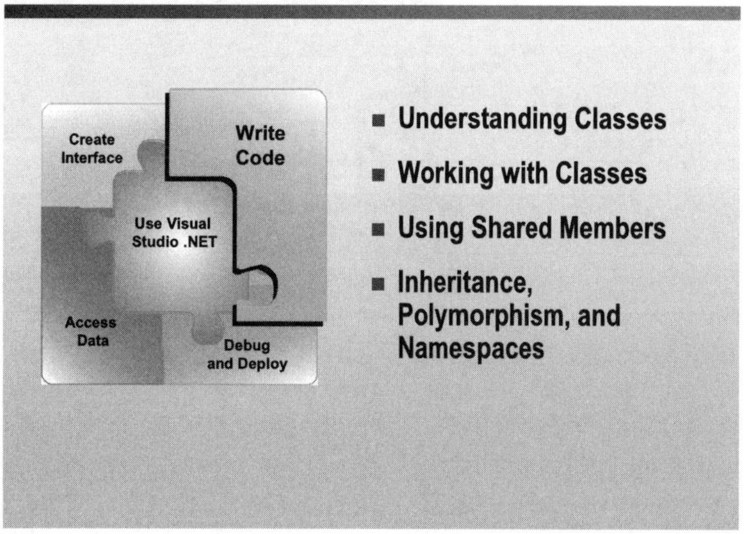

Introduction

This module explains how to create and use classes. The module provides a conceptual understanding of abstraction, encapsulation, instantiation, initialization, constructors, and destructors. This module also describes inheritance, polymorphism, and namespaces.

Objects are fundamental to Microsoft® Visual Basic® .NET programming. Forms, controls, and databases are all objects. In this module, you will learn how to create your own objects from classes you define and how you can use objects to simplify your coding and increase code reuse.

Objectives

After completing this module, you will be able to:

- Explain object-oriented programming concepts, including class, abstraction, encapsulation, and object.
- Use the Object Browser to examine available programming elements, including classes and objects.
- Create a new class, including its methods, properties, and data members.
- Create and use an instance of a class, including instance and shared data members, and shared and non-shared methods.
- Explain how constructors and destructors work.
- Explain inheritance, polymorphism, and namespaces.

Multimedia: Introduction to Object-Oriented Concepts

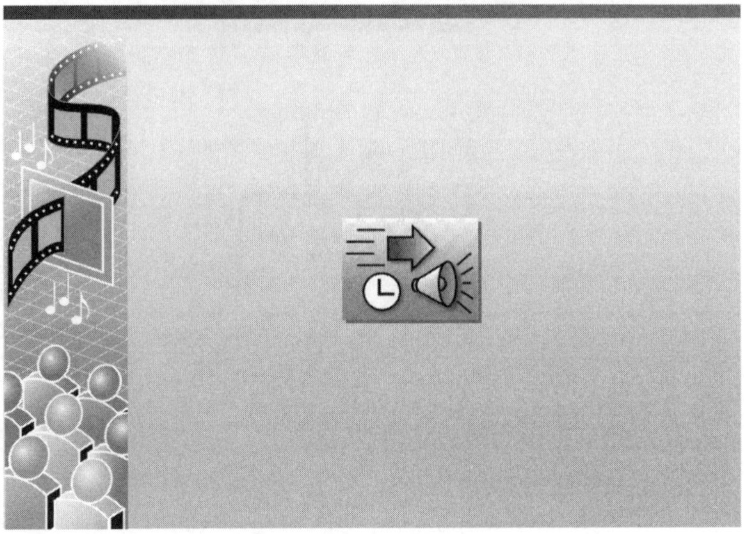

Introduction

This animation introduces you to fundamental elements you will be using in Visual Basic .NET and throughout this module, including classes and objects.

Animation script

In Visual Basic .NET, you can use object-oriented programming elements such as classes and objects.

A class can be a concrete entity, like a clock, or an abstract entity, like time.

Think of a class as a template or blueprint that has variables, methods, properties, and events.

An object is an instance of the class. For example, this blueprint for a house is like a class—the **House** class—and each of the actual houses built from the blueprint is like an instance of the **House** class.

In Visual Basic .NET, you can extend your class by inheriting from it. The class you inherit from is called a *base class*. The class you extend is called a *derived class*. Derived classes inherit and can extend the properties, methods, and events defined in the base class.

Lesson: Understanding Classes

Introduction

This lesson describes basic object-oriented programming concepts, including classes, abstraction and encapsulation, and objects. Understanding these concepts enables you to use the powerful object-oriented features of Visual Basic .NET. In addition, this lesson describes how to use the Object Browser to examine classes, objects, and other programming elements.

Lesson agenda

This lesson includes the following topics:

- What Is a Class?
- What Is an Object?
- How to Use the Object Browser

Lesson objectives

After completing this lesson, you will be able to:

- Describe classes and objects.
- Explain the role of abstraction and encapsulation in creating classes.
- Use the Object Browser to examine classes, objects, and other programming elements.

What Is a Class?

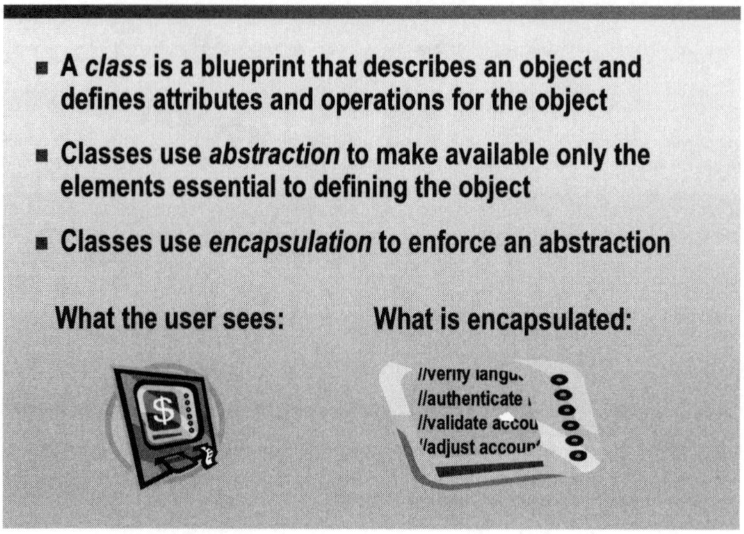

Introduction

In object-oriented programming, you use abstraction and encapsulation to create well-designed classes.

Definition

A *class* is a template or a blueprint for an object. This blueprint defines attributes for storing data and defines operations for manipulating that data. A class also defines a set of restrictions to allow or deny access to its attributes and operations.

Using abstraction

To create a well-designed class, you will use *abstraction.* In implementing abstraction, you will define a concept by using a minimal set of carefully considered functionality that provides the essential behavior of the class in an easy-to-use manner. Unfortunately, creating good software abstractions is not easy. Finding good abstractions usually requires a deep understanding of the problem being solved by the class and its context, great clarity of thought, and plenty of experience.

Example of abstraction

The Visual Basic .NET form you have been working with is a good example of abstraction. The essential properties of a form, such as caption and background color, have been abstracted in the **Form** class. Some essential operations that have been abstracted are open, close, and minimize.

Using encapsulation

Abstraction is enforced by means of *encapsulation.* Encapsulation is the packaging of attributes and functionality to create an object that is essentially a "black box"—an object whose internal structure remains private. You package the details of the abstraction and provide access to only the elements that need to be accessible. Other objects can access the services of an encapsulated object only by means of messages passed by a clearly defined interface.

Example of encapsulation

An automatic teller machine (ATM) provides an example of encapsulation. The interface of the ATM is appropriately simple for the ATM customer, and the internal workings are hidden. In the same way, a **BankAccount** class would encapsulate the methods, fields, and properties that describe a bank account. Without encapsulation, you would need to declare separate procedures and variables to store and manage information for the bank account, and it would be difficult to work with more than one bank account at a time. Encapsulation lets users use the data and procedures in the **BankAccount** class as a unit, without knowing the exact code encapsulated in the class.

Object 3 Parts

Identity / State / Behavior

ISB

What Is an Object?

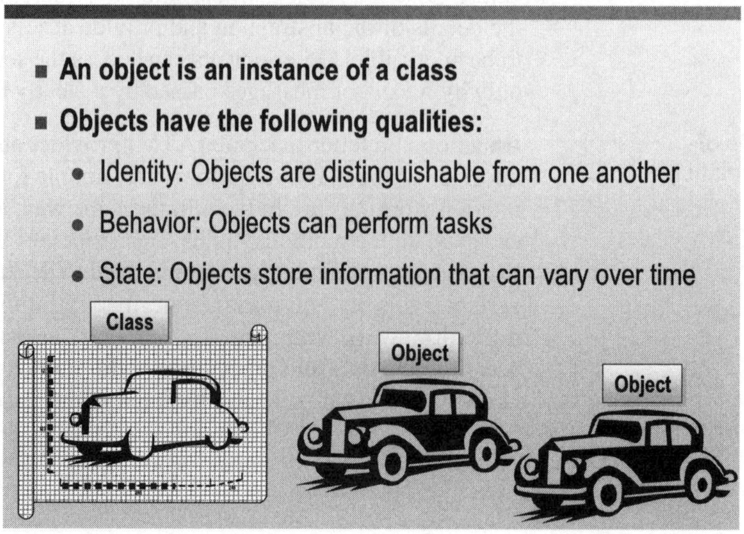

Introduction

In general, to execute the methods and use the properties of a class, you need to create an *instance* of the class. An instance of a class is called an object. The words *class* and *object* are used so much in object-oriented programming that it is easy to get the terms mixed up. Think of a class as an abstract representation of something and an object as a usable example of the thing the class represents.

Definition

An *object* is a unit of software that contains a collection of related methods and data. An object is a specific instance of a class, and includes the characteristics of that class.

Example of an object

The word *car* has different meanings in different contexts. Sometimes the word refers to the general concept of a car or the set of all cars. Using the word in this way is analogous to using the word *class*. Sometimes the word *car* refers to a specific car. Using the word in this way is analogous to using the word *object*.

Identity

Objects have identity. *Identity* is the characteristic that distinguishes one object from all other objects.

Behavior

Objects provide behavior. *Behavior* is the characteristic that makes objects useful. Objects exist to provide behavior. For example, most of the time you can ignore the inner workings of a car and think about its behavior. Cars are useful because you can drive them. The inner workings exist, but they are mostly inaccessible. It is the behavior of an object that is accessible. Objects of the same class share the same behavior. A car is a car because you can drive it.

State

Objects have state. *State* is the characteristic that refers to the inner workings of an object that enable it to provide its defining behavior. A well-designed object keeps its state inaccessible. State is closely related to abstraction and encapsulation. You do not care *how* an object performs its actions, but you do care *that* it performs those actions. Two objects might coincidentally contain the same state, but they are still two different objects.

How to Use the Object Browser

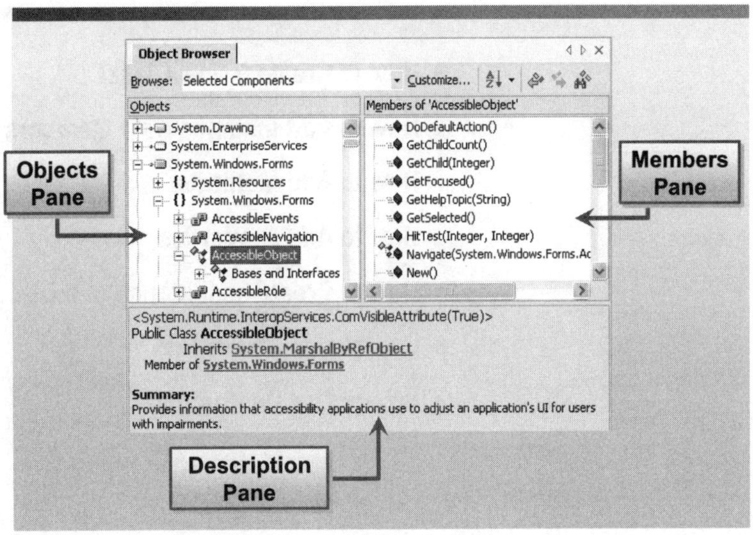

Introduction

You can use the Object Browser to examine a component's programming elements (namespaces, classes, modules, structures, and so on) and the members of those elements (properties, methods, events, variables, and so on). The components you examine can be projects in your solution, referenced components in those projects, or external components.

Using the Object Browser

To open the Object Browser, either press CTRL+ALT+J or, on the **View** menu, point to **Other Windows** and then click **Object Browser**.

The Object Browser is composed of three panes:

- The *Objects pane* displays all container objects in the browsing scope in a tree view. When you expand an element by double-clicking it or by clicking the plus sign (+) next to its name, the elements defined within it appear.
- The *Members pane* displays the members of an element when you select the element in the Objects pane.
- The *Description pane* displays detailed information about the currently selected element or member.

A specific icon represents each programming element in the Object Browser. The following table illustrates some of the icons that are used.

Icon	Description	Icon	Description
{}	Namespace		Module
	Class		Structure

Lesson: Working with Classes

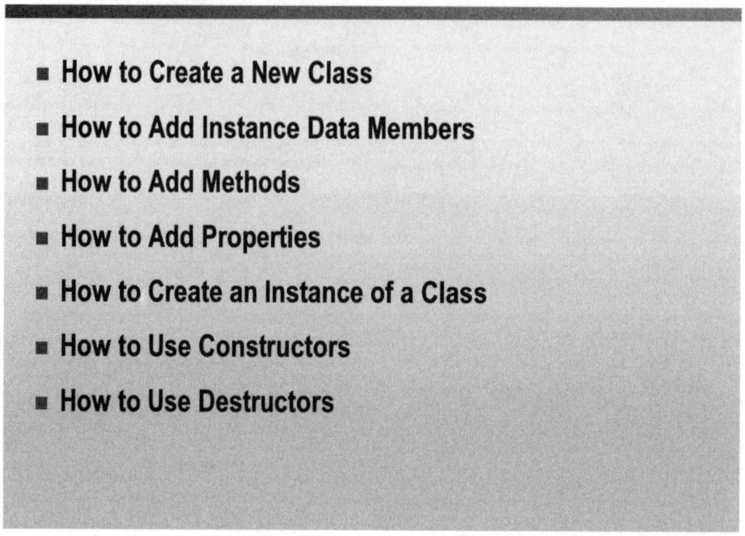

Introduction

The Microsoft .NET platform provides the Microsoft .NET Framework class library, but you can also create your own classes. This lesson describes how to create a new class, add data members, methods, and properties to the class, and set public and private access modifiers. This lesson also describes how to create an instance of a class and how to initialize and un-initialize objects.

Lesson agenda

This lesson includes the following topics and activities:

- How to Create a New Class
- How to Add Instance Data Members
- How to Add Methods
- How to Add Properties
- How to Create an Instance of a Class
- Practice: Creating a Class
- How to Use Constructors
- How to Use Destructors

Lesson objectives

After completing this lesson, you will be able to:

- Create a new class.
- Add instance data members to a new class.
- Add methods to a new class.
- Add properties to a new class.
- Create an object.
- Use constructors to initialize new objects.
- Use destructors to un-initialize objects.

How to Create a New Class

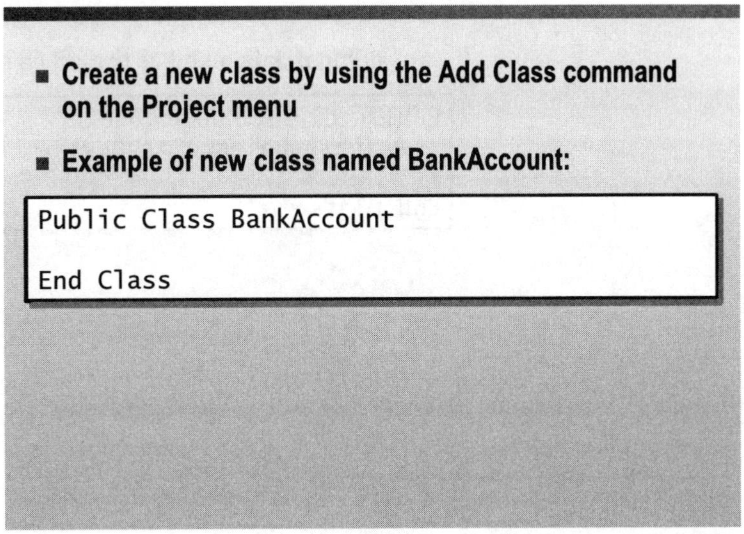

Introduction

After you use the process of abstraction to determine the relevant entities for a business problem, you are ready to create classes that reflect the entities in the abstraction.

Creating a new class

► **To create a new class**

1. Open a project in Microsoft Visual Studio® .NET (if one is not already open).
2. On the **Project** menu, click **Add Class**.
3. In the **Name** box, type the name of your new class, and then click **Open**.

   The Code Editor provides programming statements that mark the beginning and ending statements for your class, as follows:

```
Public Class ClassName

End Class
```

How to Add Instance Data Members

- **Adding a data member named *balance***

```
Public Class BankAccount
  Private balance As Double

End Class
```

Keyword	Definition
Public	Accessible everywhere
Private	Accessible only within the type itself
Protected	Accessible only by classes which inherit from the class

Introduction

After you add a new class to your project, you can add data members to your class. A data member specific to an instance of the class is called an *instance data member*. When you add instance data members to a class, you specify the level of access by setting the access modifiers.

Instance data members

Instance data members include member variables and constants. Member variables are also called *fields*.

Example

In the following example, a data member of type **Double** named *balance* is added to the class:

```
Private balance As Double
```

Me keyword

You can also refer to the data member *balance* by using the **Me** keyword, as shown in the following example:

```
Me.balance
```

The **Me** keyword behaves like an object variable referring to the current instance of a class. When a class can have more than one instance, the **Me** keyword provides a way to refer to the specific instance of the class in which the code is currently running.

Access modifiers

You can control the accessibility of entities inside this class: some will be accessible only from the inside and others will be accessible from the inside and the outside. Those members of the entity that are accessible from only the inside are private. Those members of the entity that are accessible from both the inside and the outside are public. For example, you would need to make the instance data member *balance* private so the balance of the account could not be changed except from inside the **BankAccount** class.

You can also use the **Protected** keyword to limit accessibility to classes that *inherit* from this class. You will learn more about inheritance in the last lesson in this module.

How to Add Methods

- **Adding a method named Deposit**

```
Public Class BankAccount

   Private balance As Double

   Public Sub Deposit(ByVal amount As Double)
       balance += amount
   End Sub

End Class
```

- **Overloaded methods: two or more methods with the same name but different signatures**
  Example: MessageBox.Show

Introduction

You can add methods to a class. When you add methods, you specify the level of access by setting the access modifier. Methods include functions and **Sub** procedures.

Example

In the following example, a method called **Deposit** is added to the class:

```
Public Sub Deposit(ByVal amount As Double)
  Balance +=amount
End Sub
```

In this example, the **Deposit** method is public so that the users of this class can deposit money into an account by using the **Deposit** method.

Overloading methods

Method overloading occurs when a class contains two or more methods with the same name but different signatures. An example of an overloaded method is the **MessageBox.Show** method. The **Show** method provides twelve overloads. These overloads make the method more flexible for users of the method.

To overload a method, use the **Overloads** keyword. The **Overloads** keyword declares a property or method with the same name as an existing member, but with a parameter list that is different from the original member.

The following example shows an overloaded method named **Execute**. The first **Execute** method does not take any parameters. The second one takes a string as a parameter.

```
Public Overloads Sub Execute( )
   ...
End Sub
Public Overloads Sub Execute(ByVal connection As String)
   ...
End Sub
```

How to Add Properties

- **Adding a property:**

```
Public Class BankAccount
    Private customerName As String

    Public Property Name( ) As String
        Get
            Return customerName
        End Get
        Set(ByVal Value As String)
            customerName = Value
        End Set
    End Property

End Class
```

Introduction

You can add properties to a new class in your project. You can assign the property, and you can retrieve the value of the property from the class.

Adding properties

To add property members to a class, you usually define a private data member and public property procedures. You can perform two types of procedures on properties in Visual Basic .NET: **Get** and **Set**.

- The **Get** procedure retrieves the property value from the class. It should not change the value.
- The **Set** procedure assigns the property.

Example

In the following example, a property called **Name** is added to the **BankAccount** class:

```
Public Class BankAccount
    Private customerName As String

    Public Property Name( ) As String
        Get
            Return customerName
        End Get
        Set(ByVal Value As String)
            customerName = Value
        End Set
    End Property

End Class
```

ReadOnly and WriteOnly

Use the **ReadOnly** specifier in the property declaration to create only the **Get** property. Use the **WriteOnly** specifier in the property declaration to create only the **Set** property.

How to Create an Instance of a Class

- **Using the New keyword to create an instance of the BankAccount class:**

```
Module Bank

   Sub Main
      Dim account As New BankAccount( )
      account.Deposit(500.00)
   End Sub

End Module
```

Introduction

To execute the methods and use the properties of a class, you must create an instance of the class. An instance of the class is called an object.

Syntax

To create an instance of a class, you declare a variable of the type of the class and use the **New** keyword, as shown in the following line of code:

```
Dim objectname As New objecttype( )
```

Example

The following example shows how to create an instance of the **BankAccount** class by using the **New** keyword:

```
Sub Main
  Dim account As New BankAccount( )
  account.Deposit(500.00)
End Sub
```

Practice: Creating a Class

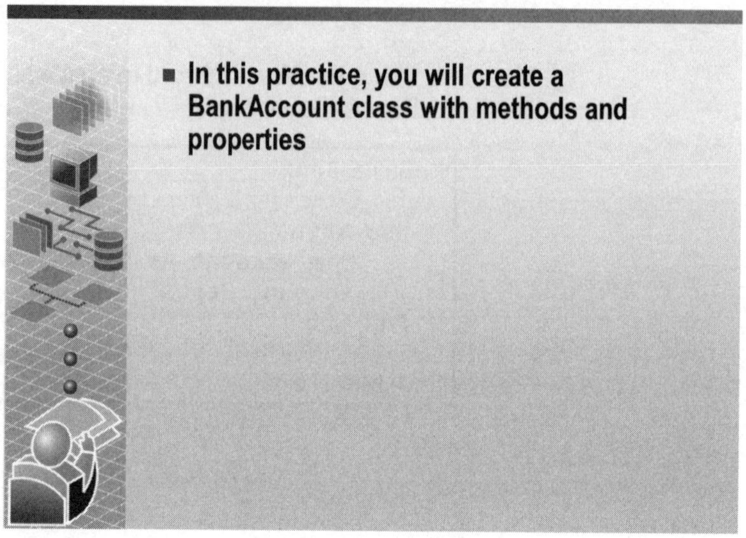

In this practice, you will create a **BankAccount** class with methods and properties.

► **Add a new class to a project**

1. Open a new Microsoft Windows® application in Visual Basic .NET. Set the project name to **SimpleClass** and the location to *install_folder*\Practices\Mod07\CreatingClass.
2. On the **Project** menu, click **Add Class**.
3. In the **Add New Item** dialog box, change the class name to **BankAccount.vb**, and then click **Open**.

► **Add data members, methods, and properties to the class**

1. Add a private data member named *customerBalance* of type **Double**, as shown in the following line of code:

```
Private customerBalance As Double
```

2. Add another private data member named *customerName* of type **String**, as shown in the following line of code:

```
Private customerName As String
```

3. Create a public method named **Deposit** that takes an **amount** parameter of type **Double** by value, as follows:

```
Public Sub Deposit(ByVal amount As Double)
End Sub
```

4. In the method, increment the value of the balance by adding *amount* to it, as follows:

```
customerBalance += amount
```

5. Create a public property called **Name**, as follows:

```
Public Property Name( ) As String

End Property
```

6. In the **Get** block of the property, return **customerName**, as follows:

```
Get
   Return customerName
End Get
```

7. In the **Set** block of the property, assign **Value** to **customerName**, as follows:

```
Set(ByVal Value As String)
   customerName = Value
End Set
```

8. Create a read-only property called **Balance** that returns the current balance, as follows:

```
Public ReadOnly Property Balance( ) As Double
   Get
      Return customerBalance
   End Get
End Property
```

The completed code for the **BankAccount** class should look like the following:

```
Public Class BankAccount
    Private customerBalance As Double
    Private customerName As String

    Public Sub Deposit(ByVal amount As Double)
        customerBalance += amount
    End Sub

    Public ReadOnly Property Balance( ) As Double
        Get
            Return customerBalance
        End Get
    End Property

    Public Property Name( ) As String
        Get
            Return customerName
        End Get
        Set(ByVal Value As String)
            customerName = Value
        End Set
    End Property
End Class
```

► **Create a test harness to test the BankAccount class**

1. Add a module named TestHarness.vb to the project.
2. Create a public **Sub** procedure called **Main**, as follows:

```
Public Sub Main( )
End Sub
```

3. Inside the **Sub Main**, create an instance of the **BankAccount** class, as follows:

```
Dim account As New BankAccount( )
```

4. Use the **Name** property to assign the name to the account, as follows:

```
account.Name = "Joe"
```

5. Use the **Deposit** method to deposit money into the account, as follows:

```
account.Deposit(500)
```

6. Use a message box to display the account name and balance, as follows:

```
MessageBox.Show ("Name: " & account.Name & _
". Balance: $" & account.Balance( ))
```

7. Change the startup object for the project to use **Sub Main**.
8. Build and run the program.

The completed code for the TestHarness module should look like the following code:

```
Module TestHarness

Public Sub Main( )
  Dim account As New BankAccount( )

  account.Name = "Joe"
  account.Deposit(500)

  MessageBox.Show("Name: " & account.Name & _
  ". Balance: $" & account.Balance( ))

  End Sub
End Module
```

Solution files

The solution files for this practice are located in the *install_folder*\Practices\Mod07\CreatingClass\Solution folder.

I disposable

use instead of clean

How to Use Constructors

- **Executes code when object is instantiated**

```
Public Sub New( )
    ' Perform simple initialization
    value = 1
End Sub
```

- **Can overload, but does not use Overloads keyword**

```
Public Sub New(ByVal i As Integer)
   ' Overloaded without Overloads keyword
    ' Perform more complex initialization
    value = i
End Sub
```

Introduction

In Visual Basic .NET, you control the initialization of new objects by using constructors. To create a constructor for a class, create a procedure named **Sub New** anywhere in the class definition.

Features of Sub New

The **Sub New** constructor has the following features:

- The code in the **Sub New** block will always run before any other code in a class.
- The **Sub New** constructor will only run once, when an object is created.

Example of Sub New

The following example shows how to use the **Sub New** constructor:

```
Public Sub New( )
    ' Perform simple initialization
    intValue = 1
End Sub
```

The following line of code creates an object from a class named **BankAccount**, which is already defined in the application.

```
Dim myAccount As New BankAccount( )
```

You can overload **New** and create as many class constructors as you require. This is useful if you want to initialize your object when you create it.

Overloading constructors

You can overload constructors just as you can overload any other method in a class. However, you cannot use the **Overloads** keyword when overloading constructors. The following example shows how to overload **New** and create multiple class constructors:

```
Class BankAccount
  Private balance as Double

  Sub New( )
     ' Initialize balance
     balance = 0.0
  End Sub

  Sub New(ByVal amount As Double)
     balance = amount
  End Sub
End Class
```

One of the constructors in the above example takes a parameter. If you are creating an object from such a class, you can include its parameters in the declaration. The following example shows how to call the **New** method that takes a parameter.

```
Dim myAccount As New BankAccount(120.00)
```

How to Use Destructors

- **Used for resource cleanup**
- **Called by runtime before destroying object**
  - Important: Destruction might not happen immediately

```
Protected Overrides Sub Finalize( )
    ' Can close connections or other resources
    conn.Close
End Sub
```

Introduction

In Visual Basic .NET, you can control what happens during the destruction of objects by using procedures called *destructors*.

Finalize and Dispose

The system calls the **Finalize** destructor before releasing the object. You can use it to clean up open resources, such as database connections, or to release other resources. However, there is a delay between when an object loses scope and when the **Finalize** destructor is called.

Running **Sub Finalize** causes a slight loss in performance, so you should define a **Sub Finalize** method only when you need to release objects explicitly.

Note Visual Basic .NET allows for a second kind of destructor, named **Dispose**, which can be explicitly called at any time to release resources immediately. **Dispose** is beyond the scope of this course. For more information about **Dispose**, see "Object Lifetime: How Objects Are Created and Destroyed" in the Visual Studio .NET documentation.

Example of Sub Finalize

The following example shows how to use the **Finalize** destructor:

```
Protected Overrides Sub Finalize( )
    ' Can close connections or other resources
    conn.Close
End Sub
```

Protected is an access modifier that sets the level of accessibility.

Lesson: Using Shared Members

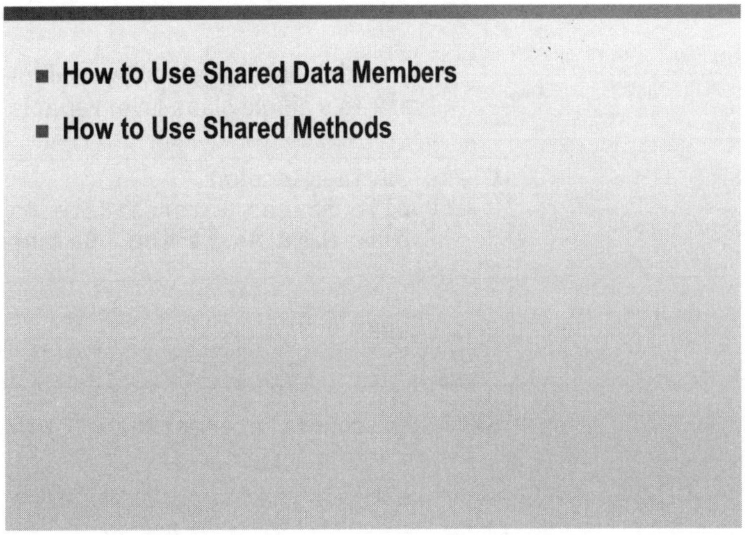

Introduction

This lesson describes how to use shared data members and shared methods. You can use shared members for counters or for any common data or common methods required by all instances of a class.

Lesson agenda

This lesson includes the following topics and activities:

- How to Use Shared Data Members
- How to Use Shared Methods
- Practice: Creating Shared Methods

Lesson objectives

After completing this lesson, you will be able to:

- Use shared data members to share data across class instances.
- Use shared methods.

How to Use Shared Data Members

- **Shared data members allow multiple class instances to refer to a single class-level variable**

```
Class SavingsAccount
    Public Shared InterestRate As Double
    Public Name As String, Balance As Double
. . .

End Class
```

```
SavingsAccount.InterestRate = 0.03
```

Introduction

In Visual Basic .NET, you can use shared data members to allow multiple instances of a class to refer to a single class-level variable.

Syntax

Use the following syntax to declare shared data members:

```
AccessLevel Shared DataMember As DataType
```

Access levels

Shared data members are directly linked to the class, and you can declare them as public or private. If you declare data members as public, they are accessible to any code that can access the class. If you declare data members as private, you provide public shared properties to access the private shared property.

Example

The following example shows how to create a savings account class that uses a public shared data member to maintain interest rates for a savings account:

```
Class SavingsAccount
    Public Shared InterestRate As Double

    Public Function CalculateInterest( ) As Double
        ...
    End Function
End Class
```

The value of the *InterestRate* data member of the **SavingsAccount** class can be set globally regardless of how many instances of the class are in use. This value is then used to calculate the interest on the current balance.

Calling shared data members from a client

After you create a class that uses public shared data members, you can call the data members of that class from a client application. The following code shows how to call the **SavingsAccount** class and its data members from a client application:

```
Sub Test( )
    SavingsAccount.InterestRate = 0.03

    Dim myAccount As New SavingsAccount( )
    Dim yourAccount As New SavingsAccount( )

    MessageBox.Show(myAccount.CalculateInterest( ))
    MessageBox.Show(yourAccount.CalculateInterest( ))
End Sub
```

As you examine this code, note the following:

- *InterestRate* can be set before and after any instances of the **SavingsAccount** class are created.
- Any changes to *InterestRate* will apply to all instances of the **SavingsAccount** class.

Shared properties

You can also create shared properties in your classes. The following example shows how to declare a shared property called **Rate** in the **SavingsAccount** class:

```
Class SavingsAccount
    Private Shared interestRate As Double

    Shared Property Rate( ) As Double
        Get
            Return interestRate
        End Get
        Set(ByVal Value As Double)
            interestRate = Value
        End Set
    End Property
End Class
```

Calling shared properties from a client

After you declare the shared property **Rate**, you can use it in a client application instead of directly accessing the shared data member *interestRate*. You can call a shared property by qualifying it either with the class name or with the variable name of a specific instance of the class.

The following code shows how to call a shared property by qualifying it with the class name:

```
SavingsAccount.Rate = 0.03
```

The following code shows how to call a shared property by using the variable name of a specific instance of the class:

```
myAccount.Rate = 0.04
```

How to Use Shared Methods

- Can be used without declaring a class instance
- Can only access shared data

```
' TestClass code
Public Shared Function GetComputerName( ) As String
    ...
End Function
```

```
' Client code
MessageBox.Show(TestClass.GetComputerName( ))
```

Introduction

You can use shared procedure members to design functions that can be called without creating an instance of the class. Shared procedures are class methods that are not associated with a specific instance of a class. Shared procedure members can only access data that is marked with the **Shared** keyword. For example, a shared method cannot refer to an instance member of a class.

Example of using a shared procedure member

The following example shows how a commonly used function, such as **GetComputerName**, can be created as a shared procedure member so that a client application can easily use it. The client only needs to reference the method prefixed by the class name, because no instance of the class is required.

```
' TestClass code
Public Shared Function GetComputerName( ) As String
...
End Function

' Client code
MessageBox.Show(TestClass.GetComputerName( ))
```

Also note that, in the above code, **Show** is a shared method of the **MessageBox** class.

Practice: Creating Shared Methods

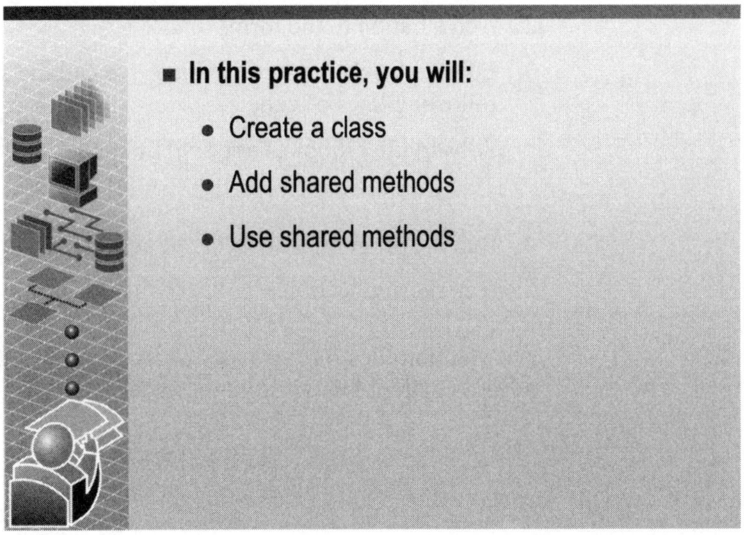

In this practice, you will create and use a class that has a shared method to convert degrees Fahrenheit to degrees Celsius.

► **Create a new class**

1. Open a new Windows application in Visual Basic .NET. Set the project name to **TemperatureApplication** and the location to *install_folder*\Practices\Mod07\SharedMethod.
2. Create a new class and name it **TemperatureConverter**.
3. Add a shared method named **FahrenheitToCelsius** to the new class, as follows:

```
Public Shared Function FahrenheitToCelsius _
   (ByVal degreesFahrenheit As Double) As Double

End Function
```

4. Use the following formula in your function to calculate the temperature in degrees Celsius. Return the result from the function.

```
(degreesFahrenheit - 32) * 5 / 9
```

Your code should look like the following code:

```
Public Shared Function FahrenheitToCelsius _
   (ByVal degreesFahrenheit As Double) As Double

   Return (degreesFahrenheit - 32) * 5 / 9

End Function
```

► Call methods of the class

1. Open Form1 in your project.
2. Add a button to the form.
3. Edit the **Click** event of the button to call the shared method, as shown in the following lines of code:

```
MessageBox.Show(TemperatureConverter.FahrenheitToCelsius _
   (212))
```

4. Run the program and check the result.
5. Quit the application.

Solution files

The solution files for this practice are located in the *install_folder*\Practices\Mod07\SharedMethod\Solution folder.

Lesson: Inheritance, Polymorphism, and Namespaces

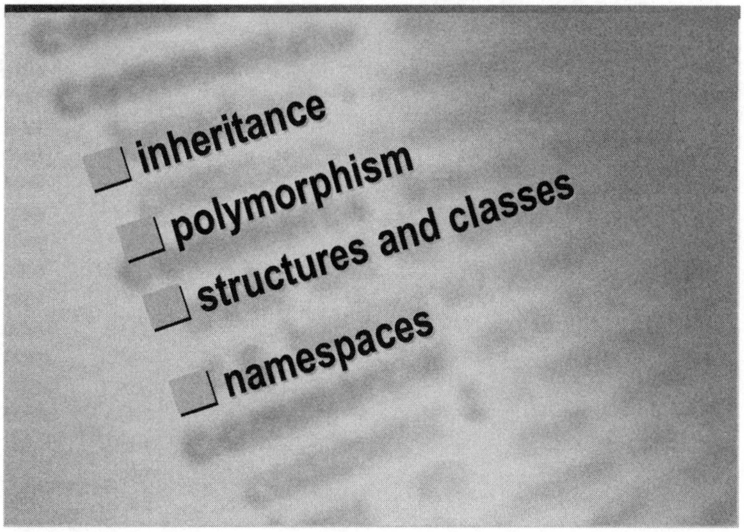

Introduction

You can add functionality to the classes in the Microsoft .NET Framework or to your own classes by using inheritance and polymorphism. This lesson describes inheritance and polymorphism. This lesson also compares classes to structures.

Lesson agenda

This lesson includes the following topics and activities:

- What Is Inheritance?
- How to Inherit from a Class
- What Is Polymorphism?
- Comparing Classes to Structures
- How to Organize Classes into Namespaces

Lesson objectives

After completing this lesson, you will be able to:

- Explain the concept of inheritance.
- Explain the concept of polymorphism.
- Compare classes to structures.
- Explain namespaces.

What Is Inheritance?

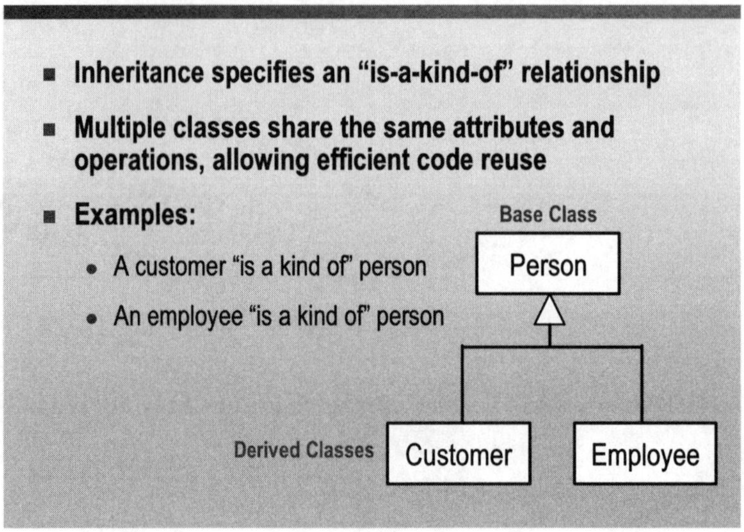

Introduction

In object-oriented programming, you can share the characteristics of a base class in other classes derived from the base class. This is called inheritance.

Definition

Inheritance is the concept of reusing common attributes and operations from a base class in a derived class.

Example of inheritance

Imagine three classes: **Customer**, **Employee**, and **Person**. The attributes and operations of the **Person** base class can be applied to **Customer** or **Employee** too. Reusing these attributes and operations is an efficient technique.

Visual Basic .NET supports single inheritance at the class level. That is, a class can only inherit from a single base class. This is shown in the example in the previous illustration. Other languages, such as C++, allow a class to inherit from multiple classes.

Default Simple Inheritance

How to Inherit from a Class

- **A derived class inherits from a base class**
- **Properties, methods, data members, events, and event handlers can be inherited (dependent on scope)**
- **Keywords**
  - **Inherits** – inherits from a base class
  - **NotInheritable** – cannot be inherited from
  - **MustInherit** – instances of the class cannot be created; must be inherited from as a base class

---

Introduction

In Visual Basic .NET, you can use inheritance to derive a class from an existing base class. The derived class can inherit all the base class properties, methods, data members, events, and event handlers, making it easy to reuse the base class code throughout an application.

Inherits keyword

You use the **Inherits** keyword to define a derived class that will inherit from an existing base class.

Example

The following example shows how to use the **Inherits** keyword:

```
Public Class CheckingAccount
   Inherits BankAccount
   Private Sub ProcessCheck( )
      ' Add code to process a check drawn on this account
   End Sub
End Class
```

Note You can use the **MyBase** keyword to call methods in a base class when you are overriding methods in a derived class. You can also use the **MyBase** keyword to call the base class constructor and destructor in your derived class.

NotInheritable keyword

You use the **NotInheritable** keyword to define a class that cannot be used as a base class for inheritance. A compiler error is generated if another class attempts to inherit from this class.

Example

The following example shows how to use the **NotInheritable** keyword:

```
Public NotInheritable Class TestClass
...
End Class
Public Class DerivedClass
' The following line generates a compiler error
    Inherits TestClass
...
End Class
```

MustInherit keyword

You use the **MustInherit** keyword to define classes that are not intended to be used directly as instantiated objects. The resulting class must be inherited as a base class for use in an instantiated derived class object.

Example

The following example shows how to use the **MustInherit** keyword:

```
Public MustInherit Class BaseClass
...
End Class
...
```

If the client code attempts to create an instance of this type of class, a compiler error is generated, as shown in the following example:

```
' Client code
' The following line generates a compiler error
Dim x As New BaseClass( )
```

Protected keyword

You use **Protected** access to limit the scope of a property, method, data member, event, or event handler to the defining class and any derived class based on that base class.

Example

The following example shows how to use the **Protected** keyword:

```
Public Class BaseClass
    ' Accessible anywhere
    Public counter As Integer

    ' Accessible only in this class or a derived class
    Protected name As String
...
End Class
```

What Is Polymorphism?

Many forms of same Thing

Inheritance or Interface

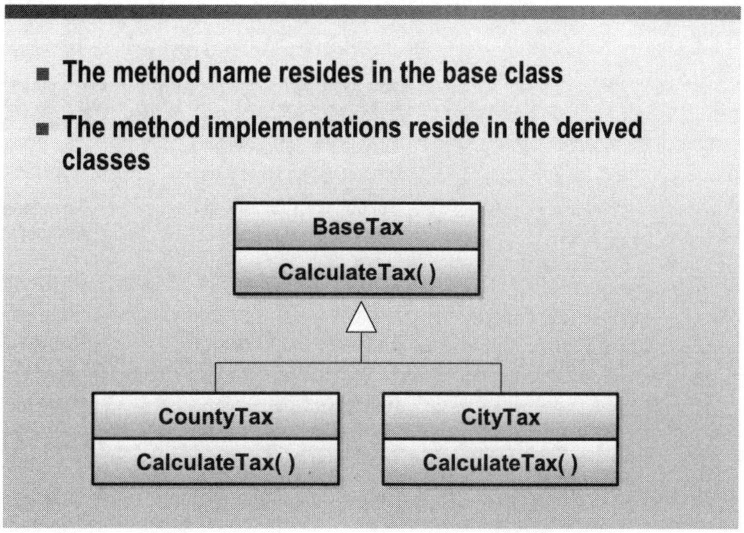

Introduction

Most object-oriented programming systems provide polymorphism by means of inheritance. Inheritance-based polymorphism involves defining methods in a base class and overriding them with new implementations in derived classes.

Definition

Polymorphism refers to the ability to define multiple classes with different functionally but identically named methods or properties that can be used interchangeably by client code at run time. The method name resides in the base class. The method implementations reside in the derived classes. To manage this, only the name of the method (not the code that provides the method's functionality) can be declared in the base class.

Example of polymorphism

Suppose you define a class named **BaseTax** that provides basic functionality for computing sales tax in a state. Classes derived from **BaseTax**, such as **CountyTax** or **CityTax**, could implement methods such as **CalculateTax**.

Polymorphism refers to the fact that the implementation of the **CalculateTax** method might be different in each of the derived classes. The county tax rate might be different from the city tax rate, for example. Any class that inherits from **BaseTax** will have a **CalculateTax** method, but the way that the tax is actually calculated might vary in each of the derived classes.

Comparing Classes to Structures

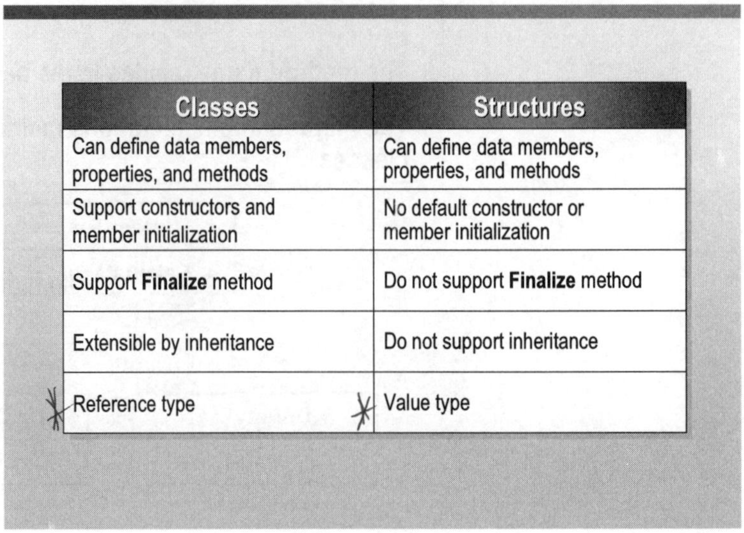

Classes	Structures
Can define data members, properties, and methods	Can define data members, properties, and methods
Support constructors and member initialization	No default constructor or member initialization
Support **Finalize** method	Do not support **Finalize** method
Extensible by inheritance	Do not support inheritance
Reference type	Value type

Introduction

Classes and structures are similar in several ways: both can define data members, properties, and methods. However, classes provide some advanced features that you can use.

The following table compares classes to structures.

	Classes	Structures
Initialization	Support constructors and member initialization.	No default constructor and no initialization of members.
Finalize method	Support **Finalize** method.	Do not support **Finalize** method. You must manually release resources.
Inheritance	Extensible by inheritance.	Do not support inheritance.
Data type	Reference data type. When an object variable is passed to a function, the address reference of the data is passed rather than the data itself. Assigning one class variable to another points both variables to the same object. Any updates to either variable will therefore affect the other.	Value data type. When a structure variable is passed to a function, the actual data must be copied to the function. Assigning one structure variable to another creates an actual copy of the structure. Updates to one of the variables will therefore not affect the other. The difference in data type has a significant effect on application performance. A class with a lot of internal data will perform better than a large data structure under these conditions.

How to Organize Classes into Namespaces

- **Namespaces are an organizational system**
- **Namespaces provide fully qualified names for classes**
  - Example: **System.Windows.Forms.Button**
- **To import a namespace:**
  - At the project level, add a reference to the DLL that contains the namespace
  - Use the **Imports** keyword

Introduction

Namespaces are used as an organizational system—a way to present logically related program components that are available to other programs and applications. A namespace can contain both other namespaces and types.

Example of a namespace

An example of a namespace is the **System.Windows.Forms** namespace. This namespace provides the relevant classes required to create forms. The **Forms** namespace is contained in the **Windows** namespace, which is contained in the **System** namespace.

Fully qualified names

To refer to a class by using its fully qualified name, you prefix the class name with the namespace that contains the class. For example, the fully qualified name of the **Button** class is **System.Windows.Forms.Button**. By using fully qualified names, you can declare two classes with the same name in different namespaces without conflict. By default, every executable file you create with Visual Basic .NET contains a namespace with the same name as your project.

Accessibility

Namespaces are always **Public**, so you cannot declare a namespace with an access modifier. However, the components in the namespace can have **Public** or **Friend** access. If the access modifier is not stated, the default access type is **Friend**.

Defining a namespace

In Visual Basic .NET, you use the **Namespace** statement to define a new namespace, which encapsulates the classes that you create, as shown in the following example:

```
Namespace CompVB
     Public Class StringComponent
     ...
     End Class
End Namespace
```

Using a namespace

At the project level, you must include a reference to the dynamic-link library (DLL) that contains the namespace. In Visual Basic .NET, you use the **Imports** statement to import the types contained in the given namespace so that they can be referenced directly. The following code shows the use of the **Imports** statement:

```
Imports System.Windows.Forms

Public Class Form1
    Inherits Form
```

If you omit the **Imports** statement, you will need to use the fully qualified name of the namespace, as shown in the following example:

```
Public Class Form1
  Inherits System.Windows.Forms.Form
```

Review

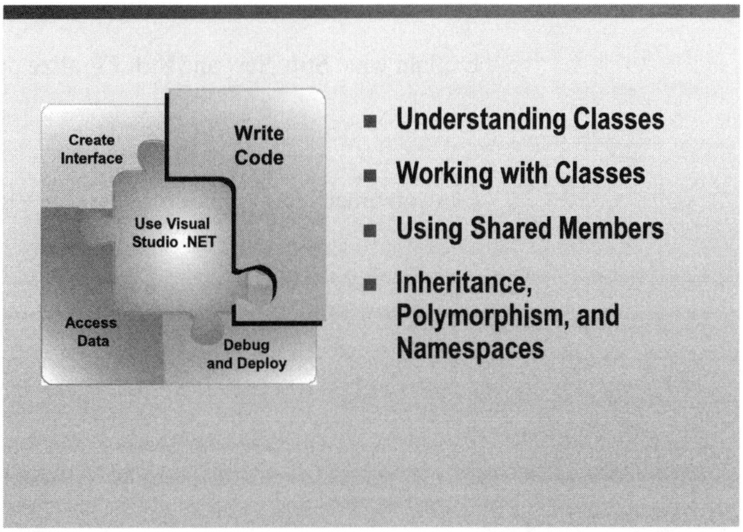

1. In designing a direct deposit application, developers analyze all the relevant objects and disregard all the irrelevant objects. What is this process called?

   abstraction – process of

2. In a direct deposit application, the inner workings and implementation are hidden from the user. What is this process called?

   Incapsolation

3. Write the code to create a public class called **Student** that has a private instance data member named *testScore* of type **Integer**.

   Public Class Student
   Private Test Score As Integer

4. Write code to add a read-only property called **Score** to the **Student** class.

5. Explain what **Sub New** and **Sub Finalize** do.

Initialize varables and Distroy

6. Can you inherit from multiple classes in Visual Basic .NET?

No

Single

Lab 7.1: Creating a Derived Class

Objectives

After completing this lab, you will be able to create a derived class that has methods.

Note This lab focuses on the concepts in this module and as a result may not comply with Microsoft security recommendations.

Prerequisites

Before working on this lab, you must be able to:

- Create a class in Visual Basic .NET.
- Declare data members and methods in a class.

Solution files

The solution files for this lab are in the *install_folder*\Labfiles\Lab071\Ex01\Solution folder.

Estimated time to complete this lab: 30 minutes

Exercise 1
Creating a Derived Form Class

In this exercise, you will create a derived form class. This class will inherit from the **System.Windows.Forms** class. You will add data members, a method, and a constructor to create a simple form application that displays the current date and time.

► Create a new project

1. Start Visual Studio .NET and create a new Visual Basic project based on the Empty Project template.
2. Name the project **SimpleWindowsApplication**, set the folder location to *install_folder*\Labfiles\Lab071\Ex01\Starter, and then click **OK**.

► Add references to the project

- In Solution Explorer, right-click **References**, and then click **Add Reference**. In the **Add Reference** box, on the **.NET** tab, select **System.dll**, **System.Drawing.dll**, and **System.Windows.Forms.dll**. Click **Select** after each one, and then click **OK**.

► Add a new class to the project

1. Add a new class named **Clock** to the project.
   a. On the **Project** menu, click **Add New Item**.
   b. In the **Add New Item** dialog box, click **Class**.
   c. In the **Name** box, type **Clock.vb** and then click **Open**.
2. Add the **Imports** statement at the beginning of the Clock.vb file to import the **System.Windows.Forms** namespace. Your code should look as follows:

```
Imports System.Windows.Forms
   Public Class Clock

   End Class
```

► Inherit the Clock class from the System.Windows.Forms.Form class

- Modify the **Clock** class declaration to inherit from the **System.Windows.Forms.Form** class, as follows:

```
Public Class Clock
    Inherits Form

End Class
```

▶ Add data members to the Clock class

1. Add a private data member named *displayTimeLabel* of type **System.Windows.Forms.Label**, as follows:

```
Private displayTimeLabel As Label
```

2. Add a private data member named *getTimeButton* of type **System.Windows.Forms.Button**, as follows:

```
Private WithEvents getTimeButton As Button
```

Note The **WithEvents** keyword allows an object variable to raise events.

▶ Add a method to the Clock class

1. Add the following method to the class definition.

Method name	Type	Parameters
Initialize	`Private Sub`	None

2. Create an instance of the **Label** type by using the **New** keyword. Your code should look as follows:

```
Private Sub Initialize( )
   Me.displayTimeLabel = New Label( )

End Sub
```

3. Write code to set the properties for **displayTimeLabel** as shown in the following table.

Property	Value
BorderStyle	**BorderStyle.Fixed3D**
Left	**104**
Top	**56**
Height	**30**
Width	**130**

Your code should look as follows:

```
Me.displayTimeLabel.BorderStyle = BorderStyle.Fixed3D
Me.displayTimeLabel.Left = 104
Me.displayTimeLabel.Top = 56
Me.displayTimeLabel.Height = 30
Me.displayTimeLabel.Width = 130
```

4. Add **displayTimeLabel** to the control collection of the form, as follows:

```
Me.Controls.Add(displayTimeLabel)
```

5. Create an instance of the **Button** type, as follows:

```
Me.getTimeButton = New Button( )
```

6. Write code to set the properties for **getTimeButton** as shown in the following table.

Property	Value
FlatStyle	FlatStyle.Flat
Left	128
Top	104
Text	Date Time

Your code should look as follows:

```
Me.getTimeButton.FlatStyle = FlatStyle.Flat
Me.getTimeButton.Left = 128
Me.getTimeButton.Top = 104
Me.getTimeButton.Text = "Date Time"
```

7. Add **getTimeButton** to the control collection of the form, as follows:

```
Me.Controls.Add(getTimeButton)
```

Your completed code for the **Initialize** method of the **Clock** class should look like the following code:

```
Private Sub Initialize( )
   Me.displayTimeLabel = New Label( )
   Me.getTimeButton = New Button( )

   Me.displayTimeLabel.BorderStyle = BorderStyle.Fixed3D
   Me.displayTimeLabel.Left = 104
   Me.displayTimeLabel.Top = 56
   Me.displayTimeLabel.Height = 30
   Me.displayTimeLabel.Width = 130
   Me.Controls.Add(displayTimeLabel)

   Me.getTimeButton.FlatStyle = FlatStyle.Flat
   Me.getTimeButton.Left = 128
   Me.getTimeButton.Top = 104
   Me.getTimeButton.Text = "Date Time"
   Me.Controls.Add(getTimeButton)

End Sub
```

► **Add a constructor to the Clock class**

1. Create a constructor for the **Clock** class, as follows:

```
Sub New( )

End Sub
```

2. In the constructor, add a call to the base class constructor and the Initialize method, as follows:

```
MyBase.New( )
Initialize( )
```

► Add code to the Click event of getTimeButton

1. Create an event handler for the **Click** event of **getTimeButton**.
2. Add code to display the current date and time in the **displayTimeLabel** control. Your code should look as follows:

```
Private Sub getTimeButton_Click (...)
   Me.displayTimeLabel.Text = Now( )
End Sub
```

► Change the startup object

- In Solution Explorer, right-click the **SimpleWindowsApplication** project, and then click **Properties**. In the **Startup object** box, change the startup object to **Clock**.

► Test the application

1. Compile and run the application. Click the **Date Time** button to display the current date and time.
2. Quit the application.

msdn® training

Module 8: Handling Errors and Exceptions

Contents

Microsoft®

Overview

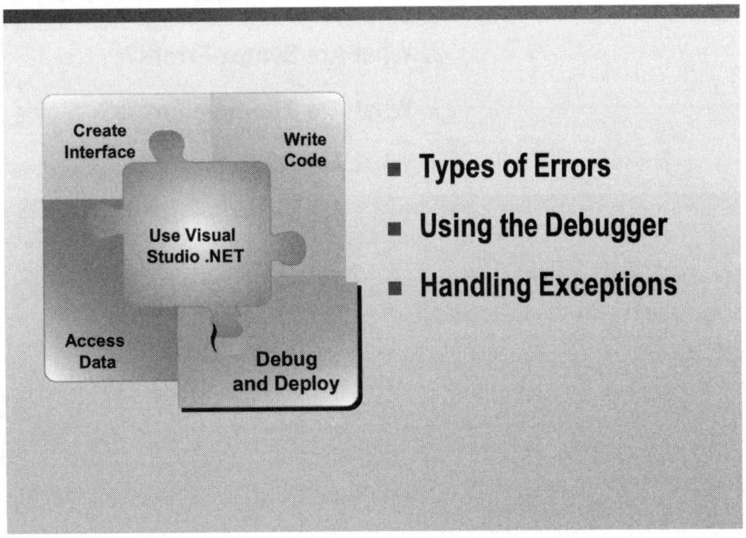

Introduction

As programs become bigger and more complex, a certain number of errors are inevitable. Even careful programming can result in unintended errors, called *bugs*. Finding and removing these bugs is called *debugging*.

In this module, you will learn about the types of errors that can occur in a program, and how to use the Microsoft® Visual Studio® .NET debugger, various debugging windows, and structured exception handling to help you diagnose, correct, and handle errors.

Objectives

After completing this module, you will be able to:

- Define and give examples of syntax, run-time, and logic errors.
- Debug code by using the Visual Studio .NET debugger.
- Implement structured exception handling in your application.

Lesson: Types of Errors

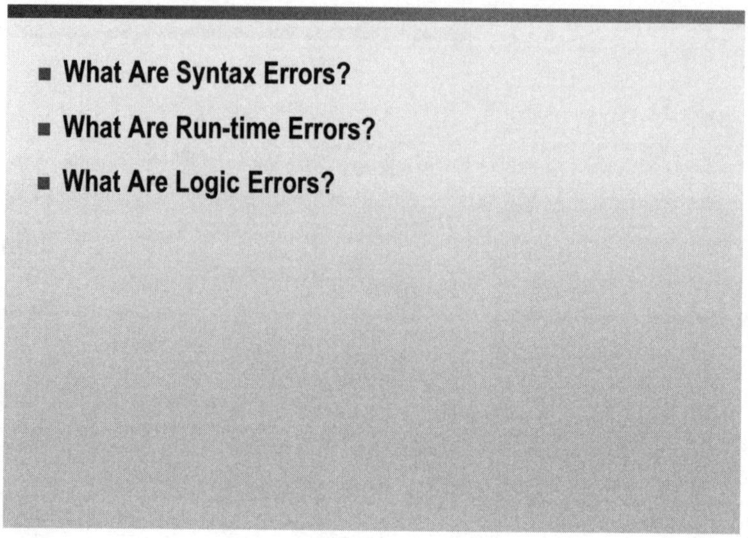

Introduction

Programming errors generally fit into three categories: syntax errors, run-time errors, and logic errors. You will use different methods and tools to find and fix each type of error.

Lesson agenda

This lesson includes the following topics and activities:

- What Are Syntax Errors?
- What Are Run-time Errors?
- What Are Logic Errors?
- Demonstration: Types of Errors

Lesson objective

After completing this lesson, you will be able to describe the difference between syntax, run-time, and logic errors.

What Are Syntax Errors?

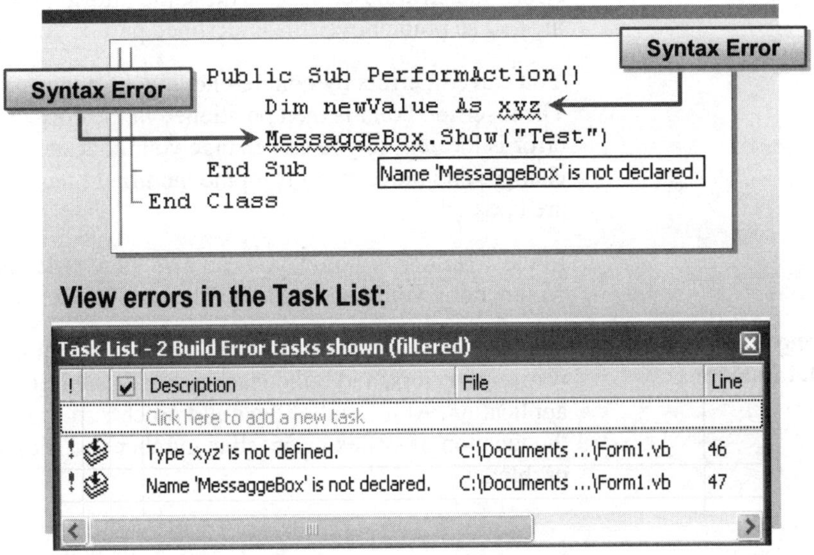

Introduction

The most obvious type of error is a *syntax error*, which occurs when you write code in a manner that is not allowed by the rules of the language. Examples include an incorrectly typed keyword, the omission of required punctuation, or an incorrect construct (such as a **For** statement without a corresponding **Next** statement, or the **If** keyword on a line without a conditional operator).

Finding syntax errors

Microsoft Visual Basic® .NET displays syntax errors while you type each statement in your application code. The portion of the code that contains the error appears with a jagged underline. When you position your mouse pointer over the underlined code, a ToolTip containing a short error description appears near the mouse pointer.

Syntax errors are caught by the compiler, which displays an error message informing you of the problem. If you ignore syntax errors while you are writing code, you can view and address them at any time in the Task List window. If you attempt to build your application without correcting syntax errors, the Task List window appears with all build errors included on the list.

Viewing errors in the Task List window

The Task List window includes an error description, the path to the file in which the error occurred, and the number of the line of code that contains the error. The error description is the same information that you see if you position the mouse pointer over the underlined part of your code in the Code Editor.

You can edit errors by double-clicking the appropriate entry in the Task List. The insertion point is then positioned in the correct file and exact line where the error is located, so you can change your code. As soon as you complete your changes and move away from the modified line, the Task List window entries are updated.

In the Task List window, you can also view tasks that you create yourself by commenting your code with the phrase **TODO**.

Viewing errors in the Output window

You can also use the Output window to view build errors. This window lists warnings, errors, and build status while Visual Studio .NET is building the application. At the end of the build process, it provides a summary, including the location of syntax errors (line number and file) and short descriptions of the problems.

What Are Run-time Errors?

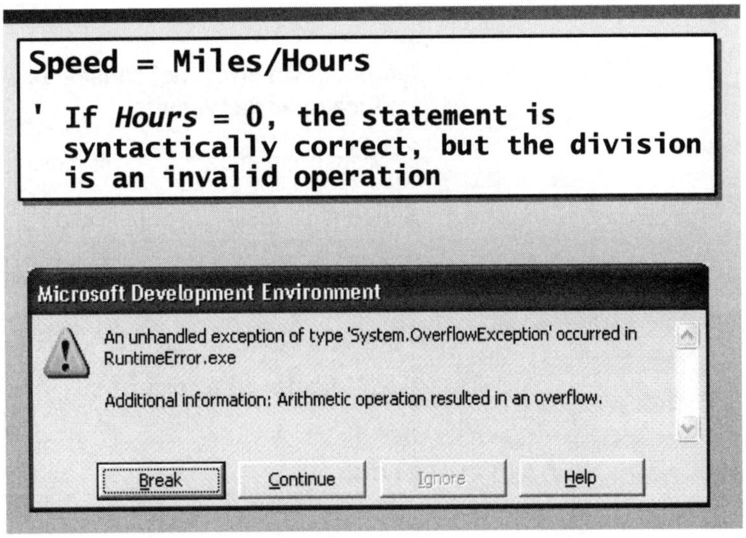

Introduction

Run-time errors are errors that occur when a statement attempts an operation that is impossible to carry out, for example, referencing an object that is inaccessible. Run-time errors appear during execution of your code.

Example of a run-time error

Run-time errors are often a result of unforeseen actions. For example, a user might forget to insert a disk into a floppy drive, or a user could select an invalid input file. One common run-time error is an attempt to divide by zero. Consider the following code:

```
Speed = Miles / Hours
```

If the variable *Hours* is equal to zero, the division is an invalid operation, even though the statement itself is syntactically correct.

Consequences of run-time errors

The compiler does not catch run-time errors. Compilers only catch errors in the structure of the code you write, not errors in the functionality.

If an unhandled run-time error occurs when your program is running as a debug build, an error message appears that lets you enter break mode and address the problem. If a run-time error occurs when your application is running as a release build, it can cause your program to stop responding with or without an error message. In colloquial terms, it can cause your program to crash or hang.

You can use Visual Studio .NET debugging tools to isolate errors and write error-handling code to handle conditions that might generate run-time errors. To handle run-time errors, you can also write exception handlers that trap errors and take a prescribed action, such as correcting the problem, prompting the user for action, or saving data before ending the program. Another way you can minimize run-time errors is to validate all forms of user input.

What Are Logic Errors?

- **Definition: An error that causes an application to produce incorrect results**
  - Might not generate an error message
  - Found by testing the application and analyzing the results

```
Dim x As Integer = 2
Do While x < 10
  ' Code statements
  x -= 1
Loop
```

Introduction

Logic errors are errors that occur when an application does not perform the way it was intended to perform. These errors are especially difficult to find because a logic error might not generate an error message. An application can have syntactically valid code and run without performing any invalid operations but still produce incorrect results.

Example of a logic error

The following code contains a logic error that will eventually result in a run-time error.


```
Dim x As Integer = 2
Do While x < 10
  ' Code statements
  x -= 1
Loop
```


In this code, the **While** loop executes as long as the value of *x* is less than 10. Inside the loop, the statement `x -= 1` contains a logic error, because the starting value of *x* is 2, and the value is decremented by 1 each time the loop executes. The condition `x < 10` will always be true, which results in an infinite loop. A run-time error will occur when the value of *x* exceeds the value that can be stored in an **Integer**.

Finding and fixing logic errors

The only way to verify that an application is working correctly is to test it and analyze the results. As part of the debugging process, you can use Visual Studio .NET debugging tools to isolate and correct logic errors in your code.

Demonstration: Types of Errors

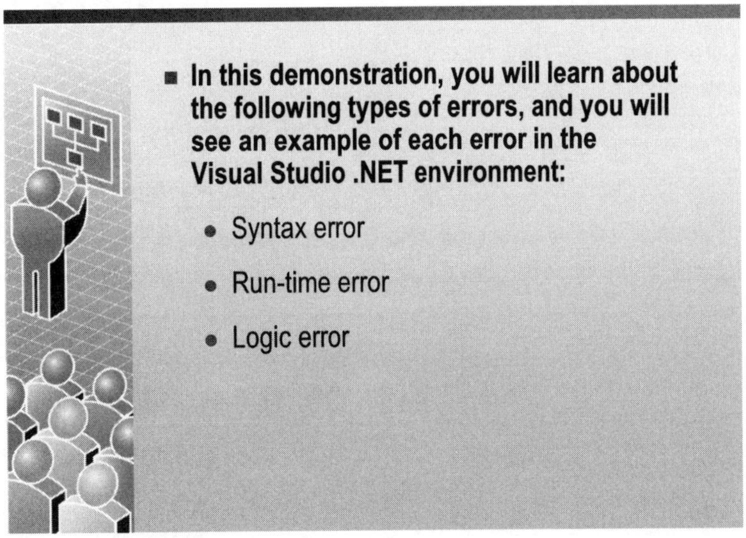

In this demonstration, you will learn about different types of errors.

Lesson: Using the Debugger

- What Is Break Mode?
- How to Use Breakpoints
- How to Modify Breakpoints
- The Debug Toolbar
- How to Step Through Code
- How to Use Debugging Windows
- How to Use the Command Window

Introduction

Debugging tools assist you in diagnosing program errors by helping you to examine the flow of your program. You can use debugging tools to stop your program at set locations in code execution, examine changes in variable and property values, and move through portions of the code step by step.

Lesson agenda

This lesson includes the following topics and activities:

- Multimedia Demonstration: How to Debug an Application
- What Is Break Mode?
- How to Use Breakpoints
- How to Modify Breakpoints
- The **Debug** Toolbar
- How to Step Through Code
- Demonstration: How to Use Debugging Windows
- How to Use Debugging Windows
- How to Use the Command Window
- Practice: Debugging Code

Lesson objectives

After completing this lesson, you will be able to:

- Set, remove, and modify breakpoints.
- Step through code by using Step commands and **Run To Cursor** syntax.
- Use the following windows to inspect your program: the Autos window, the Call Stack window, the Command window, the Locals window, and the Watch window.

Multimedia: How to Debug an Application

In this demonstration, you will learn how to debug an application by using breakpoints, stepping through code line by line, and using the Watch window to examine variables in code.

What Is Break Mode?

- **Pauses the operation of an application**
- **In break mode, you can:**
  - Step through your code line by line
  - Determine the active procedures that have been called
  - Watch the values of variables, properties, and expressions
  - Use debugging windows to change the values of variables and properties
  - Change program flow
  - Run code statements

Introduction

When you develop an application in Visual Basic .NET, you work primarily in two modes: design mode and run mode. In design mode, you create and edit code and can address syntax errors, although you cannot test for logic and run-time errors. In run mode, you can check the program's execution and test for logic and run-time errors, but you cannot make any changes to the code. A third mode—break mode—pauses the operation of an application and gives you a snapshot of its condition at any moment. Entering break mode does not end the execution of your program. Execution can be resumed at any time.

You can only enter break mode when you are running a debug build of your application. You cannot enter break mode when running a release build of an application.

Entering break mode

Visual Basic enters break mode when:

- It encounters a breakpoint that you have set in your code.
- It encounters a **Stop** statement in your code.
- A watch expression that you have placed is triggered.
- You press CTRL+BREAK on your keyboard while you are running a debug build of your program.
- You click the **Break All** button on the **Debug** toolbar while you are running a debug build of your program.
- A statement in a line of code generates an untrapped run-time error and you click **Debug** in the dialog box that appears.
- A **Debug.Assert** statement evaluates to **False**.

  You will learn more about the **Debug.Assert** statement later in this topic.

Using break mode

When you are in break mode, the text **[break]** appears in the Visual Studio title bar. The following screen shot shows an application named DebuggingApplication in break mode.

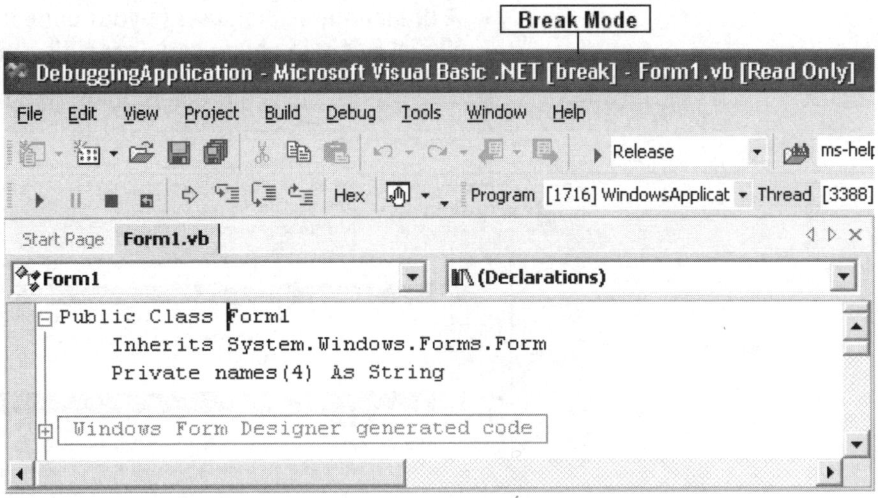

While in break mode, you can:

- Step through your code line by line.
- Determine the active procedures that have been called.
- Watch the values of variables, properties, and expressions.
- Use debugging windows to change the values of variables and properties.
- Change the program flow.
- Run code statements.

Using the Debug.Assert method

You can conditionally enter break mode by using the **Debug.Assert** method. This method uses a Boolean expression to determine whether to enter break mode. Break mode is entered when the **Debug.Assert** statement evaluates to **False**.

To employ the **Debug.Assert** method, use the following syntax:

```
Debug.Assert booleanexpression
```

In the following code, the **Debug.Assert** statement will cause Visual Basic to enter break mode when the variable *Counter* is greater than or equal to five:

```
Private Sub Count_Click( )
    Dim Counter As Integer
    For Counter = 1 To 10
      Debug.Assert Counter < 5
      'Enter break mode when this statement evaluates to False
    Next
End Sub
```

Note You can use **Debug.Assert** only in a debug build of an application. When code is compiled using a release build, method calls to **Debug** are omitted.

How to Use Breakpoints

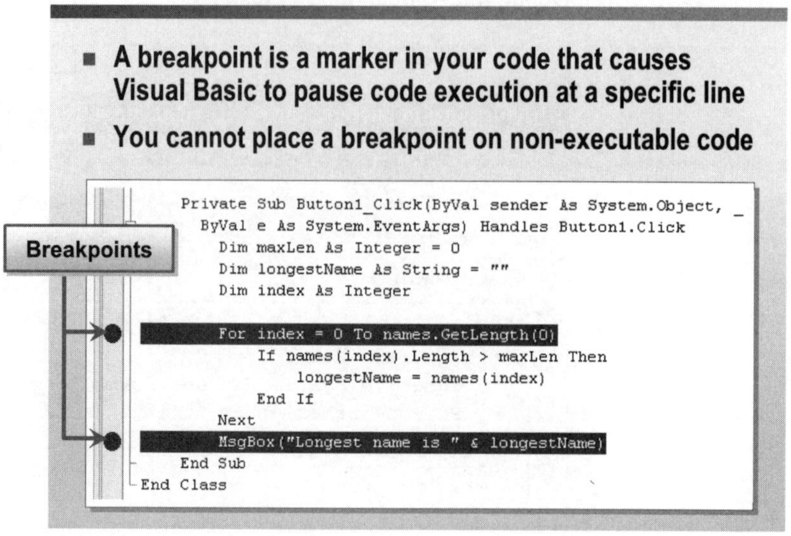

Introduction

A breakpoint is a marker in your code that causes Visual Basic to pause code execution at a specific line. Rather than stepping through your code line by line or instruction by instruction, you can allow your program to run until it encounters a breakpoint and then start to debug.

To stop your program at a location in your code where you suspect a problem, set a breakpoint at that location. You can set breakpoints at design time or during a debugging session.

Setting a breakpoint

There are several ways you can set a breakpoint:

- Click the margin to the left of the Code Editor at the line containing the statement where you want the debugger to halt.
- Place the mouse pointer on the line where you want the debugger to halt. Press F9 to switch the breakpoint on or off.
- Right-click a line of code, and then click **Insert Breakpoint** on the shortcut menu.

When you have set the breakpoint, a circular symbol (●) appears in the margin to the left of the line of code on which the breakpoint is set, and the line of code is highlighted in the same color as the breakpoint.

When the breakpoint is reached during run time, an execution indicator appears on the line that is executed next. You can move this indicator to another line if you want to do so. The following illustration shows the execution indicator.

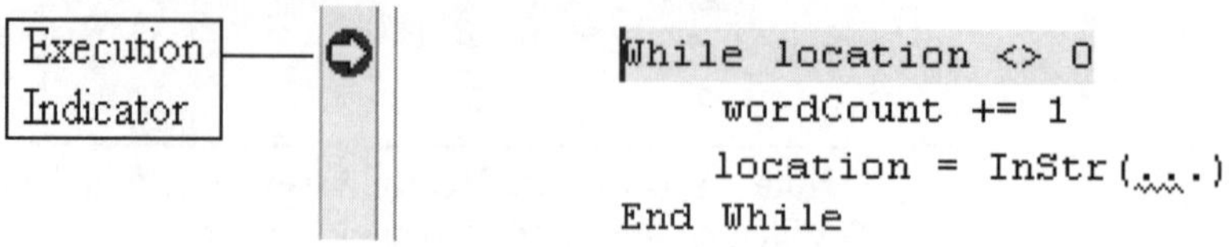

Clearing a breakpoint

There are several ways to clear a breakpoint:

- Click the breakpoint symbol (●) next to the line containing the breakpoint, in the margin to the left of the Code Editor.
- Place the cursor on the line on which the breakpoint is set, and then press F9 to switch the breakpoint off.
- Right-click the line of code on which the breakpoint is set, and then click **Clear Breakpoint** on the shortcut menu.

Note To clear all breakpoints at the same time, on the **Debug** menu, click **Clear All Breakpoints**.

The Breakpoints window

The Breakpoints window lists all breakpoints currently set in your program and displays their properties. In the Breakpoints window, you can set new breakpoints, delete breakpoints, enable or disable breakpoints, edit a breakpoint's properties, or go to the source or disassembly code corresponding to a breakpoint.

► **To open the Breakpoints window**

- On the **Debug** menu, point to **Windows**, and then click **Breakpoints**.

The following screen shot shows the Breakpoints window.

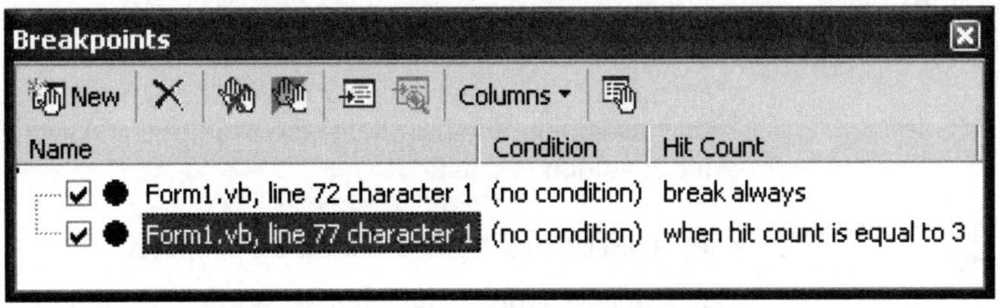

Note For more information about using the Breakpoints window, see *Using the Breakpoints Window* in the Visual Studio .NET documentation.

How to Modify Breakpoints

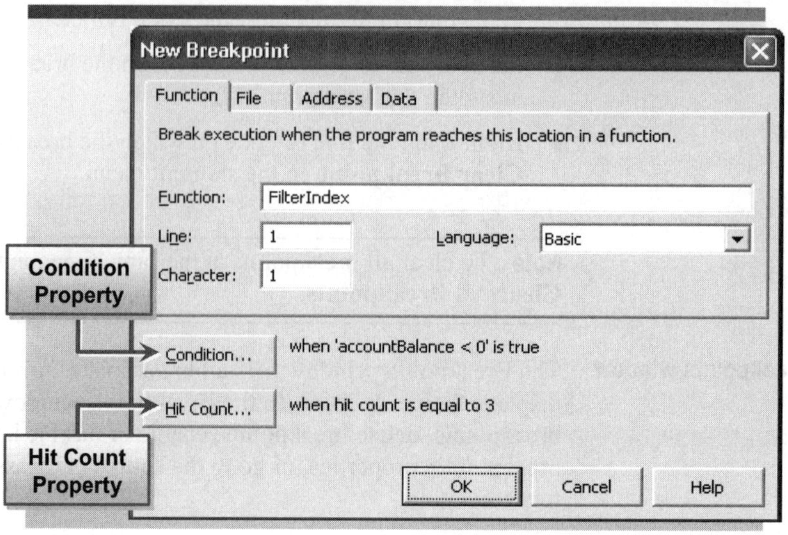

Introduction

You can set two properties that modify the behavior of a breakpoint: the **Condition** property, and the **Hit Count** property.

Using the Condition property

You can use the **Breakpoint Properties** dialog box to set a conditional breakpoint. A condition is an expression that determines whether the debugger enters break mode when it reaches the breakpoint. When the debugger reaches the breakpoint, it will evaluate the condition and switch to break mode only if the condition is satisfied.

Setting the Condition property

► **To set a breakpoint Condition property**

1. On the **Debug** menu, point to **Windows**, and then click **Breakpoints**.
2. Open the **Breakpoint Properties** dialog box by clicking the appropriate breakpoint in the Breakpoints window and then clicking **Properties**  on the Breakpoints window toolbar.
3. In the **Breakpoint Properties** dialog box, click **Condition**.
4. Type the expression that you want the debugger to evaluate.
5. Specify how the condition is satisfied by choosing one of the following:
   a. When the expression is true.
   b. When the value of the expression changes. (Click **has changed** in the **Breakpoint Condition** dialog box.)

      When you set a breakpoint condition that evaluates whether an expression has changed, the debugger does not stop the first time the breakpoint is reached. The expression is evaluated and a value is stored, but this initial store is not considered to be a change in value.

Example using the Condition property

For example, suppose you are debugging a banking program in which the account balance is never allowed to go below zero. You might set breakpoints at certain locations in the code and attach the condition `accountBalance < 0` to each one.

When you run the program, execution will break at the breakpoints only when the variable *accountBalance* is less than zero. You can examine variables and program state at the first breakpoint location, and then continue execution to the second breakpoint location, and so on. The following screenshot shows how you would set the breakpoint **Condition** property for the preceding scenario.

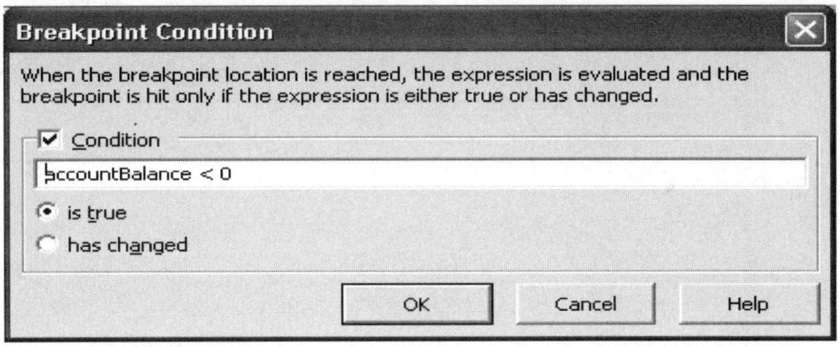

Using the Hit Count property

By default, the debugger pauses execution of code every time a breakpoint is reached. However, some bugs do not appear the first time your program executes a loop, calls a function, or accesses a variable. So you might want to halt execution only when the breakpoint has been reached a specific number of times. This number is called the *hit count*. You can use the **Hit Count** property to specify how many times the breakpoint is hit before the debugger stops execution.

Setting the Hit Count property

► **To set a breakpoint Hit Count property**

1. On the **Debug** menu, point to **Windows**, and then click **Breakpoints**.
2. Open the **Breakpoint Properties** dialog box by selecting the appropriate breakpoint in the Breakpoints window and then clicking **Properties**  on the Breakpoints window toolbar.
3. In the **Breakpoint Properties** dialog box, click **Hit Count**.
4. In the **Breakpoint Hit Count** dialog box, in the **When the breakpoint is hit** box, click the type of hit count test that you want to perform. The following choices are available:
   a. **break always**
   b. **break when the hit count is equal to**
   c. **break when the hit count is a multiple of**
   d. **break when the hit count is greater than or equal to**
5. Enter the appropriate hit count value, and then click **OK**.

Example using the Hit Count property

In the following example, the hit count is set to 3. Execution will stop the third time the breakpoint is hit. If you have set a **Condition** property, execution will stop the third time the breakpoint is hit under that condition.

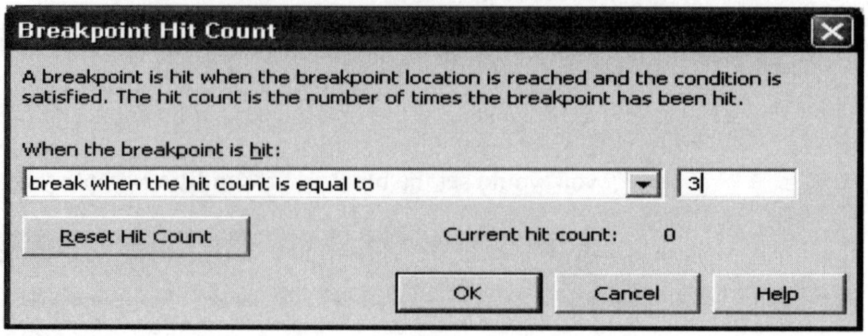

The Debug Toolbar

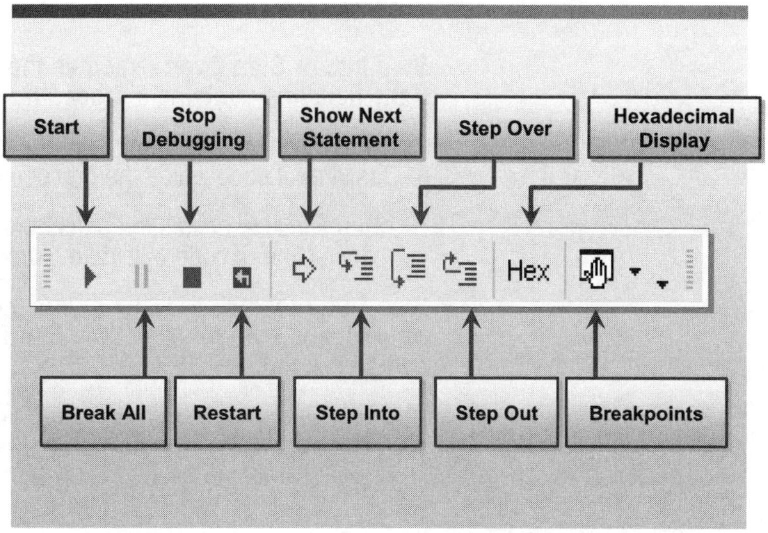

Introduction

After execution of your program is halted near a point where you think a problem is occurring, you can use the debugging tools provided by Visual Basic to investigate the problem. The **Debug** toolbar offers quick access to several of the most frequently used debugging features.

The Debug toolbar

If the **Debug** toolbar is not visible, right-click any toolbar while in design or break mode, and then click **Debug**. The following table describes the toolbar buttons you will use most frequently.

Button name	Default shortcut key	Description
Start/Continue	F5	Runs the application from the startup form (or **Sub Main**) specified on the **General** tab of the **Property Pages** dialog box. In break mode, the **Start** button's ToolTip text changes to **Continue**.
Break All	CTRL+ALT+BREAK	Stops execution of all programs running under the debugger. The programs do not exit and you can resume execution at any time.
Stop Debugging	SHIFT+F5	Stops running the program and returns to design mode.
Step Into	F11	Runs the next executable line of code, stepping through each line of code that follows. If the code calls another procedure, **Step Into** steps through each line in that procedure.
Step Over	F10	Runs the next executable line of code, stepping through each line of code that follows. If the code calls another procedure, that procedure runs completely before stepping to the next line of code in the first procedure.
Step Out	SHIFT+F11	Executes the remainder of the current procedure and breaks at the next line in the calling procedure.
Breakpoints	CTRL+ALT+B	Opens the Breakpoints window.

How to Step Through Code

- **Step Into or Step Over: executes the next line of code. If the next line contains a procedure call:**
  - **Step Into:** executes only the call, and then halts at the first line of code inside the procedure
  - **Step Over:** executes the procedure, and then halts at the first line of code outside the procedure
- **Step Out: resumes execution until the procedure returns, and then breaks at the return point in the calling procedure**
- **Run To Cursor: the debugger runs your application until it reaches the insertion point that you set**

Introduction

One of the most common debugging procedures is stepping through code, or executing code one line at a time. The **Debug** menu provides three commands for stepping through code: **Step Into**, **Step Over**, and **Step Out**. In addition, the **Run To Cursor** command allows you to run your application until the debugger reaches the insertion point that you set. You can then step through your code from this point.

Note You cannot access Step commands if your application is running. Step commands are valid only in break mode or before you start the application.

Using Step Into and Step Over

Both **Step Into** and **Step Over** instruct the debugger to execute the next line of code. These commands differ in only one respect: the way they handle procedure calls.

If the line contains a procedure call:

- **Step Into** executes only the call itself, and then halts at the first line of code inside the procedure.
- **Step Over** executes the entire procedure, and then halts at the first line of code outside the procedure.

Use **Step Into** if you want to view the procedure call. Use **Step Over** if you want to avoid stepping into procedures.

Using Step Out

Use **Step Out** when you are inside a procedure call and want to return to the calling procedure. **Step Out** resumes execution of your code until the procedure returns, and then breaks at the return point in the calling procedure.

Using Run To Cursor

You can use the **Run To Cursor** command to instruct the debugger to run your application until it reaches the insertion point that you set by clicking the Code Editor with your mouse. The **Run To Cursor** command is not available on the **Debug** menu. To execute this command, right-click in the source window, and then click **Run To Cursor** on the shortcut menu.

Starting to step through code

To start debugging an application, you can use **Start**, **Step Into**, **Step Over**, or **Run To Cursor**.

- If you click **Start**, your application starts up and runs until it reaches a breakpoint. You can break execution at any time to examine values, modify variables, and otherwise examine the state of your program.
- If you click **Step Into** or **Step Over**, your application breaks on the first executable line of code.
- If you click **Run To Cursor**, your application starts up and runs until it reaches a breakpoint or the location of the insertion point, whichever comes first. In some cases, a break does not occur. This means that execution never reached the line of code on which you set the insertion point.

Demonstration: How to Use Debugging Windows

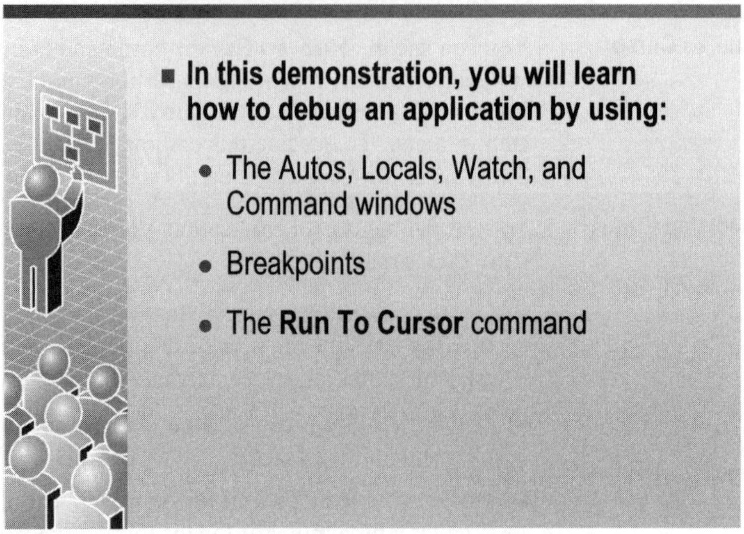

In this demonstration, you will learn how to debug an application by using the Autos, Locals, Watch, and Command windows, breakpoints, and the **Run To Cursor** command.

How to Use Debugging Windows

Window	Use this window to...
Autos	View variables in the current statement and three statements before and after the current statement
Call Stack	View the history of calls to the line of code being debugged
Locals	View and modify local variables
Watch	▪ Create a custom list of variables and expressions to monitor ▪ View and manipulate any watch expressions

Introduction

The Visual Studio .NET debugger provides a variety of windows that enable you to inspect your program in detail and modify the state of your program. The Autos, Call Stack, Locals, and Watch windows are the debugging windows you are likely to use most frequently.

Using the Autos window

You can use the Autos window to view variables in the current statement and three statements before and after the current statement. The current statement is the statement at the current execution location (the statement that will be executed next if execution continues). You can also use the Autos window to change the value of a variable.

► **To modify the value of a variable by using the Autos window**

1. On the **Debug** menu, point to **Windows**, and then click **Autos**.
2. In the **Value** column, double-click the value you want to change.
3. Type the new value, and then press ENTER.

Using the Call Stack window

You can use the Call Stack window to view the history of calls to the line of code being debugged, including any parameter types and parameter values. A *call stack* is the series of procedures called within an application.

► **To view the source code for a procedure on the call stack**

1. On the **Debug** menu, point to **Windows**, and then click **Call Stack**.
2. In the Call Stack window, right-click the procedure whose source code you want to see, and then click **Go To Source Code** on the shortcut menu.

The Call Stack window displays the name of each procedure and the programming language it is written in. The procedure name might be accompanied by optional information, such as module name, line number, byte offset, and parameter names, types, and values. The display of this optional information can be turned on or off.

► **To change the optional information displayed in the Call Stack window**

1. On the **Debug** menu, point to **Windows**, and then click **Call Stack**.
2. Right-click the Call Stack window and select or clear **Show *the desired information*** on the shortcut menu.

Using the Locals window

You can use the Locals window to view and modify variables local to the current context. This window provides explicit details about objects, such as inheritance information.

► **To modify the value of a variable by using the Locals window**

1. On the **Debug** menu, point to **Windows**, and then click **Locals**.
2. In the Locals window, double-click the value you want to edit.
3. Type the new value, and then press ENTER.

Because the Locals window shows you all the variables in the current context, it might not be the ideal window for concentrating on a few specific variables. To monitor only the variables you specify, use the Watch window.

Using the Watch window

You can use the Watch window to create your own custom list of variables or expressions to monitor while the code executes. You can then view and manipulate any watch expressions in the Watch window.

► **To add a variable to the Watch window**

- Right-click the variable in the Code Editor, and then click **Add Watch**.

► **To evaluate a variable or expression by using the Watch window**

1. On the **Debug** menu, point to **Windows**, click **Watch**, and then click **Watch 1**.
2. In the Watch window, click an empty row in the **Name** column.
3. Type or paste the variable or expression in the selected row.
4. Press ENTER. The result appears in the **Value** column.

   If you typed the name of an array or object variable, a tree control appears next to the name in the **Name** column. Click the plus (+) or minus (-) in the **Name** column to expand or collapse the variable.
5. The expression remains in the Watch window until you remove it.

Watch window or QuickWatch dialog box?

The Visual Studio .NET debugger provides a modal dialog box called **QuickWatch** that provides a quick way to evaluate or edit a single variable or expression. Because **QuickWatch** is modal, you cannot leave it open to watch a variable or expression while you step through your program. If you want to watch a variable or expression while you step through your program, add the variable or expression to the Watch window. However, if you simply want to do a quick calculation involving one or more variables, you can use **QuickWatch**.

► **To manipulate a variable by using QuickWatch**

- In break mode, in a source window, right-click a variable name and click **QuickWatch** on the shortcut menu. This automatically places the variable into the **QuickWatch** dialog box.

How to Use the Command Window

- **Use the Command window to:**
  - Issue commands (Command mode)
  - Debug and evaluate expressions (Immediate mode)

Task	Solution	Example
Evaluate expressions	Preface the expression with a question mark (?)	?myVariable
Switch to Immediate mode from Command mode	Type **immed** into the window, without the greater than sign (>)	immed
Switch back to Command mode from Immediate mode	Type >**cmd** into the window	>cmd
Temporarily enter Command mode from Immediate mode	Type the command, prefacing it with a greater than sign (>)	>alias

Introduction

The Command window is not a debugging window, but you might find it useful when debugging your code. You can use the Command window to issue commands (Command mode) or to debug and evaluate expressions (Immediate mode).

Using the Command window

► **To open the Command window**

- On the **View** menu, point to **Other Windows**, and then click **Command Window**.

The following table describes several commands that you can use in the Command window.

Task	Solution	Example
Evaluate expressions	Preface the expression with a question mark (?)	?myVariable
Switch to Immediate mode from Command mode	Type **immed** into the window, without the greater than sign (>)	immed
Switch back to Command mode from Immediate mode	Type **>cmd** into the window	>cmd
Temporarily enter Command mode while in Immediate mode (to execute a single command)	Type the command into the window, prefacing it with a greater than sign (>)	>alias

Note You must include the greater than sign (>) when issuing Visual Studio .NET commands while in Immediate mode. Commands typed in Command mode are not prefaced by the greater than sign.

Practice: Debugging Code

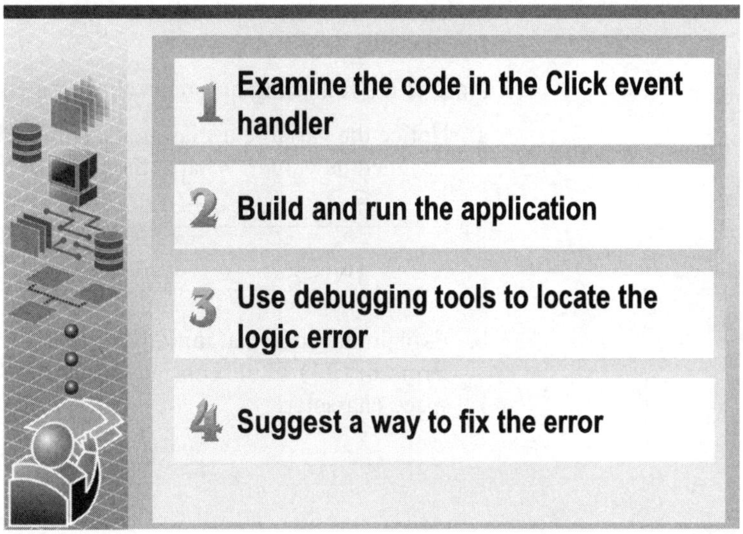

In this practice, you will work through the process of debugging a simple application. To locate a logic error in a program, you will set a breakpoint, step through code, and use the Autos window to check the values stored in variables while your code is running in break mode. You will suggest how the logic error could be fixed, and will then implement one possible solution to the error.

► Open the project

- Open the DebugApplication.sln project, which is in the *install_folder*\Practices\Mod08\Starter folder.

  This application is designed to calculate the number of words in a sentence. The user types a sentence into a text box on a form and clicks a button, and then a message box appears telling the user how many words are in the sentence that was typed.

  The following screen shot shows the running application.

► Examine the NumberOfWords_Click event handler

- Open the **NumberOfWords_Click** event handler, and examine the code to understand how the application has been written to accomplish the expected functionality.

  Answer the following questions about the code.

  a. Notice the variable declarations. How will the *sentence* variable be assigned its value? What is the purpose of the **Trim** function?

  By user

  Max Chr in String

  b. Explain the code that initially assigns a value to *location*. Note that the term `Chr(32)` in the constant declaration for *spaceDelimeter* refers to a space character.

  c. What condition will prevent the **While** loop from iterating?

  Location does not = 0

  d. What is the purpose of the *wordCount* variable?

  to Quantitate Number (whole)

  e. What is the purpose of assigning a new value to *location* in the **While** loop? Why does the location assignment using the **InStr** function occur again?

  to

f. Describe the code flow that you would expect if a user were to type the word "Test" with no spaces into **InputTextBox**. What value would the message box return?

____

____

g. Describe the code flow that you would expect if a user were to type the words "Test Me" into **InputTextBox**. What value would the message box return?

____

____

Note Check your answers before continuing to the next part of the practice. To check your answers, you can use the answers provided on the Student Materials compact disc, compare answers with another student, or show your answers to the instructor. To check your answers for the last two questions, you can also set a breakpoint at the beginning of the **While** loop and use the **Step Into** command (F11) to move through the code step by step.

► **Build and run the application**

1. Run the application in debug mode.
2. In the **Enter a sentence** box, type the word **Test** and then click **Total Words**. The message box should display 1, the correct number of words. Click **OK**.
3. In the **Enter a sentence** box, type the sentence **Test me** and then click **Total Words**. The message box should display 2, the correct number of words in this sentence. Click **OK**.
4. Modify the existing sentence in the **Enter a sentence** box by adding extra spaces between the two words.
5. Click **Total Words**. An incorrect word count appears in the message box. Click **OK**.

► **Locate the code that causes the error**

1. To locate the logic error in this application, think through the following questions:
   a. What input from the user is causing this error?

      ____

      ____

   b. What debugging tools could you use to locate the code causing the error?

      ____

      ____

2. In the **NumberOfWords_Click** event handler, on the line of code that starts the **While** Loop, set a breakpoint.
3. Run the application. In the **Enter a sentence** box, type **Test   Me** with extra spaces between the two words, and then click the **Total Words** button.

4. Use the **Step Into** command (F11) to step through the code one line at a time. As you step through the code, use the Autos window to examine the variable values and determine when the error occurs.

   You might want to use the following questions to help you locate the logic error:

   a. What is the value of *location* during the first iteration of the **While** loop?

   ____

   ____

   b. Does the value of *wordCount* increment properly after the first space is found?

   ____

   ____

   c. What is the value of *location* when the value of *wordCount* changes to 2?

   ____

   ____

   d. How many words have actually been counted if the current value of *location* is 6?

   ____

   ____

   e. Describe the problem with this code, and suggest a way to correct the error.

   ____

   ____

▶ Correct the logic error

One way to solve the problem with this code is to remove each word after it is counted and then remove the spaces from the beginning of the remaining string.

The *sentence* variable is a **String** data type, and it provides the **Remove** method to remove characters from a string. The following code shows how to use the **Remove** method and the **LTrim** function to solve the error:

```
sentence = LTrim(sentence.Remove(0, location))
```

Because you remove a word from the string with the preceding code, you also need to modify the **InStr** function call in the **While** loop and set the start position to 1 each time the code runs.

- Correct the code in the **NumberOfWords_Click** event handler. The corrected code should look similar to the following code:

```
While location < > 0
   wordCount += 1
   sentence = LTrim(sentence.Remove(0, location))
   location = InStr(1, sentence, spaceDelimeter)
End While
```

▶ Test the application

- Run and test the application in debug mode.

Solution files

The solution files are located in the *install_folder*\Practices\Mod08\Solution folder.

Lesson: Handling Exceptions

- The Exception Class
- What Is Structured Exception Handling?
- How to Use the Try...Catch Statement
- How to Use the Finally Block
- How to Throw Exceptions
- Guidelines for Using Structured Exception Handling

Introduction

Visual Basic supports structured exception handling. Structured exception handling provides a way for you to handle errors that might occur in a block of code, while still allowing your application to run. By using structured exception handling in your application, you can plan for potential errors and prevent them from interfering with the intended purpose of your application.

In this lesson, you will learn how to implement structured exception handling in Visual Basic .NET, and you will learn when to use this method of error handling.

Lesson agenda

This lesson includes the following topics and activities:

- The **Exception** Class
- What Is Structured Exception Handling?
- How to Use the **Try...Catch** Statement
- How to Use the **Finally** Block
- How to Throw Exceptions
- Guidelines for Using Structured Exception Handling
- Demonstration: Using Structured Exception Handling

Lesson objectives

After completing this lesson, you will be able to:

- Explain the purpose of structured exception handling.
- Create and use **Try...Catch...Finally** blocks.
- Throw exceptions.

The Exception Class

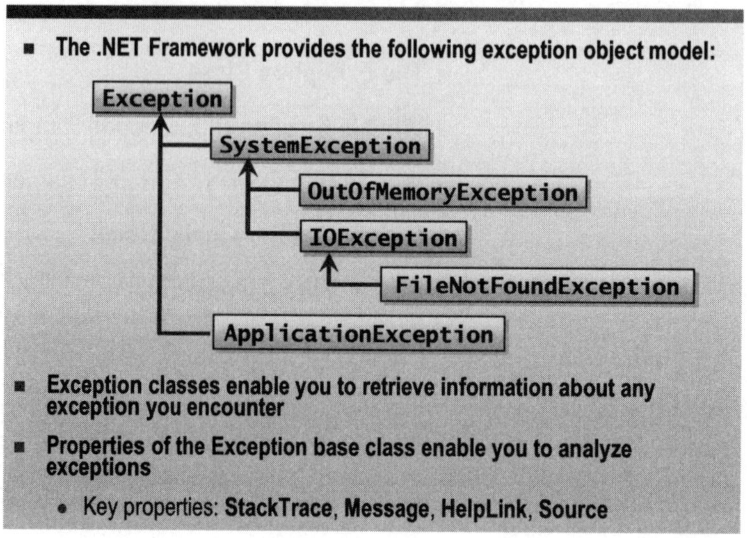

What is an exception?

An exception is any error condition or unexpected behavior that occurs during the execution of a program and requires the execution of code outside the normal flow of control. Exceptions can be raised because of a fault in your code or in code you call, because of operating system resources not being available, because of unexpected conditions that the common language runtime encounters, and so on. An exception is *thrown*—in other words, it originates—from the area of code where a problem has occurred.

The Exception class

In the Microsoft .NET Framework, the runtime creates an object to represent an exception when it occurs. Exceptions are objects that inherit from the **Exception** base class. The .NET Framework defines a range of exception classes. These classes provide information about exceptions in a meaningful manner and allow you to retrieve information about any exception you encounter. This information helps you to debug your applications effectively.

The following table describes several of the properties of the **Exception** base class that help you to identify the code location, type, and cause of an exception. Any exception that inherits from the base class will provide these properties.

Property	Description
StackTrace	Lists the called methods that led up to the exception, helping you find where the error occurs in the code.
Message	Returns a text message describing the error. Use this property to retrieve information about why an exception was thrown. You can alter the text to make a cryptic message easier to understand. If you do not supply an error message text string, the default is used.
HelpLink	Gets or sets a link to an associated Help file.
Source	Gets or sets a string containing the name of the object causing the error or the name of the assembly in which the exception originated.

What Is Structured Exception Handling?

- **Detect and respond to errors while an application is running**
- **Use Try...Catch...Finally to encapsulate and protect blocks of code that have the potential to raise errors**
  - Each block has one or more associated handlers
  - Each handler specifies some form of filter condition on the type of exception it handles
- **Advantages:**
  - Allows separation between logic and error handling code
  - Makes code easier to read, debug, and maintain

Introduction

Structured exception handling is code designed to detect and respond to errors during execution by combining a control structure (similar to **Select Case** or **While**) with exceptions, protected blocks of code, and filters.

Consequences if you do not handle exceptions

If an exception occurs in a method that is not equipped to handle it, the exception is propagated back to the calling method. If it is not handled in the calling method, the search for a handler continues up the call stack. If no handler for the exception exists, an error message appears and the application is closed.

Using structured exception handling

Using the **Try...Catch...Finally** statement, you can protect blocks of code that have the potential to raise errors.

The **Try** block encloses an expression that might generate an exception. The **Try** block has one or more associated **Catch** statements, which filter exceptions and match them with a particular action. If the exception occurs, the runtime stops normal execution and starts searching for a **Catch** block that can catch the exception, based on its type.

- If an appropriate **Catch** block is not found in the immediate procedure, the runtime proceeds up the call stack searching for the calling procedure.
- If an appropriate **Catch** block is not found there, the runtime searches for the procedure that called the calling procedure, and so on, until it finds an appropriate **Catch** block.
- If a **Catch** block is found, the exception is considered to have been caught, and execution restarts, beginning with the body of the **Catch** block.
- If no **Catch** block is found, an error message appears and the application is closed.

By using **Try** and **Catch** blocks, you separate error-handling statements from the core logic statements. This makes your program easier to read and to debug.

How to Use the Try...Catch Statement

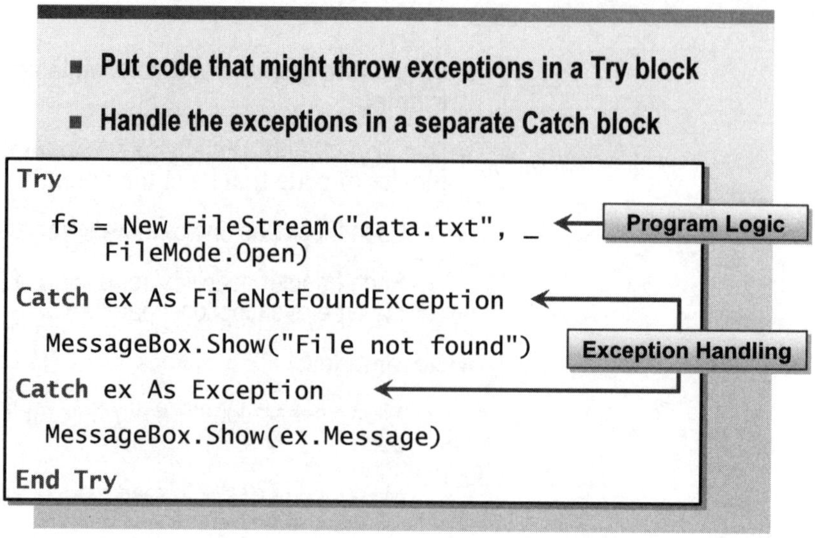

Syntax

You can implement structured exception handling in Visual Basic .NET by using the **Try...Catch** statement. The following code shows the structure of a simple **Try...Catch** statement:

```
Try
  ' Starts a structured exception handler
Catch [optional filter]
  ' This code runs if the statements listed in the Try block
  ' fail and the filter on the Catch statement is true
End Try
  ' Ends a structured exception handler
```

Where to put your code

The **Try** block of a **Try...Catch** exception handler contains the section of code that you want your exception handler to monitor. Place the sections of code that might throw exceptions in a **Try** block and place code that handles exceptions in a **Catch** block.

How the Try...Catch statement is processed

The code in the **Try** block always executes. If an error occurs during execution of any of the code in the **Try** section, Visual Basic examines each **Catch** statement in the exception handler until it matches the type of the exception that occurred to the name of the exception specified in the **Catch** statement and then transfers control to the first line of code in the **Catch** statement. If no appropriate **Catch** block is found, an error is produced.

Important Because **Catch** statements are processed in order, the order in which you write your **Catch** statements is important. You should put **Catch** blocks targeted to specific exceptions before a general exception **Catch** block.

Example using Try...Catch

The following code provides a simple example of a structured exception handler. In this example, the **Try** block executes. If there is a **FileNotFoundException** error, then code in the first **Catch** block is executed. For all other errors, the code in the second **Catch** block executes.

Note that you target specific errors in the first **Catch** block. The second **Catch** block is designed to catch any general errors.

```
Try
  fs = New FileStream("data.txt", FileMode.Open)
Catch ex As FileNotFoundException
  MessageBox.Show("File not Found")
Catch ex As Exception
  MessageBox.Show(ex.Message)
End Try
```

How to Use the Finally Block

- **Optional section; if included, it always executes**
- **Place cleanup code, such as that for closing files, in the Finally block**

```
Try
  fs = New FileStream("data.txt", FileMode.Open)
Catch ex As FileNotFoundException
  MessageBox.Show("Data File Missing")
Catch ex As Exception
  MessageBox.Show(ex.Message)
Finally
  If Not (fs Is Nothing) Then fs.Close( )
End Try
```

Introduction

The **Finally** block is an optional block of code, which if included, is always executed. In this block, you can define actions that need to take place regardless of whether an exception occurs. This might include actions such as closing files or releasing objects. The **Finally** block is most often used to clean up resources used in your code when a method fails.

The code in the **Finally** section always executes last, just before the error-handling block loses scope. If you include this block, it is executed after the **Try** block if no errors occurred, or after the appropriate **Catch** block has been processed if an exception is caught.

Example using Try...Catch...Finally

The following code provides an example of using a **Finally** block to close an open file.

In this example:

- The **Try** block always executes.
  - If there is a **FileNotFoundException** error, code in the first **Catch** block is executed next, followed by the code in the **Finally** block.
  - If there is some other type of error, the code in the second **Catch** block is executed next, followed by the code in the **Finally** block.
- If there is no error, then code in the **Finally** block executes after the code in the **Try** block.

```
Try
  fs = New FileStream("data.txt", FileMode.Open)
Catch ex As FileNotFoundException
  MessageBox.Show("Data File Missing")
Catch ex As Exception
  MessageBox.Show(ex.Message)
Finally
  If Not (fs Is Nothing) Then fs.Close( )
End Try
```

How to Throw Exceptions

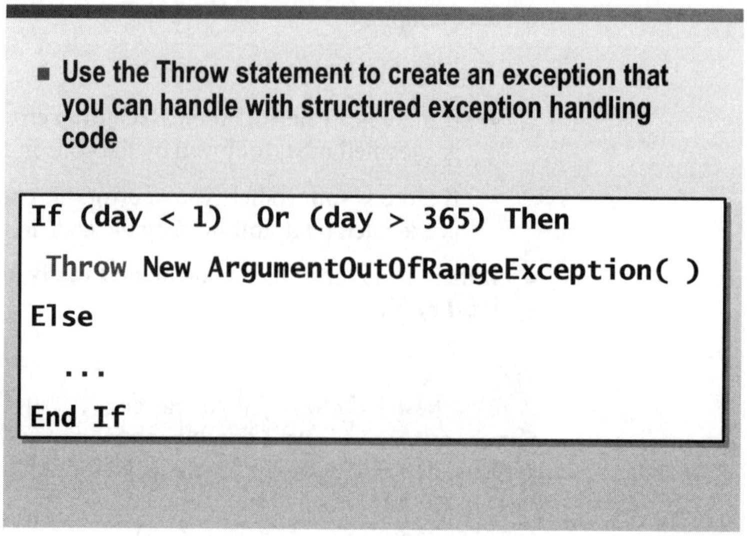

Introduction

The **Throw** statement creates an exception that you can handle with structured exception handling code. In some cases, you should use a **Throw** statement to raise an exception, which can be trapped by calling code. To understand when you might want to throw an exception, consider the following scenario.

Scenario using the Throw statement

When writing larger applications, it is common practice to write reusable code: **Function** and **Sub** procedures that can be used repeatedly in the application or in other applications. Typically, a function takes certain parameters, performs a task, and can return a value. For example, consider a function that takes the day of the year as an integer and returns the calendar date. When passed the number 33, this function is expected to return "February 2."

As the writer of this function, you need to consider how to handle a case in which your function is passed invalid data. For example, if your function is passed a negative number or a number greater than 365 for non-leap years, an error has occurred, and the return value will not be correct.

The best solution to this problem depends on the application. In a simple case, you might be able to ask the user to enter correct information. However, if this function is called by another function rather than a user, the solution is not as simple. In this case, you can write a **Throw** statement that throws the appropriate exception in a case in which the argument passed to your function is out of range.

Example using the Throw statement

The following code uses the **Throw** statement to create an **ArgumentOutOfRangeException** error:

```
If (day < 1) Or (day > 365) Then
      Throw New ArgumentOutOfRangeException( )
Else
      ...
End If
```

Guidelines for Using Structured Exception Handling

- Do not use structured exception handling for errors that are likely to occur routinely. Use other code blocks to address these errors.
  - **If...End If**, and so on.
- Return a value for common error cases.
  - Example: File I/O read methods do not throw end-of-file exception.
- Arrange **Catch** blocks from specific to general.

Introduction

Structured exception handling can be an effective way of handling possible errors in your application. However, it is important that you recognize when to use a **Try...Catch...Finally** block and when to use other code solutions to solve a problem. If a problem is likely to occur, you can programmatically check for and address the problem without using structured exception handling. When an error is truly an exception—when it is an unlikely but possible occurrence—using structured exception handling is appropriate.

Example of handling a potential error by using an If statement

The following example uses an **If** statement to check whether a connection is closed. You can use this method as an alternative to throwing an exception if the connection is not closed.

```
If conn.State <> ConnectionState.Closed Then
  conn.Close( )
End If
```

Example of handling the same error by using Try...Catch

In the following example, an exception is thrown if the connection is not closed.

```
Try
  conn.Close( )
Catch ex As InvalidOperationException
  ' Do something with the error or ignore it
End Try
```

When to use each method

The method that you choose to use to handle potential errors depends on how often you expect a particular event to occur. If the event is truly exceptional and is an error (such as an unexpected end-of-file error), using exception handling is better because less code is executed in the normal case. If the event happens routinely, using another method to check for errors is better. In that case, if an exception occurs, the exception will take longer to handle.

Other guidelines for structured exception handling

The following list describes other guidelines to follow when you implement structured exception handling:

- If you know a situation is going to happen, such as an end-of-file error, do not use an exception to signal it. Use the return value of the method instead. For example, in the .NET Framework, the file input/output (I/O) read methods do not throw an end-of-file exception. Instead, they return a value indicating that they could not read from the file.
- Always order exceptions in **Catch** blocks from the most specific to the least specific. This technique handles the specific exception before it is passed to a more general **Catch** block.
- Use **Try...Finally** blocks around code that can potentially generate an exception, and place your **Catch** statements in one location. When you do this, the **Try** statement generates the exception, the **Finally** statement closes or reallocates resources, and the **Catch** statement handles the exception from a central location.

Note For more information about when to use structured exception handling, see *Best Practices for Handling Exceptions* in the Visual Studio .NET documentation.

Demonstration: Using Structured Exception Handling

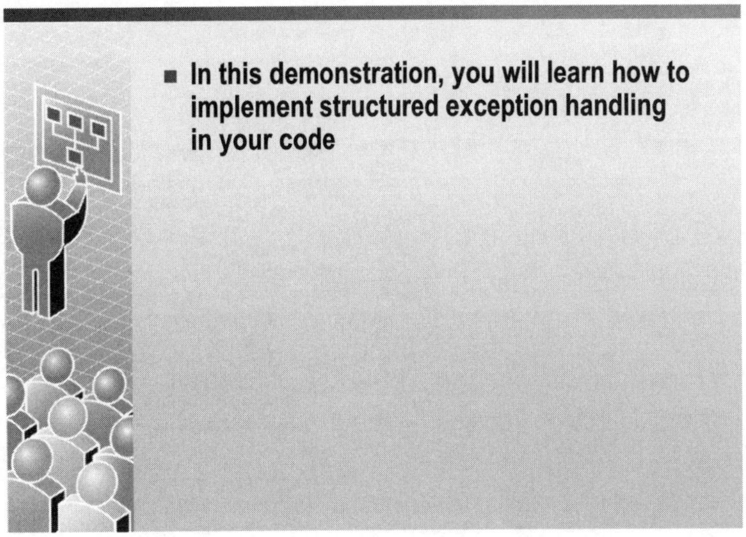

In this demonstration, you will learn how to use the **Try...Catch** statement to implement structured exception handling.

Review

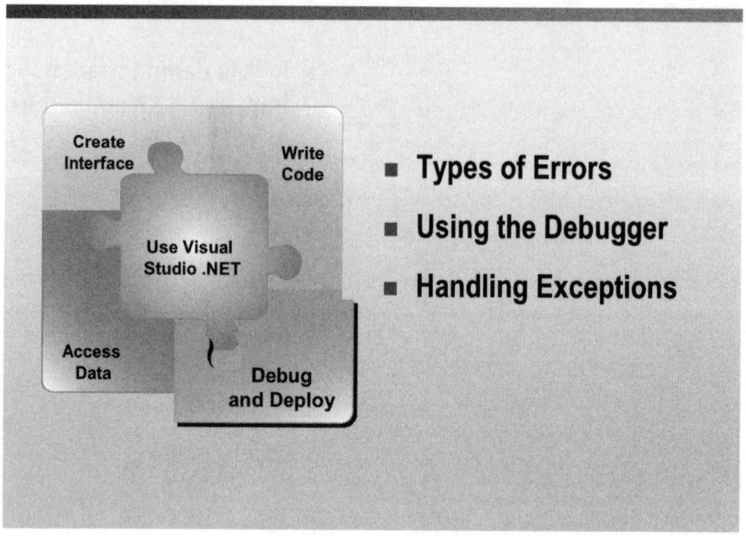

1. Explain the following terms:
   a. Syntax error
   b. Run-time error
   c. Breakpoint
   d. Call stack

2. Suppose you want to enter break mode only if a certain condition is true. How can you set this type of breakpoint?

3. Examine the following code. In what order will the statements in the **Try...Catch...Finally** block execute in each of the following cases?

   a. No exception occurs.

   b. A **FileNotFoundException** occurs.

   c. An **IOException** occurs.

```
Try
   fs = New FileStream("data.txt", FileMode.Open)
Catch ex As FileNotFoundException
   MessageBox.Show("File not found")
Catch ex As Exception
   MessageBox.Show(ex.Message)
Finally
   If Not (fs Is Nothing) Then fs.Close( )
End Try
```

4. Write a statement that throws an exception of type **ArgumentOutOfRangeException** if the variable *percent* is less than zero or greater than 100.

5. Why should structured exception handling not be used to handle an error that is likely to occur routinely?

Lab 8.1: Implementing Structured Exception Handling

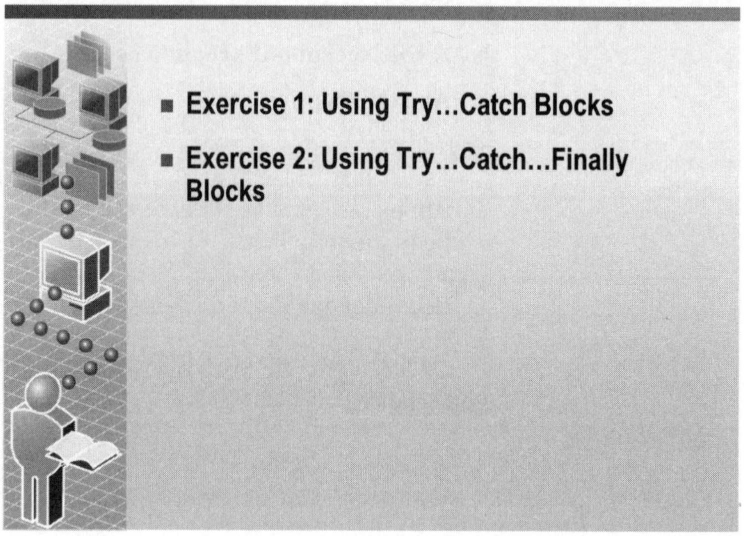

Objectives

After completing this lab, you will be able to:

- Use structured exception handling to handle exceptions.

Note This lab focuses on the concepts in this module and as a result may not comply with Microsoft security recommendations.

Prerequisites

Before working on this lab, you must:

- Be familiar with structured exception handling as an error handling technique.
- Be familiar with **Try...Catch...Finally** syntax.

Solution files

The solution files for this lab are in the *install_folder*\Labfiles\Lab081\Ex01\Solution and the *install_folder*\Labfiles\Lab081\Ex02\Solution folders.

Estimated time to complete this lab: 45 minutes

Exercise 1
Using Try...Catch Blocks

In this exercise, you will add **Try...Catch** blocks to handle exceptions in an existing program that opens and displays the contents of a text file.

▶ **Open the project**

- Open the ExceptionApplication.sln project located in the *install_folder*\Labfiles\Lab081\Ex01\Starter folder.

▶ **Examine the Sub Main procedure**

- Open the **Sub Main** procedure in FileOpen.vb and observe the following:
  a. **FileStream** is used for opening a file.
  b. **StreamReader** is used for reading lines of text from a text file.
  c. **MessageBox** is used to display the line read from the file.
  d. Finally, the **FileStream** and the **StreamReader** are closed.

▶ **Build the application**

- On the **Build** menu, click **Build Solution**.

  What happens?

  ____

  ____

► **Fix the error**

1. In Solution Explorer, right-click **References** and then click **Add Reference**. In the **Add Reference** dialog box, on the **.NET** tab, click **System.Windows.Forms.dll**. Click **Select**, and then click **OK**.
2. After fixing the errors, build the application and run it in debug mode.

   What happens when you run the application? Why?

   ____

   ____

   How would you handle the error?

   ____

   ____

3. Click **Continue** to quit the application.

► **Handle the exception by using Try...Catch**

- Modify the code in the **Sub Main** procedure by adding a **Try...Catch** block.
  a. Enclose the existing code in the **Try...End Try** block.
  b. Write a general **Catch** block to catch any exceptions. Use a message box to display a "File Not Found" message. Your code should look similar to the following code:

```
Try
  Dim file As New FileStream ("C:\test\test.txt",_
    FileMode.Open)
  Dim reader As New StreamReader (file)
  Dim line As String = reader.ReadLine ( )
  MessageBox.Show (line)
  reader.Close ( )
  file.Close ( )
Catch ex As Exception
  MessageBox.Show ("File Not Found")
End Try
```

► **Build the application**

1. Run the application in debug mode.

   What happens?

   ____

   ____

2. Click **OK** in the message box to quit the application.

► **Create a folder and a file**

1. Create a folder named Test in drive C.
2. On the **Start** menu, point to **All Programs**, point to **Accessories**, and then click **Notepad**.
3. In **Notepad**, type one line of text.
4. On the **File** menu, click **Save**.
5. In the **Save As** dialog box, browse to the C:\Test folder, and save the file as **test.txt**. Close the file.

► **Build and run the application**

1. Build and run the application in debug mode.

   What happens?

   ____

   ____

2. Click **OK** in the message box to quit the application.

► **Add another Catch block**

- Add another **Catch** block after the existing **Catch** block. The second **Catch** block should catch a **DirectoryNotFoundException**. In the **Catch** block, use a message box to display the error message "Incorrect Path."

  Your completed code should look similar to the following code:

```
Catch ex As Exception
      MessageBox.Show("File Not Found")
Catch ex As DirectoryNotFoundException
      MessageBox.Show("Incorrect Path")
```

▶ Edit the file path

- In your code, change the path to the test.txt file to C:\BadPath\test.txt. Your code should look similar to the following line of code:

```
Dim file As New FileStream ("c:\BadPath\test.txt", _
    FileMode.Open)
```

▶ Build and test the application

1. Run the application in debug mode.

   What happens? Why?

   ____

   ____

   How should you fix the error?

   ____

   ____

2. Click **OK** to quit the application.

▶ Modify the Catch blocks

1. In your code, change the path to the test.txt file to C:\test.txt. Your code should look similar to the following line of code:

```
Dim file As New FileStream ("c:\test.txt", FileMode.Open)
```

2. Move the `Catch ex As Exception` block to the end of the **Try...Catch** block. Use the message box call to display the **Message** property of the **Exception** class.
3. Add a new **Catch** block as the first **Catch** block to handle a **FileNotFoundException**. Use a message box to display an appropriate message. Your code should look similar to the following code:

```
Catch ex As FileNotFoundException
      MessageBox.Show("File Not Found")
Catch ex As DirectoryNotFoundException
      MessageBox.Show("Incorrect Path")
Catch ex As Exception
      MessageBox.Show(ex.Message)
```

► **Build and test the application**

1. Run the application in debug mode and verify that the "File Not Found" error message appears.
2. Click **OK** to quit the application.
3. In your code, change the path to the test.txt file to `A:\test.txt`. Your code should look similar to the following line of code:

```
Dim file As New FileStream ("a:\test.txt", FileMode.Open)
```

4. Run the application in debug mode again.

   The last **Catch** block handles the exception and displays the appropriate message by using the **Message** property of the **Exception** class.
5. Click **OK** in the message box to quit the application.

Exercise 2
Using Try...Catch...Finally Blocks

In this exercise, you will use **Try...Catch...Finally** blocks to handle exceptions. You will use breakpoints and the **Run To Cursor** command to debug an application. You will modify an existing program that reads a sales amount from a text file and then calculates and displays a discount.

▶ Open the project

- Open the ExceptionApplication.sln project located in the *install_folder*\Labfiles\Lab081\Ex02\Starter folder.

▶ Examine the Sub Main procedure

- Open the **Sub Main** procedure in FileOpen.vb, and observe the following:
  a. The **FileStream** function is used for opening the input.txt file located in the *install_folder*\Labfiles\Lab081\Ex02\Starter\bin folder.
  b. The **StreamReader** function is used for reading text from the file.
  c. The **CInt** function is used to convert the data read from the file to the **Integer** data type.
  d. A message box is used to calculate a discount on the amount that is read from the file, and to display the discount amount to the user.
  e. The **file** and the **reader** are closed.
  f. A **Catch** block is used to handle all exceptions.

▶ Examine the text file

- Open the input.txt file in the *install_folder*\Labfiles\Lab081\Ex02\Starter\bin folder. Note that this file contains a purchase amount of 100.

▶ Build and test the application

1. Run the application in debug mode.

   What happens?

   ____

   ____

2. Click **OK** in the message box to quit the application.

▶ Edit the text file

1. Using Notepad, open the file in the *install_folder*\Labfiles\Lab081\Ex02\Starter\bin folder. Change the amount from 100 to 100b.
2. Save and close the file.

► Build and test the application

1. Run the application in debug mode.

   What happens?

   ____

   ____

2. Click **OK** in the message box to quit the application.

► Debug the application

1. Set a breakpoint on the `MessageBox.Show` line of code.
2. Run the application in debug mode again.

   Why did the application not enter break mode at the breakpoint?

   ____

   ____

3. Click **OK** in the message box to quit the application.
4. Remove the breakpoint.
5. Place the insertion point on the **Try** line, and start the application by using the **Run To Cursor** command.
6. Use the F11 key to step through your code.

   Which line throws the exception? Why?

   ____

   ____

   Does the code for closing the **file** and the **reader** execute after the exception occurs?

   ____

   ____

How can you ensure that the code for closing the **file** and the **reader** is always executed?

____

____

7. Quit the application.

▶ Add a Finally block

1. Add a **Finally** block before the **End Try** statement.
2. In the **Try** block, delete the calls to the **Close** method.
3. In the **Finally** block, close the **file** and the **reader** objects. Your code should look similar to the following code:

```
Finally
   file.Close ( )
   reader.Close ( )
```

4. Note that this code contains two syntax errors. What is causing the errors?

____

____

5. Declare the *file* and *reader* variables outside the **Try** block, and change the code inside the **Try** block to create new instances of the **FileStream** and **StreamReader** classes and assign them to these variables. Your code should look similar to the following code:

```
Sub Main

Dim file As FileStream
Dim reader As StreamReader

Try
   file = New FileStream("input.txt", FileMode.Open)
   reader = New StreamReader(file)
   ...
Catch ex as Exception
   MessageBox.Show(ex.Message)

Finally
   ...

End Try
```

► Test the application

1. Set a breakpoint on the **Finally** statement.
2. Build and run the application in debug mode.
3. Click **OK** in the message box, and then use the F11 key to step through the code and verify that the application executes the code in the **Finally** block.
4. Quit the application.
5. Remove the breakpoint.

► Edit the file path

- Modify the file path as shown in the following line of code:

```
file = New FileStream("c:\input.txt", FileMode.Open)
```

► Test the application

1. Run the application in debug mode. In the message box that appears, click **OK**.

   Why does an unhandled exception of type **NullReferenceException** occur?

   ____

   ____

2. Click **Continue** to quit the application.
3. In the **Finally** block, before calling the **Close** method, use the **IsNothing** function to check whether the objects exist. Your code should look similar to the following code:

```
   ...
Finally
       If Not IsNothing (reader) Then reader.Close( )
       If Not IsNothing (file) Then file.Close( )
End Try
```

► Test the application

- Build and run the application.

  The application should now catch the exception, display a message box, and quit after you click **OK** in the message box.

Module 9: Enhancing the User Interface

Contents

Overview

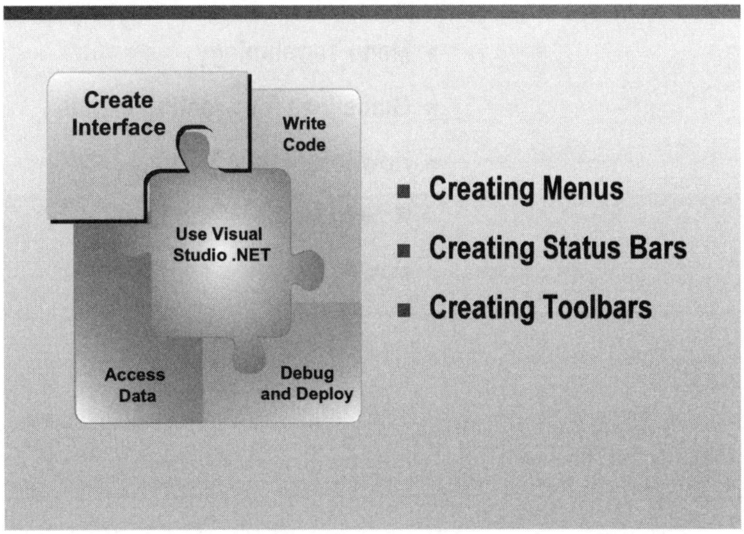

Introduction

Menus, status bars, and toolbars are all ways of making functionality available to your users or alerting them to important information in your application. Menus contain commands grouped by a common theme. Status bars indicate application state or provide information about the entity in the application that has focus, such as a menu command. Toolbars use buttons to make frequently used commands available.

In this module, you will learn how to create menus, status bars, and toolbars to enhance the usability of your application.

Objectives

After completing this module, you will be able to:

- Create custom menus to group application commands.
- Create a status bar to provide users with feedback about the application.
- Create a toolbar to provide a graphical interface with which users can access key functions of your application.

Lesson: Creating Menus

- Menu Terminology
- Guidelines for Creating Menus
- How to Create a Menu
- How to Modify Menu Items
- How to Enhance Your Menu

Introduction

If you want your application to provide a set of commands for users, menus are a convenient and consistent way for you to group commands so users can easily access them. In addition, you can use access keys and shortcut keys to make menu navigation easier for experienced users of your application.

This lesson describes how to create menus to provide a grouped set of commands for the user.

Lesson agenda

This lesson includes the following topics and activities:

- Multimedia Demonstration: How to Create Menus
- Menu Terminology
- Guidelines for Creating Menus
- How to Create a Menu
- How to Modify Menu Items
- How to Enhance Your Menu
- Practice: Creating a Menu

Lesson objectives

After completing this lesson, you will be able to:

- Create and edit menus, submenus, and menu items.
- Enhance a menu by using check marks, separator bars, access keys, and shortcut keys.

Multimedia: How to Create Menus

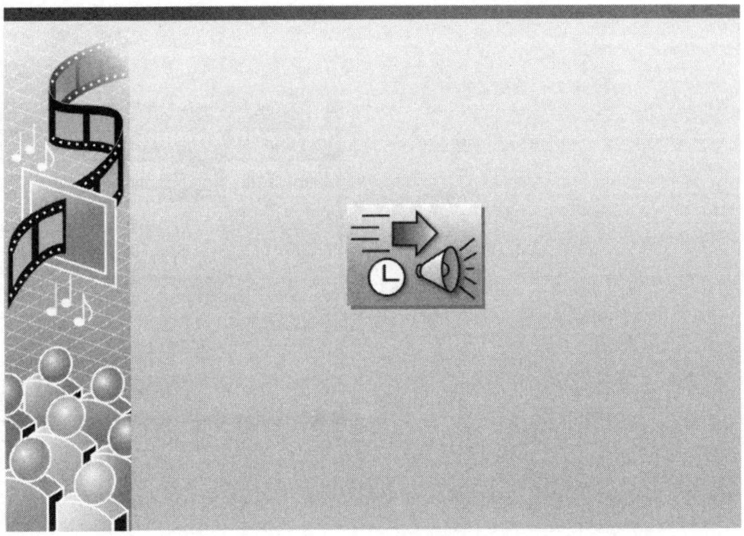

In this demonstration, you will learn how to add a **MainMenu** control to a Microsoft® Windows® Form in Microsoft Visual Basic® .NET. You will also learn how to create a hierarchy of menus and write code for the **Click** events of the items in the menu.

Menu Terminology

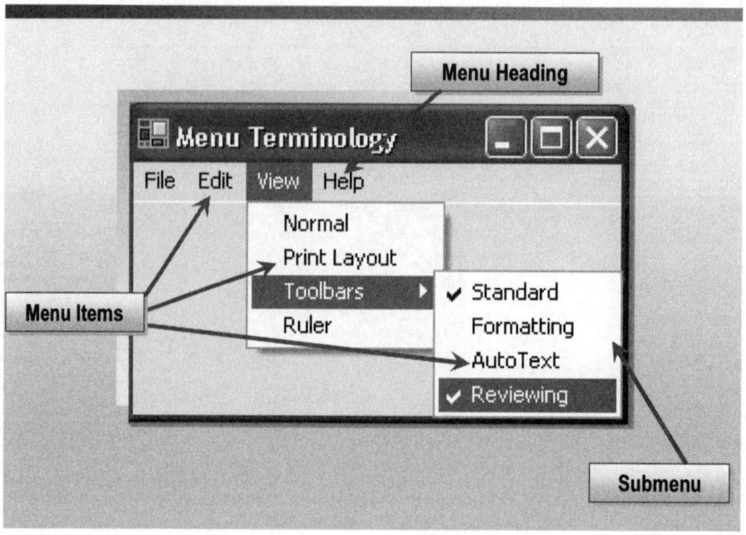

Definitions

A menu system typically consists of several related elements. The following table describes the menu elements of a typical user interface, such as those used by Windows-based applications.

Menu element	Description
Menu heading	The menu heading is the first menu item in a list of items. In most Windows-based applications, **File**, **Edit**, and **Help** are examples of menu headings.
Menu item	A menu item, also called a *command*, refers to any of the choices listed on the main menu. Each menu item is a member of the **MenuItem** class.
Submenu	A submenu, or *cascading menu*, is a menu that contains subdivisions of a menu item. The menu item associated with the cascading menu has an arrow next to it to indicate that a new menu will appear when the user points to the menu item.

Note A *context menu* is a context-sensitive menu that typically appears when you right-click an object in an application. For information about context menus, see Course 2565, *Developing Microsoft .NET Applications for Windows (Visual Basic .NET)*.

Guidelines for Creating Menus

Guideline	Example
Use initial capital letter	File, Edit, Help
Assign a unique access key	File, Edit, Help
Use consistent naming conventions	FileItem, EditItem, HelpItem
Use ellipses (...) after menu commands that require more information from the user	Save As...

Introduction

The purpose of a menu is to make using your application easy and intuitive for users. Following standard guidelines for creating menu items will help make your menu more intuitive and more useful.

Guidelines for creating menus

The following table provides guidelines for creating menus.

Guideline	Example
Use an initial capital letter when naming menu items.	**File**, **Edit**, **Help** (instead of **file**, **edit**, **help**).
Assign a unique access key for each menu item.	H is the standard access key for **Help** in Windows-based applications.
Use consistent naming conventions when you create your menu.	Name the **File**, **Edit**, and **Help** items on a menu FileItem, EditItem, and HelpItem in your program.
Use ellipses (. . .) after menu commands that require more information from the user.	The **Save As** menu item in Microsoft Word is followed by an ellipsis to indicate that more information is required. In this case, the name, location, and type of the document the user is saving are required.

How to Create a Menu

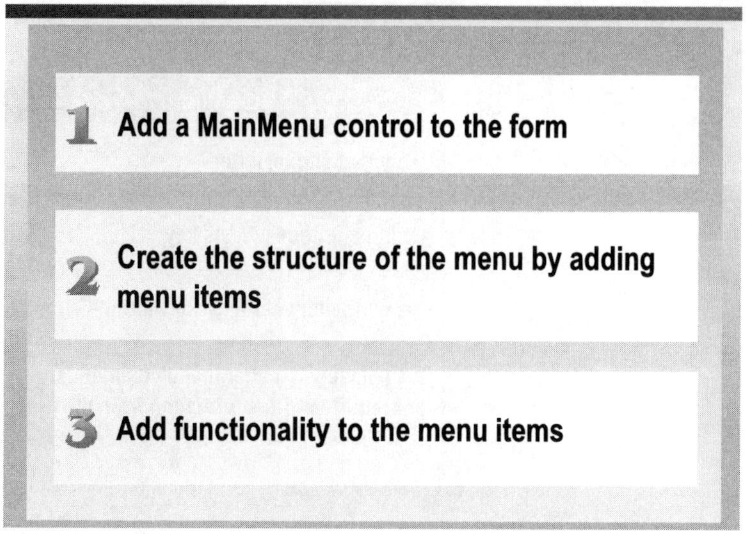

Introduction

You can create a menu on a Windows Form by adding a **MainMenu** control from the Toolbox to the form at design time. You can then create the menu items and submenus for your menu by using the Menu Designer. After your menu structure is created, you add functionality to the menu items.

Creating the menu, menu items, and submenus

► **To add a menu and menu items to a form**

1. In the Windows Forms Designer, open the form to which you want to add a menu.
2. In the Toolbox, double-click the **MainMenu** control.

   A menu is added to the form. The menu displays the text "Type Here."
3. Click the text **Type Here**, and then type the name of the desired menu item to add it to the menu.
4. The name you type is listed as the **Text** property of the menu item.

> **Note** By default, the **MainMenu** control contains no menu items, so the first menu item added to the menu becomes the menu heading.

5. To add another menu item, click another **Type Here** area in the Menu Designer.
   a. Click the area to the right of the current menu item to add a submenu. You cannot add a submenu to a menu heading.
   b. Click the area below the current menu item to add another item to the same menu.

Adding functionality to menu items

You can add functionality to menu items by adding code to the menu item **Click** event. The **Click** event occurs when a user clicks the menu item, when a user selects the item by using the keyboard and presses ENTER, or when a user clicks an access key or shortcut key associated with the menu item.

► To add functionality to the menu item

1. In the Menu Designer, click the menu item you want to add functionality to.
2. In the Properties window, change the **Name** property of the item. Rename the item. Use the naming convention you will use for all items on the menu. (For example, you might name the **Open** menu item **OpenItem**.)
3. Double-click the menu item to open an event handler for its **Click** event.
4. Write the code for the event handler.

How to Modify Menu Items

Desired change	Steps
Move	Click and drag the item in Menu Designer.
Delete	Right-click the item, and then click Delete.
Edit	Use the Properties window to change the Text property. Use the Name Editor to change the Name property.
Disable	Set the Enabled property of the item to False.
Hide	Set the Visible property of the item to False

Introduction

After you create your menu, you can easily modify it by moving, deleting, editing, disabling, or hiding items.

Moving menu items

► **To move a menu item**

- In the Menu Designer, click the menu item and drag it to its new location.

  You can place the item at the top of the menu or between other menu items, or you can add it as a new submenu of an existing item.

Deleting menu items

► **To delete a menu item**

- In the Menu Designer, right-click the menu item, and then click **Delete**.

Editing menu items

The **Text** property of the menu item sets the name that users will see. When you use the Menu Designer, you set the **Text** property for each item when you create the menu items.

► **To edit the Text property of a menu item**

- In the Menu Designer, click the menu item to select the name, and then type the new name.

The **Name** property for each item is set dynamically by the Menu Designer. The Menu Designer uses the naming system MenuItem*X*, where *X* is a number representing the order in which the menu item was created. Microsoft Visual Studio® provides a Name Editor in the Menu Designer to change the **Name** property of menu items you create.

► **To edit the Name property of menu items by using the Name Editor**

1. Right-click anywhere in the Menu Designer, and then click **Edit Names**.

   The Menu Designer switches to name-editing mode, and a menu item name appears next to the text specified in the **Text** property.
2. Change the **Name** property to the desired value.
3. To leave name-editing mode, right-click anywhere in the Menu Designer, and then click **Edit Names** again.

Disabling menu items

Menu items are enabled by default when they are created. Disabling menu items in response to user activity is a way to limit the commands a user can use. To disable a menu item, use the **Enabled** property of the menu item.

► **To disable a menu item**

1. In the Menu Designer, click the menu item you want to disable.
2. In the Properties window, set the **Enabled** property to **False**.

You can disable a menu item at run time by using the following code, where `MenuItem1` is the name of the menu item you want to disable:

```
MenuItem1.Enabled = False
```

Hiding menu items

Hiding menu items is a way to control the user interface of your application and restrict user commands. You will often want to hide an entire menu when all of the menu items on it are unavailable. This presents fewer distractions for users.

Note that it is important to both hide and disable the menu, because hiding alone does not prevent access to a menu command by means of a shortcut key.

► **To hide a menu item**

1. In the Menu Designer, click the menu item you want to hide.
2. In the **Properties** window, set the **Visible** property to **False**.

Note When the top-level menu item in a given menu is hidden or disabled, all menu items within that menu are hidden.

How to Enhance Your Menu

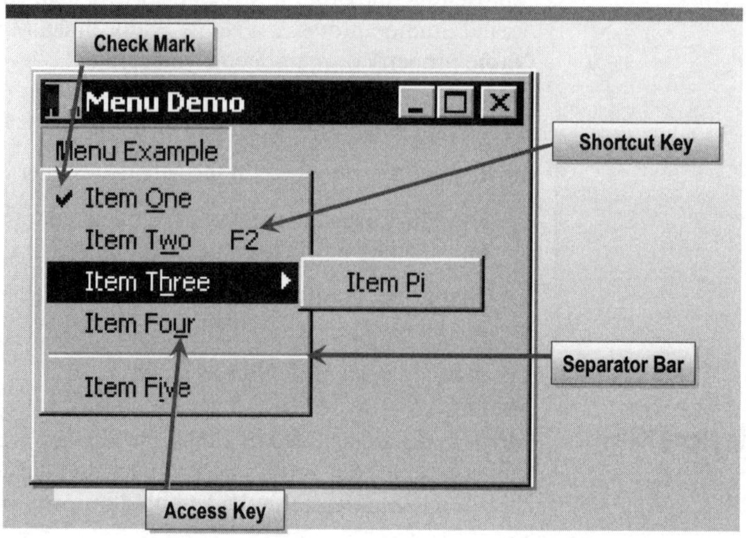

Introduction

There are four enhancements that you can add to a menu to convey information to users:

- *Check marks* can be used to designate whether a feature is turned on or off (for example, whether a ruler is displayed along the margin of a word-processing application) or to indicate which of a list of files is being displayed (such as on a **Window** menu).
- *Shortcut keys* are keyboard commands for accessing menu items in an application.
- *Access keys* allow keyboard navigation of menus. Pressing ALT and the underlined access key activates the desired menu or menu item.
- *Separator bars* are used to group related commands on a menu and to make menus easier to read.

Adding a check mark

► **To add a check mark to a menu item**

- In the Menu Designer, click the menu item, and then click the area to the left of the menu item.

  A check mark appears, indicating that the **Checked** property has been set to **True**.

  – Or –

1. In the Menu Designer, click the menu item.
2. In the Properties window, set the **Checked** property to **True**.

Note The **RadioCheck** property works in conjunction with the **Checked** property. When the **RadioCheck** property is set to **True**, a small dot (•) is displayed next to a checked menu item instead of a check mark (✓).

Assigning a shortcut key

► To assign a shortcut key to a menu item

1. In the Menu Designer, click the menu item.
2. In the Properties window, set the **Shortcut** property to one of the values offered in the drop-down list.

Assigning an access key

► To assign an access key to a menu item

- When setting the **Text** property for the menu item (either in the Properties window, in the Menu Designer, or in code), type an ampersand (&) prior to the letter you want to designate as the access key.

  For example, typing **&File** as the **Text** property of a menu item will result in a menu item that appears as File. Typing **F&ormat** will result in a menu item that appears as Format.

Note To navigate to this menu item, press ALT to give focus to the menu bar, and then press the access key of the menu name. When the menu opens and shows items with access keys, you only need to press the access key to activate the menu item.

Adding a separator bar

► To add a separator bar as a menu item

- In the Menu Designer, right-click the location where you want to place the separator bar, and then click **Insert Separator**.

  – Or –

- When setting the **Text** property for the menu item (either in the Properties window, in the Menu Designer, or in code), type a dash (–) to make that menu item a separator bar.

Practice: Creating a Menu

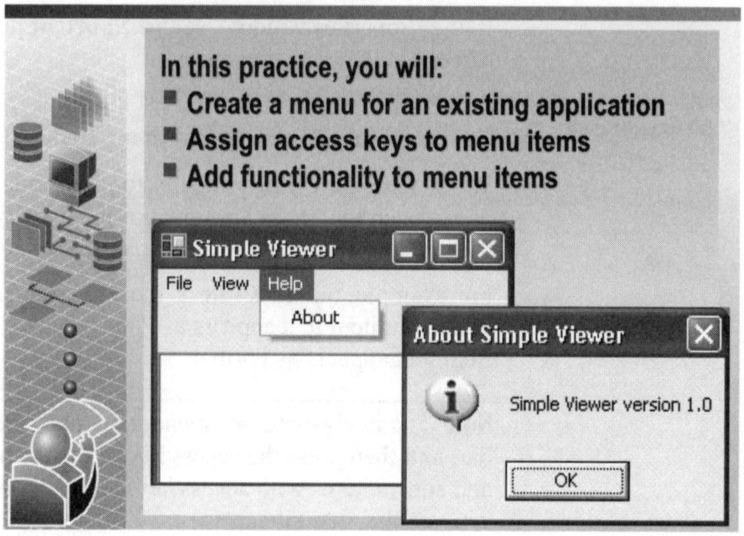

In this practice, you will add a main menu to a simple text viewer application, assign access keys to the menu items, and write code that will run when a user clicks a menu item.

▶ Open the Simple Viewer application

- The starter files are located in the *install_folder*\Practices\Mod09\Menu\Starter folder. Open the UserInterfaceApplication.sln solution.

▶ Add a main menu

1. Examine the form, controls, and code for the application.
2. Add a main menu to the SimpleViewer form.
3. Add the following menu items to the main menu, change the **Name** property of each item, and assign appropriate access keys.

Menu headings	Items below headings	Menu item names	Suggested access keys
File	**Open**	**MenuFile, MenuItemOpen**	Alt F, O
	Exit	**MenuItemExit**	X
View	**Toolbar**	**MenuView, MenuItemToolbar**	Alt V, T
	Status Bar	**MenuItemStatusBar**	S
Help	**About**	**MenuHelp, MenuItemAbout**	Alt H, A

► Add event handlers for menu items

1. Create a **Click** event handler for the **Open** menu item. Call the **loadFile** procedure to load the selected file into the **RichTextBox** control. The **loadFile** procedure is already provided for you in the code for the application.
2. Create a **Click** event handler for the **Exit** menu item. Call **Application.Exit** to quit the application.
3. Create a **Click** event handler for the **About** menu item. In the event handler, use a message box to display text. Your code should look similar to the following code:

```
MessageBox.Show("Simple Viewer version 1.0", _
   "About Simple Viewer", MessageBoxButtons.OK, _
   MessageBoxIcon.Information)
```

► Compile and test the application

1. Run the application.
2. Use the **File** menu to open a text file. A sample text file named Test.txt is provided in the *install_folder*\Practices\Mod09\Menu\Starter folder.
3. Verify that a message box appears when you click **About** on the **Help** menu.
4. Test one of your access keys by pressing ALT and the access key.
5. Quit the application by clicking **Exit**.

Solution code

The solution files are located in the *install_folder*\Practices\Mod09\Menu\Solution folder.

Lesson: Creating Status Bars

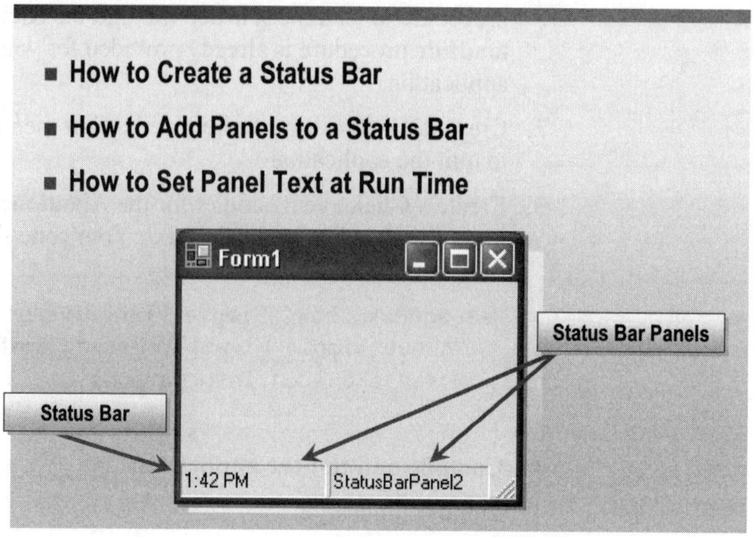

Introduction

A **StatusBar** control can be added to a form and customized to provide useful information, such as the name of a file that is currently open, the current date or time, or the status of certain keys on the keyboard. In this lesson, you will learn how to enhance an application's interface by using the **StatusBar** control.

Lesson agenda

This lesson includes the following topics and activities:

- How to Create a Status Bar
- How to Add Panels to a Status Bar
- How to Set Panel Text at Run Time
- Practice: Creating a Status Bar

Lesson objective

After completing this lesson, you will be able to create a status bar on a form to provide feedback to users.

How to Create a Status Bar

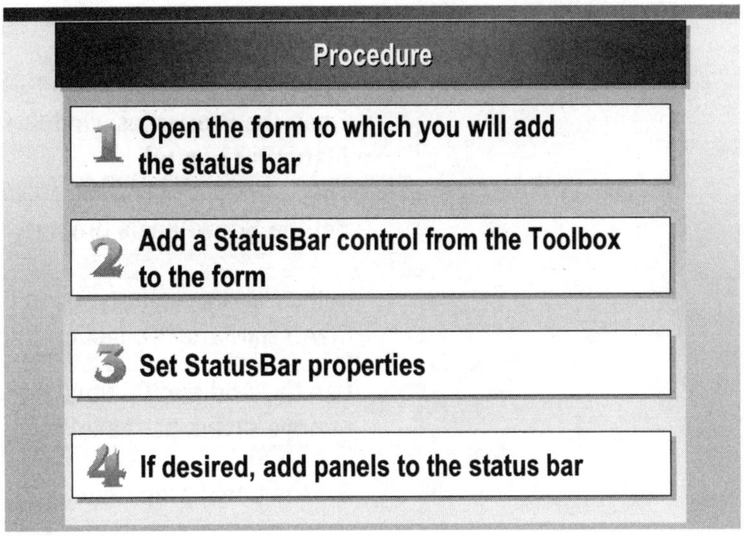

Introduction

The Windows Forms **StatusBar** control is used on forms as an area, usually displayed at the bottom of a window, in which an application can display various kinds of status information.

Adding a status bar

► **To add a status bar to your application**

1. Open the form to which you want to add the status bar.
2. Use the Toolbox to add a **StatusBar** control to the form.
3. Set the appropriate **StatusBar** properties, including **ShowPanels**.
   a. If you will not add panels to the status bar, set the **ShowPanels** property to **False** (the default), and then set the **Text** property to the text that you want to appear in the status bar.
   b. To display more than one type of information in the status bar, set the **ShowPanels** property to **True**, and then add the desired number of panels to the status bar.

StatusBar properties

The following table shows **StatusBar** properties that you will frequently use.

Property	Description
Panels	By default, a status bar has no panels. Use the **Panels** property to add panels to or remove panels from the status bar.
ShowPanels	If set to **False** (default), displays only the value of the **Text** property of the control. If set to **True**, enables you to display panels in your status bar.
SizingGrip	Displays a sizing grip on the lower right corner of the form to indicate to users that the form can be resized. Use only on a form that can be resized.
Text	Contains the text string displayed in the status bar.

How to Add Panels to a Status Bar

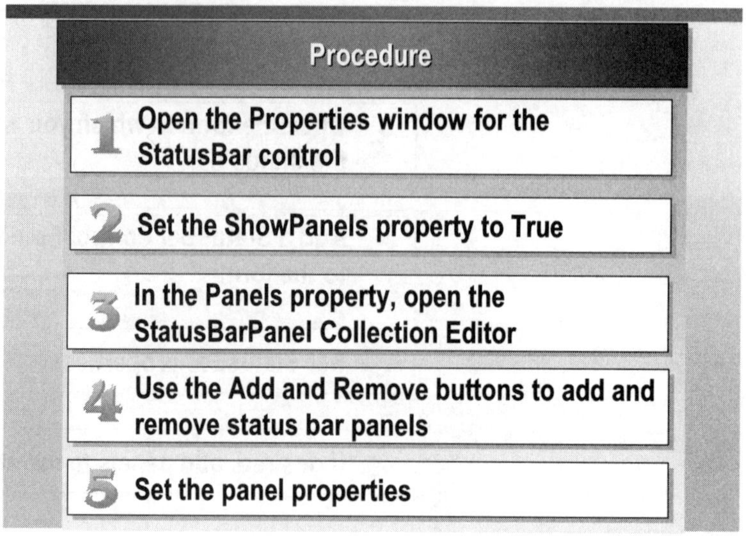

Introduction

The programmable area in a **StatusBar** control consists of instances of the **StatusBarPanel** class. You can display more than one type of information in the status bar by setting the **ShowPanels** property to **True** and adding panels to the status bar.

You can use status bar panels to display text or icons to indicate state, or to display a series of icons in an animation to indicate that a process is working. For example, a status bar panel in Word displays a small icon to indicate when a document is being saved.

Adding panels to a status bar

► **To add panels to a status bar at design time**

1. In the Properties window for the status bar, set the **ShowPanels** property to **True**.
2. Click the **Panels** property to select it, and then click the ellipsis button ... to open the StatusBarPanel Collection Editor.
3. Use the **Add** and **Remove** buttons to add panels to and remove panels from the **StatusBar** control.
4. Configure the properties of the individual panels in the Properties window that appears in the pane on the right side of the editor.
5. Click **OK** to close the dialog box and create the panels you specified.

Panel properties

The following table shows **StatusBar** panel properties that you will frequently use.

Property	Description
AutoSize	Sets the resizing behavior of the panel. The following options are available. • **Contents:** The width of the panel is determined by its contents. • **None:** The panel does not change size when the status bar control is resized. • **Spring:** The panel shares the available space on the status bar with other panels that have their **AutoSize** property set to **Spring**.
Alignment	Sets the alignment of the panel in the **StatusBar** control. Options include **Center**, **Left**, and **Right**.
BorderStyle	Sets the type of border that is displayed at the edges of the panel. The following options are available. • **None:** No border is displayed. • **Raised:** The panel is displayed with a three-dimensional raised border. • **Sunken:** The panel is displayed with a three-dimensional sunken border.
Icon	Sets the icon (.ico file) that is displayed in the panel.
MinWidth	Sets the minimum width that the panel can be when displayed in the status bar.
Style	Sets the style of the panel. The following options are available: • **OwnerDraw:** Supports the display of images or the use of a font that is different from that used by the rest of the panel objects on a status bar. • **Text:** The panel displays text in the standard font.
Text	Sets the text string displayed in the panel.
Width	Sets the width of the panel, measured in pixels. This property might change when the form is resized, depending on the setting of the **AutoSize** property.

How to Set Panel Text at Run Time

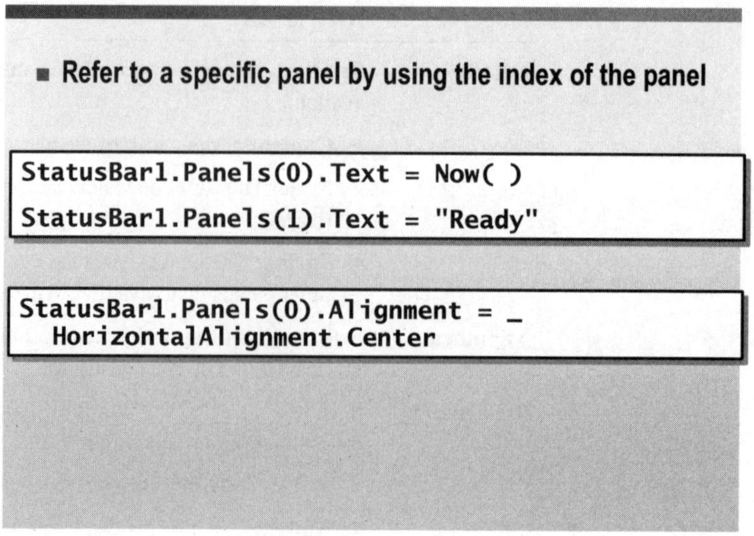

Introduction

Because the status bar is often used to show the current status of some aspect of the application, you will often want to set the panel text at run time rather than at design time.

Setting panel text at run time

To set panel text at run time, you need to refer to the panel whose property you want to set. You can refer to a specific panel by using the index of the panel. The index numbers start with 0.

For example, the following code will set the **Text** property of the first panel to the current date and time:

```
StatusBar1.Panels(0).Text = Now( )
```

To set the **Text** property of the second panel to the string "Ready", you would use the following code:

```
StatusBar1.Panels(1).Text = "Ready"
```

The following code will set the **Alignment** property of the first panel so that the panel is centered on the status bar:

```
StatusBar1.Panels(0).Alignment = HorizontalAlignment.Center
```

Practice: Creating a Status Bar

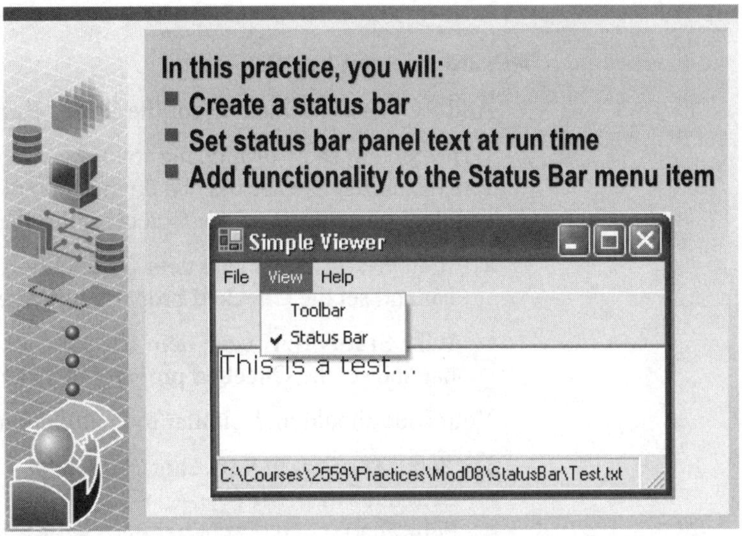

In this practice, you will add a status bar to a simple viewer application. You will set panel properties at design time, and you will also write code to set the **Text** property of the panel at run time. Finally, you will write code to respond to the **Click** event of the **Status Bar** menu item. The starter files are located in the *install_folder*\Practices\Mod09\StatusBar\Starter folder.

► Add a status bar

1. Open UserInterfaceApplication.sln. If you did not complete the practice Creating a Menu, familiarize yourself with the form and the code for the application.
2. Add a **StatusBar** control to the form.
3. Set the **Text** property of the status bar to *blank*.
4. Use the **Panels** property to add a panel to the status bar.
5. Set the **AutoSize** property of the panel to **Spring**.
6. Set the **Text** property of the panel to *blank*, and then click **OK** to close the StatusBarPanel Collection Editor.
7. Set the **ShowPanels** property of the status bar to **True**.

► Modify the MenuItemOpen_Click event handler

1. Open the **MenuItemOpen_Click** event handler.
2. After the call to the **loadFile** procedure, add the following code to display the file path in the status bar: `openFileDialogBox.FileName`. Your code should look similar to the following:

```
StatusBar1.Panels(0).Text = openFileDialogBox.FileName
```

▶ Set a menu item property

- Click the **Status Bar** menu item, and then set its **Checked** property to **True**.

▶ Add an event handler

1. Add a **Click** event handler for the **Status Bar** menu item.
2. Write code to show or hide the status bar, depending on whether the **Status Bar** menu item is checked. To do this, complete the body of the event handler by writing the code to accomplish the following:
   a. If the **Status Bar** menu item **Checked** property is **True**, hide the status bar and set the **Checked** property to **False**.
   b. If the **Status Bar** menu item **Checked** property is **False**, show the status bar and set the **Checked** property to **True**.

   Your code should look similar to the following code:

```
If MenuItemStatusBar.Checked Then
   StatusBar1.Hide( )
   MenuItemStatusBar.Checked = False
Else
   StatusBar1.Show( )
   MenuItemStatusBar.Checked = True
End If
```

▶ Test the application

1. Run the application and open a text file. A sample text file named Test.txt is provided in the *install_folder*\Practices\Mod09\StatusBar\Starter folder.
2. Use the **Status Bar** menu item to show and hide the status bar.
3. Quit the application.

Solution code

The solution files are located in the *install_folder*\Practices\Mod09\StatusBar\Solution folder.

Lesson: Creating Toolbars

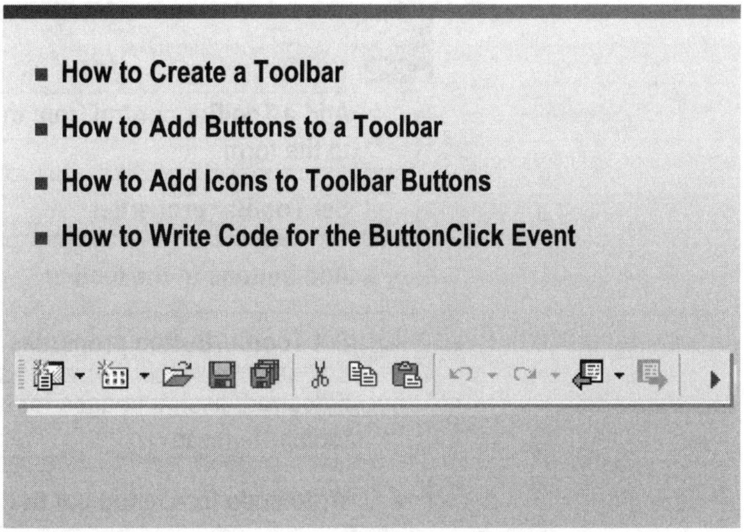

Introduction

The toolbar is a standard feature in many Windows-based applications. Toolbars display a row of buttons and drop-down menus that activate commands. Typically, the buttons and drop-down menus correspond to items in an application's menu structure, providing a graphical interface through which users have quick access to the application's most frequently used functions and commands.

Lesson agenda

This lesson includes the following topics and activities:

- How to Create a Toolbar
- How to Add Buttons to a Toolbar
- How to Add Icons to Toolbar Buttons
- How to Write Code for the **ButtonClick** Event
- Practice: Creating a Toolbar

Lesson objectives

After completing this lesson, you will be able to:

- Create a toolbar by using the **ToolBar** control.
- Add buttons to a toolbar.
- Assign an icon to a toolbar button.
- Add code to toolbar buttons that is triggered by the **ButtonClick** event.

How to Create a Toolbar

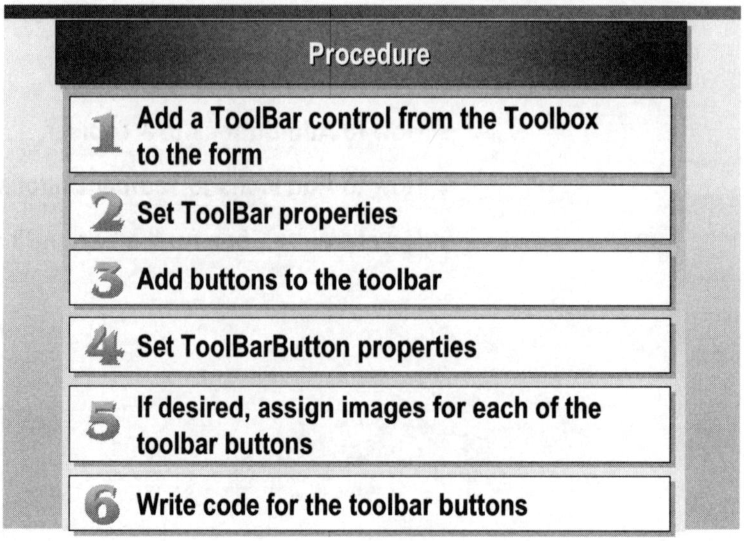

Introduction

The Windows Forms **ToolBar** control is used on forms to create a toolbar for an application.

Creating a toolbar

► **To create a toolbar for your application**

1. Open the form to which you want to add the toolbar.
2. Add a **ToolBar** control from the Toolbox to the form.
3. Set the appropriate **ToolBar** properties.
4. Add buttons to the toolbar, and then set the appropriate **ToolBarButton** properties.
5. If desired, assign images for each of the buttons on the toolbar.
6. Write code for the toolbar buttons.

ToolBar properties

The following table shows **ToolBar** properties that you will frequently use.

Property	Description
Appearance	Affects the appearance of the buttons assigned to the toolbar. The following options are available: • **Normal:** Gives the toolbar buttons a three-dimensional, raised appearance. • **Flat:** Gives the toolbar buttons a flat appearance. When the mouse pointer moves over the flat buttons, they appear raised and three-dimensional.
Buttons	Holds all the **ToolBarButton** controls assigned to the toolbar. The **Buttons** property is a zero-based indexed collection. Use this property to add buttons to or remove buttons from the toolbar.
ButtonSize	Sets the size of the **ToolBarButton** controls on the toolbar. If the **ButtonSize** property is not set by the developer, it will be set either to a default size or large enough to accommodate the image and text, whichever is greater.
ImageList	If you create an instance of the **ImageList** class and assign it to the **ImageList** property, you will be able to assign an image from the list to the **ToolBarButton** controls.
ShowToolTips	Determines whether ToolTips will be visible to users. ToolTips allow you to provide help to users when they rest the mouse pointer on a **ToolBarButton** control. The default value is **True**.

How to Add Buttons to a Toolbar

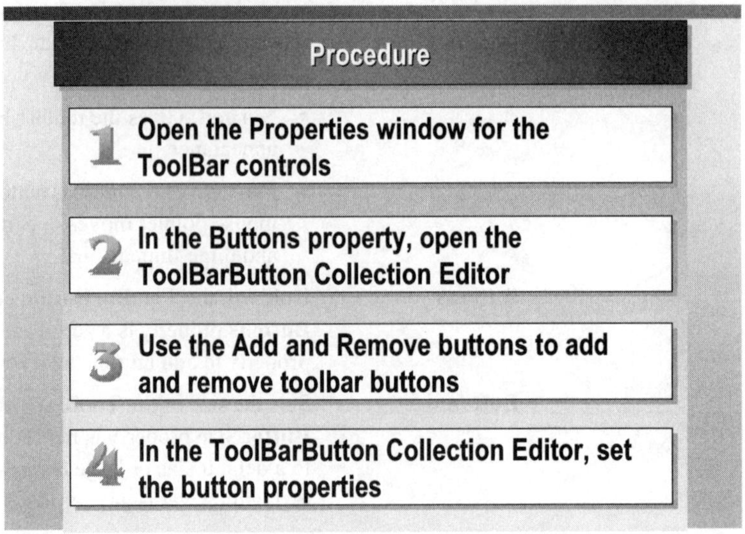

Introduction

An integral part of the **ToolBar** control are the buttons you add to it. These buttons can be used to provide access to menu commands, or they can be placed in another area of the user interface of your application to provide access to commands that are not available in the menu structure.

Adding buttons to a toolbar

► **To add buttons to a toolbar**

1. Open the Properties window for the **ToolBar**.
2. Click the **Buttons** property to select it, and then click the ellipsis button ... to open the ToolBarButton Collection Editor.
3. Use the **Add** and **Remove** buttons to add buttons to and remove buttons from the **ToolBar** control.
4. Set the properties of the individual buttons in the Properties window that appears in the pane on the right side of the editor.
5. Click **OK** to close the dialog box and create the buttons you specified.

Button properties

The following table shows toolbar button properties that you will frequently use.

Property	Description
DropDownMenu	Sets the menu that is to appear in the drop-down toolbar button. The toolbar button's **Style** property must be set to **DropDownButton**.
Pushed	Sets whether a toggle-style toolbar button is currently in the pushed state. The toolbar button's **Style** property must be set to **ToggleButton** or **PushButton**.
Style	Sets the style of the toolbar button. The following options are available: • **DropDownButton:** A drop-down control that displays a menu or other window when clicked. • **PushButton:** A standard three-dimensional button. • **Separator:** A space or line between toolbar buttons. • **ToggleButton:** A toggle button that appears sunken when clicked and retains the sunken appearance until it is clicked again.
Text	Specifies the text string displayed by the button.
ToolTipText	Specifies the text that appears as a ToolTip for the button. ToolTips allow you to provide help to users when they rest the mouse pointer on a toolbar button.

How to Add Icons to Toolbar Buttons

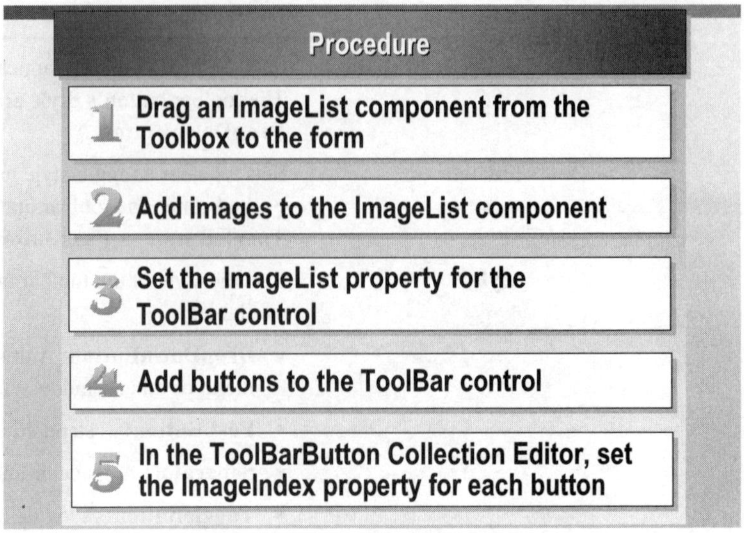

Introduction

Toolbars usually have buttons that use icons to represent a function of the application. The icons provide easy identification for users. For example, an icon of a floppy disk is commonly used to represent a file save function. Each button should have either text or an image assigned to it; you can also assign both.

To display images on your toolbar, you must first add the images to the **ImageList** component and then associate the **ImageList** component with the **ToolBar** control.

► **To set an icon for a toolbar button at design time**

1. Add an **ImageList** component from the Toolbox to your form.
2. In the Properties window for the **ImageList** component, click the **Images** property to select it, and then click the ellipsis button ... to open the Image Collection Editor.
3. Use the **Add** button to add images to the **ImageList** component, and then click **OK** to close the Image Collection Editor.
4. In the Properties window for the **ToolBar**, set the **ImageList** property to the **ImageList** component you added earlier.
5. Click the **ToolBar** control's **Buttons** property to select it, and then click the ellipsis button ... to open the ToolBarButton Collection Editor.
6. Use the **Add** button to add buttons to the **ToolBar** control.
7. In the Properties window that appears in the pane on the right side of the ToolBarButton Collection Editor, set the **ImageIndex** property of each toolbar button to one of the values in the list, which is drawn from the images you added to the **ImageList** component. Click **OK** to close the ToolBarButton Collection Editor.

How to Write Code for the ButtonClick Event

- **All buttons on a toolbar share a single Click event**
- **To determine which button was clicked, use a Select Case statement and the ToolBarButtonClickEventArgs class**

```
Protected Sub ToolBar1_ButtonClick(ByVal sender _
  As Object,ByVal e As ToolBarButtonClickEventArgs)
   Select Case ToolBar1.Buttons.IndexOf(e.Button)
       Case 0
         MessageBox.Show("First button clicked")
       Case 1
         MessageBox.Show("Second button clicked")
   End Select
End Sub
```

Introduction

All buttons on a toolbar share a single **Click** event. To add functionality to your toolbar, you need to write code to determine which button the user has clicked.

Determining which button has been clicked

To write code to determine which button the user has clicked, add an event handler for the **ButtonClick** event of the **ToolBar** control. Use a **Select Case** statement and the **ToolBarButtonClickEventArgs** class to evaluate the index number of the button that was clicked. For each case, write the code that should run for the appropriate button.

Example

In the following example, a **Select Case** statement is used to determine which of three buttons has been clicked, and a message box confirms the result. In an actual application, the executable code for the button would be written instead of the code that calls the **MessageBox** function in this example.

```
Protected Sub ToolBar1_ButtonClick(ByVal sender As Object, _
  ByVal e As ToolBarButtonClickEventArgs) Handles _
  ToolBar1.ButtonClick
' Use the Button property of the ToolBarButtonClickEventArgs
' class to determine which button has been clicked
   Select Case ToolBar1.Buttons.IndexOf(e.Button)
     Case 0
       MessageBox.Show("First toolbar button clicked")
     Case 1
       MessageBox.Show("Second toolbar button clicked")
     Case 2
       MessageBox.Show("Third toolbar button clicked")
   End Select
End Sub
```

Practice: Creating a Toolbar

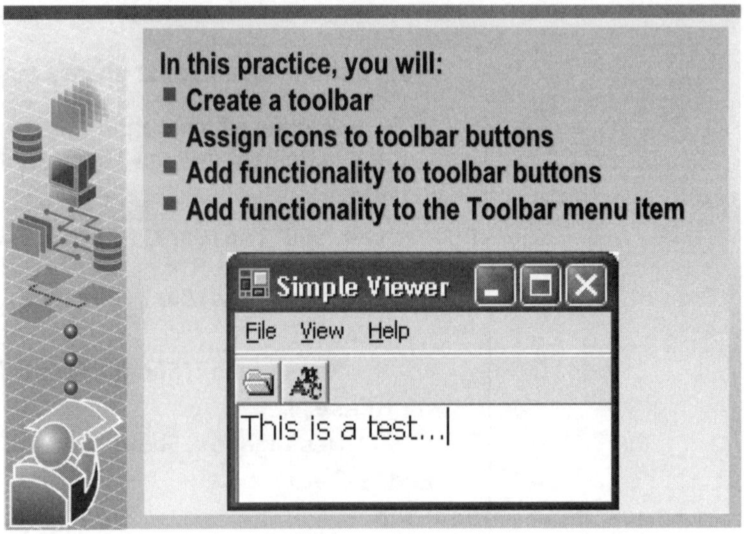

In this practice, you will add a toolbar to the simple text viewer application. You will set toolbar properties at design time, add two buttons to the toolbar, assign icons to the toolbar buttons, and write code that will run when each button is clicked. The starter files are located in the *install_folder*\Practices\Mod09\Toolbar\Starter folder.

► **Add a toolbar**

1. Open UserInterfaceApplication.sln. If you did not complete the practice Creating a Status Bar, familiarize yourself with the form and the code for the application.
2. Add an **ImageList** control to the form.
3. Add two images by using the **Images** property. The images OpenFold.ico and Font02.ico are provided in the *install_folder*\Practices\Mod09\Toolbar\Starter folder. Ensure that OpenFold.ico is assigned the index number 0, and that Font02.ico is assigned the index number 1.
4. Add a **ToolBar** control to the form.
5. Set the **ImageList** property of the toolbar to use the **ImageList** control you added earlier.
6. Add a button to the toolbar by using the **Buttons** property. Set the **ImageIndex** property of the button to **0**.
7. Add another button, and set the **ImageIndex** property of the button to **1**.
8. Click **OK** in the ToolBarButton Collection Editor.

► Set a menu item property

- On the **View** menu for the Simple Viewer application, click the menu item **Toolbar** and set its **Checked** property to **True**.

► Add an event handler for the Toolbar menu item

1. Add a **Click** event handler for the **Toolbar** menu item.
2. Complete the body of the event handler by writing code to accomplish the following:

   a. If the **Toolbar** menu item **Checked** property is **False**, then show the toolbar and set the **Checked** property to **True**.

   b. If the **Toolbar** menu item **Checked** property is **True**, then hide the toolbar and set the **Checked** property to **False**.

   Your code should look similar to the following code:

```
If Not MenuItemToolbar.Checked Then
   ToolBar1.Show( )
   MenuItemToolbar.Checked = True
Else
   ToolBar1.Hide( )
   MenuItemToolbar.Checked = False
End If
```

► Add an event handler for the toolbar

1. Add a **Click** event handler for the toolbar.
2. Complete the body of the event handler.

   a. Use a **Select Case** statement to determine which button was pressed.

   b. For the button associated with the OpenFold icon, call the **Open** menu item's existing **Click** event hander and pass **sender** and **e** as parameters.

   c. For the button associated with the Font02 icon, set the **Font** property of the **RichTextBox** control by creating a new font.

   Your code should look similar to the following code. (In this code, 0 is the index number for the **Open** button, and 1 is the index number for the **Font** button.)

```
Select Case ToolBar1.Buttons.IndexOf(e.Button)
Case 0
   MenuItemOpen_Click(sender, e)
Case 1
   RichTextBox1.Font = New System.Drawing.Font _
       ("Comic Sans MS", 12.0!, _
       System.Drawing.FontStyle.Regular, _
       System.Drawing.GraphicsUnit.Point, CType(0, Byte))

End Select
```

► **Test the application**

1. Run the application.
2. Click the **Open** button and open a text file. A sample text file named Test.txt is provided in the *install_folder*\Practices\Mod09\Toolbar\Starter folder.
3. Click the **Font** button and verify that the font of the text file changes.
4. Quit the application.

Solution code

The solution files are located in the *install_folder*\Practices\Mod09\Toolbar\Solution folder.

Review

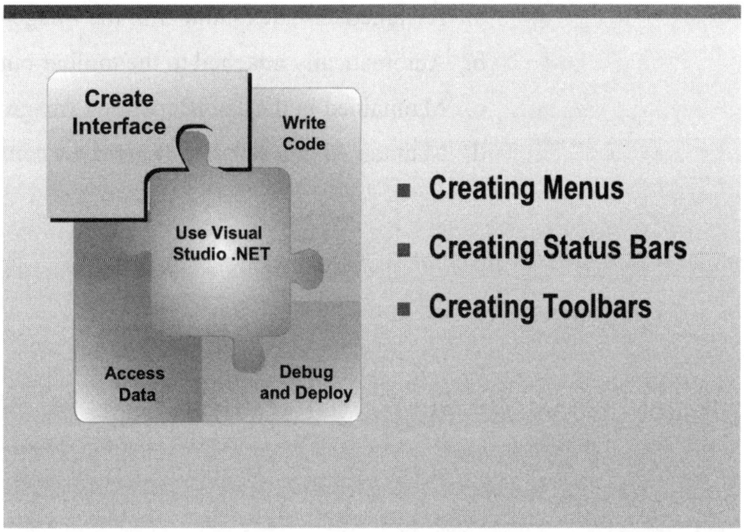

1. Explain the purpose of the following elements:
   a. Access keys
   b. Shortcut keys
   c. ToolTips

2. Determine which of the following code statements changes the contents of the first panel of a status bar named StatusBar1 to read "Press F1 for Help."
   a. `"Press F1 for Help." = StatusBar1.Panels(1).Text`
   b. `StatusBar1.Panels(1).Text = "Press F1 for Help."`
   c. `StatusBar1.Panel1.Text = "Press F1 for Help."`
   d. `StatusBar1.Panels(0).Text = "Press F1 for Help."`

3. Which statement or statements correctly complete the following sentence?

   Images for a toolbar's buttons are:

   a. Assigned an index number in the Image Collection Editor.

   b. Automatically attached to the toolbar button based on function.

   c. Maintained in the ToolBarButton Image Collection Editor.

   d. Maintained in a separate **ImageList** control.

msdn training

Module 10: Web Forms and XML Web Services

Contents

Microsoft

Overview

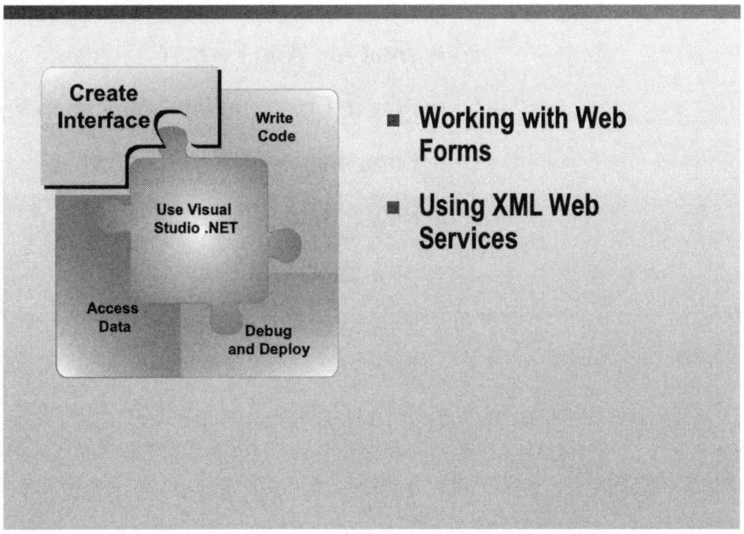

Introduction

Microsoft® Visual Studio® .NET allows you to create applications that take advantage of the World Wide Web, including traditional Web sites that use Hypertext Markup Language (HTML) pages, fully featured business applications that run on an intranet or the Internet, and sophisticated business-to-business applications providing Web-based components that can exchange data by using XML.

Web Forms are used to create applications in which the primary user interface is a browser. This includes applications intended to be available publicly by means of the World Wide Web, such as e-commerce applications.

XML Web services provide programmable application logic that can be invoked by using standard Internet protocols. XML Web services combine the best aspects of component-based development and the Web.

This module explains how to create an application that uses a Web Form, and how to invoke a simple XML Web service.

Objectives

After completing this module, you will be able to:

- Create, build, and run an application that uses Web Forms.
- Explain the process for discovering and calling XML Web services.
- Use a proxy to call an XML Web service from a Web Form.

Lesson: Working with Web Forms

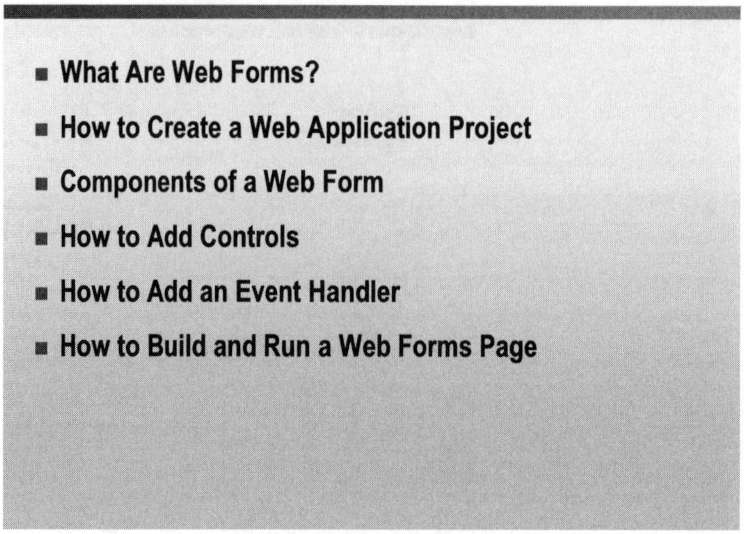

Introduction

This lesson describes how to create a Web Form, how to add controls, how to handle events, and how to build and run a Web Forms page.

Lesson agenda

This lesson includes the following topics and activities:

- What Are Web Forms?
- Demonstration: Using Web Forms
- How to Create a Web Application Project
- Components of a Web Form
- How to Add Controls
- How to Add an Event Handler
- How to Build and Run a Web Forms Page
- Practice: Creating a New Web Forms Page

Lesson objectives

After completing this lesson, you will be able to:

- Define the components of a Web Form.
- Create a new Web Application project.
- Add HTML and Web server controls to a Web Form.
- Program events to handle interactions with the user.
- Build and run a Web Forms page.

What Are Web Forms?

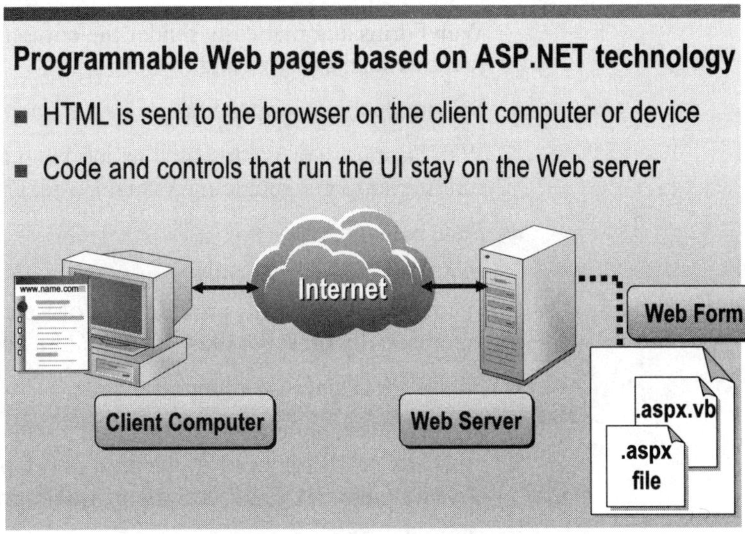

Introduction

Just as you use Microsoft Windows® Forms to create Windows-based applications, you can use Web Forms to build Web applications. Web Forms are programmable Web pages that serve as the user interface (UI) for a Microsoft ASP.NET Web Application project. Web Forms consist of a combination of HTML, code, and controls that execute on a Web server that is running Internet Information Services (IIS). A Web Form presents information to the user in any type of browser, and it also implements application logic by using server-side code.

How Web Forms work

Web Forms display a UI by generating HTML that is sent to the browser, while the supporting code and controls that run the UI stay on the Web server. This split between client-side interface and server-side code is a crucial difference between Web Forms and traditional Web pages. Whereas a traditional Web page requires all of the code to be sent to and processed by the browser, Web Forms need to send only the interface controls to the browser. The page processing is kept on the server. This splitting of the UI and code increases the range of browsers that are supported by a single set of code, and also increases the security and functionality of the Web page.

.aspx files

Web Forms are commonly referred to as ASP.NET pages or ASPX pages. Web Forms have an .aspx extension and work as containers for the text and controls that you want to display in the browser.

Web Forms are often made up of two separate files: the .aspx file contains the UI for the Web Form, while the .aspx.vb file, which is called a *code-behind page*, contains the supporting Microsoft Visual Basic® .NET code.

Features

Web Forms provide the following features:

- Run on any browser

  Web Forms automatically render the correct, browser-compliant HTML for features such as styles and layout.

- Programmable in any language

  Web Forms are programmable in any language that the common language runtime supports, including Visual Basic, C#, and Microsoft JScript® .NET.

- State management

  State refers to the information that an application needs to maintain about a Web page. Web Forms provide a set of state management features that automatically preserve the view state of a page between requests.

- WYSIWYG and RAD support

  Web Forms support WYSIWYG (what you see is what you get) editing tools and powerful rapid application development (RAD) tools, such as Visual Studio .NET, for designing and programming your forms.

- Controls

  Web Forms provide a rich set of controls that allow you to encapsulate page logic into reusable components and declaratively handle page events.

Demonstration: Using Web Forms

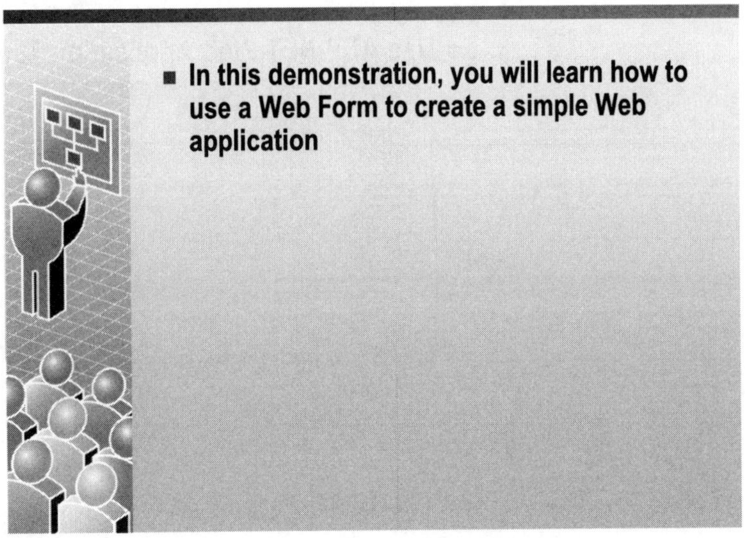

In this demonstration, you will learn how to create a simple Web application by adding controls to a Web Form, and writing code that responds to events.

How to Create a Web Application Project

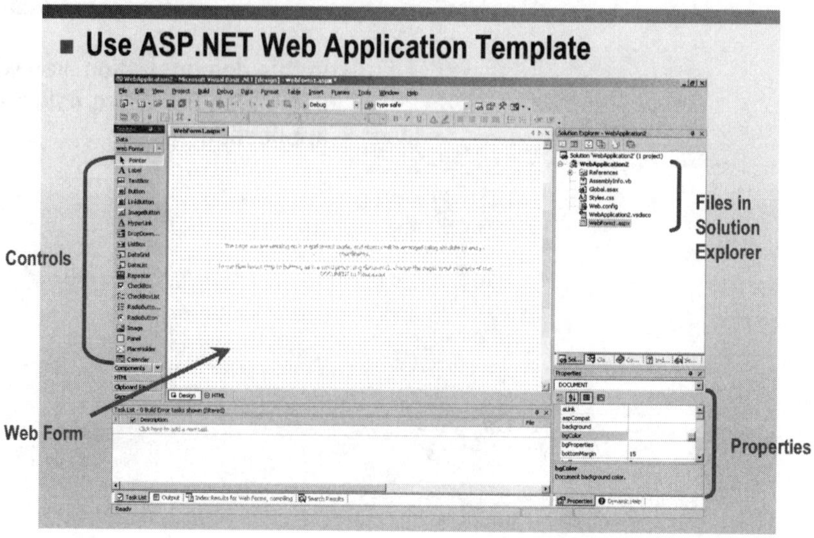

Introduction

The first step to creating a Web Forms page is to create an ASP.NET Web Application project.

Creating the project

► **To create the ASP.NET Web Application Project**

1. On the **File** menu, point to **New**, and then click **Project**.
2. In the **New Project** dialog box, perform the following steps:
   a. In the Project Types pane, click Visual Basic Projects.
   b. In the Templates pane, click ASP.NET Web Application.
   c. In the **Location** box, enter the complete Uniform Resource Locator (URL) for your application, including http://, the name of the server, and the name of your project.

      The default value for the server name is http://localhost, which assumes that your local computer is the Web server.
   d. Click **OK**.

      When you click **OK**, a new project is created at the root of the Web server that you specified. In addition, a new Web Forms page called WebForm1.aspx is displayed, in Design view, in the Web Forms Designer.

Project files created

The following table lists some of the files that are created on your local computer when you create an ASP.NET Web Application project.

File created	Description
WebForm1.aspx and WebForm1.aspx.vb files	These two files make up a single Web Forms page. The .aspx file contains the visual elements (user interface) of the Web Forms page, for example the HTML elements and Web Forms controls. The aspx.vb class file contains the code for the Web Forms page, including event-handler code.
AssemblyInfo.vb	A project information file (AssemblyInfo.vb or AssemblyInfo.cs file) that contains metadata about the assemblies in a project, such as name, version, and culture information.
Web.config	An XML-based file that contains configuration data about each unique URL resource that is used in the project.
Global.asax and Global.asax.vb files	Global.asax is an optional file for handling application-level events. This file resides in the root directory of an ASP.NET application. The Global.asax.vb class file is a hidden, dependent file of Global.asax. It contains the code for handling application events, such as the **Application_OnError** event. At run time, this file is parsed and compiled.
Styles.css	A file for a cascading style sheet to be used within the project.
.vsdisco (project discovery) file	An XML-based file that contains links (URLs) to resources providing discovery information for an XML Web service.

Viewing the files

► **To view all of the files in a project**

- Click the **Show All Files** button in the toolbar of Solution Explorer.

Components of a Web Form

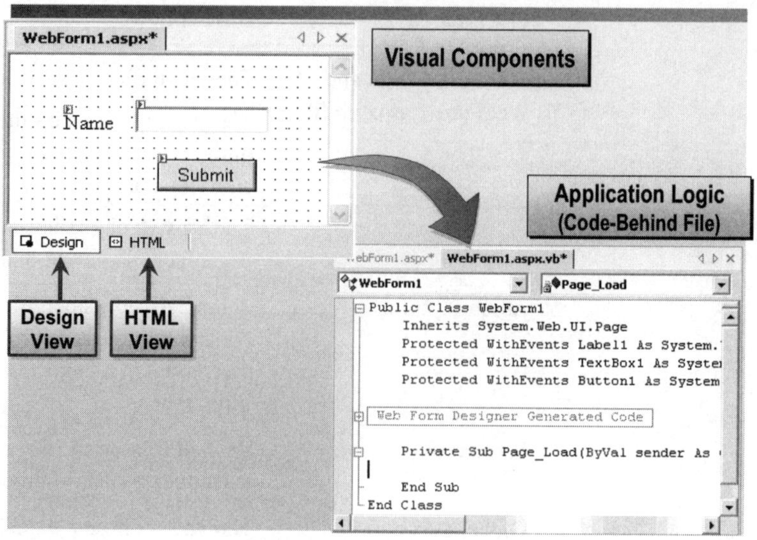

Introduction

Web Forms divide a Web application's UI into two parts: visual components and application logic. When working with the visual components of the page, you can work in either Design view or HTML view.

Web Forms code model

A Web Forms page consists of two files:

- The .aspx file, or *page*

  This file contains HTML, static text, and the server controls that make up the visual components of the page.

- The .aspx.vb file, or *code-behind* file

  When Visual Studio .NET creates a Web Form, such as WebForm1.aspx, it also creates a code-behind file, WebForm1.aspx.vb. This file contains the application logic, which is the code that you create to interact with the form. When you run the form, the code-behind class file runs and dynamically produces the output for your page.

.aspx file views

When you work with the .aspx file, you can work in one of two views: Design view or HTML view. When you switch between these views, each view is updated with the changes that you made in the other view.

Design view

The Design view shows you the WYSIWYG view of the .aspx file that you are working with. In Design view, you can drag controls from the Toolbox and use the Properties window to configure the controls to approximate what they will look like when displayed to the user by means of a Web browser.

In Design view, you can arrange UI elements in two modes, which you select by using the **pageLayout** property of the page.

- Grid layout: You can arrange objects on the page by using absolute positioning (x and y coordinates). This mode is the default mode.
- Flow layout: You can arrange elements as you would in a word-processing document, from top to bottom. As in a word-processing document, you can also add text directly to the Web Form by typing the text that you want to appear and using the **Formatting** toolbar to format the text.

You will find the **Design** tab at the bottom of the Web Forms Designer.

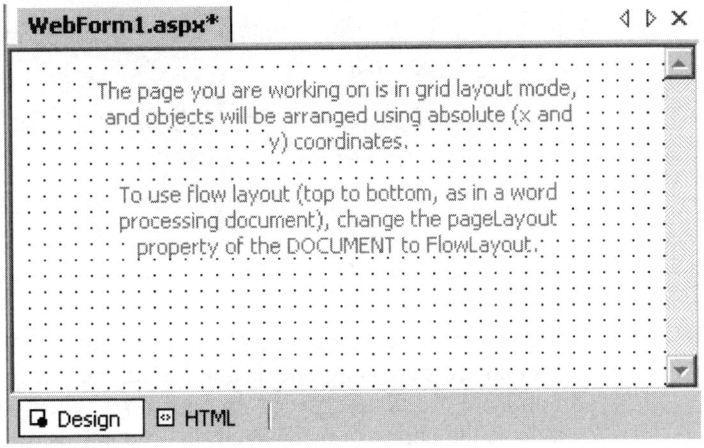

HTML view

The HTML view shows you the HTML format of the .aspx file that you are working with. In this view, you can view and edit the HTML code for the elements in your Web Form. As in other Code Editor views, the Web Forms Designer supports Microsoft IntelliSense® for elements in HTML view.

You will find the **HTML** tab at the bottom of the Web Forms Designer.

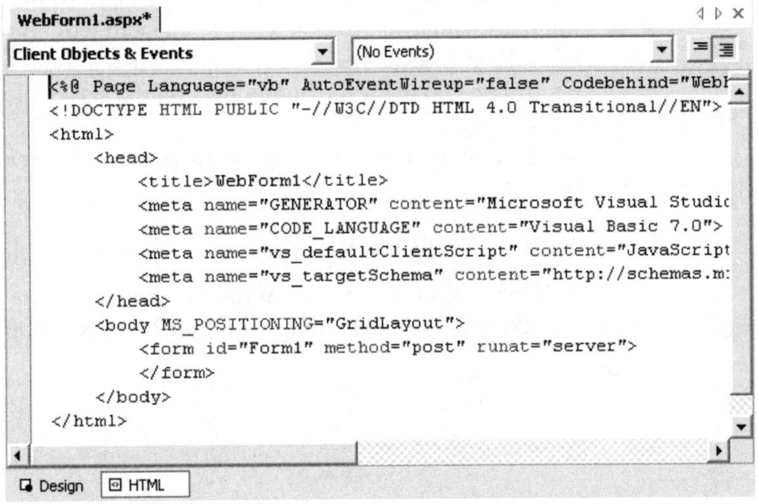

Note To display the current HTML document in the built-in internal Web browser, click **View in Browser** on the **File** menu, or right-click the .aspx file in Design or HTML view and then click **View in Browser**.

How to Add Controls

Server controls: components that run on the server

- **Web server controls:**
  - Created specifically for ASP.NET
  - Available from the **Web Forms** tab of the Toolbox
- **HTML server controls:**
  - HTML client controls that you convert to run as server controls
  - Available from the **HTML** tab of the Toolbox

Introduction

After you create a Web Form, you can add controls to build the UI. ASP.NET server controls are components that run on the server and encapsulate UI functionality and other related functionality. When you create ASP.NET pages, you have the option of using Web server controls or HTML server controls. You can mix these control types on the same page as a means of quickly updating an HTML page. However, the best practice is to avoid HTML server controls. Web server controls have a richer object model than HTML server controls.

Web server controls

Web server controls are server controls created specifically for ASP.NET. ASP.NET controls are called server controls because when the page runs, the controls are instantiated in server code as part of the **Page** class. When a user interacts with a control, the code associated with the control runs on the server after the page is posted. For example, when a user clicks an ASP.NET **Button** control, the code for the button runs on the server after the page is displayed.

► **To add Web server controls to your Web Form**

1. Open the .aspx file in Design view.
2. If the Toolbox is not open, on the **View** menu, click **Toolbox**.
3. On the **Web Forms** tab of the Toolbox, click the control that you want to add to the form and drag it to the desired location on the form.

HTML server controls

HTML server controls are modified HTML elements that run on the server instead of on the client browser. By default, HTML elements on a Web Form run on the client computer. However, adding the **runat="server"** attribute converts HTML elements to HTML server controls.

► **To add an HTML control to a Web Form and convert it to a server control**

1. Open the .aspx file in Design view.
2. If the Toolbox is not open, on the **View** menu, click **Toolbox**.
3. From the **HTML** tab of the Toolbox, drag an HTML element onto the page.
4. Right-click the element, and then click **Run As Server Control**.

   The Web Forms Designer adds the **runat="server"** attribute to the element, which alerts the server to treat the element as a server control. In Design view, an icon appears on the control to indicate that it is a server control.

How to Add an Event Handler

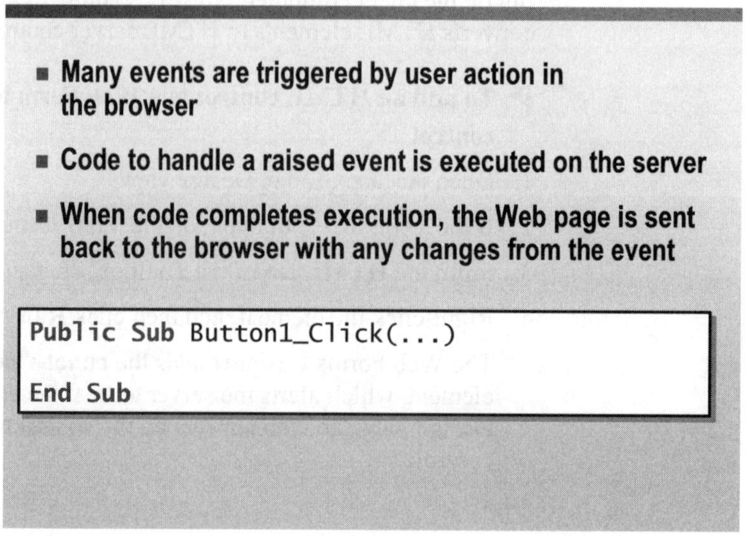

Introduction

Web Forms bring to Web applications the model of writing code in event handlers for events that occur on either the client or server. Web Forms abstract this model in such a way that the underlying mechanism of capturing an event on the client, transmitting it to the server, and calling the appropriate handler is all automatic and invisible. The result is a clear, easily written code structure.

Programming events

Interacting with users is one of the primary reasons for creating ASP.NET Web Forms. You program various events to handle these interactions. The Web page can execute code, and so can the many events raised by different objects, including all of the server controls.

You can create event handlers to handle events associated with individual controls, with a page, with an application, or with a session.

Example

Server controls on Web Forms pages can raise various events. Many events are triggered by something the user does in the browser. For example, a **Button** Web server control can raise a **Click** event when a user clicks a button on your page.

The code to handle the raised event is executed on the server. When the user clicks a button, the page is posted back to the server. The framework for the ASP.NET page parses the event information, and if you have an event handler corresponding to the event, your code is called automatically. When your code finishes, the page is sent back to the browser with any changes that the event-handler code made.

Opening an event handler

► **To open an event handler for a page or control event**

1. On the **View** menu, click **Code** to open the Code Editor for the Web Form you are working with.
2. In the **Class Name** list, click the control for which you want to write code. To write code for page events such as **Page_Load**, click **(Base Class Events)** in this list.

   The following illustration shows the **Class Name** list with **Button1** selected.

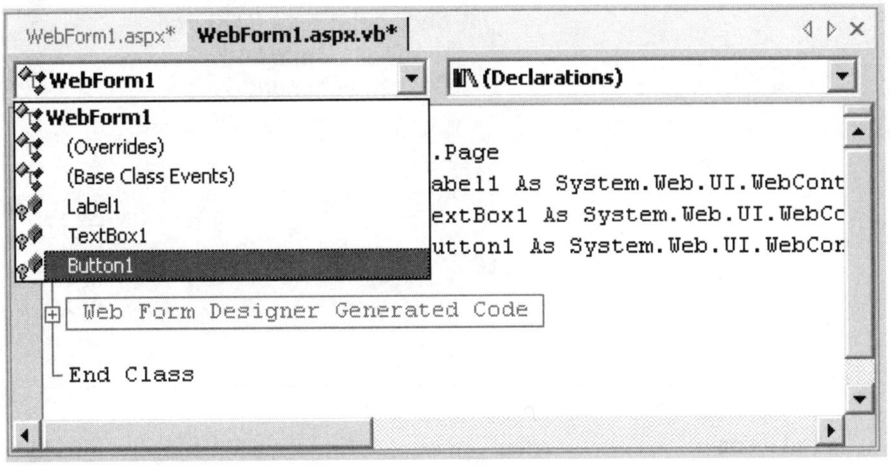

3. Open the **Method Name** list to view events available for the control. The following illustration shows a list of control events for Button1. The **Click** event is selected.

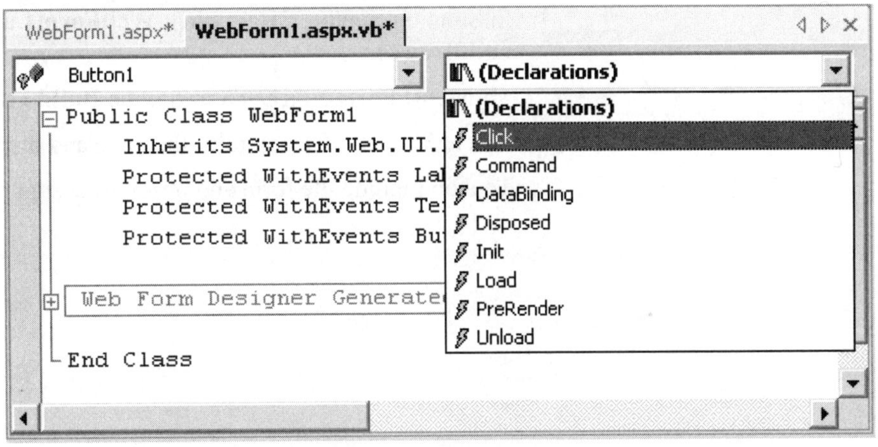

4. Click the event to open the event handler for the event.

Note For more recommendations about ASP.NET server controls, see the Visual Studio .NET documentation.

How to Build and Run a Web Forms Page

- In Solution Explorer, right-click the Web Forms page and then click Build and Browse
- Shortcut: Press CTRL+F8 to run the Build and Browse command

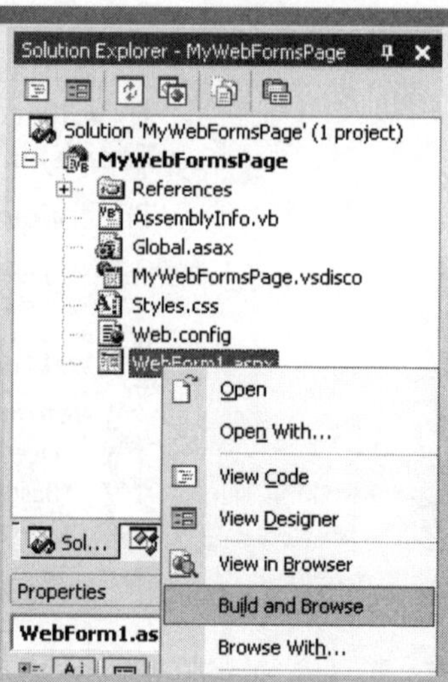

Introduction

After you create a project, add controls, and add event handlers for the controls, you can compile the class file of the page. You can then view the page in any browser.

Build and run the Web Forms page

► **To build and run your Web Forms page**

1. In Solution Explorer, right-click **WebForm1.aspx**, and then select **Build and Browse**.

   Shortcut: Press CTRL+F8 to run the **Build and Browse** command.

   Visual Studio .NET compiles the page and displays it in the **Browse** tab.

2. To stop running the form and return to design mode, close the **Browse** tab.

Practice: Creating a New Web Forms Page

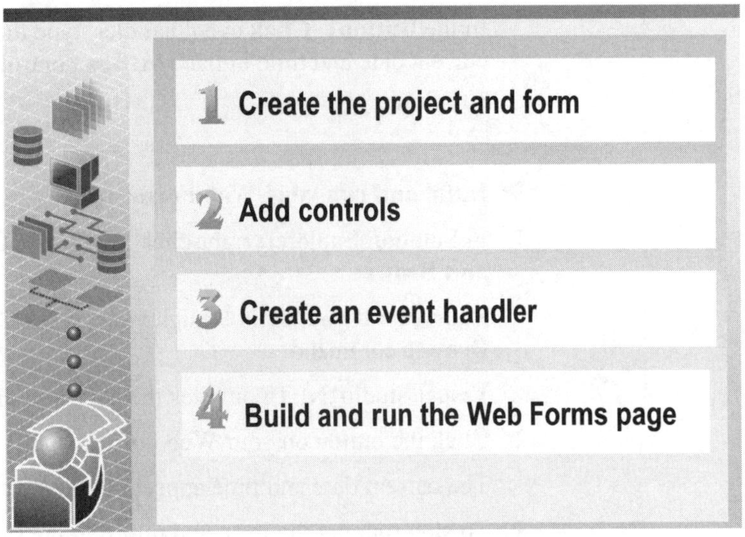

Introduction

In this practice, you will create a Web Forms page.

► **Create an ASP.NET Web Application project**

1. Start Visual Studio .NET.
2. On the **File** menu, point to **New**, and then click **Project**.
3. In the **New Project** dialog box, perform the following steps:
   a. In the Project Types pane, click Visual Basic Projects.
   b. In the Templates pane, click ASP.NET Web Application.
   c. In the **Location** box, enter the complete URL for your application: **http://localhost/MyWebFormsPage**
   d. Click **OK**.

   When you click **OK**, a new project is created at the root of the Web server that you specified. In addition, a new Web Forms page called WebForm1.aspx is displayed, in Design view, in the Web Forms Designer.

► **Add ASP.NET server controls to a Web Forms page**

1. From the **Web Forms** tab of the Toolbox, drag a **Button** control onto the page.
2. From the **Web Forms** tab of the Toolbox, drag a **TextBox** control onto the page.

► **Create an event handler for the Button control**

1. Create an event handler for the **Click** event of the **Button** control.
2. In the **Button1_Click** event handler, type the following code to display the current date and time in the **TextBox** control by setting its **Text** property.

```
TextBox1.Text = Now
```

► **Build and run your Web Forms page**

1. In Solution Explorer, right-click **WebForm1.aspx**, and then click **Build and Browse**.

   Shortcut: If you are in Design view, press CTRL+F8 to run the **Build and Browse** command.

   Visual Studio .NET compiles the page and displays it in the **Browse** tab.
2. Click the button on your Web Forms page.

   The current date and time appears in the text box.
3. To stop running the form and return to the Code Editor, close the **Browse** tab.

Solution files

The solution files for this practice are located in the *install_folder*\Practices\Mod10\MyWebFormsPage\Solution folder.

Lesson: Using XML Web Services

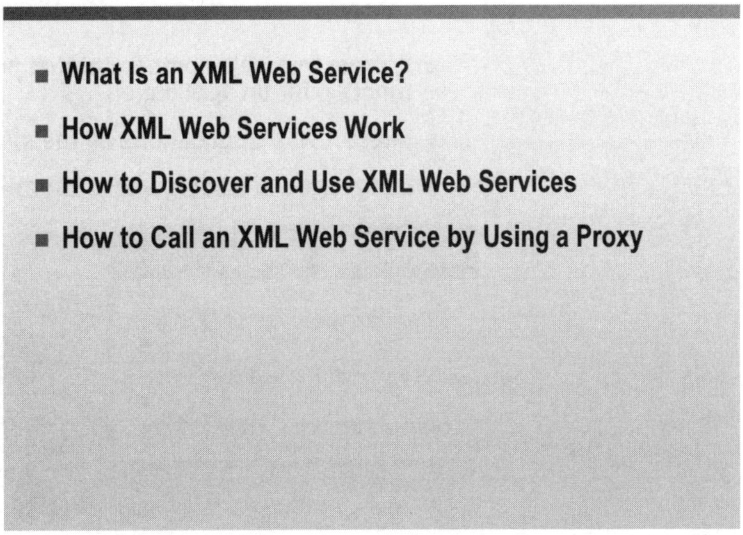

Introduction

XML Web services are applications that are hosted on a Web server and that customers can access by means of the Web. XML Web services are the basis for the move to distributed computing on the Internet. Applications can be constructed by using multiple XML Web services from various sources that work together regardless of where they reside or how they were implemented.

Lesson agenda

This lesson includes the following topics and activities:

- What Is an XML Web Service?
- How XML Web Services Work
- Demonstration: Using XML Web Services
- How to Discover and Use XML Web Services
- How to Call an XML Web Service by Using a Proxy

Lesson objectives

After completing this lesson, you will be able to:

- Explain what an XML Web service is.
- Describe how to discover existing XML Web services.
- Create a proxy to call an XML Web service.
- Invoke XML Web service methods in a simple application.

What Is an XML Web Service?

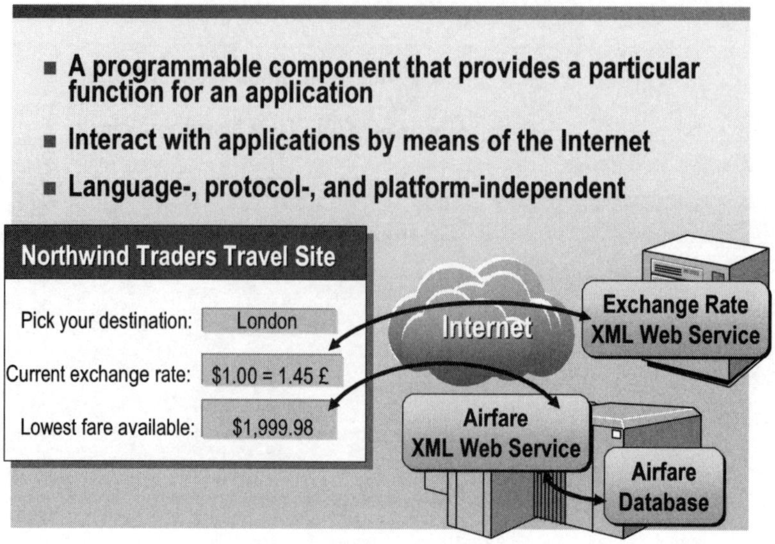

Introduction

XML Web services are similar to components in that they represent black-box functionality that developers can use to add features to Web Forms, Windows-based applications, or even other XML Web services, without worrying about how the supporting service is implemented.

Definition

An *XML Web service* is a programmable component that provides a particular function for an application, such as application logic. An XML Web service can be used internally, by a single application, or it can be used externally, by many applications that access it by means of the Internet.

Example of an XML Web service

Microsoft Passport is an example of a user identity XML Web service. An organization can subscribe to Passport and use this XML Web service to verify a user's identity before providing access to an application, rather than writing their own code to accomplish this task.

Why use XML Web services?

One of the primary advantages of the XML Web services architecture is that it allows programs written in different languages on different platforms to communicate with each other in a standards-based way. The following features of XML Web services enable you to easily provide access to your application logic or to discover an XML Web service and use it in your application.

- Language-independent

  A connection to an XML Web service can be written in any Microsoft .NET-compatible language. This means that you do not need to learn a new programming language to use an XML Web service. A component written in any .NET-compatible language and exported as an XML Web service can be used by any Visual Basic .NET-based application capable of sending and reading XML by means of the transport.

- Protocol-independent

  Unlike other component technologies, XML Web services do not use protocols that are specific to certain object models, such as the Distributed Component Object Model (DCOM) or Common Object Request Broker Architecture (CORBA). XML Web services communicate by means of standard Web protocols and data formats, such as Hypertext Transfer Protocol (HTTP) and XML. Any server that supports these Web standards can access or host XML Web services.

- Platform-independent

  XML Web services are designed to interact directly with other applications by means of the Internet. As a result, XML Web services do not have user interfaces. Instead, they provide standard defined interfaces (called contracts) that describe the services that they provide. Because XML Web services are accessible by means of a standard interface, they allow disparate systems to work together. Servers that can support Web Forms can also support XML Web services.

XML Web services example

The preceding illustration shows a hypothetical travel Web site that offers several features that are based on XML Web services. In this scenario, the user enters a destination city name, and the application code uses the city name as a parameter in calls to two XML Web services. From the user's perspective, this is a richly featured travel Web site. From a code perspective, the Web site is more of a graphical interface that combines XML Web services from unrelated companies.

This travel agency Web site, by using XML Web services, provides advantages to both the consuming Web site and the various XML Web service providers.

Advantages for the Web site providers include the following:

- The travel agency application can provide functionality that otherwise might be limited by the agency developer's programming skills, available time, or subject expertise.
- The travel agency does not bear the maintenance costs of keeping data, such as travel fares or exchange rates, up to date.
- The travel agency developers do not need to learn how the XML Web service was built and deployed in order to be able to use it.
- The Web site might be able to charge the XML Web service providers for the right to offer services to the Web site customer base.

Advantages for the XML Web service providers include the following:

- The XML Web service provider does not bear the cost of developing and marketing a Web site to the traveling public.
- By offering an application as an XML Web service, the Web service provider can access the customer base of a number of travel agencies.
- The XML Web service can be used by a wide variety of applications.
- The XML Web service provider might be able to charge the Web site for the use of the service.

Note For information about how companies are currently using XML Web services, see the Microsoft XML Web Services Case Studies Web site at http://www.microsoft.com/net/use/casestudies.asp.

How XML Web Services Work

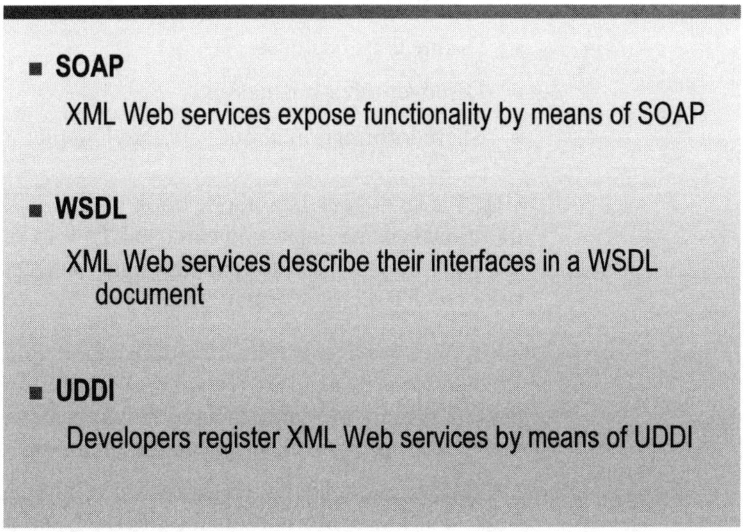

Introduction

XML Web services provide functionality on the Web by means of SOAP, are described with a Web Services Description Language (WSDL) file, and are registered through Universal Description, Discovery and Integration (UDDI).

SOAP

XML Web services provide useful functionality by means of a standard Web protocol. In most cases, the protocol used is SOAP. SOAP is a lightweight XML-based protocol that is used for information exchange. SOAP defines the XML format for messages.

WSDL

XML Web services provide a way to describe their interfaces in enough detail to enable a user to build a client application to communicate with them. This description is usually provided in an XML document called a WSDL document.

The WSDL file defines everything required to write a program to work with an XML Web service, including the following:

- Location of the URL
- XML Web service methods and properties
- Data types used
- Communication protocols

Visual Studio .NET uses the WSDL file to build proxy objects to communicate with an XML Web service.

Note For more information about WSDL files, see "XML Web Service Discovery" in the Visual Studio .NET documentation.

UDDI

XML Web services are registered by means of UDDI so that potential users can find them easily. UDDI is a comprehensive industry initiative that allows businesses to:

- Define their business.
- Discover other businesses.
- Share information about how they interact in a global registry.

UDDI is analogous to a phone book listing of XML Web services. As with a traditional phone book, you can use UDDI to search for a company that offers the services you need, to read about the services offered, and to contact someone for more information.

XML Web service developers publish descriptions and locations for their XML Web services to a UDDI Web site. After the data has been registered, it becomes freely available to anyone who needs to discover which XML Web services are provided by a particular business.

Note For more information about UDDI, see the UDDI Web site at http://www.uddi.org or the Microsoft UDDI Web site at http://uddi.microsoft.com.

Demonstration: Using XML Web Services

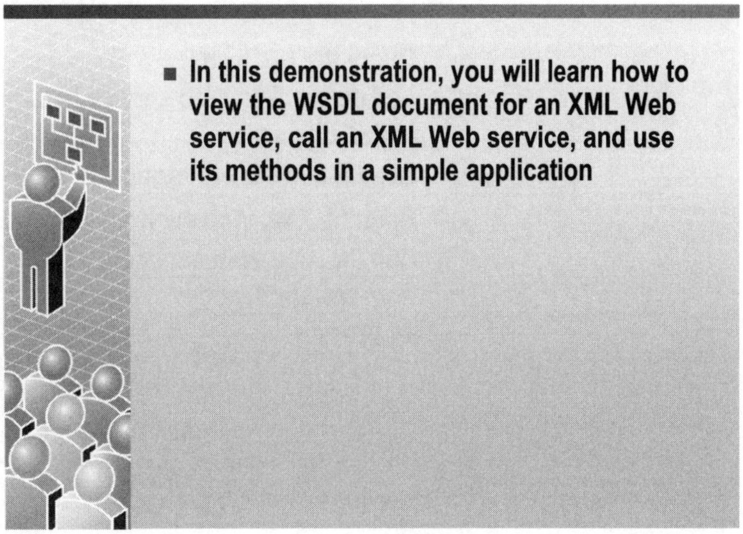

In this demonstration, you will learn how to view the WSDL document for an XML Web service, how to call an XML Web service from a simple application, and how to use the methods of the XML Web service to calculate a mortgage payment.

How to Discover and Use XML Web Services

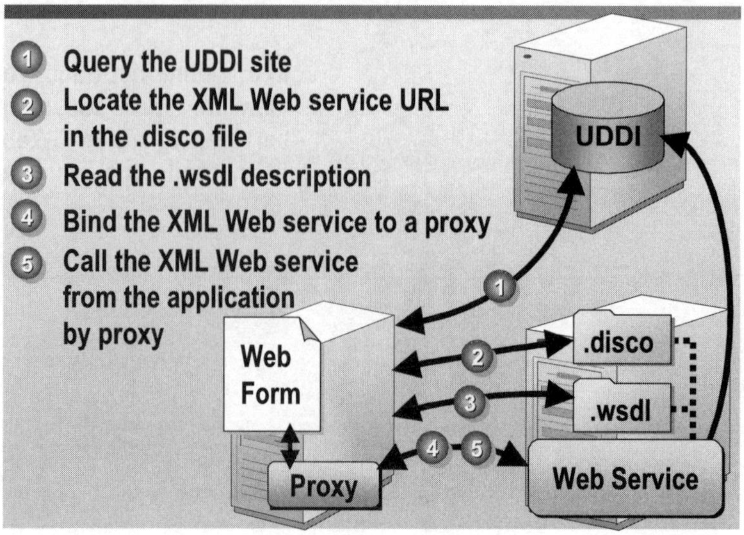

Introduction

If you are developing an application that uses an XML Web service from a business partner, it is likely that the partner will give you the URL for the XML Web service. However, you might want your application to use other XML Web services for which you do not have a URL.

The process by which you locate an XML Web service and its descriptions and learn how to interact with it is known as *discovery*. You can find existing XML Web services to add to your application by using one or more of a series of discovery services. These discovery services are evolving and changing rapidly as the development and use of XML Web services gains acceptance in the Internet community.

Process for discovering an XML Web service

The general process for discovering and calling an XML Web service is as follows:

1. Query the UDDI Web site to discover available XML Web services that meet your requirements.

   The UDDI Web site provides a listing of XML Web services that includes the discovery document (.disco file) URLs for those XML Web services.
2. Select an XML Web service and access the discovery document to locate the XML Web service URL and the related WSDL document URLs.
3. Build a proxy object from the WSDL document.

   A *proxy object* is code that behaves exactly like the class it is meant to represent. However, a proxy does not contain any of the application logic. Instead, a proxy contains marshaling and transport logic. A proxy allows a client to access an XML Web service as if it were a local object.
4. Use the proxy to bind the XML Web service.
5. Call the XML Web service by using the proxy.

Visual Studio .NET and UDDI

You can use Visual Studio .NET to connect to UDDI and search for and examine available XML Web services.

► **Use Visual Studio .NET to locate information about XML Web services**

1. On the Visual Studio .NET Start Page, click **XML Web Services**.

   If the Start Page is not visible, click **Help**, and then click **Show Start Page**.

2. On the **Find a Service** tab, click either **UDDI Production Environment** or **UDDI Test Environment**.

   Note The **UDDI Production Environment** option is selected by default. If you are developing your application, click **UDDI Test Environment**.

   ---

3. In the **Search For** box, enter a keyword for the XML Web service that you want to locate.
4. Click **Go** to start the search.

   The results of the search are displayed under the search criteria. You can use the results to display more information about an XML Web service.

   Note This procedure does not work in an environment that is not connected to the Internet.

How to Call an XML Web Service by Using a Proxy

1. **Create a Web reference for the XML Web service**
2. **Create an instance of the XML Web service**

```
Dim WebServiceName As New localhost.service1( )
```

3. **Call the Web methods of the XML Web service**

```
Label1.Text = WebServiceName.WebMethod( )
```

Example:

```
Sub GetRatingButton_Click (...)
   Dim ProxyGetStocks As New localhost.GetStocks( )
   ResultsLabel.Text = _
       ProxyGetStocks.GetRating("Contoso, Ltd.")
End Sub
```

Introduction

To call an XML Web service, in your application project, you need to add a Web reference to the XML Web service. Visual Studio .NET automatically creates the proxy object that is used to communicate with the XML Web service. This scenario will use a Web-based application. The process is the same for a Windows-based application.

Calling an XML Web service

► **To call an XML Web service from a Web Form**

1. Open the application from which you will be calling the XML Web service.
2. On the **Project** menu, click **Add Web Reference**.
3. In the **Address** field of the **Add Web Reference** dialog box, type the URL of the XML Web service that you are accessing, press ENTER, and then click **Add Reference**.

   After adding a Web reference to your project, Visual Studio .NET displays the associated files in a folder within the Web References folder of Solution Explorer. By default, the name of the Web reference will be the same as the name of the server that is hosting the XML Web service. For example, if you create a Web reference to http://localhost/Stocks/Service1.asmx, Visual Studio .NET will name the Web reference **localhost** by default.

Note Visual Studio .NET is optimized for XML Web services that are created by Visual Studio .NET. ASP.NET might not read WSDL files that are created with other programs.

---

4. In the code for the Web Form, create an instance of the proxy of the XML Web service.

   In the following example, **WebServiceName** is the name you choose for this instance of the XML Web service, **localhost** is the name of the Web reference, and **service1** is the name of the Web service.

   ```
   Dim WebServiceName As New localhost.service1( )
   ```

5. Call the Web methods of the XML Web service.

   In the following example, the method **WebMethod** is called, and the return value is assigned to the text property of a label on the Web Form.

   ```
   Label1.Text = WebServiceName.WebMethod( )
   ```

Example of calling an XML Web service

The following example is based on a Web Form with a **GetRating** button and a label named ResultsLabel. When the user clicks the **GetRating** button, an instance of the proxy of the GetStocks XML Web service is created. The second line of code calls the **GetRating** method of the XML Web service, passes the stock name “Contoso, Ltd.” as a parameter, and displays the return value to the user by using the **Text** property of ResultsLabel.

```
Sub GetRatingButton_Click (...)
  Dim ProxyGetStocks As New localhost.GetStocks( )
  ResultsLabel.Text = _
      ProxyGetStocks.GetRating("Contoso, Ltd.")
End Sub
```

Review

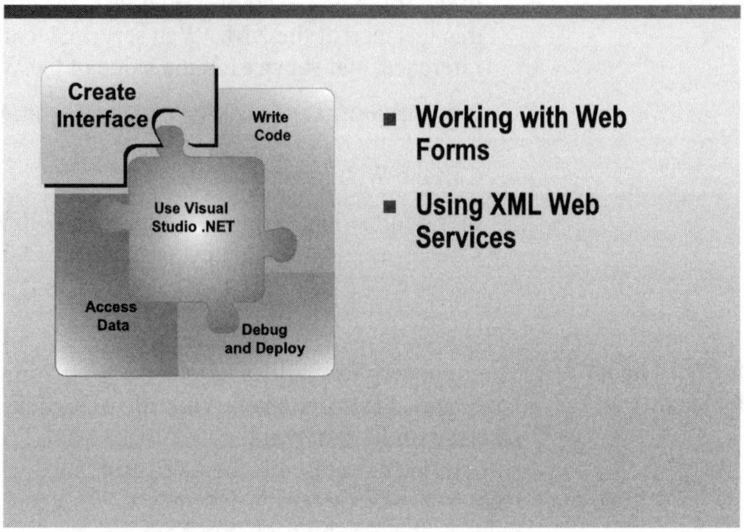

1. How can you display text to the user on a Web Forms page?

   a. In Design view, add a **Label** control to the Web Form and then type the text in the **Text** property.

   b. In Design view, in Flow layout mode, type the text directly onto the Web Form.

   c. In Design view, in Grid layout mode, type the text directly onto the Web Form.

   d. In HTML view, add the text, using the appropriate HTML tags.

2. Which of the following is the file extension for the file that contains the event-handling code for a Web Form?

   a. asmx

   b. Web.config

   c. webform1.vb

   d. aspx.vb

3. What attribute causes the server to recognize that an element is a server control?

4. What is the default name for a Web server running on a local machine?
   a. aspx
   b. localhost
   c. localserver
   d. aspx.vb

5. What is the protocol that is used to communicate between a proxy and an XML Web service?
   a. HTML
   b. WSDL
   c. SOAP
   d. UDDI

6. How do you access an XML Web service from a Web Form?

Lab 10.1: Creating a Web Application

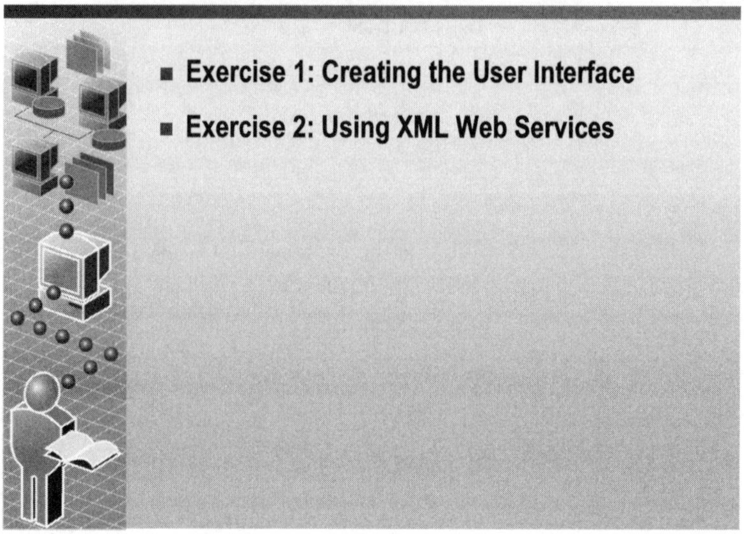

Objectives

After completing this lab, you will be able to:

- Create a Web Form and use ASP.NET server controls.
- Discover an XML Web service and use it from a Web Form.
- Write event handlers for the controls.
- Call methods that the XML Web service provides.

Note This lab focuses on the concepts in this module and as a result may not comply with Microsoft security recommendations.

Prerequisites

Before working on this lab, you must:

- Have experience writing event handlers in Visual Basic .NET.
- Be familiar with Web Forms and ASP.NET server controls.
- Be familiar with the XML Web service discovery process.

Scenario

In this lab, you will use Web Forms to create a user interface that is similar to that of the loan estimate application. You will also use an XML Web service to calculate mortgage payments on the Web Form.

Solution files

The solution files for this lab are in the *install_folder*\Labfiles\Lab101\Ex01\Solution and *install_folder*\Labfiles\Lab101\Ex02\Solution folders.

Estimated time to complete this lab: 30 minutes

Exercise 1
Creating the User Interface

In this exercise, you will create the user interface for the Web version of the loan estimate application.

▶ Create a new project

1. Start Visual Studio .NET.
2. Create a new Visual Basic ASP.NET Web application. Set the location to **http://localhost/2559/Labfiles/Lab101/Ex01/WebFormApplication** and then click **OK**.
3. Change the **File Name** property of WebForm1.aspx to **WebForm.aspx**.

▶ Add controls to the main form

- Add the following controls to the Web form:

Control name	Property	Property value
Label1	**Text**	**Loan Calculator**
	Font.Bold	**True**
	Font.Size	**X-Large**
Label2	**ID**	**LoanAmountLabel**
	Text	**Loan Amount**
Label3	**ID**	**InterestRateLabel**
	Text	**Interest Rate**
Label4	**ID**	**LoanTermLabel**
	Text	**Loan Term**
Label5	**ID**	**PaymentLabel**
	Text	**Payment**
Label6	**ID**	**AmountLabel**
	Text	*Blank*
TextBox1	**ID**	**LoanAmountTextBox**
DropDownList1	**ID**	**InterestRateDropDownList**
	Items	**4.5, 5.0, 6.0, 6.5, 7.0, 7.5, 8.0, 9.0, 10.0**
DropDownList2	**ID**	**LoanTermDropDownList**
	Items	**10, 15, 30**
Button1	**ID**	**MonthlyPaymentButton**
	Text	**Monthly Payment**
Button2	**ID**	**TotalPaidButton**
	Text	**Total Paid**

Your form should look similar to the following:

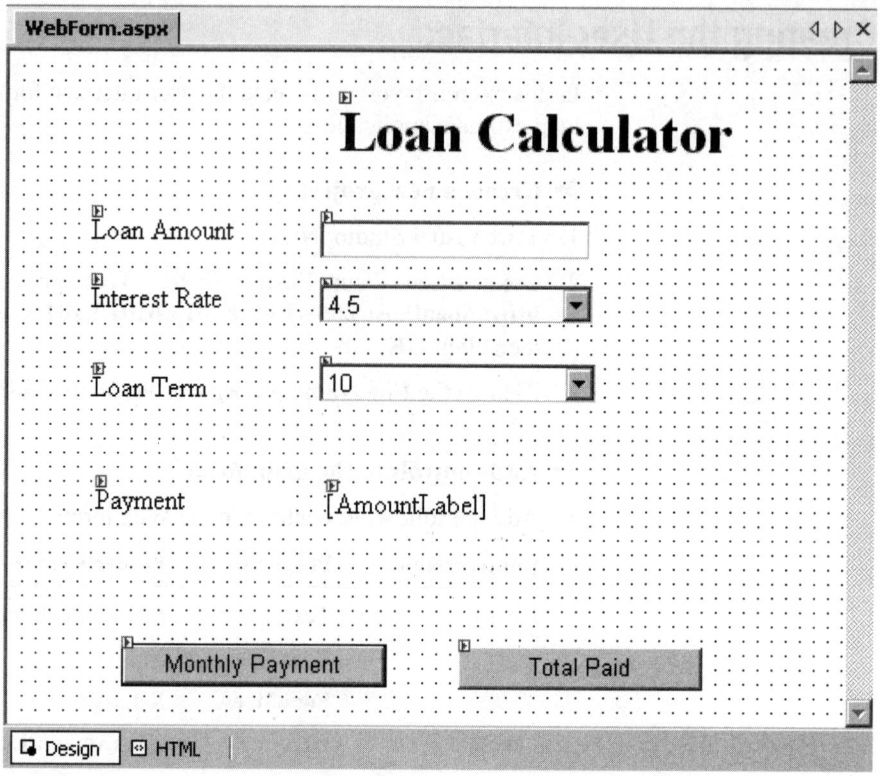

▶ **Compile and run the project**

1. Build the project.
2. Run the project in a browser.
3. Close the browser.

Exercise 2
Using XML Web Services

In this exercise, you will call the methods of an XML Web service by using a proxy, and then use the methods for calculating mortgage payments.

▶ Add a Web reference

1. Continue working with the project you created in Exercise 1. If you did not complete Exercise 1, use the WebFormApplication.sln project in the *install_folder*\Labfiles\Lab101\Ex02\Starter folder.
2. On the **Project** menu, click **Add Web Reference**, and then type in the following URL:

   http://localhost/2559/Labfiles/Lab101/Ex02/WebService/CalculationService.asmx?wsdl
3. Click the **Go** button , and then click **Add Reference**.

▶ Call the MonthlyPayment method in the event handler for the MonthlyPaymentButton

1. Add an event handler for the **MonthlyPaymentButton_Click** event.
2. Declare and instantiate a **localhost.CalculationService** variable named *payment*. Your code should look as follows:

```
Dim payment As New localhost.CalculationService( )
```

3. Call the **MonthlyPayment** method of *payment*.

   a. Use the following parameters in the call to **MonthlyPayment**.

Parameter	Value
loanAmount	**CDbl(LoanAmountTextBox.Text)**
rate	**CDbl(InterestRateDropDownList.SelectedItem.Text)**
loanLength	**CInt(LoanTermDropDownList.SelectedItem.Text)**

   b. Use the **FormatCurrency** function to format the return value of the **MonthlyPayment** method, and assign the formatted return value to the **AmountLabel.Text** property.

   Your completed code should look as follows:

```
AmountLabel.Text = FormatCurrency(payment.MonthlyPayment _
   (CDbl(LoanAmountTextBox.Text), _
   CDbl(InterestRateDropDownList.SelectedItem.Text), _
   CInt(LoanTermDropDownList.SelectedItem.Text)))
```

► Call the TotalPaid method in the event handler for the TotalPaidButton

1. Add an event handler for the **TotalPaidButton_Click** event.
2. Declare and instantiate a **localhost.CalculationService** variable named *payment*.
3. Call the **TotalPaid** method of *payment*.
   a. Use the following parameters in the call to **TotalPaid**.

Parameter	Value
loanAmount	**CDbl(LoanAmountTextBox.Text)**
rate	**CDbl(InterestRateDropDownList.SelectedItem.Text)**
loanLength	**CInt(LoanTermDropDownList.SelectedItem.Text)**

   b. Use the **FormatCurrency** function to format the return value of the **TotalPaid** method, and assign the formatted return value to the **AmountLabel.Text** property.

   Your completed code should look like the following:

```
AmountLabel.Text = FormatCurrency(payment.TotalPaid _
   (CDbl(LoanAmountTextBox.Text), _
   CDbl(InterestRateDropDownList.SelectedItem.Text), _
   CInt(LoanTermDropDownList.SelectedItem.Text)))
```

► Compile, run, and test the application

1. Right-click **WebForm.aspx**.
2. Click **Build and Browse**.

   WebForm.aspx displays in a browser window inside Visual Studio .NET.
3. Enter a loan amount, interest rate, and loan length.
4. Click **Monthly Payment** to calculate the monthly payment.
5. Click **Total Paid** to calculate the total payment.
6. Quit Visual Studio .NET.

Course Evaluation

Your evaluation of this course will help Microsoft understand the quality of your learning experience.

At a convenient time between now and the end of the course, please complete a course evaluation, which is available at http://www.CourseSurvey.com.

Microsoft will keep your evaluation strictly confidential and will use your responses to improve your future learning experience.

msdn® training

Module 11: Using ADO.NET

Contents

Microsoft®

Overview

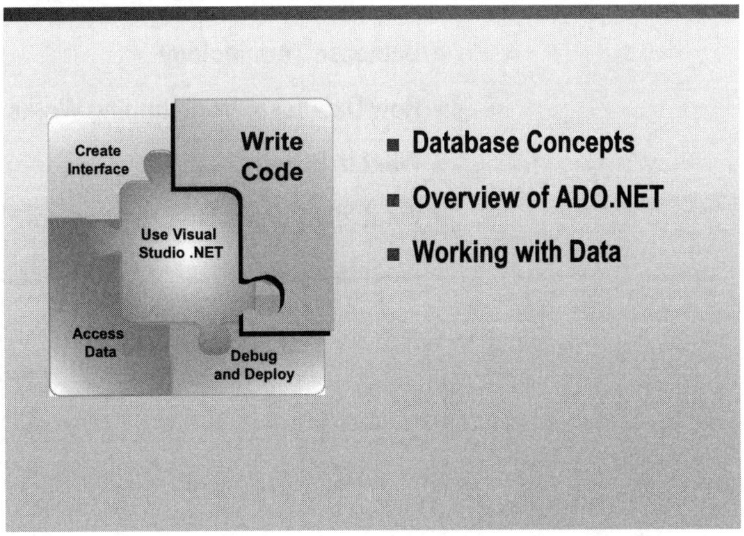

Introduction

This module explains how to use Microsoft® ADO.NET with a Microsoft Windows® Form application to create, read, update, and delete records in Microsoft SQL Server™ databases and Microsoft Access (Jet 4.0) databases.

Objectives

After completing this module, you will be able to:

- Define basic database terminology, including database, table, record, field, and key.
- Describe some commonly used ADO.NET objects.
- Create and open a connection to a database.
- Create, read, update, and delete records in a database.
- Use the Data Form Wizard to create a simple data access application.
- Display and modify data extracted from a database.

Lesson: Database Concepts

- Database Terminology
- How Database Programming Works
- What Is SQL?
- What Is a Connected Environment?
- What Is a Disconnected Environment?

Introduction

This lesson provides an overview of basic database concepts. It introduces the Structured Query Language (SQL) and explains the difference between connected and disconnected data environments.

Lesson objectives

After completing this lesson, you will be able to:

- Describe basic database elements, including database, table, record, field, and key.
- Explain the overall process of accessing data.
- Use basic SQL statements.
- Explain the difference between a connected and disconnected environment.
- Use Server Explorer to view database elements.

Lesson agenda

This lesson includes the following topics and activities:

- Database Terminology
- How Database Programming Works
- What Is SQL?
- What Is a Connected Environment?
- What Is a Disconnected Environment?
- Practice: Identifying Connected or Disconnected Data Scenarios

Database Terminology

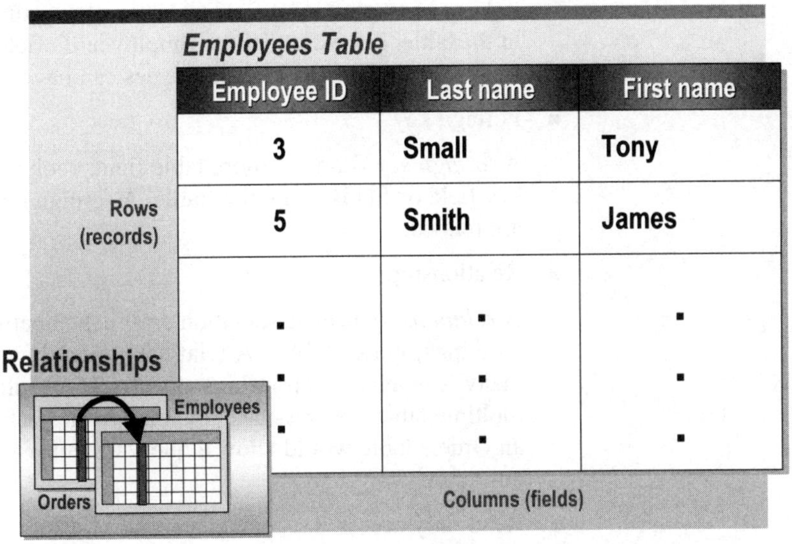

Introduction

When working with databases, it is important to understand some basic terminology.

Definitions

The following terms are defined in the context of relational databases.

- Relational database

  A *relational database* is a type of database that stores information in tables. Relational databases use matching values from two tables to relate data in one table to data in the other table. In a relational database, you typically store a specific type of data just once.

- Table

  A *table* is a database object that stores data in records (rows) and fields (columns). The data is usually about a particular category of things, such as employees or orders.

- Record

  A *record* is a collection of data about a person, a place, an event, or some other item. Records are the logical equivalents of rows in a table. For example, a record in the Employees table would have information about a particular employee.

- Field

  A record is composed of multiple fields. Each *field* in a record contains a single piece of information about the record. For example, an Employee record has fields for Employee ID, Last Name, First Name, and so forth.

- Primary key

  A *primary* key uniquely identifies each row in a table. The primary key is a field or combination of fields whose value is unique for each row (or record) in the table. For example, the Employee ID field is the primary key for the Employees table. No two employees can have the same ID.

- Foreign key

  A *foreign key* is one or more table fields (columns) that refer to the primary key field or fields in another table. A foreign key indicates how the tables are related.

- Relationship

  A *relationship* is an association established between common fields (columns) in two tables. A relationship can be one-to-one, one-to-many, or many-to-many. Relationships allow query results to include data from multiple tables. A one-to-many relationship between a Customers table and an Orders table would allow a query to return all orders for a specific customer.

- Read-only access

  Read-only access to a database means that you can retrieve (read) the data but you cannot modify (write to) the data. A read-only file or document can be displayed or printed but not altered in any way.

- Read/write access

  Read/write access to a database means that you can retrieve (read) the data and modify (write to) the data.

How Database Programming Works

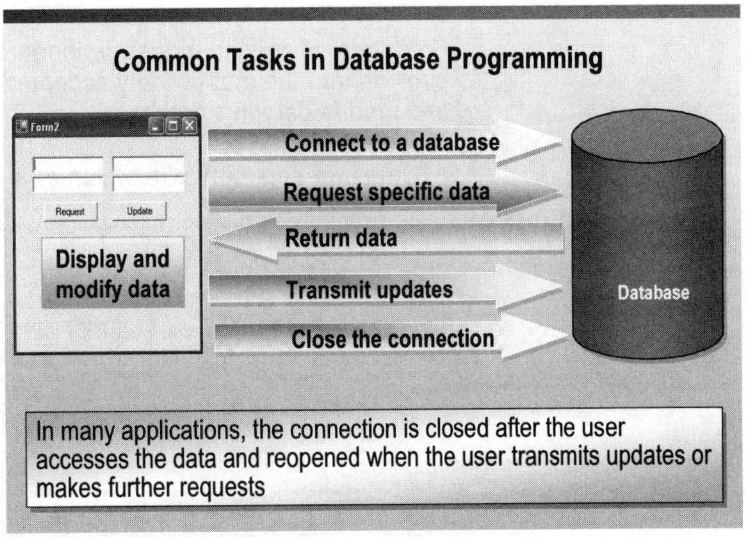

Introduction

When you develop applications, you will have different requirements for working with data. In some cases, you might simply want to display data on a form. In other cases, you might need to devise a way to share information with another organization.

Key tasks in database programming

When you work with data, you use various objects to retrieve and modify information in a database. In general, you will perform the following tasks when working with databases in ADO.NET:

1. Connect to a database.
2. Request specific data.

   Specify the data that you want to retrieve and whether you need read-only or read/write access to the data.
3. Retrieve and display the data.
4. Close the connection (in some applications).
5. Modify the retrieved data (if you have read/write access).
6. Reopen the connection (in some applications).
7. Transmit any changes made to the data back to the database.
8. Close the connection.

In later lessons in this module, you will learn more about the specific objects and tools that you can use in ADO.NET to work with data.

What Is SQL?

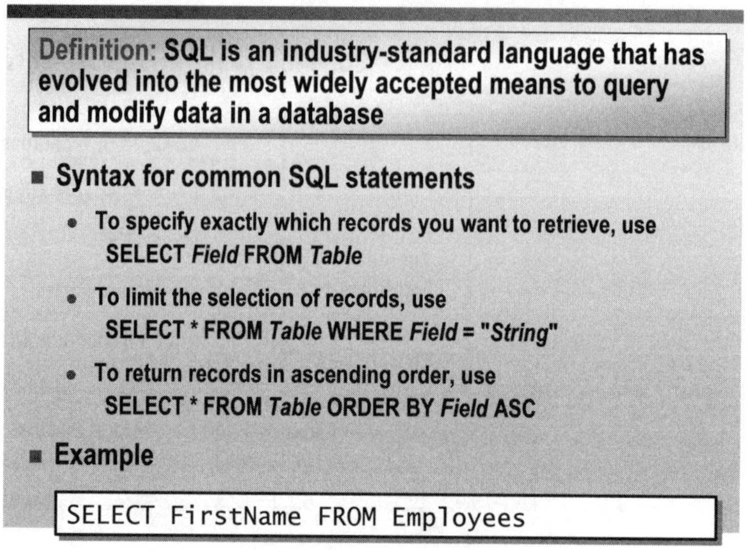

Introduction

Before you can write an application that uses data, you need to know a little bit about Structured Query Language (SQL). You use SQL to specify exactly which records to retrieve from a database.

Definition

SQL is an industry-standard language that has evolved into the most widely accepted means to query and modify data in a database.

Note SQL is defined by the American National Standards Institute (ANSI) standard. Different implementations of SQL exist for different database engines. For instance, there is one version of SQL for Microsoft Access (Jet 4.0) databases and one for SQL Server.

SELECT statement

By using SQL, you can specify exactly which records you want to retrieve and the order in which you want to retrieve them. You can create an SQL statement that retrieves information from multiple tables at once, or you can create a statement that retrieves only one specific record.

The SELECT statement returns specific fields from one or more tables in a database. The following statement retrieves the first name field for all records in the Employees table:

```
SELECT FirstName FROM Employees
```

To select all fields in the table, use an asterisk (*), as follows:

```
SELECT * FROM Employees
```

Visual Basic .NET example

When using SQL statements in Microsoft Visual Basic® .NET, you need to place quotes around the statements, as shown in the following code:

```
Dim sqlString As String
sqlString = "SELECT * FROM Employees"
```

WHERE clause

You can use the WHERE clause to limit the selection of records by using multiple fields to filter queries. The following code shows how to use the basic WHERE clause to retrieve all fields from all records in the Employees table for which the last name is equal to "Danseglio":

```
SELECT * FROM Employees WHERE LastName = 'Danseglio'
```

There are several other forms of the WHERE clause that you can use to further refine your queries, as follows:

- WHERE IN clause

  You can use the WHERE IN clause to return all records that meet specific criteria. For example, you can return employee last names from selected states, as shown in the following code:

  ```
  SELECT LastName
  FROM Employees
  WHERE Employees.State    IN ('NY','WA')
  ```

- WHERE BETWEEN clause

  You can also return a selection of records that falls between two specified criteria. Note the use of the number signs (#) surrounding the dates in the following code:

  ```
  SELECT OrderID
  FROM Orders
  WHERE OrderDate BETWEEN #01/01/93# AND #01/31/93#
  ```

- WHERE LIKE clause

  You can use the WHERE LIKE clause to return all records where a particular condition exists in a specific field. For example, the following code shows how to return all records in which the last name starts with the letter "D."

  ```
  SELECT LastName FROM Employees WHERE LastName LIKE 'D%'
  ```

ORDER BY clause

You can use the ORDER BY clause to return records in a particular order. The ASC option indicates ascending order. The DESC option indicates descending order. The following code returns all fields from the Employees table and sorts them by last name:

```
SELECT * FROM Employees ORDER BY LastName ASC
```

What Is a Connected Environment?

- **A connected environment is one in which users are continuously connected to a data source**
- **Advantages:**
  - Environment is easier to maintain
  - Concurrency is more easily controlled
  - Data is more likely to be current than in other scenarios
- **Disadvantages:**
  - Must have a constant network connection
  - Limited scalability

→ System (Server structure)
Scale out – more machines
Scale up – Larger machine

Introduction

A connected environment is one in which a user or an application is continuously connected to a data source. For much of the history of computers, the only environment available was the connected environment.

Advantages

A connected scenario provides the following advantages:

- A connected environment is easier to maintain.
- Concurrency is easier to control.
- Data is more likely to be current than in disconnected scenarios.

Disadvantages

A connected scenario has the following disadvantages:

- A constant network connection must be maintained.
- A connected scenario provides limited scalability.

Examples

The following are examples in which a continuous connection might be used:

- A factory that requires a real-time connection to monitor production output and storage.
- A brokerage house that requires a constant connection to stock quotes.

What Is a Disconnected Environment?

- **A disconnected environment is one in which data can be modified independently and changes are written to the database later**
- **Advantages:**
  - Connections are used for the shortest possible time, allowing fewer connections to serve more users
  - A disconnected environment improves the scalability and performance of applications
- **Disadvantages:**
  - Data is not always up-to-date
  - Change conflicts can occur and must be resolved

Introduction

With the advent of the Internet, disconnected environments have become commonplace, and with the increasing use of handheld devices, disconnected scenarios are becoming nearly universal. Laptop, notebook, and other portable computers allow you to use applications when you are disconnected from servers or databases.

In many situations, people do not work entirely in a connected or disconnected environment, but rather in an environment that combines the two approaches.

Definition

A *disconnected environment* is one in which a user or an application is not constantly connected to a source of data. Internet applications make frequent use of disconnected architectures. The connection to the data is opened, data is retrieved, and the connection is closed. The user works with the data in the browser and the connection is reopened for updates or further requests.

Mobile users who work with portable computers are also primary users in disconnected environments. Users can take a subset of data with them on a disconnected computer and later merge changes back into the central data store.

Advantages

A disconnected environment provides the following advantages:

- Connections are used for the shortest possible time, allowing fewer connections to serve more users.
- A disconnected environment improves the scalability and performance of applications by maximizing the availability of connections.

Disadvantages

A disconnected environment has the following disadvantages:

- Data is not always up-to-date.
- Change conflicts can occur and must be resolved.
- Transmission of data can be perceived as slower than it would be in connected environments.

Examples

The following are examples in which a disconnected environment might be used:

- An application that maintains customer data on a sales representative's laptop computer.
- An application that tracks rainfall.
- An application that a farmer uses to count livestock. The application is on the farmer's Microsoft Windows CE–based device that is running Microsoft SQL Server 2000 Windows CE Edition.

Handling updates in a disconnected application

Because multiple users can change data in the same records at the same time in a disconnected environment, your application must handle conflicts in data updates. There are several ways you can handle these conflicts:

- Allow the most recent updates to prevail.
- Allow the earliest made updates to prevail.
- Write application code that allows the users to determine which changes should be retained. Specific solutions will vary according to the business requirements for a particular application.

Note For more information about handling conflicts, see "Introduction to Data Concurrency in ADO.NET" in the Microsoft Visual Studio® .NET documentation.

Practice: Identifying Connected or Disconnected Data Scenarios

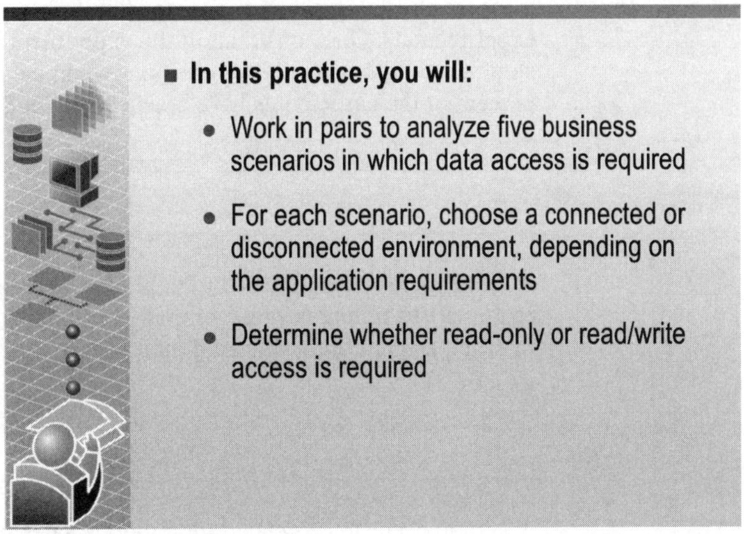

Introduction

In this practice, you will work with a partner to discuss five scenarios and determine whether they would be best implemented in a connected or disconnected scenario. You will also determine whether the scenario requires read-only or read/write access.

Instructions

1. Analyze each scenario.
2. Choose a connected or disconnected environment, depending on the application requirements.
3. Determine whether read-only or read/write data access is required.

Scenario 1

An investment-banking firm needs a system that will allow customers to use the Internet to track their own portfolios. The firm needs to provide services such as historical charts, account history, individual transaction details, and limited investment analysis.

____

____

Scenario 2

A group of scientists is conducting an experiment that requires a system that will store and display data for 50 participants. The application must continually measure physiological responses to stimuli that are coordinated by the experimenters. One constraint of the experiment is that the experimenters must stop the stimuli manually for one hour when the system alerts them that 60 percent of the participants have reached a level 8 in four of 10 measurements.

____

____

Scenario 3

A system needs to be created for a photo finishing service that allows its customers to submit scanned or mailed-in photos, pay for services over the Internet, and check the status of their orders.

____

____

Scenario 4

A system needs to be created for a mobile sales team. Each salesperson must be able to connect to the office wide area network, the company intranet, and the Internet by using mobile communication devices. The salespeople are responsible for creating and submitting customer orders in the field, after verifying availability of stock and appropriate credit availability. They will also need to check on customer shipments and order status, and submit daily reports regardless of whether they can establish an Internet connection. The system requirements state that appropriate deductions and credits to inventory and shipping must occur twice each day. The salespeople must be able to verify, but not change, credit account balances for customers.

____

____

Scenario 5

A firm of financial traders needs access to the data of three different stock markets and to a separate internal database that tracks the transactions of the traders for their customers. The internal database receives continuous downloads from the stock market data flow. Data for each trader's customers is replicated locally on the hard disk of the trader's personal computer. The trader uses this data to maintain accounts for two or three customers, plan projected trades, and complete these trades each day. What data environment and access permissions are required between the individual traders' personal computers and the internal database?

____

____

Lesson: Overview of ADO.NET

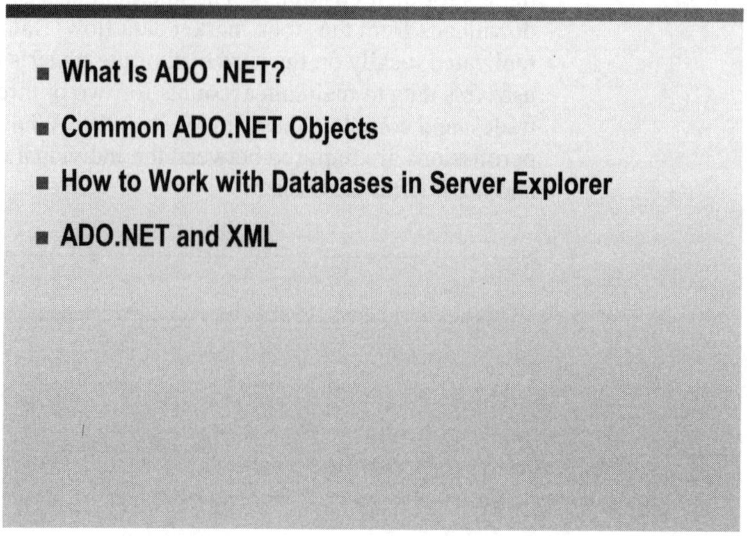

Introduction

This lesson provides an overview of ADO.NET and describes its primary role in applications that work with databases.

Lesson objectives

After completing this lesson, you will be able to:

- Describe the key components in the ADO.NET architecture.
- Explain how to work with data by using objects in the ADO.NET object model.
- Describe XML support in ADO.NET.

Lesson agenda

This lesson includes the following topics and activities:

- What Is ADO.NET?
- Common ADO.NET Objects
- Instructor-Led Demonstration: Using Server Explorer
- How to Work with Databases in Server Explorer
- ADO.NET and XML
- Practice: Accessing Read-Only Data

What Is ADO.NET?

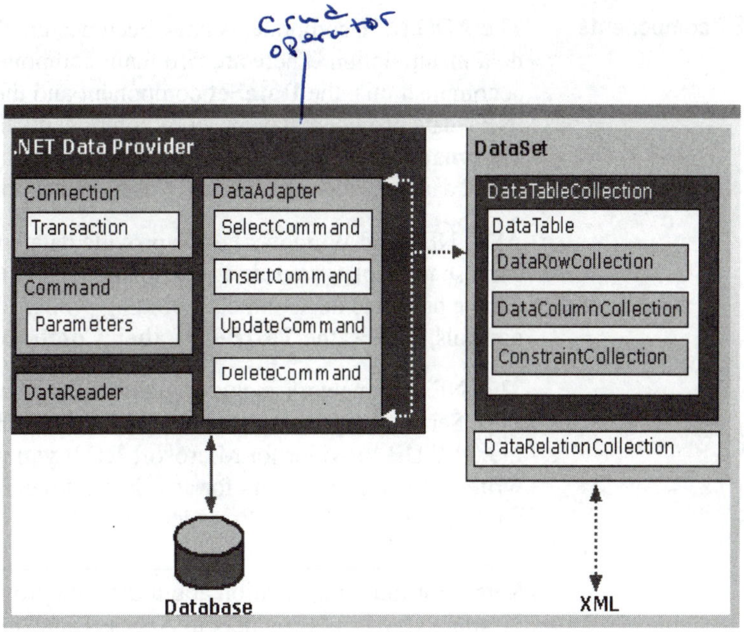

Introduction

No matter what you do with data, there are certain fundamental concepts you should understand about the data approach in ADO.NET. You might never need to know some of the details of data handling, but it is useful to understand the data architecture in ADO.NET, what the major data components are, and how the pieces fit together. This topic does not provide elaborate details, but rather introduces you to concepts related to data integration in ADO.NET.

Note For more information about using ADO.NET, see Course 2389, *Programming with ADO.NET*.

Definition

ADO.NET is a set of classes for working with data. It provides:

- A system designed for disconnected environments.
- A programming model with advanced XML support.
- A set of classes, interfaces, structures, and enumerations that manage data access from within the Microsoft .NET Framework.

ADO.NET components

The ADO.NET components have been designed to separate data access from data manipulation. There are two main components of ADO.NET that accomplish this: the **DataSet** component and the .NET data providers. The .NET data providers have a set of components that include the **Connection**, **Command**, **DataReader**, and **DataAdapter** objects. The components of the .NET data provider are explicitly designed for disconnected data manipulation.

ADO.NET and Windows Forms provide data consumer components that you can use to display your data. These include controls like the **DataGrid**, which can be bound to data, and data-binding properties on most standard Windows controls, such as the **TextBox**, **Label**, **ComboBox**, and **ListBox** controls.

The .NET Framework includes many .NET data providers, including the SQL Server .NET Data Provider, OLE DB .NET Data Provider for SQL, and the OLE DB Provider for Microsoft Jet. If you need a custom provider, you can write .NET data providers for any data source. In this module, you will focus on the OLE DB .NET Data Provider for SQL.

Note For more information about the data providers included with .NET, see "Using .NET Data Providers to Access Data" in the Visual Studio .NET documentation.

For more information about creating custom providers, see "Sample .NET Data Provider, Visual Basic Implementation" in the Visual Studio .NET documentation.

Common ADO.NET Objects

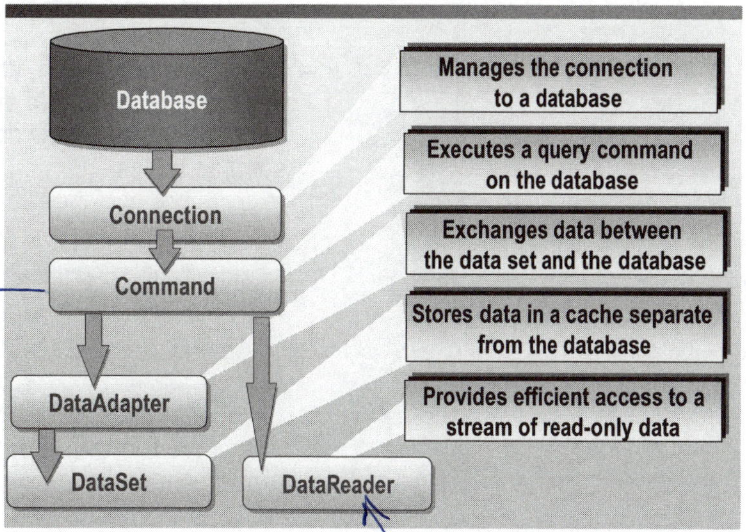

Introduction

The .NET data providers and the **System.Data** namespace provide the ADO.NET objects that you will use in a disconnected scenario.

ADO.NET objects

ADO.NET provides a common object model for .NET data providers. The following table describes the main ADO.NET objects that you will use in a disconnected scenario.

Object	Description
Connection	Establishes and manages a connection to a specific data source. For example, the **OleDbConnection** class connects to OLE DB data sources.
Command	Executes a command from a data source. For example, the **OleDbCommand** class can execute SQL statements in an OLE DB data source.
DataSet	Designed for data access independent of any data source. As a result, you can use it with multiple and differing data sources, with XML data, or to manage data local to the application. The **DataSet** object contains a collection of one or more **DataTable** objects made up of rows and columns of data, in addition to primary key, foreign key, constraint, and relation information about the data in the **DataTable** objects.
DataReader	Provides an efficient, forward-only, read-only stream of data from a data source.
DataAdapter	Uses the **Connection**, **Command**, and **DataReader** objects implicitly to populate a **DataSet** object and to update the central data source with any changes made to the **DataSet**. For example, **OleDbDataAdapter** can manage the interaction between a **DataSet** and an Access database.

Demonstration: Using Server Explorer

In this demonstration, you will learn how to use Server Explorer to add database connections and view database elements such as tables.

How to Work with Databases in Server Explorer

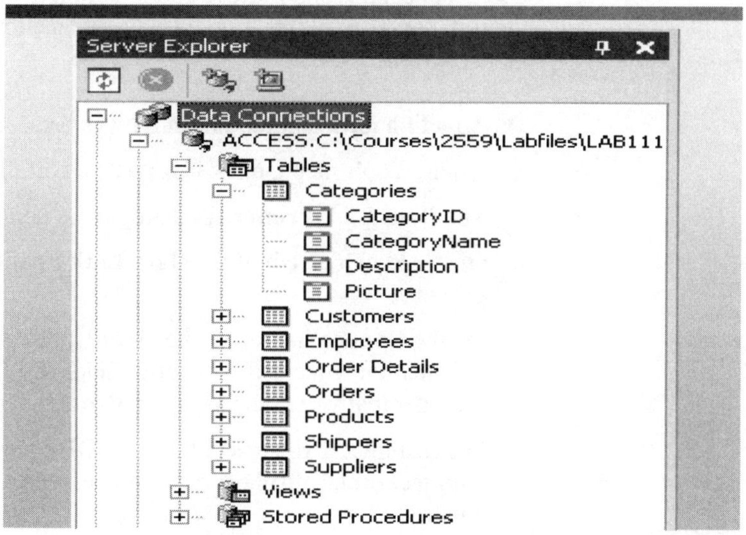

Introduction

You can use Server Explorer to view and manipulate data links, database connections, and system resources on any server to which you have network access. Using Server Explorer, you can:

- Create and open data connections to Access, and servers running SQL Server and other databases.
- Log on to servers and display their databases, tables, fields, and the data in them without exiting the development environment or using the database software.
- View system services, including event logs, message queues, performance counters, and system services.
- View information about available XML Web services and the methods and schemas that they provide.
- Store database projects and references.
- Create data components that reference the data resource or monitor its activity by dragging nodes from Server Explorer into your Visual Studio .NET projects.
- Interact with data resources by programming to those data components that are created in your Visual Studio .NET projects.

Opening Server Explorer

You can open Server Explorer at any time during the development process, while working with any type of project or item.

► **To open Server Explorer**

- On the **View** menu, click **Server Explorer**.

  – Or –

- If the **Server Explorer** tab is displayed on the left edge of the screen, click that tab.

Adding and removing data connections

Server Explorer displays database connections beneath the Data Connections node. After you have established a connection, you can design programs to open connections and retrieve and manipulate the data that is provided. By default, Server Explorer displays data connections and links to servers that you have previously used.

► **To add a data connection in Server Explorer**

1. On the **Tools** menu, click **Connect to Database**.

   The **Data Link Properties** dialog box opens.

2. On the **Provider** tab of the **Data Link Properties** dialog box, select a provider.

3. On the **Connection** tab of the **Data Link Properties** dialog box, provide the information requested. The input fields displayed vary, depending upon the provider that you selected on the **Provider** tab.

   For example, if you select the OLE DB Provider for SQL Server, the **Connection** tab displays fields for server name, type of authentication, and database.

4. Click **OK** to establish the data connection.

   The **Data Link Properties** dialog box closes, and the new data connection appears beneath the Data Connections node, named for the server and database accessed. For example, if you create a data connection to a database called NWind on a server named Server1, a new connection named Server1.NWind.dbo appears beneath the Data Connections node.

► **To remove a data connection from Server Explorer**

1. In Server Explorer, expand the **Data Connections** node.

2. Select the desired database connection.

3. Press DELETE.

   There is no effect on the database. You are removing the reference from your view.

Dragging and dropping data resources

You can drag items from Server Explorer and drop them into the Windows Forms Designer. Putting items into the Windows Forms Designer creates new data resources that are preconfigured to retrieve information from the selected data source.

► To create a new data component by using Server Explorer

You can create a data component preconfigured to reference a particular resource.

1. In Design view, open the form to which you want to add a data component.
2. In **Server Explorer**, select the data item that you want to use. An example of a data item is a field or table.
3. Drag the item from **Server Explorer** to the designer surface.

Viewing database elements

You can use Server Explorer to view and retrieve information from all of the databases installed on a server. You can list database tables, views, stored procedures, and functions in Server Explorer, expand individual tables to list their columns and triggers, and right-click a table to select the Table Designer from its shortcut menu.

ADO.NET and XML

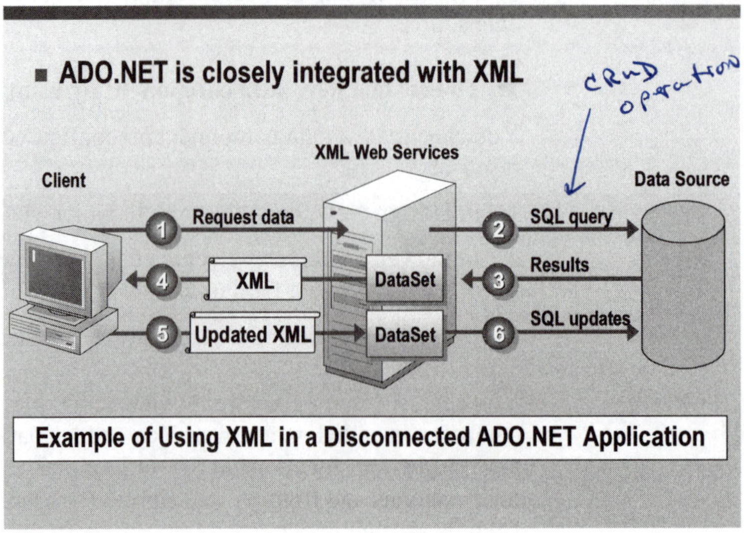

Introduction

ADO.NET is closely integrated with XML. As a result, ADO.NET makes it easy for you to convert relational data into XML format. You can also convert data from XML into tables and relations.

Importance of using XML

XML is a useful, portable way of representing data in an open and platform-independent way. An important characteristic of XML data is that it is text-based. Using text-based data, as opposed to passing binary data such as ADO Recordsets, makes it easier to pass XML data between applications and services, even if they are running on different platforms. XML also enables organizations to exchange data without further customization of each organization's proprietary software.

XML support

The ADO.NET object model includes extensive support for XML. Consider the following facts and guidelines when using the XML support in ADO.NET:

- You can read data from a **DataSet** in XML format. The XML format is useful if you want to pass data between applications or services in a distributed environment.
- You can fill a **DataSet** with XML data. This is useful if you receive XML data from another application or service and want to update a database by using this data.
- You can create an XML Schema for the XML representation of the data in a **DataSet**. You can use the XML Schema to perform tasks such as serializing the XML data to a stream or file.

- You can load XML data from a stream or file into a Document Object Model (DOM) tree. You can then manipulate the data as XML or as a **DataSet**. To do this, you must have an XML Schema to describe the structure of the data to the **DataSet**.
- You can create typed **DataSets**. A typed **DataSet** is a subclass of **DataSet**, with added properties and methods to make the functionality of the **DataSet** available. To describe the XML representation of the typed **DataSet**, Visual Studio generates an equivalent XML Schema definition for this **DataSet**.

Example of using XML in a disconnected application

This example describes how to use XML in a disconnected ADO.NET application. You can use XML to pass data between the different parts of the system as follows:

1. The client application invokes an XML Web service to request data from a database.
2. The XML Web service queries a data source to obtain the requested data.
3. The XML Web service loads the results into a **DataSet**.
4. The XML Web service translates the data into XML format and returns the XML data to the client application.
5. The client application processes the XML data in some way. For example, the client can load the XML data into a **DataSet** and bind it to a user-interface control such as a **DataGrid**. When the client application is ready, it invokes an XML Web service to update the data source with the data changes.
6. The XML Web service loads the new XML data into a **DataSet** and uses the new data to update the data source.

Note For more information about how to populate a **DataSet** with an XML stream, see "**DataSet** Class, XML" in the Visual Studio .NET documentation.

For more information about obtaining data as XML from SQL Server, see "SQL Server .NET Data Provider, XML" in the Visual Studio .NET documentation.

Practice: Accessing Read-Only Data

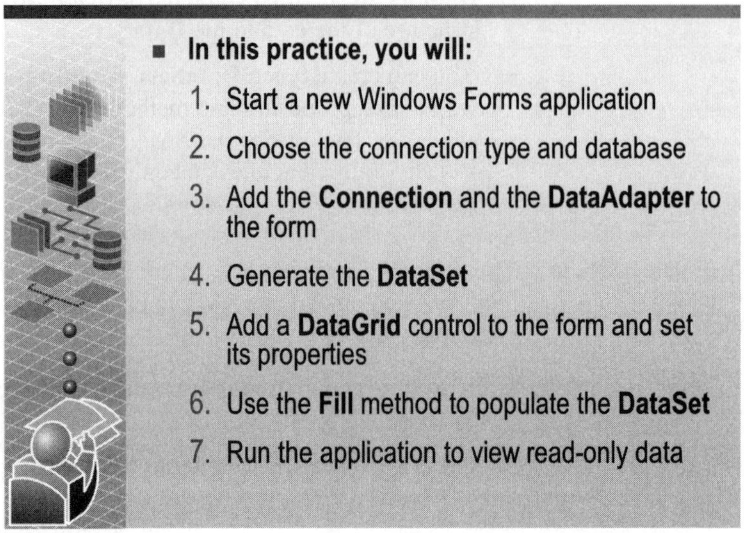

Introduction

In this practice, you will open a new project and use the drag-and-drop functionality provided with Server Explorer to create a dataset and populate a data grid with read-only data.

Note This practice focuses on the concepts in this lesson and as a result may not comply with Microsoft security recommendations. For instance, this practice does not comply with the recommendation that individual user accounts be used rather than administrator accounts, or the recommendation that all accounts use strong passwords.

Instructions

► **Create a new project**

1. Start a new Visual Basic .NET project based on the Windows Application template.
2. Name the project **PubsDataGrid**, set the folder location to *install_folder*\Practices\Mod11, and then click **OK**.

► **Add the Connection and the DataAdapter to the form**

1. In Server Explorer, under Servers, expand the ***your_pc_name*** node (**London** for the instructor), expand the **SQL Servers** node, and then expand the ***your_pc_name*/NetSDK** node so that all SQL databases available on your computer are displayed.
2. Expand the **Pubs** database node, and then expand the **Tables** node under Pubs.
3. Drag the **Authors** table to **Form1**.

   When you drag the table to the form, **SqlConnection1** and **SqlDataAdapter1** will be created and added to the component tray.
4. In the Properties window, change the **Name** property of **SqlConnection1** to **PubsConn** and change the **Name** property of **SqlDataAdapter1** to **PubsSqlDataAdapter**.
5. Expand the **InsertCommand** property of the **PubsSqlDataAdapter**. Verify that the **Connection** property is set to **PubsConn**. Notice that the **DataAdapter** and **Connection** you added are already connected to each other.

► **Generate the DataSet for the Products table**

1. In the Properties window, in the description area at the bottom of the properties list, click **Generate Dataset**.
2. In the **Generate Dataset** dialog box, type **PubsDataSet** in the **New** text box.
3. In all other text boxes, leave the default values. Click **OK**.

   PubsDataSet1 should appear in the component tray.

► **Add a DataGrid to the form and set its properties**

1. From the **Windows Forms** tab of the Toolbox, add a **DataGrid** control to the form.
2. In the Properties window, name the **DataGrid** control **PubsDataGrid**.
3. In the Properties window, set the **DataSource** property of the **DataGrid** control to **PubsDataSet1**, and set the **DataMember** property to **Authors**.
4. Size the form and the **DataGrid** control so that all of the rows and columns are visible.

   The data grid should display the field names for the Authors table.

▶ Populate the DataSet with the Authors table data

- Open an event handler for the **Form1_Load** event. In the **Form1_Load** event handler, call the data adapter's **Fill** method to populate the Authors table with data. Your code should look as follows:

```
PubsSqlDataAdapter.Fill(PubsDataSet1)
```

▶ Test the application

1. Run the application.

   The Authors data should populate the data grid.
2. Navigate through the data by using the scroll bars in the data grid.

Note Although you have created a working application that displays read-only data from a data source, it has limited functionality. For example, navigation can only be accomplished by means of the scroll bars in the data grid. In a real application, you would probably want to further modify the selection of fields to be displayed. To add more functionality to your form, you might allow users to view product details. You might also allow users to select an item, go to another form that inherits data from this one, and then create an order or view existing orders.

Solution files

The solution files for this practice are located in the *install_folder*\Practices\Mod11\Solution folder.

Lesson: Working with Data

- How to Use a Connection Object
- How to Use a DataAdapter Object
- How to Use a DataSet Object
- How to Use a DataGrid Control
- How to Use the Data Form Wizard

Introduction

ADO.NET provides all of the necessary components to connect to data sources and work with data in your applications. In this lesson, you will learn how to use ADO.NET objects to connect to a database, retrieve data, modify data, and transmit updated data back to the database. You will also learn how to display data on a Windows Form by using the **DataGrid** control. Finally, you will learn how to use the Data Form Wizard to automate the process of working with data. The wizard reduces the task of adding controls and setting properties to a few easy steps.

Lesson objectives

After completing this lesson, you will be able to:

- Establish a connection to a data source by using the **Connection** object.
- Retrieve data from a data source by using the **DataAdapter** and **DataSet** objects.
- Transmit updates to a data source by using the **DataAdapter** and **DataSet** objects.
- Use a **DataGrid** control to display data.
- Use the Data Form Wizard to add a new data-bound form to a project.

Lesson agenda

This lesson includes the following topics and activities:

- How to Use a **Connection** Object
- How to Use a **DataAdapter** Object
- How to Use a **DataSet** Object
- How to Use a **DataGrid** Control
- How to Use the Data Form Wizard

How to Use a Connection Object

- **You use Connection to:**
  - Choose the connection type
  - Specify the data source
  - Open the connection to the data source
  - Close the connection to the data source
- **Example of connection to a SQL Server database**

```
Dim PubsSQLConn As SqlClient.SqlConnection
PubsSQLConn = New SqlClient.SqlConnection( )
PubsSQLConn.ConnectionString = "Integrated Security=True;" & _
      "Data Source=local;Initial Catalog=Pubs;"
PubsSQLConn.Open( )
```

Introduction

Before you can work with data, you first need to establish a connection with a data source. To connect to a data source, you choose the connection type, specify the data source, and open the connection to the data source. When you are finished working with the data, you will close the connection.

Choosing the connection type

You can use the **Connection** object to connect to a specific data source. You can use either **SqlConnection** to connect to SQL Server databases or **OleDbConnection** to connect to other types of data sources.

Specifying the data source

After you choose the connection type, you use a **ConnectionString** property to specify the data provider, the data source, and other information used to establish the connection. The format of these strings differs slightly between the **SqlClient** namespace and the **OleDb** namespace.

Opening and closing the data connection

The **Connection** object supports an **Open** method that opens the connection after the connection properties have been set, and a **Close** method that closes the connection to the database after all transactions have cleared.

SQL example

The following example shows how to use a **Connection** object, the **ConnectionString** property, and the **Open** method to connect to a SQL Server database by using the SQL Server .NET Data Provider:

```
Dim PubsSQLConn As SqlClient.SqlConnection
PubsSQLConn = New SqlClient.SqlConnection( )
PubsSQLConn.ConnectionString = "Integrated Security=True;" & _
  "Data Source=local;Initial Catalog=Pubs;"
PubsSQLConn.Open( )
```

Jet 4.0 example

The following example shows how to connect to an Access database by using the Jet 4.0 OLE DB .Data Provider:

```
Dim NWindOleDbConn As OleDb.OleDbConnection
NWindOleDbConn = New OleDb.OleDbConnection( )
NWindOleDbConn.ConnectionString = _
  "Provider=Microsoft.Jet.OLEDB.4.0;Data Source=c:\NWind.MDB"
NWindOleDbConn.Open( )
```

How to Use a DataAdapter Object

- **To create a DataAdapter**
  - Declare with the **Dim** keyword
  - Pass a query string and a **Connection** object as parameters

```
Dim PubsAdapter As SQLDataAdapter = New SQLDataAdapter _
       ("Select * from Titles", PubsSQLConn)
```

- **Key methods of DataAdapter:**
  - **Fill** method populates a data set
  - **Update** method transmits changes to the data store

Introduction

After you establish a connection with a data source, you can use a data adapter to exchange data between the data source and a dataset. In many applications, this means reading data from a database into a dataset by means of the data adapter, and then writing changed data from the dataset to the data adapter and back to the database. However, a data adapter can move data between any source and a dataset. For example, there could be an adapter that moves data between a server running Microsoft Exchange and a dataset.

Types of data adapters

Visual Studio makes available two primary data adapters for use with databases:

- **OleDbDataAdapter** is suitable for use with any data source that an OLE DB provider provides.
- **SqlDataAdapter** is specific to SQL Server. Because it does not have to go through an OLE DB layer, it is faster than the **OleDbDataAdapter**. However, it can only be used with SQL Server version 7.0 or later.

Creating the DataAdapter

You can instantiate the **DataAdapter** by using the **Dim** keyword and passing a query string and a **Connection** object as parameters. The **DataAdapter** will check whether the **Connection** is open, and, if it is not open, it will open it for you and close it when your method call is complete. This approach is useful if you have already set the properties of a **Connection** object in your application and only need the connection to be opened to populate the data tables.

Examples

The following examples show how to create an instance of an **Sql Client DataAdapter** class. The code for creating an instance of the **DataAdapter** class is shown in bold.

SQL example

The following example shows how to access the Titles table in the Pubs database:

```
Dim PubsSQLConn As SqlClient.SqlConnection
PubsSQLConn = New SqlClient.SqlConnection( )
PubsSQLConn.ConnectionString = "Integrated Security=True;" & _
  "Data Source=local;Initial Catalog=Pubs;"

Dim PubsAdapter As SQLDataAdapter = New SQLDataAdapter _
  ("Select * from Titles", PubsSQLConn)

  ' Code to populate the dataset
Dim titlesDataset As DataSet = New DataSet
PubsAdapter.Fill(titlesDataset)

  ' Code to bind the dataset to form controls might go here
```

Jet 4.0 example

The following example shows how to access the Customers table in the Northwind database by using the OLE DB Provider for Microsoft Jet:

```
Private NWindOleDbConn as OleDb.OleDbConnection

Private Sub Form1_Load(...) Handles MyBase.Load
  NWindOleDbConn = New OleDb.OleDbConnection( )
  NWindOleDbConn.ConnectionString = "Provider= " & _
      "Microsoft.Jet.OLEDB.4.0;Data Source=c:\NWind.mdb"

  Dim NWindAdapter As New OleDb.OleDbDataAdapter _
  ("Select * from Customers", NWindOleDbConn)

  ' Code to populate the DataSet might go here
  ' Code to bind the DataSet to form controls might go here
```

Key methods

DataAdapter supports specific methods to move the data back and forth between the dataset and the data source. You can use a data adapter to perform the following operations:

- Retrieve rows from a data store and populate them into corresponding data tables in a dataset.

  To retrieve rows from a data store and populate a dataset, use the **Fill** method of **SqlDataAdapter** or **OleDbDataAdapter**. When you invoke the method, it invokes a SQL SELECT statement on the data store. Executing this method will open and close the connection object.

- Transmit changes made to a dataset table to the corresponding data store.

  To transmit the changes in a dataset table to the data store, use the adapter's **Update** method. When you invoke the method, it executes whatever SQL INSERT, UPDATE, or DELETE statements are needed, depending on whether the affected record is new, changed, or deleted. Executing this method will open and close the connection object.

Example

```
' Code to manipulate the data locally by using the DataSet
  ' goes here

' Update the database by means of the data adapter

PubsAdapter.Update (PubsDataSet)
```

Jet 4.0 example

```
' Create the Connection, the DataAdapter, and the DataSet,
  ' and populate the dataset

Dim NWindConn As OleDb.OleDbConnection
NWindConn = New OleDb.OleDbConnection( )
NWindConn.ConnectionString = "Provider= " & _
  "Microsoft.Jet.OLEDB.4.0;Data Source=c:\NWind.mdb"

Dim NWindAdapt As New OleDb.OleDbDataAdapter("SELECT * " & _
  "from Customers", NWindConn)

Dim NWindDataSet As DataSet = New DataSet( )
NWindAdapt.Fill(NWindDataSet, "customersTable")

' Code to manipulate the data locally by using the DataSet
  ' goes here

' Update the database by means of the data adapter

NWindAdapt.Update (NWindDataSet.Tables("customersTable"))
```

How to Use a DataSet Object

- **How DataSets work**
  - Store data in a disconnected cache
  - Use a hierarchical object model of tables, rows, and columns
- **You can populate a DataSet by:**
  - Using the **Fill** method
  - Manually populating the tables
  - Reading an XML document or stream
  - Merging or copying the contents of another **DataSet**

Introduction

After you specify the data that you want to retrieve, the next step is to populate a dataset with data from the database. Datasets store data in a disconnected cache. The structure of a dataset is similar to that of a relational database. A dataset makes available a hierarchical object model of tables, rows, and columns. In addition, it contains constraints and relationships that are defined for the dataset.

Populating datasets

A dataset is a container, so you need to populate it with data. You can populate a dataset in a variety of ways:

- Call the **Fill** method of a data adapter. Calling this method causes the adapter to run an SQL statement or a stored procedure and populate a table in the dataset with the results. If the dataset contains multiple tables, you probably have separate data adapters for each table, and must therefore call each adapter's **Fill** method separately.
- Manually populate tables in the dataset by creating **DataRow**s and adding them to the table's **Rows** collection. You can do this only at run time. You cannot set the **Rows** collection at design time.
- Read an XML document or stream into the dataset.
- Copy the contents of another dataset. This technique can be useful if your application obtains datasets from different sources (different XML Web services, for example), but needs to consolidate them into a single dataset.

Example

You use a **DataAdapter** to access data stored in a database and to store the data in **DataTable**s within a **DataSet** in your application.

SQL example

The bold statements in the following example show how to populate a **Dataset** called PubsDataset with data from a SQL database by using a **DataAdapter**. There is only one table, and the dataset will refer to it by using an index number. The **Update** command uses the same table to update changes to the database.

```
' Create the Connection, the DataAdapter, and the DataSet,
  ' and populate the dataset

Dim PubsSQLConn As SqlClient.SqlConnection
PubsSQLConn = New SqlClient.SqlConnection( )
PubsSQLConn.ConnectionString = "Integrated Security=True;" & _
  "Data Source=local;Initial Catalog=Pubs;"

Dim PubsAdapter As SQLDataAdapter = New SQLDataAdapter _
  ("Select * from Authors", PubsSQLConn)
Dim PubsDataSet As DataSet = New DataSet( )
PubsAdapter.Fill(PubsDataSet)

' Code to manipulate the data locally by using the DataSet
  ' goes here

' Update the database by means of the data adapter

PubsAdapter.Update (PubsDataSet.Tables("authorsTable"))
```

Jet 4.0 example

The bold statements in the following example show how to populate a **DataSet** called NWindDataSet with data from an OLE DB database by using a **DataAdapter**.

```
' Create the Connection, the DataAdapter, and the DataSet,
  ' and populate the dataset:

Dim NWindConn As OleDb.OleDbConnection
NWindConn = New OleDb.OleDbConnection( )
NWindConn.ConnectionString = "Provider= " & _
  "Microsoft.Jet.OLEDB.4.0;Data Source=c:\NWind.mdb"

Dim NWindAdapt As New OleDb.OleDbDataAdapter("SELECT * " & _
  "from Customers", NWindConn)
Dim NWindDataSet As DataSet = New DataSet( )
NWindAdapt.Fill(NWindDataSet)

' Code to manipulate the data locally by using the DataSet
  ' goes here

' Update the database by means of the data adapter

NWindConn.Open( )
NWindAdapt.Update (NWindDataSet)
NWindConn.Close( )
```

How to Use a DataGrid Control

- **Use a DataGrid control to display data from a single data source or multiple data sources**
  - From the Toolbox, add a **DataGrid** control to a form
  - Set the properties of the **DataGrid** control

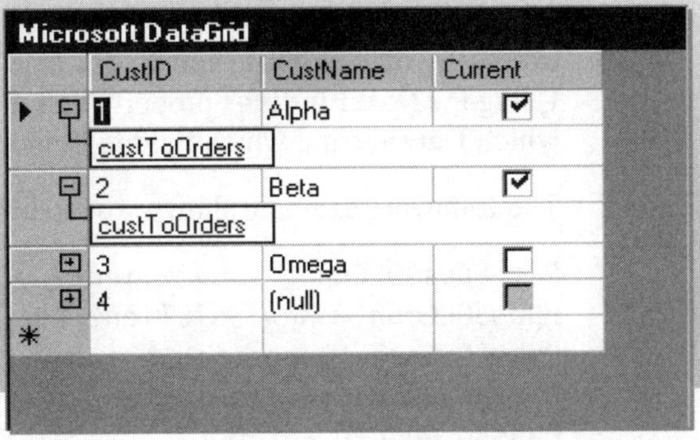

Introduction

After you populate a dataset, you can view and modify data by using the Windows Forms **DataGrid** control. The **DataGrid** displays data in a series of rows and columns. The simplest case is when the grid is bound to a data source with a single table containing no relationships. In that case, the data appears in simple rows and columns, as in a spreadsheet.

How the DataGrid control works

If the **DataGrid** is bound to data with multiple related tables, and if navigation is enabled on the grid, the grid will display expanders in each row. An expander allows navigation from a parent table to a child table. Clicking a node displays the child table, and clicking the **Back** button displays the original parent table. In this fashion, the grid displays the hierarchical relationships between tables.

The **DataGrid** can provide a user interface for a dataset, navigation between related tables, and rich formatting and editing capabilities.

The display and manipulation of data are separate functions: The control handles the user interface, while data updates are handled by the Windows Forms data-binding architecture and by ADO.NET data providers. Therefore, multiple controls bound to the same data source will stay synchronized.

Binding data to the control

For the **DataGrid** control to work, you must bind it to a data source by using the **DataSource** and **DataMember** properties at design time or the **SetDataBinding** method at run time. This binding links the **DataGrid** to an instantiated data-source object (such as a **DataSet** or **DataTable**), and the **DataGrid** control is updated with the results of actions that are performed on the data.

Most data-specific actions are not performed by means of the **DataGrid**. They are performed by means of the data source.

▶ To bind the DataGrid control to a single table in the designer

1. Set the control's **DataSource** property to the object containing the data items to which you want to bind.
2. If the data source is a dataset, set the **DataMember** property to the name of the table to which you want to bind.
3. If the data source is a dataset or a data view based on a dataset table, add code to the form to populate the dataset.

Simple binding

You use simple binding to link a control to a single field in a **DataSet**. For example, you would use simple binding for a **TextBox** or a **Label** control. Using the **DataBindings** property of a data-aware control, you can specify which **DataSet** and which field to bind to which property.

SQL example

The following example shows how to bind data to a **TextBox** control:

```
Dim PubsSQLConn As SqlClient.SqlConnection
PubsSQLConn = New SqlClient.SqlConnection( )
PubsSQLConn.ConnectionString = "Integrated Security=True;" & _
  "Data Source=local;Initial Catalog=Pubs;"
PubsSQLConn.Open( )

Dim PubsAdapter As SQLDataAdapter = New SQLDataAdapter _
  ("Select * from Titles", PubsSQLConn)

Dim PubsDataSet As DataSet = New DataSet( )
PubsAdapter.Fill(PubsDataSet)

TextBox1.DataBindings.Add(New Binding("Text", _
  PubsDataSet, "Authors.FirstName"))
```

Jet 4.0 example

The **TextBox** code does not differ when you use a Jet 4.0 provider. Only the **Connection** and **DataAdapter** code differs, as shown in previous examples.

Complex binding

You use complex binding to link a control to multiple fields in a **DataSet**. For example, you use complex binding for a **DataGrid** control. Using the **DataSource** property of these controls, you can specify the table to be used.

Jet 4.0 example

The following example shows how to use the **DataSource** property of a **DataGrid** control for a Jet 4.0 database. The code that sets the property is formatted in bold.

```
Dim NWindOleDbConn As OleDb.OleDbConnection = _
  New OleDb.OleDbConnection( )
Dim NWindAdapter As New OleDb.OleDbDataAdapter _
  ("Select * from Customers", NWindOleDbConn)
Dim NWindDataSet As DataSet = New DataSet( )

NWindOleDbConn.ConnectionString = "Provider= " & _
  "Microsoft.Jet.OLEDB.4.0;Data Source=c:\NWind.mdb"
NWindOleDbConn.Open( )
NWindAdapter.Fill(NWindDataSet)

DataGrid1.DataSource = NWindDataSet
DataGrid1.DataMember = "Customers"
```

SQL example

The **TextBox** code does not differ when you use a SQL provider. Only the **Connection** and **DataAdapter** code differs, as shown in previous examples.

How to Use the Data Form Wizard

Introduction

The Data Form Wizard helps you create a Windows Forms application with data-bound controls. The controls display data from any data source that you specify.

Running the Data Form Wizard

Running the Data Form Wizard is like adding an item to an existing project.

▶ **To run the Data Form Wizard**

1. Create or open a Windows Forms application.

> **Note** The wizard can create a form only in a project type that supports forms.

2. From the **File** menu, click **Add New Item**.

   The **Add New Item** dialog box appears.
3. In the **Templates** pane, click **Data Form Wizard**.
4. Name the data form and click **Open**.

   The wizard starts.
5. Follow the steps of the wizard.

What the wizard does

The Data Form Wizard leads you through the entire process of creating the data-bound form. When you have finished, you will have:

- A Windows Form.
- Data-bound controls on the form.
- All necessary data components for the form.
- Methods that you can call to read and, for Windows Forms, write data.

The form and controls

To display data, the wizard-generated form includes controls that are bound to a data source. For example, the form can contain a grid control.

In a Windows Form, you can choose between a grid or individual controls that show one record at a time. You can also generate buttons that allow users to navigate between records, and include buttons to save changes to records and to add new records.

Data elements

The Data Form Wizard can create new data components or use components that are already available in your project. A data component for the form consists of several discrete elements:

- A connection to a data source, such as a database.
- A data adapter that references an SQL statement or stored procedure to obtain data.
- A typed dataset to hold the records that are retrieved from the database. The dataset includes a schema, a dataset class file, and an instance of the dataset on the form.

If you use the wizard to create a data source, it will automatically connect your application to the specified database. Within the database, the wizard can access tables or views.

The wizard can optionally create and use a reference to an XML Web service as the data source. In that scenario, the XML Web service is assumed to be able to return a dataset.

You can use the wizard to access multiple tables and establish relationships between them. In such a case, the controls on the form allow you to view both parent and child records.

Fill and Update methods

One of the tasks that you need to perform is to fill the dataset with data from the database. By default, to fill the dataset, the wizard generates a **Load** button that calls code to perform the fill operation. If you are creating a new dataset with the wizard, the wizard generates the **Fill** method automatically. If you are working with an existing dataset, the wizard offers you these options for creating a **Fill** method:

- Select an existing method

  If your project provides a method that returns a dataset (either as the return value of a function or as a parameter), you can select that method and the wizard generates code to call that method.

- Skip the method

  Choose this option if you want to fill the dataset yourself rather than having the fill code be called automatically.

If you are generating a Windows Form, the wizard can also generate an **Update** method that you can call to send changes from the dataset back to the data source.

Additional steps

When the wizard is finished and you have a new form, the form is ready to run. There are a few additional steps that you might want to take, and a variety of ways in which you can expand on what the wizard has done.

For example, to work with the form that you just created, you need to set the form as the startup form so that you can test it.

► **To set the startup form in Windows Forms**

1. In **Solution Explorer**, right-click the project, and then click **Properties**.

   The **Project** property page opens with the **General** properties displayed.
2. Select the form that you want as the startup form from the **Startup Object** list.

The wizard creates controls and data elements and all the code required to run the form. You can read and modify this code as necessary. You might want to perform the following tasks to enhance the form that the wizard creates:

- Change the look and arrangement of controls on the form.
- If you do not want to use the **Load** button to fill the dataset, you can move the fill code to another location. A typical example is to move it from the button event handler to the form initialization method so that the dataset is filled automatically when the form runs.
- Refine the queries that the wizard generates for the data adapter to retrieve a subset of the data and to add or modify parameters to the adapter's commands.
- Add validation or business logic to the form.
- Add navigation logic to prevent exceptions from occurring when you move beyond the first and last records.

Review

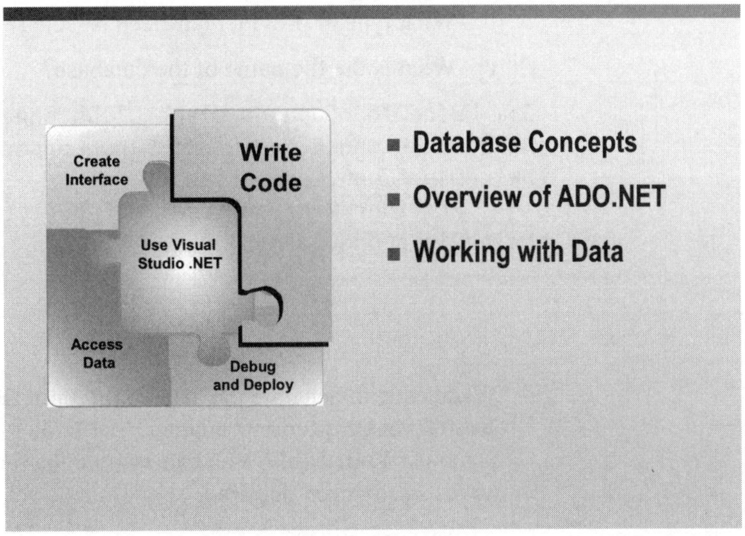

1. What is the primary difference between a connected and disconnected environment?

2. Write an SQL statement that will select all fields from a table named Customers.

3. Identify the ADO.NET object that you use to manage the communication between a connection and a dataset.

4. Examine the following code and answer these questions.
   a. What is the name of the connection object?
   b. What type of provider has been selected?
   c. What is the file name of the database?

```
Dim NWindOleDbConn As OleDb.OleDbConnection
NWindOleDbConn = New OleDb.OleDbConnection( )
NWindOleDbConn.ConnectionString = _
    "Provider=Microsoft.Jet.OLEDB.4.0;DataSource=c:\NWind.MDB"
NWindOleDbConn.Open( )
```

5. Write code to generate the dataset for **YourDataSet** by using the **YourDataAdapter** data adapter. The table from which you extract the data is named **YourTable**. You can assume that both the dataset and adapter have already been declared.

6. What is the name of the Windows Forms control that you can use to display multiple records retrieved from a data source?

7. What properties of the **DataGrid** control can you use at design time to bind it to a data source?

Lab 11.1: Accessing Data with ADO.NET

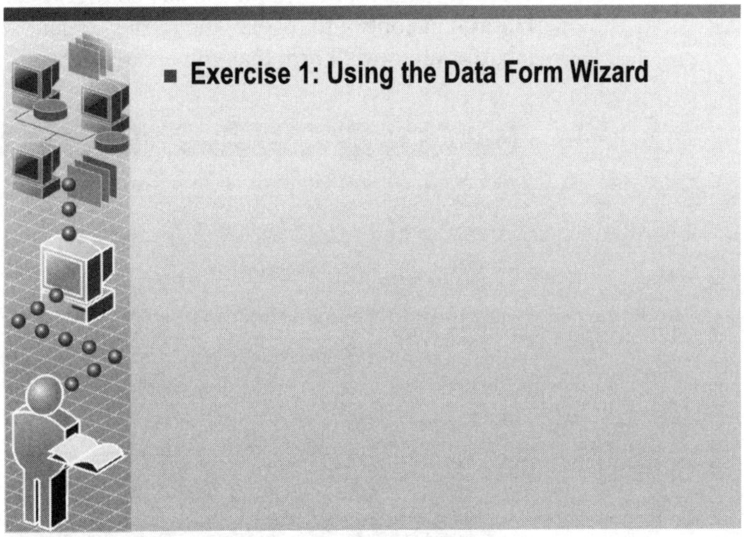

Objectives

After completing this lab, you will be able to use the Data Form Wizard to:

- Establish a connection to a database.
- Configure and create a dataset.
- Load, display, and update the retrieved data by using the buttons provided by the Data Form Wizard.

Note This lab focuses on the concepts in this module and as a result may not comply with Microsoft security recommendations.

Prerequisites

Before working on this lab, you must be familiar with the following:

- Basic database terminology
- Common ADO.NET objects, including **Connection**, **DataAdapter**, and **DataSet**
- The **DataGrid** control

Scenario

In this lab, you will use the Data Form Wizard to create a Windows Form in which you can work with data from a database. By using the wizard, you will connect to the Northwind database, configure and retrieve a dataset, and use a **DataGrid** control to display the retrieved data. When you are finished with the lab, the Windows Form that you create will look similar to the following form:

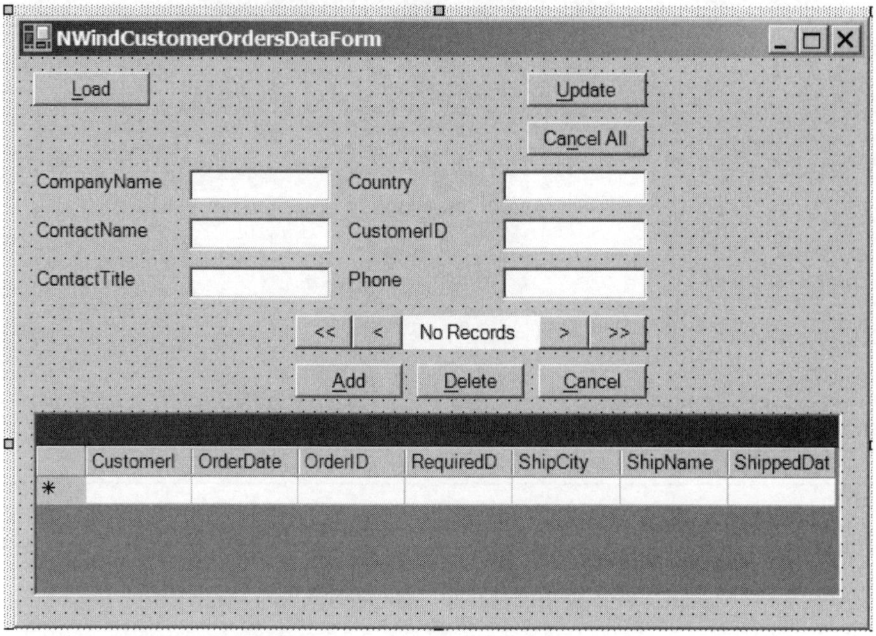

Solution files

The solution files for this lab are in the *install_folder*\Labfiles\Lab111\Ex01\Solution folder.

Estimated time to complete this lab: 30 minutes

Exercise 1
Using the Data Form Wizard

In this exercise, you will:

- Use the Data Form Wizard to create a data form that displays two related tables.
- Test run-time database functionality (add, delete, update, navigate) by using the buttons provided by the wizard.

▶ Create a new project

1. Start Visual Studio .NET and create a new Visual Basic project based on the Windows Application template.
2. Name the project **NorthwindData**, set the folder location to *install_folder*\Labfiles\Lab111\Ex01, and then click **OK**.

▶ Start the Data Form Wizard

1. In Solution Explorer, right-click **NorthwindData**, point to **Add**, and then click **Add New Item**.

   –Or–

   On the **Project** menu, click **Add New Item**.
2. Under **Templates** in the **Add New Item** dialog box, click **Data Form Wizard**.
3. In the **Name** field, type **NWindCustomerOrdersDataForm.vb** and then click **Open**.
4. In the **Welcome to the DataForm Wizard** dialog box, click **Next** to start the wizard.

▶ Choose the dataset you want to use

- In the **Create a new dataset named** box of the **Choose the dataset you want to use** dialog box, type **NorthwindDataSet** and then click **Next**.

▶ Choose a data connection

1. In the **Choose a data connection** dialog box, click **New Connection** to display the **Data Link Properties** dialog box.
2. On the **Connection** tab in Step 1, type the SQL Server name for your computer, in the format *pc_name*\NetSDK. Note that SQL Server names are case-sensitive.

Note When you install the SQL Server Desktop Engine, a SQL Server node named *pc_name*\NetSDK is created. You view this node in Server Explorer. All SQL Server database files are stored under this node, as if the computer were a server running SQL Server.

---

3. On the **Connection** tab in Step 2, click **Use Windows NT Integrated security**.

4. On the **Connection** tab in Step 3, click **Northwind**, and then click **Test Connection**. Click **OK** in the **Test connection succeeded** message box, and then click **OK** in the **Data Link Properties** dialog box.
5. In the **Which connection should the wizard use?** list, click the new connection: ***pc_name*****NetSDK.Northwind.dbo**.
6. Click **Next** in the **Choose a data connection** dialog box.

► **Assign tables to the DataAdapter**

1. In the **Choose tables or views** dialog box, under **Available item(s)**, click **Customers** and then click the  button to add the item to the **Selected item(s)** pane.
2. Add the Orders table to the **Selected item(s)** pane, and then click **Next**.

► **Create a relationship between tables**

1. In the **Create a relationship between tables** dialog box, type **CustomerOrdersRelation** in the **Name** box.
2. In the **Parent table** list, click **Customers**, and in the **Keys** list, under **Customers**, click **CustomerID**.
3. In the **Child table** list, click **Orders**, and in the **Keys** list, under **Orders**, click **CustomerID**.
4. Click the  button to add the **CustomerOrdersRelation** relation to the **Relations** box.
5. Click **Next**.

► **Choose tables and columns to display from the Customers and Orders tables**

1. In the **Choose tables and columns to display on the form** dialog box, in the **Columns** list, under **Customers**, clear **Address**, **City**, **Region**, **PostalCode**, and **Fax**.
2. In the **Columns** list, under **Orders**, clear **EmployeeID**, **ShipVia**, **Freight**, **ShipAddress**, **ShipRegion**, **ShipPostalCode**, and **ShipCountry**,
3. Click **Next**.
4. In the **Choose the display style** dialog box, select **Single record in individual controls**.
5. Under **What additional controls do you want on the form?**, leave all the boxes checked.
6. Click **Finish**.

7. Resize the form and the **DataGrid** control so that all fields in the data grid are displayed. Your data form should look as follows:

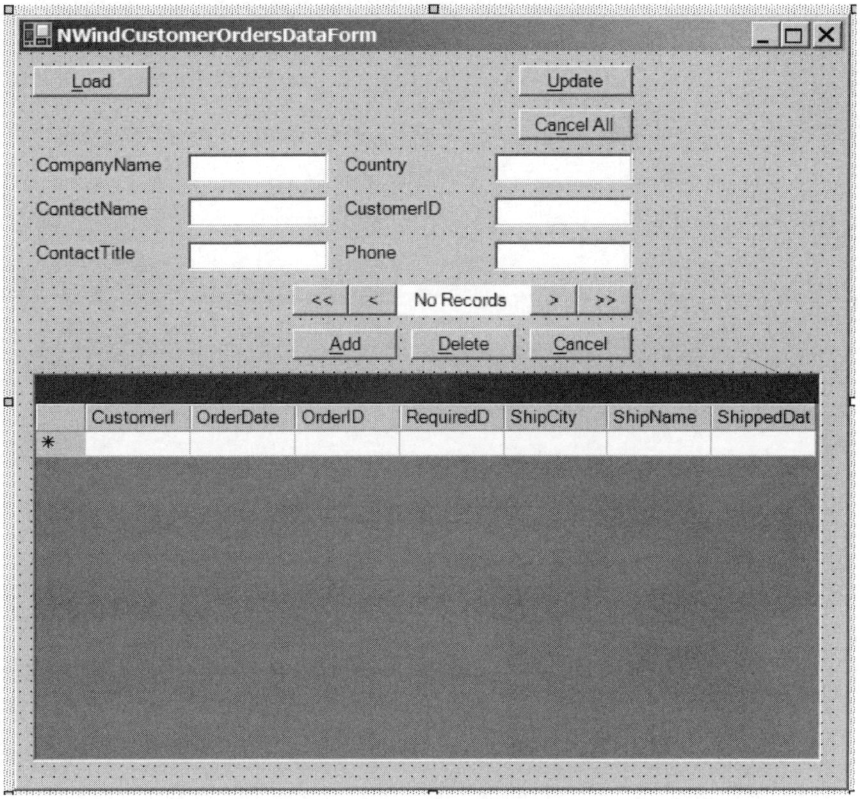

▶ **Test the data editing functionality of the form**

1. In Solution Explorer, right-click **NorthwindData**, and then click **Properties**.
2. In the **Property Pages** dialog box, change the **Startup object** to **NWindCustomerOrdersDataForm** and then click **OK**.
3. Run the application.
4. Click **Load** to load the data into the form.
5. Change the **CompanyName** field to **Microsoft**, and then click **Update**. Note the total number of records here: __________.
6. Click **Add**, and enter some sample data for the **Customer** fields. (Use 1111 or higher for the **CustomerID** field.) Note the new number of records in the form here: ___________. Move to a previous record.
7. Move back to your new record, click **Cancel All**, and then move back to the previous record. Verify that the number of records in the form is the same as you noted in Step 5.

Tip The **Cancel All** button will only cancel changes made since **Update** was clicked.

---

8. Quit the running application.

msdn® training

Module 12: Deploying Applications

Contents

Microsoft®

Overview

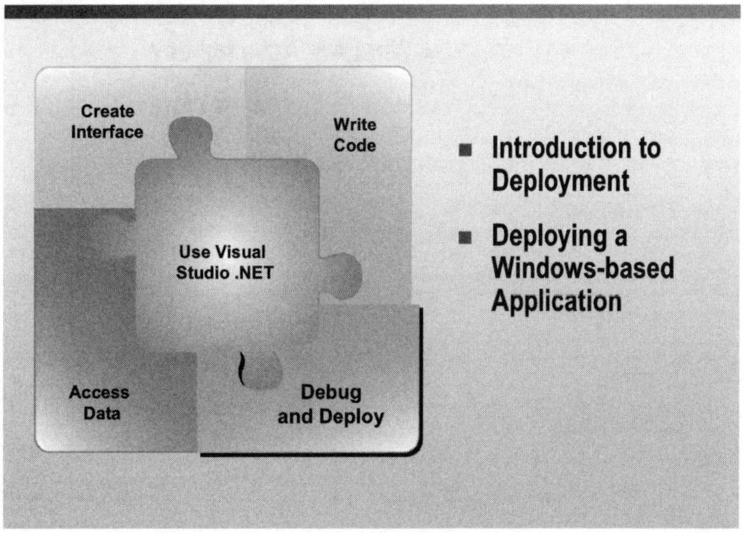

Introduction

After you create and test an application, you will most likely want to distribute it for use on other computers. The users might be end users running a Web application or a Microsoft® Windows®-based application, or they might be other developers using a code library. Deployment is the process by which you distribute a finished application or component to be installed on other computers.

In this module, you will learn about various deployment options available in Microsoft Visual Basic® .NET, and how to use some of these options to deploy Windows-based applications.

Objectives

After completing this module, you will be able to:

- Describe how applications can be deployed using Microsoft Visual Studio® .NET.
- Create and customize a Setup program for a Windows-based application.

Lesson: Introduction to Deployment

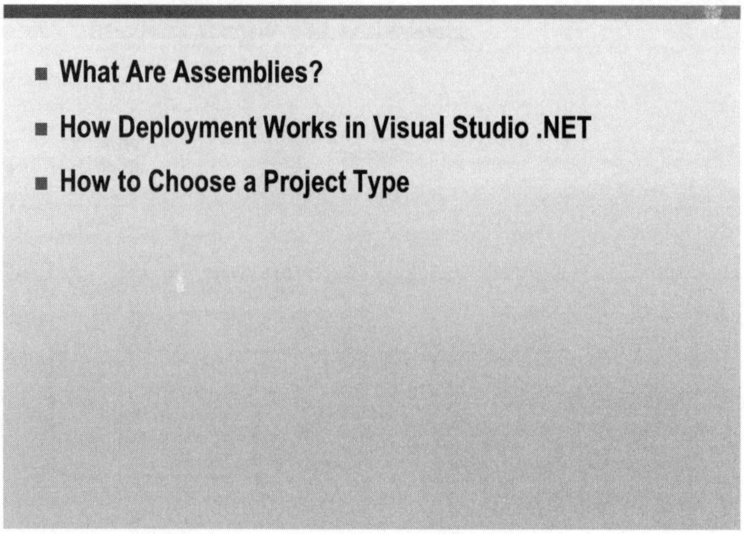

Introduction

In this lesson, you will learn about the role of assemblies in deployment, the process of deployment, and the deployment projects that are available to you in Visual Studio .NET.

Lesson agenda

This lesson includes the following topics and activities:

- What Are Assemblies?
- How Deployment Works in Visual Studio .NET
- How to Choose a Project Type

Lesson objectives

After completing this lesson, you will be able to:

- Describe assemblies.
- Explain the packaging and distribution options available in Visual Studio .NET.
- Choose appropriate deployment options for specific scenarios.

What Are Assemblies?

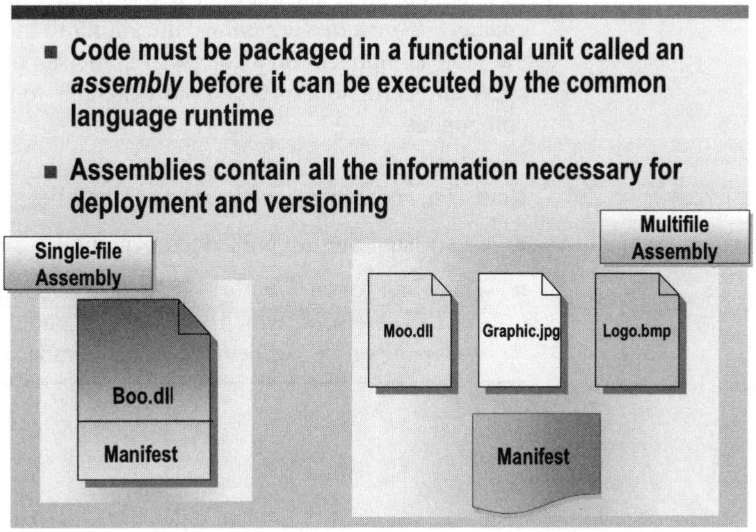

Introduction

In the Microsoft .NET Framework, code must be packaged in a functional unit called an *assembly* before it can be executed by the common language runtime. Assemblies contain all the information necessary for deployment and versioning.

Assembly structure

Applications in the .NET Framework consist of one or more assemblies. In the simplest case, an application consists of one assembly. In most cases, however, an application consists of multiple assemblies.

An assembly can be packaged as a single portable executable (PE) file, such as an executable (.exe) or dynamic-link library (.dll) file, or it can be made up of multiple PE files and external resource files, such as bitmaps. Applications are most often compiled into a single PE file.

The following elements might be contained in an assembly:

- Assembly metadata (the manifest)

  The metadata describing an assembly is called the *manifest*. The manifest provides the assembly title, a description of the assembly, version information, and so on. It also provides information about linking to the other files in the assembly, and enables the assembly to be self describing.

- Type metadata

  Type metadata provides information about available classes, interfaces, methods, and properties.

- Microsoft intermediate language (MSIL) code to be executed

  MSIL is a CPU-independent set of instructions that can be efficiently converted to native code. MSIL is converted to CPU-specific code by a just-in-time (JIT) compiler.

- Any required resources, such as graphics, or resource files for localization or other purposes

Assemblies and versioning

One of the primary goals of assemblies is versioning. Specifically, assemblies provide a means for developers to specify version rules between different software components and to have those rules enforced at run time. Assemblies enable *side-by-side versioning:* the ability to install and run multiple versions of the same component on a computer at the same time. This means that different applications running on a computer are able to use different versions of a shared component.

Note For more information about assemblies, see the following resources:

- The Visual Studio .NET documentation
- The white paper, *Simplifying Deployment and Solving DLL Hell with the .NET Framework,* which you can find under **Additional Reading** on the Web page on the Student Materials compact disc

How Deployment Works in Visual Studio .NET

- **Packaging options**
  - As portable executable files (.dll and .exe files)
  - As .cab files
  - As a Windows Installer package
- **Deployment**
  - Based on Windows Installer technology
- **Deployment alternatives**
  - XCOPY
  - The Copy Project command

Introduction

Deployment involves both packaging the code and distributing the packages. You can distribute your applications on floppy disks, CD-ROMs, across networks, or over the Internet or an intranet.

Packaging

There are several methods you can use to package applications created in Visual Studio .NET:

- As portable executable files (.dll and .exe files)

  The easiest way to package your application is to create a release build of the application. When you build your application, the code is packaged into assemblies. The resulting .exe files can be distributed by copying the files. For example, you could copy all the assembly files to a CD-ROM, write a batch file to copy the files to a directory on the user's hard disk, and then the user could simply run the application.

- As cabinet (.cab) files

  You can use .cab files to compress your application. This option is typically used for Internet download scenarios to reduce download time.

- As a Windows Installer package

  With this option, you create Windows Installer packages (.msi files) for use with the Windows Installer.

Benefits of Windows Installer

In Visual Studio .NET, deployment is based on Windows Installer technology. Windows Installer provides all installation data and instructions in a single package. With Windows Installer, each computer keeps a database of information about every application that it installs. This includes files, registry keys, and components.

Using Windows Installer provides the following benefits when you deploy an application:

- When an application is uninstalled, the computer's database is checked to ensure that no other applications rely on a file, registry key, or component before removing it. This functionality prevents you from making one application inoperable when you remove another application.
- Windows Installer supports self-repair—the ability for an application to automatically reinstall missing files that the user might have deleted inadvertently.
- Windows Installer provides the ability to roll back an installation. For example, if an application relies on a specific database and the database is not found during installation, the user can stop the installation and return the computer to its preinstallation state.
- Windows Installer allows automated configuration and creation of Internet Information Services (IIS) directory settings, NTFS security settings, network shares, and Active Directory® directory service User and Group accounts.
- Windows Installer allows automated creation of desktop shortcuts, automated addition of programs to the **Add or Remove Programs** list, and automated creation of **Start** menu entries.

Deployment process

To deploy an application, you first create a setup project and set deployment project properties that determine where and how the installer will be built.

- For deployment using traditional media, you would then copy the .msi file from the build location to a floppy disk, CD-ROM, or other media.
- To deploy to an intranet or Internet location, you would create a Web Setup project. After building the installer, you would copy it to the server computer, where it could then be downloaded over the network.

Deployment alternatives

Deploying simple applications with no dependencies can be as easy as copying the application to the destination computer. To uninstall the application, you simply delete the folder from the system. The .NET Framework provides the following options for copying applications:

- XCOPY

  Because common language runtime applications are self-describing and require no registry entries, you can use the **Xcopy** command to copy the application to an appropriate directory. The application can then be run from that directory.

  XCOPY is a simple way to copy a project or application from one location to another. However, you should only consider using XCOPY in the simplest cases. XCOPY does not register or verify the location of assemblies, and for Web projects, it does not automatically configure IIS directory settings. It does not provide the user with a graphical interface to install and uninstall the application. More importantly, if you use XCOPY to deploy an application, you do not have access to the file management features of Windows Installer. These features enable you to avoid file conflicts and prevent you from overwriting files and removing shared files.

- The Copy Project command

  For Web projects, the **Copy Project** command is available on the **Project** menu. Copying a project, rather than deploying it, is the simpler way to move your project's content to a destination Web server. However, copying does not automatically configure IIS directory settings. In most cases, you should deploy your project rather than copying it, so you can take advantage of deployment project management features, such as registration and IIS configuration.

Note For more information about XCOPY, see the article, *Determining When to Use Windows Installer Versus XCOPY,* under **Additional Reading** on the Web page on the Student Materials compact disc.

How to Choose a Project Type

Setup project

- Builds an installer for a Windows-based application (.msi file)

Web Setup project

- Builds an installer file for a Web application (.msi file)

Merge module project

- Packages components that might be shared by multiple applications (.msm file)

CAB project

- Creates a .cab file for downloading to a Web browser

Introduction

Before you can deploy a solution, you need to specify in Visual Studio .NET what to deploy, and where and how to deploy it. You do this by adding one or more deployment projects to your solution. Each deployment project specifies instructions for installing files and components on a destination computer.

Creating a new deployment project

Visual Studio .NET includes templates for four types of deployment projects. In addition, a Setup Wizard is provided to guide you through the process of creating deployment projects.

► **To create a new deployment project**

- In the **New Project** dialog box, click **Setup and Deployment Projects**, as shown in the following screen shot.

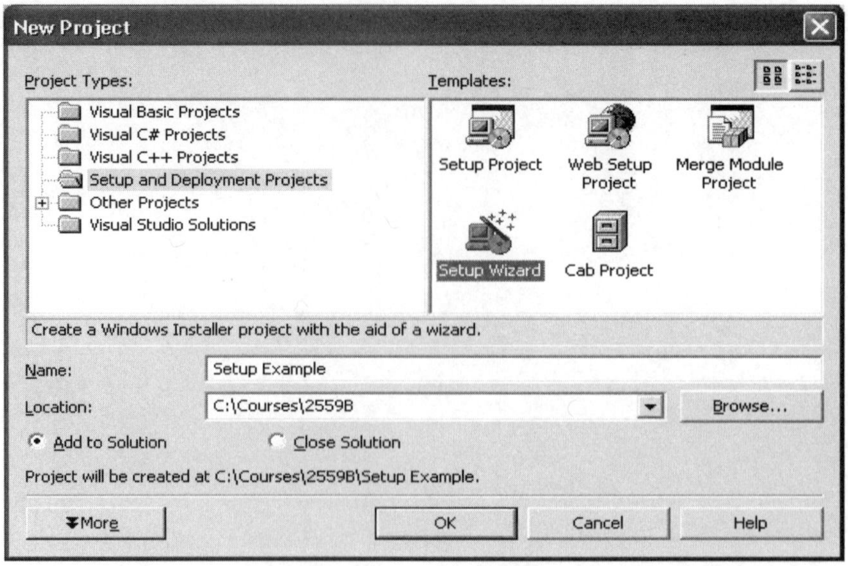

Choosing a project type

The following table provides guidelines for choosing the right project type for your deployment project.

Project type	Description	Use this project to…
Setup project or Web Setup project	Setup projects create a Windows Installer (.msi) file that contains the application; any dependent files; information about the application, such as registry entries; and instructions for installation. For a Setup project, the installer will install files into a Program Files directory on the destination computer. For a Web Setup project, the installer will install files into a virtual root directory on a Web server.	Setup project: Create an installer for a Windows-based application. Web Setup project: Create an installer for a Web-based application.
Merge module project	A merge module (.msm) file is a single package that contains all files, resources, registry entries, and setup logic necessary to install a component. Merge modules cannot be installed alone. They must be used within the context of a Windows Installer file.	Package files or components into a single module to facilitate sharing. The resulting .msm files can be included in any other deployment project.
CAB project	CAB projects create a .cab file to package Microsoft ActiveX® controls that can be downloaded from a Web server to a Web browser.	Create a .cab file for downloading to a Web browser.

Difference between Windows Installers and merge modules

In Visual Studio .NET, you can create two different types of installers: Windows Installer (.msi) files for Windows-based or Web-based applications, and merge modules (.msm).

The main distinction between the two types of installers is the target audience:

- Windows Installers are used to install applications and files on another computer. Anything that will be used directly by the end user of the application (.exe files, documents, HTML pages) should be packaged in a Windows Installer.
- Merge modules are used to install components that are shared by multiple applications. Components such as .dll files, controls, and resources can be packaged in a merge module, which will then be merged into the Windows Installer for each application that uses that component. When the applications are distributed to end users, the component is installed consistently for all of them.

Lesson: Deploying a Windows-based Application

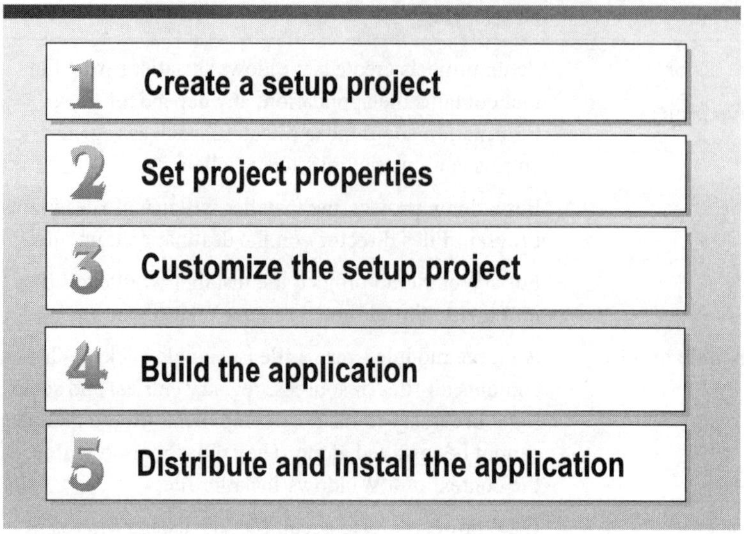

Introduction

This lesson discusses the steps that you use to create and customize a Windows Installer setup project to deploy a Windows-based application.

Lesson agenda

This lesson includes the following topics and activities:

- Multimedia: Deploying a Windows-based Application
- How to Create a Windows Installer Setup Project
- How to Set Project Properties
- Deployment Editors
- How to Use the File System Editor
- How to Build the Setup Project

Lesson objectives

After completing this lesson, you will be able to:

- Create a setup project for a Windows-based application by using the Setup Wizard.
- Configure your setup project by setting project properties and using the deployment editors.
- Deploy a Windows-based application.

Multimedia: Deploying a Windows-based Application

In this demonstration, you will learn how to deploy a Windows-based application, how to add a setup project to a solution, and how to set project properties. You will also learn how to add a program group and a shortcut to the user's desktop.

How to Create a Windows Installer Setup Project

Introduction

You can use the Setup Project template to create Windows Installer packages for Windows-based applications. The Setup Wizard can lead you through the process of gathering the necessary information to create a setup project.

Creating a new setup project using the Setup Wizard

► **To add a new setup project to a solution**

1. On the **File** menu, point to **Add Project**, and then click **New Project**.
2. In the Add New Project dialog box, click the Setup and Deployment Projects folder.
3. Click Setup Wizard.

Using the Setup Wizard, you will complete the following steps to create a setup project and add it to your solution:

1. Choose the project type.

   The type of project you choose determines where and how files will be installed on the destination computer. Creating a Setup program to install a Windows-based application is the default in the Setup Wizard.

2. Choose project outputs to include.

   Visual Studio .NET projects are used as containers within a solution to logically manage, build, and debug the items that make up your application. The output of a project is usually an .exe file, a .dll file, or a module.

The types of outputs available to add to your deployment project are dependent on the type of project you have selected. The following table describes the project outputs that you can use for deployment of a Windows-based application. Note that you can select more than one type of output.

Project output	Description
Primary output	Contains the .dll or .exe file built by the project. In general, you will select this output to include in any deployment.
Localized resources	Contains the satellite assemblies for each culture's resources. You might include this option for an application that will be deployed in multiple countries.
Debug Symbols	Contains the debugging files for the project. You might include this output in projects that will be debugged further.
Content Files	Contains all content files in the project, for example, HTML pages. You might include this output in a project that will be used by other developers.
Source Files	Contains all source files in the project. You might include this output in a project that will be used by other developers who need access to the source code, or with control files that will be compiled into the final application by another developer.

3. Choose files to include.

   You can add files such as ReadMe files or HTML pages to a setup project. In addition, if you plan to include a shortcut to your application, any icon associated with the shortcut must be included in the application setup files.

4. Create the project.

   Before creating the setup project, the Setup Wizard provides a summary of the choices you have made. This gives you the opportunity to make any modifications before adding the setup project to your solution.

How to Set Project Properties

- **Properties window**
  - Set general properties
  - Examples: **Author, Manufacturer, ProductName**
- **Deployment Properties dialog box**
  - Set configuration-dependent properties
  - Examples: **Bootstrapper, Compression, Output file name, Package files**
  - When installing to versions of Windows previous to Windows XP for the first time, you must include a bootstrapper in the installer

---

Introduction

Deployment projects have two categories of properties: general project properties and configuration-dependent properties. To set general properties, use the Properties window. General properties apply to all project configurations. To set configuration-dependent properties, use the **Deployment Properties** dialog box.

General properties

1. In the Properties window, you can set project properties such as **Author**, **Description**, **Manufacturer**, **ProductName**, **Title**, and **Version**.

Configuration-specific properties

2. To open the **Deployment Properties** dialog box, click **Property Pages** on the **View** menu when a setup project is selected in Solution Explorer, and then click **Build** in the **Configuration Properties** list.
3. The following table describes some of the key configuration properties.

Property	Description
Bootstrapper	Specifies whether a bootstrapper (bootstrapping application) will be included in an installer. A bootstrapper includes the files needed to install Windows Installer 1.5 on the destination computer if it is not already installed.
Compression	Specifies compression settings for files included in an installer.
Output file name	Specifies the location where the .msi files or .msm files will be placed when built.
Package files	Specifies how the files will be packaged within the installer file.

Note Windows Installer 1.5 is the default version for Windows XP. When installing to earlier versions of Windows for the first time, you must include the bootstrapper in the installer.

Deployment Editors

- **Use the deployment editors to configure the installer that you create**
  - File System Editor
  - Registry Editor
  - File Types Editor
  - User Interface Editor
  - Custom Actions Editor
  - Launch Conditions Editor

Introduction

Deployment editors are used to configure the installer that you create with a deployment project. Each setup project includes six editors: the File System Editor, the Registry Editor, the File Types Editor, the User Interface Editor, the Custom Actions Editor, and the Launch Conditions Editor.

Note Unlike the other deployment project types, there are no editors provided for working with CAB projects. You can add files and project outputs to a CAB project in Solution Explorer, and you can set properties in the Properties window or in the Project Property pages.

Opening the editors

You can open the deployment editors in Solution Explorer by clicking the setup project and then using the toolbar buttons, as shown below:

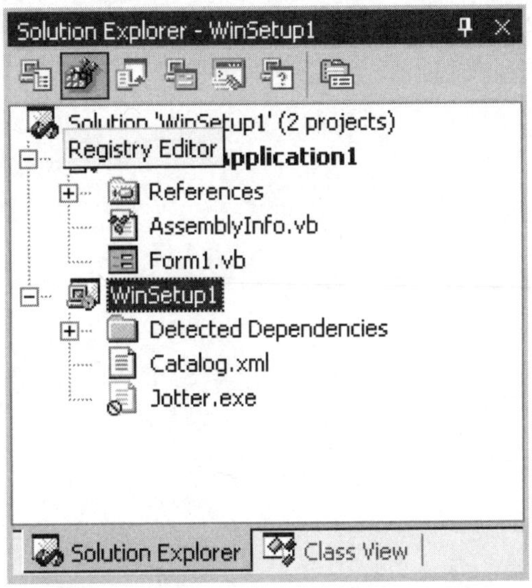

File System Editor

By using this editor, you can add project outputs and other files to a deployment project, specify the locations where files will be installed on a destination computer, and create shortcuts on a destination computer.

Registry Editor

By using this editor, you can gain access to the commonly used registry keys. These keys vary according to whether your application is a Windows-based or Web-based application. In this editor, you can define your own keys and write their default values during the installation process.

File Types Editor

By using this editor, you can establish file associations on the destination computer by associating file extensions with your application and specifying the actions allowed for each file type.

User Interface Editor

By using this editor, you can customize messages and images in the dialog boxes that the user sees in the Installation Wizard. You can customize both the standard and administrative installation programs.

You can also add extra dialog boxes to the installation process. For example, you can request user preferences by using text boxes and option buttons, request user information for registration purposes, or display license agreements.

Custom Actions Editor

By using this editor, you can include custom actions in your main Setup program. These actions can be performed during installation, commit, rollback, or uninstall. They can include running any .exe file, .dll file, or script file; adding users to or removing users from a database; or adding a support contact to the address book in Microsoft Outlook®.

Launch Conditions Editor

By using this editor, you can define conditions for installing the application or performing custom actions. For example, if a database is not present on the server, you will not want to add users to it and may not want to install the application. You can check for files, registry keys, and Windows Installer installations. You can also customize the message presented to the user if a particular condition is not satisfied.

How to Use the File System Editor

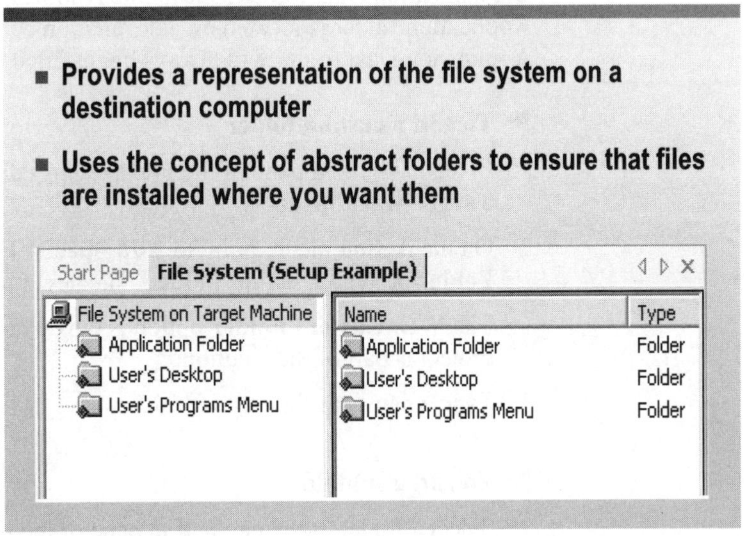

Introduction

The organization of the file system can differ from one computer to another, and folder names can also differ. The File System Editor uses the concept of virtual folders to ensure that files are installed where you want them. Virtual folders in the File System Editor are representations of Windows system folders. Windows tracks the location of system folders, so no matter where the folder is located or what it is named, files placed in the Desktop folder will always end up in the Desktop system folder.

Layout of the File System Editor

The File System Editor is divided into two parts: a navigation pane on the left and a detail pane on the right. The navigation pane contains a hierarchical list of folders that represent the file system on a destination computer. When a folder is selected in the navigation pane, any files and shortcuts that will be installed in that folder are displayed in the detail pane. When the top-level **File System on Target Machine** node is selected, the detail pane contains a list of folders.

Default folders

The following table describes the purpose of the default folders displayed in the File System Editor.

Folder name	Purpose
Application folder	This folder corresponds to a folder beneath the Program Files folder where the application will be installed. Use the Application folder to install the files used to run the application.
User's Desktop folder	Use this folder to install a desktop shortcut for the application.
User's Programs Menu folder	Use this folder to install a program menu shortcut for the application.

Creating your own folders

In the File System Editor, you can create your own folders and subfolders and place them in a location beneath any system folder. For example, if you create an Application Data folder beneath the Application folder, no matter where the Application folder is located on a destination computer, files placed in your Application Data folder will always be installed in the same relative location.

► To add a custom folder

1. In the navigation pane of the File System Editor, select the **File System on Target Machine** node.
2. On the **Action** menu, point to **Add Special Folder**, then click **Custom Folder** or **Web Custom Folder**. The new folder is selected in the folder list.

   The **Web Custom Folder** option is only available when a Web setup project is part of the solution.
3. Type a name for the custom folder.

► To add a subfolder

1. Select a folder in the navigation pane of the File System Editor.
2. On the **Action** menu, point to **Add**, and then click **Folder**. The new folder is created beneath the previously selected folder in the folder list.
3. Type a name for the new folder.

Creating shortcuts

The File System Editor supports the creation of shortcuts, allowing you to place files in one folder and link to them from a shortcut on the desktop or in another folder. For example, you might want to allow a user to start an .exe file by placing shortcuts to it on the user's desktop and program menu.

► To add a shortcut to a file or folder

1. In the File System Editor, right-click the file or folder to which you want to create a shortcut (for example, the .exe file for the application).
2. Click **Create Shortcut to *Name***. The shortcut appears in the file list.
3. Type a name for the shortcut, and then press ENTER.
4. Drag the shortcut from the file list to the folder in which you want the shortcut to appear on the destination computer, for example, the User's Desktop folder.

To associate an icon with a shortcut that you create, you can set the **Icon** property of the shortcut in the Properties window. Note that to assign an icon to the shortcut, you must first add the icon file to the setup project for the application.

► To add files to the application folder

- In the navigation pane of the File System Editor, right-click the **Application Folder**, point to **Add**, and then click **File**.

How to Build the Setup Project

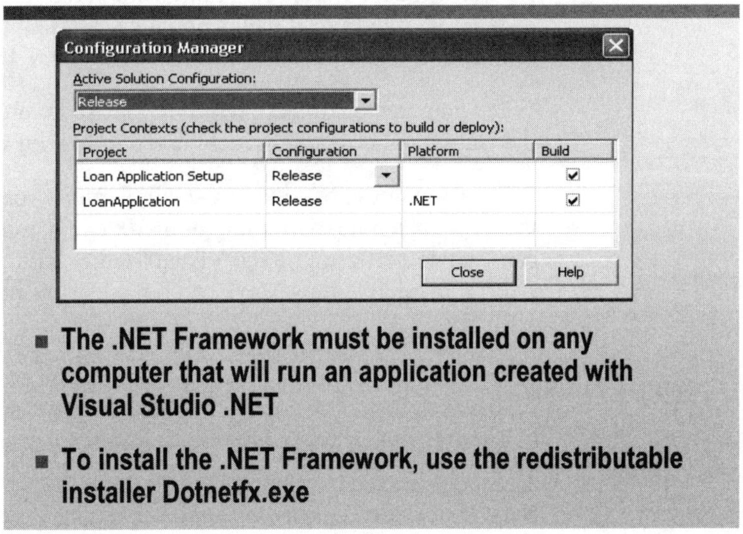

Introduction

After you configure settings for your Setup program by using the deployment editors, you can build the project so that it will be ready for deployment. Up to this point, it is likely that you have built debug builds of your application; builds that can be run, tested, and modified in the development environment. When your application is ready for deployment, you need to create a release build of all the projects in your solution.

Creating a release build

► **To create a release build of your application**

1. On the **Build** menu, click **Configuration Manager**.
2. In the **Configuration Manager** dialog box, change the Active Solution Configuration from **Debug** to **Release**.
3. In the **Build** column, select the check boxes for the projects that you want to build (including the setup project), and then click **Close**. For a final build, you will want to select the check boxes for all projects in the solution.
4. On the **Build** menu, click **Build Solution**.

Understanding setup files

Building the setup project creates the following files in the Project directory or the Release directory.

File name	Description
MyProject.msi	The Windows Installer information file, used by Setup.exe.
Setup.exe	A copy of the standard Setup application.
Setup.ini	The setup initialization file with information specific to your application.
InstMsiA.exe	The installation files needed to install Windows Installer.
InstMsiW.exe	
MyProject.vdproj	The Visual Studio .NET deployment project file used by the development environment. Created in the Project directory, not the Release subdirectory.

Installing the .NET Framework

Applications and controls written for the .NET Framework require that the .NET Framework be installed on the computer on which the application or control will run. The .NET Framework version 1.0 provides one redistributable installer, Dotnetfx.exe, which contains the common language runtime and .NET Framework components necessary to run .NET Framework applications.

When you create a release build of your setup project, the build log displayed in the Output window might include the following warning:

"This setup does not contain the .NET Framework which must be installed on the target machine by running dotnetfx.exe before this setup will install. You can find dotnetfx.exe on the Visual Studio .NET 'Windows Components Update' media. Dotnetfx.exe can be redistributed with your setup."

If your destination computer already has the .NET Framework installed, you can ignore this warning. If the destination computer does not have the .NET Framework installed, you can include the Dotnetfx.exe file in your setup files, or the user can download the file from the Internet.

Note For more information about installing Dotnetfx.exe, see ".NET Framework Deployment Guide" under **Internet Links** on the Web page on the Student Materials compact disc.

Review

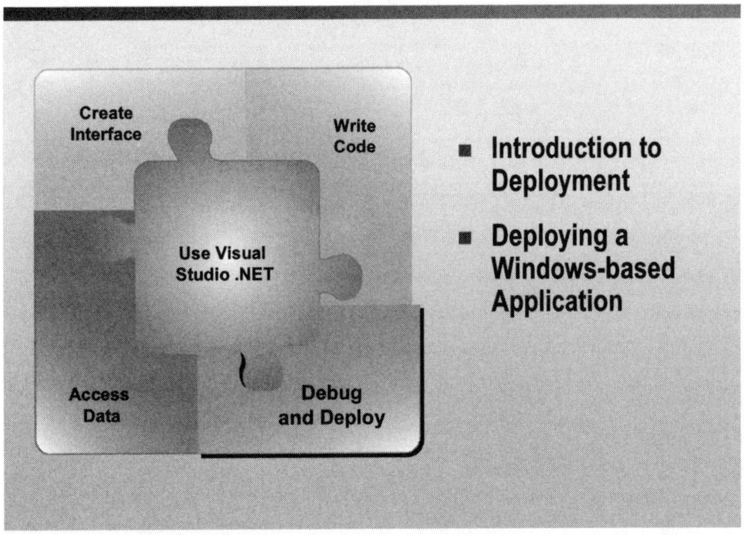

1. Which of the following options can you use to package your code for distribution? (Select all true answers.)
   a. As .cab files
   b. As XCOPY project files
   c. As a Windows Installer package
   d. As a Microsoft .NET Solution Installer package

2. Evaluate whether each of the following statements is true or false. For any false statement, explain why it is false.
   a. You must package merge modules within a Windows Installer for distribution to end-users.
   b. You can uninstall any Windows-based application by using the **Add or Remove Programs** option in Control Panel.
   c. You must include a bootstrapper in an installer if your application will be installed on versions of Windows previous to Windows XP.

3. What is the purpose of the Dotnetfx.exe file?

Lab 12.1: Deploying an Application

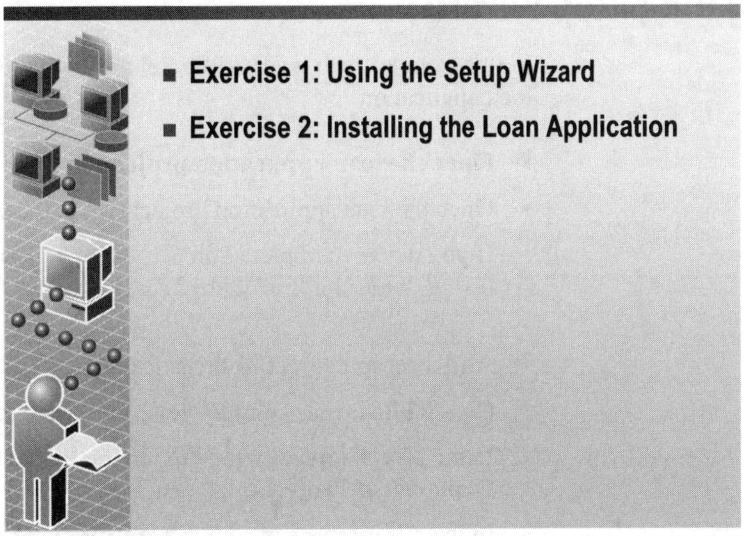

Objectives

After completing this lab, you will be able to:

- Create a Setup program for a Windows-based application by using the Setup Wizard.
- Install and remove a Windows-based application.

Note This lab focuses on the concepts in this module and as a result may not comply with Microsoft security recommendations.

Prerequisites

Before working on this lab, you must be familiar with the deployment options available in Visual Basic .NET.

Scenario

In the labs for Modules 2, 4, 5, 6, and 12 of Course 2559B, *Introduction to Visual Basic .NET Programming with Microsoft .NET*, you will create a loan payment estimate application. You will create the full application in stages, each stage building on the code created in the previous lab. At the beginning of each lab, you can either continue with your own files or start with the files provided for you.

In Lab 12.1, Deploying an Application, you will create a Setup program for the loan application.

Solution files

The solution files for this lab are in the *install_folder*\Labfiles\Lab121\Ex01\Solution folder.

Estimated time to complete this lab: 30 minutes

Exercise 1
Using the Setup Wizard

In this exercise, you will use the Setup Wizard to create a Setup program for the loan application.

▶ Open the loan application project

- Open the loan application project that you completed in Lab 6.1.

  If you did not complete Lab 6.1, open the LoanApplication.sln file in the *install_folder*\Labfiles\Lab121\Ex01\Starter folder.

▶ Add a setup project to the solution

1. On the **File** menu, point to **New**, and then click **Project**.
2. In the **New Project** dialog box, in the **Project Types** pane, click **Setup and Deployment Projects**.
3. In the **Templates** pane, click **Setup Wizard**.
4. In the **Name** box, type **Loan Application Setup** and then click **Add to Solution**.
5. In the **Location** box, type *install_folder***Labfiles\Lab121\Ex01\Starter** and then click **OK**.
6. In the Setup Wizard, on the **Welcome to the Setup Project Wizard** page, click **Next**.
7. On the **Choose a project type** page, accept the default by clicking **Next**.
8. On the **Choose project outputs to include** page, click **Primary output from LoanApplication**, and then click **Next**.
9. On the **Choose files to include** page, click **Add**.
10. In the **Add Files** dialog box, browse to the *install_folder*\Labfiles\Lab121\Ex01\Starter folder, click **App.ico**, and then click **Open**.
11. On the **Choose files to include** page, click **Next**.
12. On the **Create Project** page, click **Finish**.

▶ Set setup project properties

1. In Solution Explorer, verify that **Loan Application Setup** is selected.
2. In the Properties window, set the properties for the Loan Application Setup project as shown in the following table.

Property	New value
Manufacturer	Northwind Traders
ProductName	Loan Application
Title	Loan Application Setup

► **Add a program group and shortcut**

1. In the File System Editor, in the left pane, click **Application Folder**.
2. In the list of items contained in the Application Folder, right-click **Primary output from LoanApplication (Active)**, and then click **Create Shortcut to Primary output from LoanApplication (Active)**. Type **Loan Application**, and then press ENTER.
3. In the Properties window, click **Icon**, click the down arrow button, and then click **Browse**.
   a. In the **Icon** dialog box, click **Browse**.
   b. In the **Select Item in Project** dialog box, double-click **Application Folder**.
   c. Click **App.ico**, and then click **OK**.
   d. In the **Icon** dialog box, click **OK**.
4. In the Properties window, click **Folder**, and then click the ellipsis button.
5. In the **Select Folder** dialog box, click **User's Programs Menu**, and then click **OK**.

► **Add a shortcut to the user's desktop**

1. In the File System Editor, click **Application Folder**.
2. In the list of items contained in the Application Folder, right-click **Primary output from LoanApplication (Active)**, and then click **Create Shortcut to Primary output from LoanApplication (Active)**. Type **Loan Application** and then press ENTER.
3. In the Properties window, click **Icon**, click the down arrow button, and then click **Browse**.
   a. In the **Icon** dialog box, click **Browse**.
   b. In the **Select Item in Project** dialog box, double-click **Application Folder**.
   c. Click **App.ico**, and then click **OK**.
   d. In the **Icon** dialog box, click **OK**.
4. In the Properties window, click **Folder**, and then click the ellipsis button.
5. In the **Select Folder** dialog box, click **User's Desktop**, and then click **OK**.

► Build the setup project

1. On the Build menu, click **Configuration Manager**.
2. In the **Configuration Manager** dialog box, change the Active Solution Configuration from **Debug** to **Release**, and then click **Close**.
3. In Solution Explorer, right-click **Loan Application Setup**, and then click **Build**.

Note Ignore the build warning about including Dotnetfx.exe. This Setup program will only be installed on computers that have Visual Studio .NET already installed.

► Quit Visual Studio .NET

- On the **File** menu, click **Exit**.

Exercise 2
Installing the Loan Application

In this exercise, you will use the Setup program to install the loan application.

► **Install the application**

- Double-click the **Setup.exe** file located in the *install_folder*\Labfiles\Lab121\Ex01\Starter\Loan Application Setup\Release folder to install the application. Perform the setup by using the default options.

► **View the application folder**

- Confirm that the application is installed in the C:\Program Files\Northwind Traders\Loan Application folder.

► **Run the application by using the desktop shortcut**

1. Run the application by using the shortcut located on the desktop.
2. Quit the application.

► **Run the application by using the Start menu**

1. Click **Start**, point to **All Programs**, and then click **Loan Application**.
2. Quit the application.

► **Uninstall the application**

- Remove the application by using **Control Panel**.

Course Evaluation

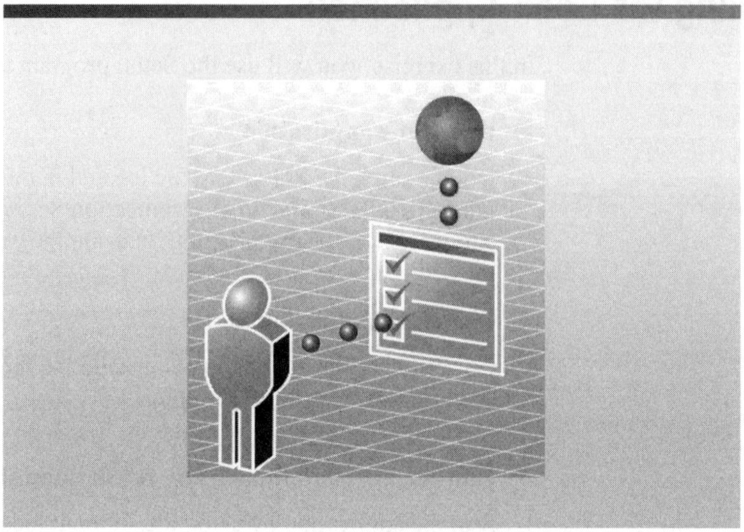

Your evaluation of this course will help Microsoft understand the quality of your learning experience.

To complete a course evaluation, go to http://www.CourseSurvey.com.

Microsoft will keep your evaluation strictly confidential and will use your responses to improve your future learning experience.

ADO
Active Data Access objects

JIT complies
Just in Time

Notes

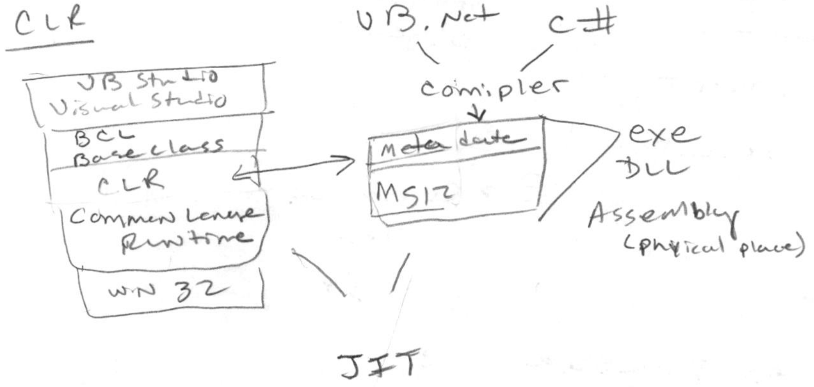

Name space = logical Grouping of source code (Location)

Class = Text file   object = instace of class

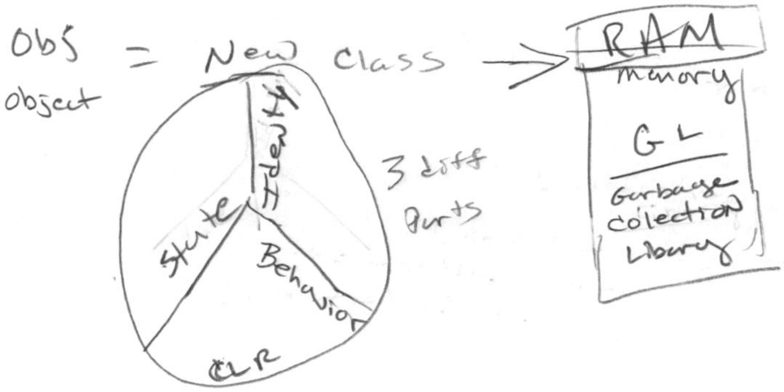

ADO.Net

Property verse Method
↓ Identity
↓ action (Behavior)

Handles
Wires.

Add Handler

Delegates = (handlers - Stactic
Dynamic)

CTS - Common Type System (two types)

chapter 3 page 5

VP Dot Net
Default
Explisit
verse
Implisis

Three Types Procedures = property, function, subroutean

SQL enviroment

Notes

Connection object

Conect - incert
Read - select
Update
D delete

=> Command
Text
SP

Two Types DataBase

1) connected -
Advantage
- get close
- Real Time
- Log data
cursor locking
- Pessimitic
disadvantage
slow

2) disconnected - ADO.Net
- Data can Be outdated
- Does not Req open connection
- Optimistic Locking (two actions)
Delect Differense
Resolve Differenses.

Data Set
in memory data Base
adaptor

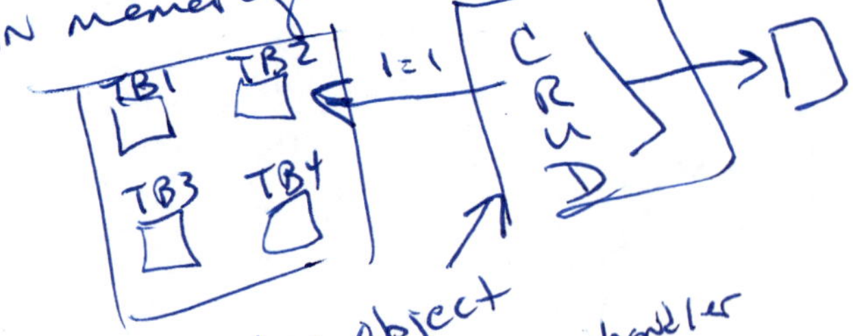

Adaptor object

Adapter spesific handler

Book Fritz Onion
Essential Asp. Net
~~Dot Net~~
.Net Reflector

(2373)

Notes

SXD. EXE

ACID
Atomic consistant

Notes

Notes

Notes

MSM2559BCP/C90-03140
0 99751 06502 4